Mark Roberts

English for
ECONOMICS

in Higher Education Studies
Teacher's Book

Series editor: Terry Phillips

English for Specific Academic Purposes

Garnet
EDUCATION

Published by
Garnet Publishing Ltd.
8 Southern Court
South Street
Reading RG1 4QS, UK

First published 2012

ISBN 978 1 85964 449 2

British Cataloguing-in-Publication Data
A catalogue record for this book is available from the British Library.

Production
Series editor: Terry Phillips
Project management: Claire Forsyth
Editorial team: Anne Abel-Smith, Penny Analytis, Claire Forsyth, Karen Kinnair-Pugh
Specialist review: Jim O'Hare
Design: Henry Design Associates and Mike Hinks
Photography: Sally Henry and Trevor Cook, alamy.com, clipart.com, corbis.com, gettyimages.com, greenpeace.org, london2012.com, nissanpress.co.uk, oxfam.org, unicef.org, wikipedia.org

Audio recorded at Motivation Sound Studios produced by EFS Television Production Ltd.

The authors and publisher would like to thank the following for permission to reproduce copyright material:
Graph on page 24 from the Office for National Statistics, licensed under the Open Government Licence v.10; table on page 33 compiled from data from the International Monetary Fund (2009). *Crisis and Recovery*, April 2009. ©2009 International Monetary Fund, available at http://www.imf.org/external/pubs/ft/weo/2009/01; results listings on page 78 with kind permission of Google; figure 3 on page 100 from the Office for National Statistics, licensed under the Open Government Licence v.10; figure 1 on page 146 from HM Treasury, licensed under the Open Government Licence v.10; figure 2 on page 146 from the Office for National Statistics, licensed under the Open Government Licence v.10; table on page 219 from Australian Bureau of Statistics, licensed under the Creative Commons Attribution 2.5 Australia License; table 1 on page 239 from the Office for National Statistics, licensed under the Open Government Licence v.10.

Every effort has been made to trace copyright holders and we apologize in advance for any unintentional omission. We will be happy to insert the appropriate acknowledgements in any subsequent editions.

Printed and bound in Lebanon by International Press: interpress@int-press.com

Contents

Book map

Unit	Topics
1 Economics in the modern world Listening · Speaking	• why economics is important • the role of economists • how economics shapes our lives
2 How economics is organized Reading · Writing	• divisions of economics • economic stakeholders • macro and microeconomics
3 Market economies Listening · Speaking	• market principles • concepts in markets • market equilibrium • marginality
4 Economics and technology Reading · Writing	• technology and economic change • the use of computers in economics and finance
5 Economics, globalization and sustainability Listening · Speaking	• the global economy • the role of foreign direct investment • emerging markets and comparative advantage • multinational corporations
6 Macroeconomics ... but microfinance! Reading · Writing	• growth • microfinance • fair trade • case study in microfinance
7 Saving, spending ... borrowing and lending! Listening · Speaking	• aggregate demand • expenditure • budget deficits
8 The economics of agriculture Reading · Writing	• price elasticity of demand • buffer stocks • food security • commodity prices
9 The economics of health care Listening · Speaking	• welfare economics • vertical equity • Pareto efficiency • health care indicators
10 The economics of sport Reading · Writing	• funding • legacy effects • staging mega-events • investment in sport • derived demand • complementary products
11 Labour markets Listening · Speaking	• trafficking • migration • demographic factors • labour market trends
12 Strategy, policy and economic change Reading · Writing	• SMART framework • Corporate Social Responsibility (CSR) • economics and ecosystems

Vocabulary focus	Skills focus		Unit
• words from general English with a special meaning in economics • prefixes and suffixes	Listening	• preparing for a lecture • predicting lecture content from the introduction • understanding lecture organization • choosing an appropriate form of notes • making lecture notes	**1**
	Speaking	• speaking from notes	
• English–English dictionaries: headwords · definitions · parts of speech · phonemes · stress markers · countable/uncountable · transitive/intransitive	Reading	• using research questions to focus on relevant information in a text • using topic sentences to get an overview of the text	**2**
	Writing	• writing topic sentences • summarizing a text	
• stress patterns in multi-syllable words • prefixes	Listening	• preparing for a lecture • predicting lecture content • making lecture notes • using different information sources	**3**
	Speaking	• reporting research findings • formulating questions	
• computer jargon • abbreviations and acronyms • discourse and stance markers • verb and noun suffixes	Reading	• identifying topic development within a paragraph • using the Internet effectively • evaluating Internet search results	**4**
	Writing	• reporting research findings	
• word sets: synonyms, antonyms, etc. • the language of trends • common lecture language	Listening	• understanding 'signpost language' in lectures • using symbols and abbreviations in note-taking	**5**
	Speaking	• making effective contributions to a seminar	
• synonyms, replacement subjects, etc., for sentence-level paraphrasing	Reading	• locating key information in complex sentences	**6**
	Writing	• reporting findings from other sources: paraphrasing • writing complex sentences	
• compound nouns • fixed phrases from economics • fixed phrases from academic English • common lecture language	Listening	• understanding speaker emphasis	**7**
	Speaking	• asking for clarification • responding to queries and requests for clarification	
• synonyms • nouns from verbs • definitions • common 'direction' verbs in essay titles (*discuss, analyze, evaluate,* etc.)	Reading	• understanding dependent clauses with passives	**8**
	Writing	• paraphrasing • expanding notes into complex sentences • recognizing different essay types/structures: descriptive · analytical · comparison/evaluation · argument • writing essay plans • writing essays	
• fixed phrases from economics • fixed phrases from academic English	Listening	• using the Cornell note-taking system • recognizing digressions in lectures	**9**
	Speaking	• making effective contributions to a seminar • referring to other people's ideas in a seminar	
• 'neutral' and 'marked' words • fixed phrases from economics • fixed phrases from academic English	Reading	• recognizing the writer's stance and level of confidence or tentativeness • inferring implicit ideas	**10**
	Writing	• writing situation–problem–solution–evaluation essays • using direct quotations • compiling a bibliography/reference list	
• words/phrases used to link ideas (*moreover, as a result,* etc.) • stress patterns in noun phrases and compounds • fixed phrases from academic English • words/phrases related to labour market issues	Listening	• recognizing the speaker's stance • writing up notes in full	**11**
	Speaking	• building an argument in a seminar • agreeing/disagreeing	
• verbs used to introduce ideas from other sources (*X contends/suggests/asserts that* …) • linking words/phrases conveying contrast (*whereas*), result (*consequently*), reasons (*due to*), etc. • words for quantities (*a significant minority*)	Reading	• understanding how ideas in a text are linked	**12**
	Writing	• deciding whether to use direct quotation or paraphrase • incorporating quotations • writing research reports • writing effective introductions/conclusions	

Introduction

The ESAP series

The aim of the titles in the ESAP series is to prepare students for academic study in a particular discipline. In this respect, the series is somewhat different from many ESP (English for Specific Purposes) series, which are aimed at people already working in the field, or about to enter the field. This focus on *study* in the discipline rather than *work* in the field has enabled the author to focus much more specifically on the skills which an economics student needs.

It is assumed that prior to using titles in this series students will already have completed a general EAP (English for Academic Purposes) course such as *Skills in English* (Garnet Publishing, up to the end of at least Level 3), and will have achieved an IELTS level of at least 5.

English for Economics

English for Economics is designed for students who plan to take an economics course entirely or partly in English. The principal aim of *English for Economics* is to teach students to cope with input texts, i.e., listening and reading, in the discipline. However, students will also be expected to produce output texts in speech and writing throughout the course.

The syllabus concentrates on key vocabulary for the discipline and on words and phrases commonly used in academic English. It covers key facts and concepts from the discipline, thereby giving students a flying start for when they meet the same points again in their faculty work. It also focuses on the skills that will enable students to get the most out of lectures and written texts. Finally, it presents the skills required to take part in seminars and tutorials and to produce essay assignments. For a summary of the course content, see the book map on pages 4–5.

Components of the course

The course comprises:
- the student Course Book
- this Teacher's Book, which provides detailed guidance on each lesson, full answer keys, audio transcripts and extra photocopiable resources
- audio CDs with lecture and seminar excerpts

Organization of the course

English for Economics has 12 units, each of which is based on a different aspect of economics.

Odd-numbered units are based on listening (lecture/seminar extracts). Even-numbered units are based on reading.

Each unit is divided into four lessons:

Lesson 1: vocabulary for the discipline; vocabulary skills such as word-building, use of affixes, use of synonyms for paraphrasing

Lesson 2: reading or listening text and skills development

Lesson 3: reading or listening skills extension. In addition, in later reading units, students are introduced to a writing assignment which is further developed in **Lesson 4**; in later listening units, students are introduced to a spoken language point (e.g., making an oral presentation at a seminar) which is further developed in Lesson 4

Lesson 4: a parallel listening or reading text to that presented in Lesson 2, in which students have to use their new skills (Lesson 3) to decode; in addition, written or spoken work is further practised

The last two pages of each unit, *Vocabulary bank* and *Skills bank*, are a useful summary of the unit content.

Each unit provides between four and six hours of classroom activity with the possibility of a further two to four hours on the suggested extra activities. The course will be suitable, therefore, as the core component of a faculty-specific pre-sessional or foundation course of between 50 and 80 hours.

Vocabulary development

English for Economics attaches great importance to vocabulary. This is why one lesson out of four is devoted to vocabulary and why, in addition, the first exercise at least in many of the other three lessons is a vocabulary exercise. The vocabulary presented can be grouped into two main areas:
- key vocabulary for economics
- key vocabulary for academic English

In addition to presenting specific items of vocabulary, the course concentrates on the vocabulary skills and strategies that will help students to make sense of lectures and texts. Examples include:
- understanding prefixes and suffixes and how these affect the meaning of the base word
- guessing words in context
- using an English–English dictionary effectively
- understanding how certain words/phrases link ideas
- understanding how certain words/phrases show the writer/speaker's point of view

Skills development

Listening and reading in the real world involve extracting communicative value in real time – i.e., as the spoken text is being produced or as you are reading written text. Good listeners and readers do not need to go back to listen or read again most of the time. Indeed, with listening to formal speech such as a lecture, there is no possibility of going back. In many ELT materials second, third, even fourth listenings are common. The approach taken in the ESAP series is very different. We set out to teach and practise 'text-attack' skills – i.e., listening and reading strategies that will enable students to extract communicative value at a single listening or reading.

Students also need to become familiar with the way academic 'outputs' such as reports, essays and oral presentations are structured in English. Conventions may be different in their own language – for example, paragraphing conventions, or introduction–main body–conclusion structure. All students, whatever their background, will benefit from an awareness of the skills and strategies that will help them produce written work of a high standard.

Examples of specific skills practised in the course include:

Listening

- predicting lecture content and organization from the introduction
- following signposts to lecture organization
- choosing an appropriate form of lecture notes
- recognizing the lecturer's stance and level of confidence/tentativeness

Reading

- using research question to focus on relevant information
- using topic sentences to get an overview of the text
- recognizing the writer's stance and level of confidence/tentativeness
- using the Internet effectively

Speaking

- making effective contributions to a seminar
- asking for clarification – formulating questions
- speaking from notes
- summarizing

Writing

- writing notes
- paraphrasing
- reporting findings from other sources – avoiding plagiarism

- recognizing different essay types and structures
- writing essay plans and essays
- compiling a bibliography/reference list

Specific activities

Certain types of activity are repeated on several occasions throughout the course. This is because these activities are particularly valuable in language learning.

Tasks to activate schemata

It has been known for many years, since the research of Bartlett in the 1930s, that we can only understand incoming information, written or spoken, if we can fit it into a schemata. It is essential that we build these schemata in students before exposing them to new information, so all lessons with listening and reading texts begin with one or more relevant activities.

Prediction activities

Before students are allowed to listen to a section of a lecture or read a text, they are encouraged to make predictions about the contents, in general or even specific terms, based on the context, the introduction to the text or, in the case of reading, the topic sentences in the text. This is based on the theory that active listening and reading involve the receiver in being ahead of the producer.

Working with illustrations, diagrams, figures

Some tasks require students to explain or interpret visual material. This is clearly a key task in a field which makes great use of such material to support written text. Students can be taken back to these visuals later on in the course to ensure that they have not forgotten how to describe and interpret them.

Vocabulary tasks

Many tasks ask students to group key economics terms, to categorize them in some way or to find synonyms or antonyms. These tasks help students to build relationships between words which, research has shown, is a key element in remembering words. In these exercises, the target words are separated into blue boxes so you can quickly return to one of these activities for revision work later.

Gap-fill

Filling in missing words or phrases in a sentence or a text, or labelling a diagram, indicates comprehension both of the missing items and of the context in which they correctly fit. You can vary the activity by, for example, going through the gap-fill text with the whole class first orally, pens down, then setting the same task for individual completion. Gap-fill activities can be photocopied and set as revision at the end of the unit or later, with or without the missing items.

Breaking long sentences into key components

One feature of academic English is the average length of sentences. Traditionally, EFL classes teach students to cope with the complexity of the verb phrase, equating level with more and more arcane verb structures, such as the present perfect modal passive. However, research into academic language, including the corpus research which underlies the *Longman Grammar of Spoken and Written English*, suggests that complexity in academic language does not lie with the verb phrase but rather with the noun phrase and clause joining and embedding. For this reason, students are shown in many exercises later in the course how to break down long sentences into kernel elements, and find the subject, verb and object of each element. This receptive skill in then turned into a productive skill, by encouraging students to think in terms of kernel elements first before building them into complex sentences.

Activities with stance marking

Another key element of academic text is the attitude (or stance) of the writer or speaker to the information which is being imparted. This could be dogmatic, tentative, incredulous, sceptical, and so on. Students must learn the key skill of recognizing words and phrases marked for stance.

Crosswords and other word puzzles

One of the keys to vocabulary learning is repetition. However, the repetition must be active. It is no good if students are simply going through the motions. The course uses crosswords and other kinds of puzzles to bring words back into the students' consciousness through an engaging activity. However, it is understood by the writers that such playful activities are not always seen as serious and academic. The crosswords and other activities are therefore made available as photocopiable resources at the back of the Teacher's Book and can be used at the teacher's discretion, after explaining to the students why they are valuable.

Methodology points

Setting up tasks

The teaching notes for many of the exercises begin with the word *Set ...* . This single word covers a number of vital functions for the teacher, as follows:

- Refer students to the rubric (instructions).
- Check that they understand **what** to do – get one or two students to explain the task in their own words.
- Tell students **how** they are to do the task, if this is not clear in the Course Book instructions – as individual work, pairwork or in groups.
- Go through the example, if there is one. If not, make it clear what the target output is – full sentences, short answers, notes, etc.
- Go through one or two of the items, working with a good student to elicit the required output.

Use of visuals

There is a considerable amount of visual material in the book. This should be exploited in a number of ways:

- before an exercise, to orientate the students, to get them thinking about the situation or the task, and to provide an opportunity for a small amount of pre-teaching of vocabulary (be careful not to pre-empt any exercises, though)
- during the exercise, to remind students of important language
- after the activity, to help with related work or to revise the target language

Comparing answers in pairs

This is frequently suggested when students have completed a task individually. It provides all students with a chance to give and explain their answers, which is not possible if the teacher immediately goes through the answers with the whole class.

Self-checking

Learning only takes place after a person has noticed that there is something to learn. This noticing of an individual learning point does not happen at the same time for all students. In many cases, it does not even happen in a useful sense when a teacher has focused on it. So, learning occurs to the individual timetable of each student in a group. For this reason, it is important to give students time to notice mistakes in their own work and try to correct them individually. Take every opportunity to get students to self-check to try to force the noticing stage.

Confirmation and correction

Many activities benefit from a learning tension, i.e., a period of time when students are not sure whether something is right or wrong. The advantages of this tension are:

- a chance for all students to become involved in an activity before the correct answers are given

- a higher level of concentration from the students (tension is quite enjoyable!)
- a greater focus on the item as students wait for the correct answer
- a greater involvement in the process – students become committed to their answers and want to know if they are right and, if not, why not

In cases where learning tension of this type is desirable, the teacher's notes say, *Do not confirm or correct (at this point)*.

Feedback

At the end of each task, there should be a feedback stage. During this stage, the correct answers (or a model answer in the case of freer exercises) are given, alternative answers (if any) are accepted, and wrong answers are discussed. Unless students' own answers are required (in the case of very free exercises), answers or model answers are provided in the teacher's notes.

Highlighting grammar

This course is not organized on a grammatical syllabus and does not focus on grammar specifically. It is assumed that students will have covered English grammar to at least upper intermediate level in their general English course. However, at times it will be necessary to focus on the grammar, and indeed occasionally the grammar is a main focus (for example, changing active to passive or vice versa when paraphrasing).

To highlight the grammar:

- focus students' attention on the grammar point, e.g., *Look at the word order in the first sentence.*
- write an example of the grammar point on the board
- ask a student to read out the sentence/phrase
- demonstrate the grammar point in an appropriate way (e.g., numbering to indicate word order; paradigms for verbs; time lines for tenses)
- refer to the board throughout the activity if students are making mistakes

Pronunciation

By itself, the mispronunciation of a single phoneme or a wrong word stress is unlikely to cause a breakdown in communication. However, most L2 users make multiple errors in a single utterance, including errors of word order, tense choice and vocabulary choice. We must therefore try to remove as many sources of error as possible. When you are working with a group of words, make sure that students can pronounce each word with reasonable accuracy in phonemic terms, and with the correct stress for multiple syllable words.

Many researchers have found that getting the stress of a word wrong is a bigger cause of miscommunication than getting individual phonemes wrong.

Pair and group activities

Pairwork and group activities are, of course, an opportunity for students to produce spoken language. As mentioned above, this is not the main focus of this course. But, the second benefit of these interactional patterns is that they provide an opportunity for the teacher to check three points:

- Are students performing the correct task, in the correct way?
- Do students understand the language of the task they are performing?
- Which elements need to be covered again for the benefit of the class, and which points need to be dealt with on an individual basis with particular students?

Vocabulary and Skills banks

Each unit has clear targets in terms of vocabulary extension and skills development. These are detailed in the checks at the end of the unit (*Vocabulary bank* and *Skills bank*). However, you may wish to refer students to one or both of these pages at the start of work on the unit, so they have a clear idea of the targets. You may also wish to refer to them from time to time during lessons.

1 ECONOMICS IN THE MODERN WORLD

This introductory unit relates to the study and practice of economics in the modern world. By listening to a short lecture, students will gain insight into what economics actually entails and why it is important. They will also be able to reflect on their studies and how these might prepare them for their future role or career as an economist. A series of shorter lectures introduces a number of key aspects of economics, from types of financial trading to advantages and disadvantages of financial regulation. The content of these mini-lectures will be explored in more depth in later units.

Note that students will need dictionaries for some exercises in this unit.

Skills focus

🎧 Listening
- preparing for a lecture
- predicting lecture content from an introductory section
- understanding lecture organization
- choosing an appropriate form of notes
- making lecture notes

Speaking
- speaking from notes

Vocabulary focus

- words from general English with a special meaning in economics
- prefixes and suffixes

Key vocabulary

activity	econometrics	instrument	quantitative
asset	efficiency	interdependent	reassess
bundle	elasticity	interest	revenue
capital	expenditure	investment	security
compete	fraud	irrational	shares
cooperate	futures	misjudge	specialization
corporate	growth	overestimate	sub-prime
debt	harmful	practitioner	supervision
demand	index	predictable	unemployment
deregulation	influential	property	utility

1.1 Vocabulary

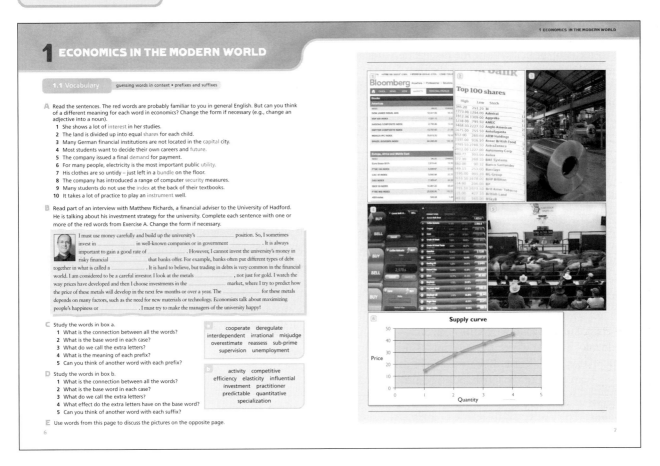

General note

Read the *Vocabulary bank* at the end of the Course Book unit. Decide when, if at all, to refer students to it. The best time is probably at the very end of the lesson or the beginning of the next lesson as a summary/revision.

Lesson aims

- identify words for the discipline in context, including words which contain affixes
- gain fluency in the target vocabulary

Introduction

Write the following sentences on the board:

1 *Spending only the money that you really have is just basic economics.*

2 *Economics is a really popular subject to study at university.*

3 *Development economics examines how investment might help countries to plan sustainable growth.*

4 *The ideas of 'supply' and 'demand' are basic principles of economics.*

5 *The economics of reducing government borrowing are extremely complicated.*

Ask students in which sentences the focus is on everyday activity (sentence 1 and, to some extent, sentence 5). Encourage students to identify differences in meaning and use of *economics* in the five sentences. Differences and similarities are not so clearly defined, but students should be able to point out some.

- In sentence 1, the focus is on everyday activity and how people should be aware of their position as consumers. Some students may have credit cards, so this aspect might be discussed.

- In sentence 2, the subject area or discipline is emphasized, but until we start to define the subject further, we only have a general idea of what is meant.

- Sentence 3 provides an example of a specific part of a broader discipline.

- Sentence 4 refers to concepts which are fundamental to any discussion on economics.

- Sentence 5 refers to how economics is about the money involved in a particular issue or area, *'the economics of defence/health'*, etc.

Note: Don't spend too much time on these consolidation activities.

Students should note that *economics* can be used quite generally to relate to everyday saving and spending. Its more specialist usage derives from contexts where economic principles will be applied. Remind students that the adjective *economic* is normally used when referring to ideas or policies from the discipline, and relating to the way goods, money, people and associated theories interact. There are, however, some restrictions. Ask students if we can say:

economic progress	YES
economic policy	YES
economic activity	YES
economic crisis	YES
economic books	NO
economic meaning	NO
economic ideas	YES
economic disagreement	POSSIBLY > YES!
economic solutions	YES
economic payments	NO
economic articles	NO

The university subject and discipline *economics* is singular. It may also be worth mentioning at this point that some related words or collocations have rather specialized meanings. Put the left-hand list on the board.

Word/phrase related to *economics*	Meaning
economize	to save money on certain things
economical	using less than expected/saving *an economical car* = cheap to run with low fuel consumption *an economical holiday* = cheap; probably good value for money
economies	plural of *economy*: e.g., *The economies of many sub-Saharan African countries are very vulnerable.*
economies of scale	usually means reducing something, e.g., *We need to introduce economies of scale in our distribution network.*

If there is time, ask students to write a few sentences or collocations using some of the items above. Check that they are using the vocabulary correctly.

Exercise A

Set for individual work and pairwork checking. Point out that these sentences introduce some important basic vocabulary related to economics – although it may not seem like that, at first glance. Do the first one as an example: *In general English, having an interest in something means an enthusiasm for/keenness about/involvement in something you enjoy. In English used in economics, it means the rate of money you receive on savings or an investment.*

Remember that the concept of *interest* is not acceptable in Islamic finance and banking, and a number of

alternative ways are available to provide loans or mortgages. These follow strict religious practice guidelines.

Point out, too, that there is often a connection between the general English usage and the way the term is used in economics. This may help students to guess certain meanings, e.g., *index* or *futures*. Tell students that some meanings are very specialized and they should not worry if they don't know the meaning at this time. Remind students to change the word form if necessary to complete the exercises.

Feed back, putting the English used in economics meanings in a table on the board. Tell students to use these structures where possible:

- *a(n) X is (a(n))* ... to define a noun
- *to X is to Y* to define a verb

Make sure students can say the words correctly. For example:

- /ʃ/ in <u>*uti*</u>*lity*
- schwa /ə/ in d<u>e</u>*mand*
- syllabic /l/ (or schwa) in *capit<u>al</u>*

Answers

See table at top of opposite page.

Exercise B

Set for individual work and pairwork checking. Do the first sentence as an example.

Feed back with the whole class. Ask students for any other words they know which have a special meaning in economics.

Answers

Model answers:

I must use money carefully and build up the university's <u>capital</u> position. So, I sometimes invest in <u>shares</u> in well-known companies or in government <u>securities</u>. It is always important to gain a good rate of <u>interest</u>. However, I cannot invest the university's money in risky financial <u>instruments</u> that banks offer. For example, banks often put different types of debt together in what is called a <u>bundle</u>. It is hard to believe, but trading in debts is very common in the financial world. I am considered to be a careful investor. I look at the metals <u>index</u>, not just for gold. I watch the way prices have developed and then I choose investments in the <u>futures</u> market, where I try to predict how the price of these metals will develop in the next few months or over a year. The <u>demand</u> for these metals depends on many factors, such as the need for new materials or technology. Economists talk about maximizing people's happiness or <u>utility</u>. I must try to make the managers of the university happy!

Examples of other possible words:

Word	Meaning	Comments
bundle	a package of financial products or items which are put together and traded	link to the more general usage is quite clear
capital	money and other assets used in starting, developing or expanding a company/business	singular uncountable use only
demand	the desire to own something and actually acquire that item = *effective demand* in economics	the verb – which is quite common in general English – is less frequently used in economics
futures	form of trading in currencies or commodities based on calculating the likely future price of these items	this might be used in an apparently 'singular' way as an area of activity, e.g., '... *futures is a highly complex form of trading*'
index	statistical table showing performance of the stock market or special funds	similar to general English, as an index is a *list*
instrument	product, such as shares or bonds, which can be traded	a financial instrument has a special function or role, for example, a long-term investment bond
interest	money paid on savings or investment	singular use only. To make it plural, we need to say '*various rates of interest*'.
securities	usually government-issued bonds with low level of risk; sometimes referred to as *gilts*	plural indicates that these are countable items rather than the uncountable noun *security* in general English which means safety
shares	special type of investment to raise capital where the investor receives shares or portions in a company or business, depending on the amount invested	note in compounds, it is usual to say '... *of shares*', e.g., *acquisition of shares, issue of shares, sale of shares*
utility	concept in economics where a consumer makes choices to gain most economic satisfaction	'*utility*' in general English refers to a public supply of, for example, water, gas or electricity but can also be the supply of a landline telephone

invest – place money, cf., *He really invests a lot of time and energy into his hobbies.*

return – interest or dividends received for an investment

accelerator – an economic term to show the influence of one factor on another (e.g., how new investment in a company might be driven by consumer change of income)

curve – mathematical/statistical figure showing trends

disposable – available to be spent by consumers

elastic – principle in the calculation of prices and the effect of price changes

ceiling – highest level at a particular time

Exercise C

Set the first question for pairwork. See which pair can work out the answer first.

Set the remainder for pairwork. Feed back, building up the table in the Answers section on the board.

Answers

Model answers:

1 They all have a base word + extra letters at the beginning/prefixes.

2 See table below.

3 A prefix.

4 See table below.

5 See table below.

Prefix	Base word	Meaning of prefix	Another word
co	operate	with, together	co-exist, coordinate, correlate, correspond (N.B. spelling)
de	regulate	gives the opposite meaning of base word	destabilize, denationalize
inter	dependent	between	interact, international, intervention
ir	rational	opposite, not	irreplaceable, irregular
mis	judge	do wrongly or incorrectly	miscalculate, misinterpret
over	estimate	do more than necessary or more than enough	overcharge, overpay, overwork
re	assess	do again	rearrange, rethink, reinforce
sub	prime	below, under	substandard, subscription
super	vision	over or bigger than	supermarket, supertanker (also, superior)
un	employ(ment)	not, opposite, absence of	unexpected, unfinished, unlimited

Language note

English is a lexemic language. In other words, the whole meaning of a word is usually contained within the word itself, rather than coming from a root meaning plus prefixes or suffixes (affixes). In most texts, written or spoken, there will only be a tiny number of words with affixes. However, these often add to a base meaning in a predictable way and it is important that students learn to detach affixes from a new word and see if they can find a recognizable base word.

Some words beginning with letters from prefixes are NOT in fact base + prefix, e.g., *refuse*, *discipline*. In other cases, the base word does not exist anymore in English and therefore will not help students, e.g., *transfer*, *transit*, although even in these cases the root meaning of the prefix may be a guide to the meaning of the whole word.

Exercise D

Repeat the procedure from Exercise C.

Answers

Model answers:

1 They all have a base word + extra letters at the end/suffixes.

2 See table below.

3 A suffix.

4 See table below.

5 See table below.

Letters shown in brackets indicate how the base word has changed in order to add the suffix.

Language note

Note that with prefixes we rarely change the form of the base word. However, with suffixes, there are often changes to the base word, so students must:

- take off the suffix
- try to reconstruct the base word

Exercise E

Set for pairwork. Try to elicit more than just the words from this lesson. Encourage students to use other forms, too (e.g., adjectives as well as nouns) and to try different collocations (*economic difficulties/problems/ issues/solutions; government programmes/policies/ intervention/lending/borrowing*). Students should describe the pictures as fully as they can at this stage.

Students may use the following words in their discussion of each picture:

Picture 1 – **index, shares, futures, securities, instrument, quantitative**

Picture 2 – **investment, interest, instrument,** products

Picture 3 – **capital, investment, competitive,** debt

Picture 4 – **futures, commodities**

Picture 5 – **demand, overestimate, misjudge,** risk

Picture 6 – curve, **quantitative,** supply, **demand, predictable, elasticity, utility**

Base word	Suffix	Effect/meaning of suffix	Another word
activ(*e*)	ity	adjective → noun	ability, accessibility, advisability, intensity
compet(*ition*)	(*i*)tive	noun → adjective to show the adjective fulfils a verbal action N.B. noun (~*ion*) formed from verb and adjective formed from noun construct, produce, reflect, repeat	constructive, productive, reflective, repetitive
efficien(*t*)	cy	adjective → noun	redundancy
elastic	ity	adjective → noun/having this quality	diversity
influen(*ce*)	tial	noun → adjective/having the features of	spatial, initial, partial
invest	ment	verb → noun/having that status, role or responsibility	employment, management, supplement
practi(*ce*)	tioner	person who does an activity or is associated with a special status or duty more usually ~*sioner*	pensioner, commissioner
predict	able	verb → adjective to show the verbal action *can be (done)* (*predicted*) (*replaced*), etc.	affordable, renewable, replaceable
quantit(*y*)	ative	noun → adjective/having the characteristics of ...	qualitative, argumentative, demonstrative
specializ(*e*)	ation	verb → noun/process or result of something happening	globalization, urbanization, standardization

Closure

If you have not done so already, refer students to the *Vocabulary bank* at the end of Unit 1. Tell students to explain how this lesson can help them deal with new words in context. If you wish, make three groups. Group A looks at the first section, *Using related words*. Group B looks at the second section, *Removing prefixes*. Group C looks at the third section, *Removing suffixes*. Then make sets of three with an ABC in each to explain to each other.

1.2 Listening

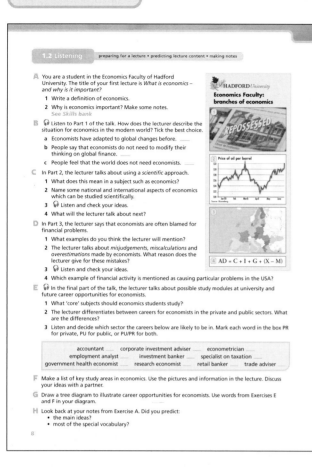

1.2 Listening   preparing for a lecture • predicting lecture content • making notes

A You are a student in the Economics Faculty of Hadford University. The title of your first lecture is *What is economics – and why is it important?*
  1 Write a definition of economics.
  2 Why is economics important? Make some notes.
      See Skills bank

B 🎧 Listen to Part 1 of the talk. How does the lecturer describe the situation for economics in the modern world? Tick the best choice.
  a Economists have adapted to global changes before. ____
  b People say that economists do not need to modify their thinking on global finance. ____
  c People feel that the world does not need economists. ____

C In Part 2, the lecturer talks about using a *scientific* approach.
  1 What does this mean in a subject such as economics?
  2 Name some national and international aspects of economics which can be studied scientifically.
  3 🎧 Listen and check your ideas.
  4 What will the lecturer talk about next?

D In Part 3, the lecturer says that economists are often blamed for financial problems.
  1 What examples do you think the lecturer will mention?
  2 The lecturer talks about *misjudgements, miscalculations* and *overestimations* made by economists. What reason does the lecturer give for these mistakes?
  3 🎧 Listen and check your ideas.
  4 Which example of financial activity is mentioned as causing particular problems in the USA?

E 🎧 In the final part of the talk, the lecturer talks about possible study modules at university and future career opportunities for economists.
  1 What 'core' subjects should economics students study?
  2 The lecturer differentiates between careers for economists in the private and public sectors. What are the differences?
  3 Listen and decide which sector the careers below are likely to be in. Mark each word in the box PR for private, PU for public, or PU/PR for both.

accountant	corporate investment adviser	econometrician
employment analyst	investment banker	specialist on taxation
government health economist	research economist	retail banker	trade adviser

F Make a list of key study areas in economics. Use the pictures and information in the lecture. Discuss your ideas with a partner.

G Draw a tree diagram to illustrate career opportunities for economists. Use words from Exercises E and F in your diagram.

H Look back at your notes from Exercise A. Did you predict:
  • the main ideas?
  • most of the special vocabulary?

HADFORD *University*

Economics Faculty: branches of economics

Price of oil per barrel

AD = C + I + G + (X – M)

8

General note

The recording should only be played once, since this reflects what happens in a real lecture. Students should be encouraged to listen for the important points, since that is what a native speaker would take from the text. However, students can be referred to the transcript at the end of the lesson to check their detailed understanding and word recognition, or to try to discover reasons for failing to comprehend.

Read the *Skills bank* at the end of the Course Book unit. Decide when, if at all, to refer students to it. The best time is probably at the very end of the lesson or the beginning of the next lesson, as a summary/revision.

Lesson aims

● prepare for a lecture
● predict lecture content
● make notes

Introduction

1 Show students flashcards of some or all of the words from Lesson 1.1. Tell students to say the words correctly and quickly as you flash them. Give out one word each to the students. Say the words again. The student with the word must hold it up. Repeat the process saying the words in context.

2 Refer students to the photos on page 8 of the Course Book unit. Briefly elicit ideas of what they depict. (They will look at the different career opportunities for economists in Exercise E.)

Exercise A

1 Set for pair or group work. Feed back, but do not confirm or correct at this time.

2 Set for pairwork. Elicit some ideas but do not confirm or correct.

Methodology note

You may want to refer students to the *Skills bank – Making the most of lectures* at this point. Set the following for individual work and pairwork checking. Tell students to cover the points and try to remember what was under each of the Ps – Plan, Prepare, Predict, Produce. Then tell students to work through the points to make sure they are prepared for the lecture they are about to hear.

🎧 Exercise B

Give students time to read the choices. Point out that they are only going to hear the introduction once, as in an authentic lecture situation. Play Part 1. Feed back. If students' answers differ, discuss which is the best answer and why.

Answers

Model answer:
  a Economists have adapted to global changes before.

Transcript 🎧 1.1

Part 1

Good morning everyone and welcome to the Faculty of Economics. I am very pleased that you have chosen this subject and I hope this first lecture will help you to understand more about the importance of economics as a discipline and its relevance to the modern world.

Right, before I ask a couple of essential questions, I want to mention an important fact which influences our thinking nowadays. Many people worldwide are trying to assess or, more accurately, reassess the position of economics globally as a result of the financial crisis which began in late 2008. Now, this situation is not new. Economists have modified their ideas and perspectives several times, especially in the last 80–90 years, because of changing world circumstances. You will go into more depth on the history of economic thought later in your course. But please keep this reassessment process in mind as you study. It might take a number of years before economics is again in a confident and stable position, but this is a challenge we must face! I am optimistic that economists will make an important contribution to world recovery and future growth.

🎧 Exercise C

1/2 Set for pairwork discussion before listening. Tell students to make notes.

3/4 Play Part 2 for students to check their ideas and listen for question 4. Feed back, building up a diagram on the board. Explain that this is a form of classification diagram. Finally, check the answer to question 4.

Answers

Model answers:

1/2 These questions consider economics as a scientific discipline. Students might mention observation, analysis, interpretation, prediction (of economic data), as well as mathematical and statistical approaches.

See diagram below.

4 The lecturer will talk about why people blame economists.

Transcript 🎧 1.2

Part 2

So, let's look at a number of key questions. Firstly, 'What is economics?' It sounds simple, but it is really quite complex! To answer this, we need to think of economics as a science, such as physics or chemistry but also as a *social* science, like geography or history. Scientists notice what happens, then they analyze these events and try to interpret them. They try to predict outcomes and test their ideas. Well, economists do more or less the same. Your studies will help you to understand, in a scientific way, how economics has developed. It is this approach to economics which allows us to call it a scientific discipline. In economics, it is important for students and practitioners – bankers, analysts, investment advisers, traders and so on – to behave in a rational and responsible way to maintain the reputation of economics.

There are so many branches of economics so, for today's lecture, I will divide the main areas into five sections, although this is really an over-simplification.

Firstly, you will learn about how economies develop, how nations compete and cooperate. As part of this process, you will find out about international agreements, related to the supervision of world trade. You can then understand better why government intervention is sometimes acceptable and necessary.

Secondly, you will understand about economic growth nationally and internationally and how this growth might be sustainable. I mean, continued into the future.

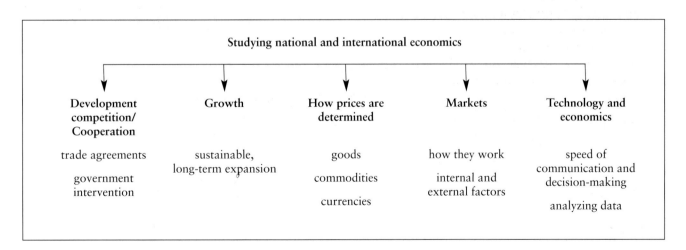

Studying national and international economics

Development competition/ Cooperation	Growth	How prices are determined	Markets	Technology and economics
trade agreements	sustainable, long-term expansion	goods	how they work	speed of communication and decision-making
government intervention		commodities	internal and external factors	
		currencies		analyzing data

Thirdly, you will learn how prices are determined for goods, commodities and currencies. As part of this process, you will understand about topics such as supply and demand, inflation and deflation, employment, unemployment and many more.

Fourthly, you will find out about how markets work for goods and services and the internal and external influences on them.

Finally, and to complement these four areas of study, you will learn how technology has changed the face of economics by making communication and decision-making so much faster. You will also learn how you can use this technology to analyze and predict.

Economics depends, as I mentioned, on a scientific approach to real events that have consequences for everyone. You will start to recognize the rational nature of economics ... and the irrational side! If there is growth in the world economy, people are generally satisfied. When things go wrong, people look for someone to blame. Economists are not supermen, or superwomen, but merely human beings! So, like all humans, they can make mistakes and misjudge situations. This is what I will discuss in the next part of my lecture.

🎧 Exercise D

1 Set for pairwork discussion before listening. Tell students to make notes of their ideas.

2 Ensure that students recall the meanings of these words if necessary. Elicit an example, e.g., using the word *growth* (*Economists might misjudge the growth rate of an economy*). Set for pairwork and ask students to keep a record of their ideas, especially the reason for mistakes.

If you have time, write the words in the left-hand column of the table on the board before the students listen. Remember to make grammatical adjustments if you ask students for answers after listening.

misjudge (**misjudged**)	financial markets
make (**made**)	unlimited profits
overestimate(**d**)	market growth
miscalculate(**d**)	demand
create(**d**)	risky financial instruments

Answers

Model answers:

1 Use the table to verify student understanding and clarify where necessary.

2/3 The lecturer emphasizes that economists, bankers, analysts, industrialists and even governments were criticized.

4 The American sub-prime housing market.

Transcript 🎧 1.3

Part 3

If there is an economic decline, then people often need to blame someone – the government, the bankers, industrialists, people making too much profit and, very often, economists. Let's consider the economic crisis which began in 2008. As in many human decision-making situations, economic analysts, bankers and investors, etc., made harmful errors. At that time, they misjudged financial markets. Bankers thought they could make unlimited profits. Analysts overestimated market growth. Producers miscalculated demand. Investment institutions created financial instruments which carried too much risk – and these professional economists made other human errors.

One example was the American sub-prime housing market, which many people say was the main cause of the 2008 financial crisis. The sequence of events was this. Firstly, banks were happy to give loans or credit to borrowers to buy a house. These loans are called mortgages. That is M-O-R-T-G-A-G-E by the way. But the second point is that these loans were given to borrowers who were not really in a strong financial position. The banks knew these borrowers would find repayment of interest difficult. Many people were sub-prime borrowers – 'sub' means 'below' and prime means 'top-quality'. So, it was predictable that these mortgages could never be repaid. That is one example of a misjudgement. But to find a solution to the economic illnesses, we always need to remember that we are dealing with human factors!

Methodology note

Up to this point, you have not mentioned how students should record information. Have a look round to see what students are doing. If some are already using good methods, make a note and mention this later in the unit.

🎧 Exercise E

1/2 Set for pairwork and ask students to make a note of their ideas.

3 Give students plenty of time to look at the words in the box, then play Part 4. Feed back. This is a post-listening discussion activity and is most suitable for pairwork. The text does not specify whether the public or private sectors or both are likely to attract economists, but some answers are more 'correct' than others.

Answers

Model answers:

1 This question asks students to predict core areas in economics which they might study. Students might realistically talk about world trade (international economics), taxation (macroeconomics, financial economics), money markets (finance and investment, capital market economics), government spending (macroeconomics) and consumer behaviour (demand and supply in markets). The lecture touches on these and other topics.

2 There is no qualitative discussion in Part 4 of the differences between being an economist in the public or private sector so this answer depends on the students. If they do not suggest any differences, you could prompt with questions such as:

Is it better to work for a private company or for a government department?

Who gets paid more? Whose job is safer? Who has more pressure? Whose job is more competitive? Who is more concerned with making profits? Who is concerned with spending money efficiently? Who has more responsibility? Who uses statistics more?

3

accountant	PR/PU
corporate investment adviser	PR
econometrician	PU
employment analyst	PU
investment banker	PR
specialist on taxation	PU/PR
government health economist	PU
research economist	PU
retail banker	PR
trade adviser	PU

Transcript 🎧 1.4

Part 4

So, we've looked briefly at the challenges for economics. Now let's turn to your studies. So, first of all, what are you likely to study over the next two or three years? Well, you have to study some core subjects – quantitative, mathematical and international economics. Then you will learn how international markets work. You will also understand how economic unions or organizations work, such as the EU or the World Trade Association. Later, you will learn to differentiate between public and private sector finances in applied economics. If you are interested in mathematics and statistics, you are likely to study more about econometrics. Other specializations are possible, such as environmental, health or agricultural economics. You might examine an area such as corporate social responsibility. So, there is a wide range of topics to stimulate you in the coming years!

Right, now what about jobs? It's never too early to think about a career in one of the many branches of economics. Let's start with the public sector – the government departments which create policies and are responsible for revenue, expenditure and analysis. There are also many economists in local government, too, who analyze income and expenditure or investment locally. In the private sector, many retail or High Street banks employ economists to give ordinary customers financial advice and support. Some banks have no retail outlets and only have investment activities. Nowadays, independent financial consultants or asset managers are responsible for trading and investing in different markets, usually for corporate clients. You would probably need several years' experience before you could work in this branch. Insurance is another branch where economists are employed. It might not sound very exciting but it is a very competitive business, especially after globalization. Many aspects of trade, shipping, aviation or property are linked to insurance. Finally, there are many economists who work in private companies or retail businesses. They may be analysts, advisers, buyers, accountants or supply chain specialists, amongst others.

So, I hope that this introductory lecture has given you a few things to think about. And I hope, too, that you can now begin to answer those two important questions, 'What is economics – and why is it important?'

Exercise F

Set for individual work and pairwork checking. Feed back, building up a list on the board.

Answers

Possible answers:

Key study areas in economics:

quantitative/mathematical economics

international economics

how markets work

economic organizations

public and private sector finances

resources analysis

policy development

econometrics (statistics)

specializations such as health/environmental/agricultural economics

corporate social responsibility (CSR)

Exercise G

Set for pairwork. Feed back to the whole class, building up a tree diagram using words from Exercises E and F on the board.

Answers

Possible answers:

Economists					
Research	Specializations	Banking	Government departments	Independent	Business
econometrics	health	retail	taxation	adviser	analysis
analysis	environmental	investment	revenue	asset manager	accountant
	agricultural				supply chain
	CSR				

Exercise H

Refer students back to their notes from Exercise A.

Closure

1 Look at the pictures in Exercise A related to different aspects of economics. Put the list of words on the board and ask students to discuss which words apply to the different pictures (suggestions in brackets).

   commodity (2), quantitative (4), theoretical (4), recession (1), supply (3), investment (3), index (2), mortgage (1), growth (4)

2 Refer students to the *Skills bank* if you have not done so already and work through the section *Making the most of lectures*.

1.3 Extending skills

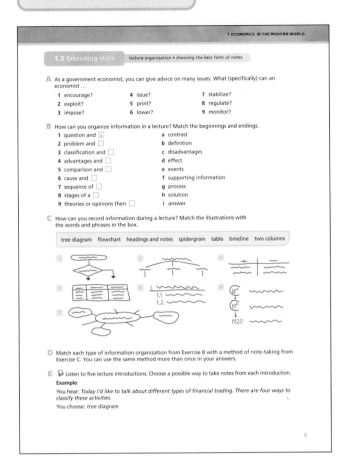

3 impose   taxation, regulations, restrictions, tariffs

4 issue   securities (bonds), money, laws

5 print   money

6 lower   taxes, interest rates, duties, tariffs

7 stabilize   the economy, the markets, the currency

8 regulate   the banking industry, trade

9 monitor   growth, inflation, import/export balance

Exercise B

Point out that you can understand a lecture better if you can predict the order of information. Point out also that there are many pairs and patterns in presenting information, e.g., question and answer, or a sequence of events in chronological order.

Set for pairwork. Feed back orally. Check pronunciation. Point out that lecturers may not actually use these words but if you recognize that what a lecturer is saying is the first of a pair or the beginning of a sequence, you are ready for the second or next stage later in the lecture.

Answers

1	question and	answer
2	problem and	solution
3	classification and	definition
4	advantages and	disadvantages
5	comparison and	contrast
6	cause and	effect
7	sequence of	events
8	stages of a	process
9	theories or opinions then	supporting information

Exercise C

Identify the first form of notes – a flowchart. Set the rest for individual work and pairwork checking. Feed back using an OHT or other visual medium if possible.

Answers

1 flowchart

2 tree diagram

3 two columns

4 table

5 headings and notes

6 timeline

7 spidergram

Lesson aims

- identify different types of lecture organization
- use the introduction to a lecture to decide the best form of notes to use

Introduction

Tell students to build up the four Ps of preparing for and attending a lecture: Plan, Prepare, Predict, Produce. You could put students into four groups, each group working on one of the stages, then feeding back to the rest of the class.

Exercise A

These words will occur in the listening texts. Set for pairwork. Feed back orally. The more the students can say about these words, the better. Accept anything correct but let students explain their choice if they choose a combination not given below.

Answers

Possible answers:

1 encourage   investment, growth, trade (exports)

2 exploit   resources, trade advantages

Methodology note

You might like to make larger versions of the illustrations of different note types and pin them up in the classroom for future reference.

Exercise D

Work through the first one as an example. Set for pairwork.

Feed back orally and encourage discussion. Demonstrate how each method of note-taking in Exercise C can be matched with an organizational structure. Point out that:

- a tree diagram is useful for hierarchically arranged information, such as when the information moves from general to specific examples. (Remind students of Lesson 1.2 Exercise G, although a spidergram would also have been appropriate here.)

- a spidergram is more fluid and flexible, and can be used to show connections between things, such as interactions or causes and effects.

Answers

Possible answers:

1 question and answer = headings and notes

2 problem and solution = headings and notes or two-column table

3 classification and definition = tree diagram or spidergram

4 advantages and disadvantages = two-column table

5 comparison and contrast = table

6 cause and effect = spidergram

7 sequence of events = timeline or flowchart

8 stages of a process = flowchart (or circle if it is a cycle)

9 theories and opinions then supporting information = headings and notes or two-column table

🎧 Exercise E

Explain that students are going to hear the introductions to several different lectures. They do not have to take notes, only decide what type of organization of information they are going to hear. Work through the example.

Play each introduction. Pause after each one and allow students to discuss then feed back. Students may suggest different answers in some cases. Establish that sometimes lecturers move from one information organization to another, e.g., classification then cause and effect.

Answers

Model answers:

1 tree diagram (classification and definition)

2 two-column table (advantages and disadvantages)

3 spidergram (classification and definition/exemplification)

4 timeline (sequence of events/historical sequence)

5 flowchart (stages in a process); note that this could also be a circular diagram to show a cycle.

Transcript 🎧 1.5

Introduction 1

Today I'd like to talk about different types of financial trading. There are four ways to classify these activities. I am only going to talk very briefly about each, so that you can understand some of the basic principles and specialized terminology that is used. The first form of trading is called equities. Secondly, we have securities. The third type is called commodities. Finally, we have currencies. So, that's *equities, securities, commodities* and *currencies*. Later in your course, you will be looking at each form of financial trading in more depth.

Introduction 2

Good morning everybody. Today we're going to look at the regulation of the banking and finance industries. We'll also consider some of the advantages and disadvantages of controls. Regulation means that the government or independent bodies have a lot of control over the banking industry. Yes, 'bodies' here means organizations, authorities or committees. These bodies are usually appointed by the government. Some economists believe that governments in advanced economies have allowed too much *de*regulation in the industry over the past 20 years or so. This has been a factor in the recent economic and banking crisis.

Introduction 3

Good afternoon everybody. Today's lecture topic is government revenue and how governments can raise money to finance their budgets. Because I am most familiar with the UK economy, I will use the UK as an example, but there are, of course, differences between most countries. *Revenue* means money that is paid to the state for different reasons. In Britain, the Treasury is responsible for revenue and expenditure. I will try to mention the most important ways in which the government takes money off its citizens! You may already know some of these sources of revenue, but some may be a bit surprising or unexpected. Most economies have different ways of raising revenue. In some countries, the government still controls industries and resources such as gas or electricity. It may also be responsible for extractive industries such as mining or drilling for oil. This government control is known as *state ownership*, but it is not found everywhere. So, I will concentrate on the other main sources of revenue in a mixed economy without considering state-owned industries.

Introduction 4

Good morning everyone. Today I want to provide you with a brief historical overview of the development of economic thought. I will cover a period approximately from the middle of the 18th century to around 1890. Most economists would accept that the four thinkers I have chosen are very influential. By the end of this lecture, I hope that you will know more about David Hume, spelt H-U-M-E. He lived from 1711 to 1776. Then there is Adam Smith who lived from 1723 to 1790. And David Ricardo – I will spell that for you, R-I-C-A-R-D-O – who lived from 1772 to 1823. They were all British, but not all English! In addition, you should know about Karl Marx, that's K-A-R-L M-A-R-X, who was born in 1818 and died in 1883. As you may know, he was German, although he spent a lot of time in England. So, you see, there is a period of approximately 150 years to the present, so I'd better get started.

Introduction 5

In today's lecture, I am going to talk about the interrelationships or interdependence between economic factors in that period when an economy does not grow and when production declines. This is known, officially, as a *recession*. We can see the relationship between the different factors as 'cause and effect', but it is often very difficult to say which 'cause' is responsible for starting a recession. As you know, most economies go through cycles where they might grow for a certain time and then, for many possible reasons, the economy starts to slow down. My lecture today will concentrate on the specific factors present in a recession in an advanced economy and how they interrelate.

Closure

1 Test students on the pairs from Exercise B. Correct pronunciation again if necessary.
2 Refer students to the *Skills bank – Making perfect lecture notes*.

1.4 Extending skills

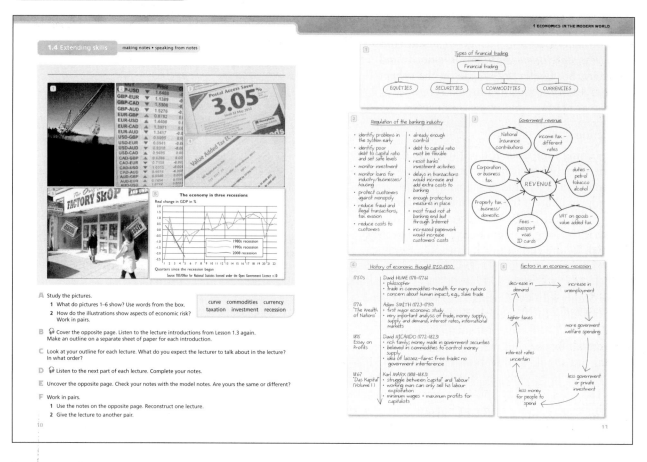

Lesson aims

- make outline notes from lecture introductions
- make notes from a variety of lecture types
- speak from notes

Further practice in:

- predicting lecture content

Introduction

Elicit as much information from the lecture notes in Lesson 1.2 as possible. If necessary, prompt students by reading parts of the transcript and pausing for students to complete in their own words.

Exercise A

Set for individual work and pairwork checking. Feed back orally but still do not confirm or correct. Point out that students are going to hear about these things in today's lesson. You will return to these illustrations at the end.

For reference, the images show:

1 exploiting of **commodities** – drilling for oil, mining or other extractive industries

2 **currency** trading with the rates shown

3 financial products to attract **investment**/customers

4 **taxation** as a method for the government to obtain revenue

5 **recession**, unemployment, economic problems

6 **curve** showing economic trends, here a **recession**

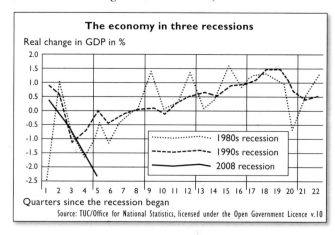

Methodology note

It is best that students close the book at this stage, so they are not tempted to look at the model notes. You can give the instructions for the next few stages orally as required.

🎧 Exercise B

Make sure students understand that they are going to hear the introductions from Lesson 1.3 again. Ask them briefly if they can remember any of the content from the introductions. Spend a few minutes on this if students are able to contribute. Elicit suggestions for types of notes (Lesson 1.3, Exercise E).

Explain that this time they must create an outline using an appropriate type of notes. (You can refer them again to the *Skills bank – Making perfect lecture notes*.) Make sure students understand that they don't need to write a lot at this stage – outlines may consist of just a few words, e.g., the start of a spidergram, the first part of a table or diagram. Play each introduction in turn and give students time to choose a note-type, make the outline and check it with other students.

Feed back, getting all the outlines on the board – you may wish to copy them from the first part of the model notes on the right-hand page, or you may prefer to follow your students' suggestions. Clarify the meaning of new words and check pronunciation.

Transcript 🎧 1.5

Introduction 1

Today I'd like to talk about different types of financial trading. There are four ways to classify these activities. I am only going to talk very briefly about each so that you can understand some of the basic principles and specialized terminology that is used. The first form of trading is called equities. Secondly, we have securities. The third type is called commodities. Finally, we have currencies. So, that's *equities*, *securities*, *commodities* and *currencies*. Later in your course, you will be looking at each form of financial trading in more depth.

Introduction 2

Good morning everybody. Today we're going to look at the regulation of the banking and finance industries. We'll also consider some of the advantages and disadvantages of controls. Regulation means that the government or independent bodies have a lot of control over the banking industry. Yes, 'bodies' here means organizations, authorities or committees. These bodies are usually appointed by the government. Some economists believe that governments in advanced economies have allowed too much *de*regulation in the industry over the past 20 years or so. This has been a factor in the recent economic and banking crisis.

Introduction 3

Good afternoon everybody. Today's lecture topic is *government revenue* and how governments can raise money to finance their budgets. Because I am most familiar with the UK economy, I will use the UK as an example but there are, of course, differences between most countries. *Revenue* means money that is paid to the state for different reasons. In Britain, the Treasury is responsible for revenue and expenditure. I will try to mention the most important ways in which the government takes money off its citizens! You may already know some of these sources of revenue, but some may be a bit surprising or unexpected. Most economies have different ways of raising revenue. In some countries, the government still controls industries and resources such as gas or electricity. It may also be responsible for extractive industries such as mining or drilling for oil. This government control is known as *state ownership*, but it is not found everywhere. So, I will concentrate on the other main sources of revenue in a mixed economy without considering state-owned industries.

Introduction 4

Good morning everyone. Today I want to provide you with a brief historical overview of the development of economic thought. I will cover a period approximately from the middle of the 18th century to around 1890. Most economists would accept that the four thinkers I have chosen are very influential. By the end of this lecture, I hope that you will know more about David Hume, spelt H-U-M-E. He lived from 1711 to 1776. Then there is Adam Smith who lived from 1723 to1790. And David Ricardo, I will spell that for you R-I-C-A-R-D-O who lived from 1772 to 1823. They were all British, but not all English! In addition, you should know about Karl Marx, that's K-A-R-L M-A-R-X, who was born in 1818 and died in 1883. As you may know, he was German, although he spent a lot of time in England. So, you see, there is a period of approximately 150 years to the present, so I'd better get started.

Introduction 5

In today's lecture, I am going to talk about the interrelationships or interdependence between economic factors in that period when an economy does not grow and when production declines. This is known, officially, as a *recession*. We can see the relationship between the different factors as 'cause and effect', but it is often very difficult to say which 'cause' is responsible for starting a recession. As you know, most economies go through cycles where they might grow for a certain time and then, for many possible reasons, the economy starts to slow down. My lecture today will concentrate on the specific factors present in a recession in an advanced economy and how they interrelate.

Methodology note

Spiral bound or stitched/stapled notebooks are not the best way to keep lecture notes. It is impossible to reorganize or add extra information at a later date, or make a clean copy of notes after a lecture. Encourage students, therefore, to use a loose-leaf file, but make sure that they organize it in a sensible way, with file dividers, and keep it tidy. Tell students to use a separate piece of paper for each outline in this lecture.

Exercise C

Set for pair or group work. Feed back, but do not confirm or correct. Students should be able to predict reasonably well the kind of information which will fit into their outline.

🎧 Exercise D

Before you play the next part of the lecture, refer students to their outline notes again. Tell them to orally reconstruct the introduction from their notes. They don't have to be able to say the exact words, but they should be able to give the gist.

Remind students that they are only going to hear the next part of each lecture once. Play each extract in turn, pausing if necessary to allow students to make notes but not replaying any section. Tell students to choose an appropriate type of notes for this part of the lecture – it could be a continuation of the type they chose for the introduction, or it could be a different type.

Transcript 🎧 1.6

Lecture 1

Let's expand on the different types of trading activity, starting with *equities*. Equities are usually in the form of shares in larger companies. Companies issue them to increase their own capital. This happens when new capitalization is needed. Company analysts or accountants suggest that new capital is necessary. This will help the company to expand or produce more. Investors can buy and sell shares in the company and the price on the stock market may change from day to day. There is usually no problem in finding investors. They will want to buy the new issue in a company which is strong.

Government bonds or *securities* are further examples of trading in a whole range of instruments which are negotiable. That means they have a value and can be traded easily, for example, the German government bonds. These are called 'bund'. Another famous bond is the US Treasury bond. Gilts, bund and US bonds are quoted

separately on the financial markets. These are very safe and provide a strong guarantee for the investor. However, there are two disadvantages. The first is the relatively low rate of interest. Secondly, these are long-term bonds. 'Long-term' indicates the lifetime of the bond, perhaps 10, 20 or even 50 years! This means that inflation can affect the value of the securities. The end of the lifetime of a bond is called the maturity. So, many people sell bonds before maturity because of inflation. There are many other financial instruments such as debt or credit bundles. But many instruments are related to mortgages and other property-related assets.

In the *commodities* markets, traders buy and sell a wide range of commodities, including oil, or coffee, metals such as copper or gold and other agricultural or mineral products. Now, trading in commodities often depends on very large investments as prices do not usually change very much from day to day. Of course, there can be dramatic events which cause sudden price changes. This is an advantage for the large investor. However, it means that small investors cannot easily trade in commodities. Another factor is that the investor is usually 'buying forward'. This is why economists talk about futures. It means that the investor speculates about the future price for the commodity and accepts the risks.

Finally, let's move on to *currency trading*. There are a number of world currencies – the dollar, yen, pound and euro – plus several additional strong trading currencies such as the Swiss franc or the Chinese yuan. One advantage is that trading involves a fairly simple conversion. Conversion means the value of one currency compared to another, on a day-to-day basis. Another advantage is that the currency market can help a government to develop its own currency reserves and stabilize the economy. A government can release some of its currency reserves to increase investment or to solve economic problems at home. An advantage for the large investor is that even very small fluctuations in the price of one currency can mean large profits. However, there are some disadvantages related to currency dealing. Speculators can force the price of a particular currency up or down by buying or selling amounts of the currency. This may be independent of the real value of the currency and the strength of that nation's economy.

🎧 1.7

Lecture 2

So what are the arguments for and against regulation? I will try and present each argument in favour of regulation and match it with a counter-argument from the point of view of the banks.

Regulation means that it is possible to identify problems in the financial systems early and take action. However, the banks say that there is already enough control.

Next, regulators want to make sure that the banks do not lend too much money compared with their assets. This is known as the debt to capital ratio. Regulators say that a safe ratio must be set for all banks. The banks have a different view and say that the debt to capital ratio must be flexible to allow them to invest without restriction.

Regulators want to monitor the types of loans for industry, business or housing, but banks say that regulation would add extra costs to all transactions and discourage borrowers. Banks also say that there would be more delays.

Regulators say that customers need more protection against unfair bank practices, but the banks argue that many regulations to protect customers are already in place.

Fraud is another worry for regulators. This involves illegal transfers of money, as well as people or businesses that avoid paying tax on their investments. However, the view of the banks is that most fraud takes place through the Internet. The banks say controls on transfers and accounts are already very strict.

Finally, regulators say that banks need to reduce costs to customers. However, the banks argue that regulations increase paperwork and, as a result, this increases costs to customers.

We will have to see how things develop in the next few years, as obviously there are two quite different viewpoints!

🎧 **1.8**

Lecture 3

As you may be aware, most advanced economies have a form of income tax. Usually, there are different rates of income tax to make the system as fair as possible, especially for people who have low incomes. Rich people always complain about high tax rates but they don't always get much sympathy. Income tax usually provides the government with a large proportion of its revenue.

Next, we will look at *duties*. This is a special form of tax which a government places on certain items such as tobacco, petrol, alcohol and, in Britain, stamp duty which is paid when buying a house.

Most countries, including Britain, have Value Added Tax – VAT. This is simply an extra tax added to the price of an item, such as clothes, cosmetics, household articles, etc. You have to pay VAT on some foods, but not all. Most people dislike VAT, but it is an easy way for the government to increase revenue.

Governments also receive fees for different documents, such as passports, but also for visas and registration fees. Perhaps some of you have paid the, usually rather high, visa fees for entry into the UK!

Most people have to pay a form of property tax, either domestic or commercial. In the UK, property tax is called council tax and is based on the size of the house. It is calculated locally. This makes it fairer because property prices vary in different parts of the UK. Business property is taxed at a different rate from domestic houses and low business property taxes can encourage expansion.

Businesses also have to pay tax on their profits at a special national rate. Of course, this tax can be a problem if the tax is much lower in one country than in others and businessmen often complain that the competition is not always fair in such situations.

Finally, the UK government obtains revenue through National Insurance Contributions or NICs, which are not really taxes. People who work pay a proportion of their income as NICs, usually about 15–20% of their salary. However, these payments also fund the National Health Service, and provide unemployment or child benefit. NICs also help to provide a state pension for people when they retire from work. So, it is understandable that governments want to have the maximum amount of revenue. But it is equally understandable that people complain a lot about taxation!

🎧 **1.9**

Lecture 4

Now, of the key economic thinkers, David Hume is perhaps better known as a philosopher. Hume said that it was commodities, materials such as cotton, pepper or gold, and not capital, that really mattered. Hume said that commodities should be more freely traded so that more nations could benefit. This would increase the wealth for more people in more countries. On the other hand, Hume was also concerned about the impact of trade on human behaviour. Many European countries had become competitors for the expanding world markets, particularly in the 18th century. They established trading posts in other countries or took control of other places by making them colonies. They fought wars to defend their colonies and to expand trade, especially the terrible slave trade between Africa and America. Hume was not a supporter of the slave trade. We can see why Hume was considered a bit of a revolutionary economist.

Adam Smith used Hume's analysis and expanded his ideas. In 1776, Smith published the extremely influential *The Wealth of Nations,* which is considered the first detailed study on economics. Smith produced a complete analysis of trade. This included an examination of the division of labour, the value of wages, money supply, as well as the principles of supply and demand. Smith proposed theories on interest rates, investment and much more. England was at war for much of Smith's life, so his ability to include examples and information from other economies – France, Holland, India, China and America – makes his work a very impressive study for the period. *The Wealth of Nations* can be seen as socio-economic history, but its influence is unquestioned. Smith certainly provided the platform for modern economic analysis!

So, the last English economist we will look at is David Ricardo. He was, officially, English, but his family came from mixed nationalities and had been involved in trade and banking. He became rich by arranging and dealing in government securities, usually to fund the wars Britain fought! Ricardo had time to think and write about many aspects of economics. During his lifetime, remember he lived from 1772 to 1823, England fought many wars, and lost the American colonies. But it also became a major industrial power. Europe had seen the 1789 French Revolution, as well as huge social change. Like Smith, Ricardo believed that economic wealth and stability depended on commodities, not money. He also wrote that the government should not print and circulate money unless it was supported by the availability of commodities at the right price. Markets and money supply should be allowed to develop without government intervention. The economic theory which Ricardo began is generally called laissez-faire, which is a French term meaning 'Let it be' or 'Don't interfere' or 'Don't take any action'. 'Laissez-faire' ideas support free trade with limited government protection of industry or agriculture, in other words no government intervention.

Now we come to our final economist. Karl Marx's writing and economic analysis were the beginnings of communism. He emphasized that the working class should control production and also political power. A number of communist states tried to put his ideas into practice, but this was not always successful. However, there is still a lot of support for some of Marx's ideas. Again, you should think about the social and political background of the time when Marx was writing. Many new nations were emerging, and old ideas were changing. Machinery had been introduced to build up industrial economies. In Europe, working people wanted freedom. Marx was German but spent many years in England. He was interested in the condition of the English working class. The workers lived in very poor conditions and were exploited by the factory owners. Marx considered that production was a struggle between capitalists – factory owners, bankers, financiers – and 'labour'. By this, Marx means the workers had nothing except their ability to work. He wrote about his ideas in a famous book *Das Kapital*. The first volume was published in 1867. In this book, Marx said that workers only ever receive the value of their labour. Marx said that capitalists would always exploit workers because the maximum profit is linked to the minimum of wages. So, for Marx, it was a struggle between two opposing sides – capital and labour. This was a viewpoint that worried governments and capitalists, but appealed to ordinary working people.

🎧 **1.10**

Lecture 5

As I said, an economy can move into recession after a period of growth. A very deep recession is known as a *slump*, spelt S-L-U-M-P. This presents many problems to governments. The changes or fluctuations during a recession are often measured according to the country's GDP – Gross Domestic Product – as you probably already know. After a recession, the economy begins to pick up again, but it is always uncertain how long a recession will last.

Let's analyze how a recession starts. This is a rather simplified version of a recession and you will learn more complicated ways to analyze economic trends later in your course. To analyze a recession, we need a starting point, so let's select *demand* as the starting factor. If demand decreases, it means that people are spending less on goods and services. Factories do not produce so much and service industries do not provide so many services. This means that unemployment increases. When this happens, the government has to pay more unemployment benefit and spend more on social welfare. As a result, there is less money for the government to encourage investment. In addition, businesses are worried about the fall in demand and do not take the risk of investing. In this situation, there is often a need for the government to increase revenue, usually by raising taxes. Because the economy is not very healthy, the government must decide what to do about interest rates. If interest rates are high, people will save, not spend. Moreover, it is expensive for businesses to borrow money in order to expand production. If interest rates are low, borrowing for investment might increase, but businesses often think that demand will not increase quickly enough. The usual result is that people have less money to spend which, in turn, leads to a decrease in demand. In a recession, it is difficult for a government to know *how*, *where* and *when* to intervene.

Exercise E

Allow students to uncover the opposite page or open their books. Give them plenty of time to compare their answers with the model notes. Feed back on the final question.

Exercise F

1 Ask students to work in pairs. Assign a set of notes to each pair. They must try to reconstruct the lecture orally – including the introduction – from the notes.

2 Put the pairs together in groups of four, with different topics. Each pair should give their lecture to the other pair.

Closure

1 Work on any problems you noticed during the pairwork (Exercise F).

2 Refer back to the pictures at the top of the Course Book page. Students should now be able to discuss them with greater confidence.

Extra activities

1 Work through the *Vocabulary bank* and *Skills bank* if you have not already done so, or as a revision of previous study.

2 Use the *Activity bank* (Teacher's Book additional resources section, Resource 1A).

A Set the crossword for individual work (including homework) or pairwork.

Answers

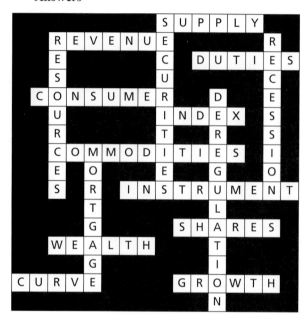

B Play noughts and crosses in pairs. There are two boards. The first board contains words with affixes, the second contains ideas and concepts from economics.

Teach students how to play noughts and crosses if they don't know. Then they take it in turns to choose a word and try to use the word/phrase in context or explain what it means. If they succeed, they can put a symbol – a nought **0** or a cross **X** – in that box.

If a student gets three of his/her own symbols in a row, he/she wins.

First board: Tell students to remove the affixes to find the base word in each case. Make sure that they can tell you the meaning of the base word (e.g., *care* for *careful*) but don't elicit the meaning of the affixed word at this stage. Put students in pairs to play the game. Monitor and adjudicate.

Second board: Put students in different pairs to play the second game. Clearly, this time they have to actually remember the facts from the lectures. Don't let them look back at the notes.

3 Each of the mini-lectures from Lesson 4 can lead on to a great deal more work. Tell students they should research one of the following, according to which group they ended in. Explain that they must come back and report to the rest of the class in the next lesson/next week.

Lecture	Research
1	Students might find out some prices in shares, commodities or bonds or currency rates and compare movements over a few days. They can tell their colleagues which websites they found useful.
2	This is rather a specialized area, but this topic could be broadened to look at, e.g., the FSA in UK or the equivalent in the USA or in a European country. More details on money laundering and illegal activities will be dealt with later in the course. It might be useful for students to look at the 'small print' in some products for consumers or to look at interest rates at banks.
3	Students might choose an economy (World Bank statistics or country profiles would be a good starting point) and try to verify how revenue is obtained in those countries. A few examples of different economies might be very useful.
4	Students could find out more about the ideas of these thinkers and/or the society in which they were living when they wrote their major works.
5	Look at past recessions in advanced economies, especially the Great Depression of 1930–1934. Look at the 2008 recession and how governments acted/reacted.

4 Brainstorm note-taking techniques. For example:

- use spacing between different ideas and points
- use abbreviations
- use symbols
- underline headings
- use capital letters (for emphasis)
- use indenting
- make ordered points
- use different colours
- use key words only

2 HOW ECONOMICS IS ORGANIZED

Unit 2 looks at different organizational principles within the field of economics. These are not clear-cut distinctions and, for ease of understanding, the term 'branches' and 'divisions' have been used. Please mention to students that there are many other areas of economics and this organizational approach is simple, but useful. The essential division between macroeconomics and microeconomics is outlined briefly but the overlap should also be mentioned to students.

The first reading text discusses the scientific nature of economics and possible divisions within economics. It should give students the chance to reflect on the status of the discipline. The second reading text looks at economic stakeholders and their roles. It is important for students to become familiar with this terminology, and in particular for students not to confuse 'stakeholder' and 'shareholder'. They will encounter these topics in more detail in subsequent units.

Note that students will need dictionaries for some exercises in this unit.

Skills focus

Reading

- using research questions to focus on relevant information in a text
- using topic sentences to get an overview of the text
- identifying paragraph structure

Writing

- writing topic sentences
- summarizing a text

Vocabulary focus

- English–English dictionaries:
  headwords
  definitions
  parts of speech
  phonemes
  stress markers
  countable/uncountable
  transitive/intransitive

Key vocabulary

benefit (n and v)	empirically	lend	predict
capitalism	employment	lending rate	produce (n and v)
communism	enterprise	leverage	resources
competitors	entrepreneur	liable	shareholder
consumers	equation	liquid (adj)	stakeholder
econometrics	industrialized	liquidity	subsidy
economics	insurance	macroeconomics	theoretical
economist	intervene	microeconomics	welfare
economy	issue (n and v)	opportunity cost	

2.1 Vocabulary

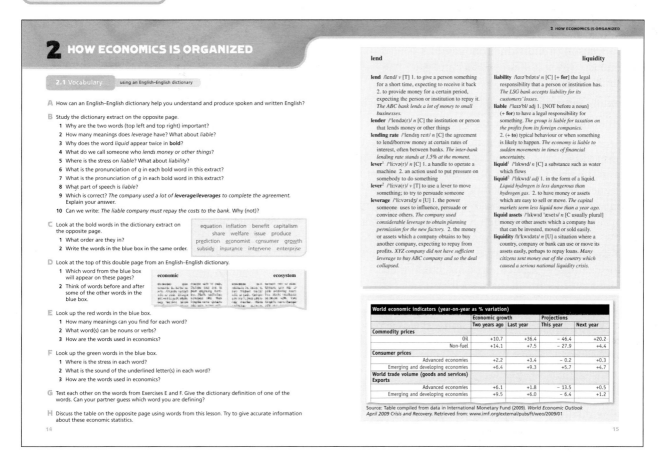

General note

Take in a set of English–English dictionaries.

Read the *Vocabulary bank* at the end of the Course Book unit. Decide when, if at all, to refer students to it. The best time is probably at the very end of the lesson or the beginning of the next lesson, as a summary/revision.

Lesson aims

- learn how to make full use of an English–English dictionary
- gain fluency in the target vocabulary

Introduction

1 Revise the vocabulary from the last unit. Check:
   - meaning
   - pronunciation
   - spelling

2 Ask students whether they use a translation (bilingual) dictionary or an English–English (monolingual) dictionary. Elicit the advantages and disadvantages of a translation dictionary.

Answers

Possible answers:

Advantages	Disadvantages
good when you know the word in your own language and need a translation into English	not good when there is more than one possible translation of a word – which is the correct one?
when you look up an English word, the translation into your language is easy to understand	English–English dictionaries often have more examples and precise definitions of each word

Methodology note

Recent research has shown that, despite the insistence of generations of language teachers on the use of English–English dictionaries in class, nearly 90 per cent of students use a translation dictionary when studying on their own.

Exercise A

Ask the question as a general discussion. Confirm but do not explain anything. Point out that the next exercise will make the value of this kind of dictionary clear.

Answers

Model answers:

The following information is useful for spoken English:

- stress
- pronunciation of individual phonemes – particularly when a phoneme has multiple pronunciations

The following information is useful for written English:

- information about the type of word – C/U; T/I
- the spelling – students might make the point that if you don't know the spelling, you can't find the word in the first place, but point out that you can often guess the possible spelling – for example, *economics*, *macro … and micro …* exist in many European languages but such words are often spelt with 'k' rather than 'c'. Therefore, students need to learn alternative spellings of common sounds like /k/, for example *c*, *k* or *ck*. Students could then look up a word with all three spellings.
- examples of the word in use to memorize
- some synonyms for lexical cohesion – this is a very important point, although you may not want to elaborate on this now

Exercise B

Set for individual work and pairwork checking. Feed back, ideally using an OHT or other visual display of the dictionary extract to highlight points. You might suggest that students annotate the dictionary extract in their books, highlighting symbols, etc., and writing notes on the meaning and value.

Answers

Model answers:

1 They tell you the first and last words on the pages to help you locate the word you want.

2 *leverage* – two meanings; *liable* – two meanings

3 Because the same word can be a noun or an adjective.

4 A *lender*.

5 *liable* – on the first syllable; *liability* – on the second syllable.

6 /kw/. As a guide, 'qu' combination in English spelling is almost always /kw/ – *question*, *quantity*, *quite*, *quarter*, *quiet*, etc. However, very occasionally, with words of French origin, there are other pronunciations – *queue* /kjuː/, *quay* /kiː/.

7 Two pronunciations: /dʒ/ or /g/. Remind students of the 'soft' *g* in English, usually in words of Latin or French origin after vowels, for example /dʒ/ in *badge*, /dʒ/ in *large*, /dʒ/ in *manage*, /dʒ/ in *hedge*.

8 Adjective.

9 The company used a lot of *leverage* to complete the agreement. Leverage is uncountable so cannot be used in the plural.

10 No. Explain to students that *liable* is a predicative adjective not an attributive adjective and can only be used as part of the predicate after such verbs as *be*, *become*, *appear*, *seem*, *prove*.

Exercise C

Note: If students are from a Roman alphabet background, you may want to omit this exercise.

1 Students should quickly be able to identify alphabetical order.

2 Set for individual work and pairwork checking. Feed back, getting the words on the board in the correct order. Don't worry about stress and individual phonemes at this point – students will check this later with their dictionaries.

Language note

It may seem self-evident that words in a dictionary are in alphabetical order. But students from certain languages may not automatically recognize this. In the famous Hans Wehr dictionary of written Arabic, for example, you must first convert a given word to its root and look that up, then find the derived form. So *iqtisad* which means 'economy' in Arabic will not be found under *I* but under *Q* because the root is *q-s-d*.

Another issue is the *lend/borrow* difference in English which does not apply in some languages.

Please point out to students:

lend = give temporarily (with more focus on the giver/owner/lender)

borrow = take temporarily (with more focus on the borrower)

Of course, the borrower can see the situation from his/her perspective, as in:

The bank lent me the money at quite a low interest rate.

Exercise D

1 Set for pairwork. Feed back orally, explaining the principle if necessary.

2 Set for pairwork. Ask students to find words connected with economics if they can. Feed back orally.

Answers

1 *Economist* will appear on the double page spread.

2 Answers depend on which words students choose.

Red word	Part of speech	Type	Main meaning in economics	Main meaning(s) in general English
equation	n	C	mathematical formula to show relationships of equality	general situation or condition
inflation	n	U	situation when prices increase and money loses value	process when air or gas is pumped into a tyre or a balloon, for example
benefit*	v	T	create utility for someone, i.e. to create the economic environment that provides maximum benefit for the maximum number	produce or create an advantage for someone
benefit	n	C	utility; well-being	payment or advantage that a person receives
capitalism	n	U	economic system which has the central ideas of: making profit, private ownership of production and distribution, as well as allowing free financial and market activities	similar meaning but often used to contrast with another economic system, e.g., communism, where state control (rather than private enterprise) is a central idea
share*	n	C	a financial holding in a company which can be traded	a portion or piece of something
share	v	T	to divide up	similar meaning
welfare	n	U	economic concept (based on decisions according to equity and efficiency)	money that the government pays regularly to people who are poor, unemployed or sick
issue*	n	C	availability of shares, bonds or other financial instruments	matter; topic or subject
issue	v	T	to emit or release financial instruments	to announce publicly or officially
produce* N.B. /prəˈdjuːs/	v	T	to manufacture	to lead to or result in something
produce N.B. /ˈprɒdjuːs/	n	U	crops which are grown	similar meaning

Exercise E

Give out the dictionaries, if you have not already done so.

Remind students that dictionaries number multiple meanings of the same part of speech and multiple parts of speech. Remind them also of the countable/uncountable and transitive/intransitive markers. (Note that different dictionaries may use different methods for indicating these things. *The Oxford Advanced Learner's Dictionary*, for example, uses [V] for intransitive verbs and [Vn] for transitive verbs.)

Set for pairwork. Feed back, building up the table in the Answers section on the board. (Students' answers will vary – accept any appropriate meanings and definitions.)

Answers

Model answers:

See table above, *means the word is used in the text in this way.

Exercise F

Remind students how stress and the pronunciation of individual phonemes are shown in a dictionary. Refer them to the key to symbols in the dictionary if necessary. Write the headings of the table in the Answers section on the board, and work through the first word as an example.

Set for pairwork. Feed back, building up the table in the Answers section on the board.

Answers

Model answers: See table on next page.

Exercise G

Demonstrate how to do the exercise by giving a few definitions and getting students to tell you the word (without reading from the board or their books, if possible). Stick to economics rather than general English definitions and encourage students to do the same. Mention to students that learners' dictionaries usually use a limited set of words to give the definitions, e.g. *a person who ...*, *a kind of ...*, *a type of ...*, *a place where ...*, *a method of ...ing*, etc.

Give students examples using such words and ask them to identify what you are defining. For example: *insurance: a type of payment a person or company makes regularly to protect against loss or damage.*

Stress	Sound	Part of speech	Type	Main meaning in economics
pre'diction	/prɪˈdɪkʃn/	n	C	forecast of financial or economic outcomes or results
e'conomist	/ɪˈkɒnəmɪst/	n	C	an expert who works in an area of economics
con'sumer	/kənˈsjuːmə(r)/	n	C	a person who consumes, i.e. buys goods or services
'growth	/grəʊθ/	n	U	amount of expansion (or contraction) in the economy
'subsidy	/ˈsʌbsədɪ/	n	C	official payments to an institution or an individual to support them financially and protect from competition
in'surance	/ɪnˈʃʊərəns/	n	usually U	regular payments made to protect an individual or company in case of a negative outcome such as loss or damage
inter'vene	/ɪntəˈviːn/	v	T	when a government takes action to prevent or reduce an economic problem; where the free market does not decide
'enterprise	/ˈentəpraɪz/	n	C	another word for companies or businesses, usually associated with free market

Exercise H

Look at the table. Discuss with students what the statistics show and the difference between certainty and prediction. Discuss why it is important for economists to use predictions.

This is an opportunity to assess whether students have the grammar control to describe economic trends and developments. The statistics relate to the years 2007–2010 and were compiled in early 2009. The table has no dates but students can use dates or the language of the table to express chronology. Point out that 'economic growth' can be about 'past growth', in which case the past tense is used. Current or predicted growth requires expressions such as: *is/are likely to …*; *is predicted to …*; or *is expected to …* Future growth predictions may use future with 'will' (*will grow by …*; *will fall by …*) or the same forms as for current growth. Remind students that growth can be 'negative growth', too, so it is useful to remind students of verbs such as *decline*, *decrease* or *fall* and associated prepositional phrases.

Students should be encouraged to discuss the table, using key language such as:

The price of oil increased by 10.7% two years ago.

Consumer prices in emerging and developing economies rose by 9.3% last year.

Exports in advanced economies are predicted to fall by 13.5% this year.

Consumer prices in advanced economies are likely to fall by 0.2% this year.

Prices for non-fuel commodities are predicted to rise by 4.4% next year.

World trade volume increased by 9.5% in emerging and developing countries two years ago.

Exports in emerging and developing countries will increase by 1.2% next year.

Closure

1 Remind students that you can identify the part of speech of an unknown word by looking at the words before or after the word, i.e.,

- nouns often come before and after verbs, so if you know that X is a verb, the next content word before or after is probably a noun
- nouns often come immediately after articles
- verbs often come after names and pronouns
- adjectives come before nouns or after the verb *be*

Come back to this point when you are feeding back on the reading texts in this unit.

2 Point out that dictionaries often use a small set of words that help to define, e.g., *person, place, type, system, theory, institution, principle, process*, etc.

Give definitions using these words and ask students to identify what you are defining. For example:

It's a system for paying for health or unemployment benefits. (insurance); *It's a type of legal responsibility for institutions or individuals.* (liability); *It's the level of economics concerned with growth on a larger scale.* (macroeconomics)

2.2 Reading

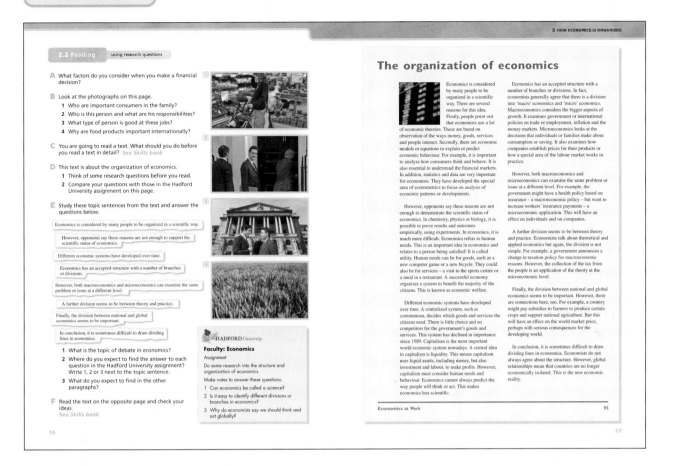

General note

Take in an English–English dictionary.

Read the *Skills bank* section on doing reading research at the end of the Course Book unit. Decide when, if at all, to refer students to it. The best point is probably at the very end of the lesson or the beginning of the next lesson, as a summary/revision.

Lesson aims

- prepare for reading research
- use research questions to structure reading research

Introduction

1 Hold up an English–English dictionary and say a word from Lesson 2.1. Ask students where approximately they will find it in the dictionary – i.e., beginning, middle, two-thirds of the way through, etc. Follow their advice and read the word at the top left. Ask students if the target word will be before or after. Continue until you get to the right page. Repeat with several more words from Lesson 2.1.

2 Give definitions of some of the words from economics in Lesson 2.1 for students to identify.

Exercise A

Set the question for pairwork. Feed back ideas and then expand briefly to discuss issues around making decisions about other people's money!

Answers

Emphasize the role of banks and investment institutions and the idea of lending money responsibly.

Exercise B

Refer students to the photographs. Point out that the photographs refer to economic activities they will learn more about later.

Discuss Photo 1 with the whole class. Why is the family an important idea in economics? In what ways are they consumers? Who makes the decisions about consumption? What types of goods and services do the different family members choose? Do the members of the family consume in the same way? What sort of goods and services do they demand?

Point out that consumer choice is a fundamental part of a market economy. What about consumption in a developing country?

Ask students to discuss the remaining photographs in pairs and then feed back.

Then discuss answers for the first question with the whole class. Set the remaining questions for pairwork. General discussion to check answers.

Answers

Possible answers:

1 Families make economic decisions – they choose to buy one thing instead of another.

2 Governments make budgets and decide how much to raise and spend in a particular period.

3 The Bank of England is the central bank of the UK. It maintains price stability and supports the economic policies of the government.

4 Governments support agriculture in many countries through subsidies.

Exercise C

Students may or may not be able to articulate preparation for reading. Elicit ideas. One thing they must identify – reading for a purpose. Point out that they should always be clear about the purpose of their reading. A series of questions to answer, or **research questions**, is one of the best purposes.

Refer students to the *Skills bank* at this stage if you wish.

Exercise D

1 Set for pairwork. Elicit some ideas, but do not confirm or correct.

2 Refer students to the Hadford University research questions at the bottom of the page. Check comprehension, especially of the word *branches*. If students have come up with better research questions, write them on the board for consideration during the actual reading.

Exercise E

Remind students about topic sentences if they haven't mentioned them already in Exercise C. Give them time to read the topic sentences in this exercise. Point out that the topic sentences are in order, so they give a rough overview of the whole text. Some topic sentences clearly announce what the paragraph will be about. Others may only give a hint of how it will develop.

1 Set for group discussion.

2 Remind students of the research questions. Look at the first research question as an example. Then set for pairwork. Point out that students may match a research question to more than one topic sentence, and that some topic sentences may not relate to the research questions (i.e., they don't have to write a number for each topic sentence).

3 Explain that here students look at the topic sentence(s) they *didn't* number in question 2, and try to work out the likely content of each paragraph. Do the first as an example, then set for pairwork. Feed back, eliciting and checking that they are reasonable possibilities, based on the topic sentence. You can accept multiple ideas for the same paragraph provided they are all possible.

Answers

Possible answers:

1 Is economics a science?

2

Economics is considered by many people to be organized in a scientific way.	1
However, opponents say these reasons are not enough to support the scientific status of economics.	1
Different economic systems have developed over time.	–
Economics has an accepted structure with a number of branches or divisions.	2
However, both macroeconomics and microeconomics can examine the same problem or issue at a different level.	2
A further division seems to be between theory and practice.	2
Finally, the division between national and global economics seems to be important.	3
In conclusion, it is sometimes difficult to draw dividing lines in economics.	2

3 Answers depend on the students. Discuss.

Exercise F

Point out, if students have not already said this, that the topic sentences are normally the first sentences of each paragraph. Tell students to compare the contents of each paragraph with their predictions. Encourage them to take notes as they read.

If necessary, the reading can be set for homework.

Closure

1 Unless you have set the reading for homework, do some extra work on oral summarizing as a comprehension check after reading (see *Skills bank – Using topic sentences to summarize*). Students work in pairs. One student says a topic sentence and the other student summarizes the paragraph from memory in his/her own words, or if necessary reads the paragraph again and then summarizes it without looking.

2 You may also want to redo the text as a jigsaw – the text is reproduced in the additional resources section at the back of this Teacher's Book (Resource 2B) to facilitate this.

3 As a further activity after reading, remind the students of the note-taking skills practised in Unit 1. Discuss appropriate note-taking forms for this text. They can then write notes on the text. Tell them to keep their notes, as they will be useful for the summary exercise in Lesson 2.3.

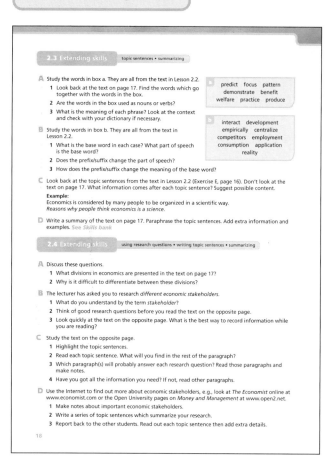

Introduction

Test students on the factual information in the text from the previous lesson, e.g. *What is an important difference between natural sciences and economics?* (Can be tested empirically; does not rely on human behaviour and actions); *What is economic theory based on?* (Observations of patterns; models and equations); *What division in economics is generally accepted by economists?* (Macro- and microeconomics).

If a student says, accurately, *I didn't read about that. It wasn't relevant to my research*, accept it and praise the student.

Exercise A

1 Set for pairwork. Feed back orally, asking students for the location of the phrase.

2 Feed back orally. (Students' answers will vary – accept any appropriate meanings and definitions.)

3 Encourage students to explore the other meanings and usage that are listed in the dictionary. Some examples are given in the table at the top of the opposite page.

Methodology note

Don't help students to find words in a text. It's a key reading skill to be able to pattern match, i.e., get a word in your mind's eye and then find it on the page.

Answers

Possible answers:

See table at top of opposite page.

Exercise B

Set for individual work and pairwork checking. Students can check these points in a dictionary. Feed back, taking apart the words and showing how the affixes can change the meaning.

Answers

Model answers:

See table at bottom of opposite page.

General note

Take in a set of English–English dictionaries.

Lesson aims

- identify paragraph structure
- produce good topic sentences
- summarize a text

Further practice in:

- vocabulary from Lesson 2.2

Word	Part of speech	Meaning	Combination in text
predict	v [T]	say what you think will happen in the future	predict the behaviour of
focus	v (usually with prep *on*)	concentrate on/pay attention to	focus on analysis
focus	n [U]	the centre of attention; what someone is concentrating on	(not used as noun in the text)
pattern	n [C]	the shape or form of actions or things that happen, usually linked to each other	economic patterns or developments
demonstrate	v [T]	show or indicate	demonstrate the scientific status of economics
benefit	v [T]	to give advantages or help to individuals, groups or institutions	to benefit the majority of the citizens
benefit	n [C]	the official financial support and advantage people get from the government	(not used as noun in the text)
welfare	n [U]	care and support given by the state to its citizens	This (system of benefits) is known as economic welfare.
practice	n [U]	opposite of theory; when an idea is applied in the real world	A further division seems to be between theory and practice.
pro'duce N.B. word stress /prə'djuːs/	v [T]	to make or manufacture goods; to grow crops	to produce certain crops and support national agriculture
'produce N.B. word stress /'prɒdjuːs/	n [U]	things that are grown such as fruit or vegetables, cf. *products*: the items that are manufactured or produced	(not used as noun in the text)

Exercise C

Ideally, display the topic sentences (or give them on a handout) so that students do not have to turn back to pages 16 and 17. The topic sentences are reproduced in the additional resources section to facilitate this (Resource 2C). Work through the example, showing that you can deduce (or in this case to some extent remember) the contents of a paragraph from the topic sentence. Do another example orally. Set for pairwork.

Feed back, eliciting possible paragraph contents and sample information. Only correct ideas which are not based on the topic sentence. Allow students to check back with the text and self-mark.

Answers

Possible answers:

See table at top of next page.

Word	Base word	Affix and meaning
interact (v)	act (v)	*inter* = *between*; other examples: *intervene, interchange,* interfere as well as adjectives such as *international* or *intermediate*
development (n)	develop (v)	*ment* = process of something happening or taking place
empirically (adv)	empirical (adj) N.B. not from empire	*ly* = adverb (based on experiments and experience not on theory)
centralize (v)	central (adj)	*ize*; verb shows the process related to the adjective itself; other examples: *nationalize, harmonize, equalize, organize*
competitors (n)	compete (v)	*or* = the person(s) who perform(s) an action
employment (n)	employ (v)	*ment* (as explained above); other examples: *adjustment, refinement, requirement, government*
consumption (n)	consume (v)	*ption* = action from the verb itself; limited and unusual suffix; other examples: *resume → resumption, assume → assumption, presume → presumption*
application (n)	apply (v)	*cation*; not very common noun form of the specific verb which usually ends in *ate*; other examples: *communication, replication; duplication* but also *specification*
reality (n)	real (adj)	*ity* = the state of being (+ adjective); other examples: *equality, purity, liquidity*

Topic sentence	Possible paragraph content	Supporting information/example(s)
Economics is considered by many people to be organized in a scientific way.	ways in which economics may be categorized as a science	theory based on observation; models and equations; use of statistics
However, opponents say these reasons are not enough to demonstrate the scientific status of economics.	reasons why the scientific view of economics is not always accepted	discussion of how economics is based on human needs and consumer/human decisions
Different economic systems have developed over time.	information about these economic systems	details about evolution of economies such as capitalism or communism
Economics has an accepted structure with a number of branches or divisions.	how economics can be organized	examples of possible divisions, including the main branches
However, both macroeconomics and microeconomics can examine the same problem or issue at a different level.	an indication of how the main branches overlap or interrelate	examples of such overlapping or connections
A further division seems to be between theory and practice.	another apparent division in economics	discussion of whether this distinction or differentiation is completely clear
Finally, the division between national and global economics seems to be important.	a further division or apparent differentiation	discussion of the division
In conclusion, it is sometimes difficult to draw dividing lines in economics.	final statement on the status of economics	important for students to know that the dividing lines are not always clear

Discourse note

In academic writing, topic sentences often consist of a general point. The sentences that follow then support the general statement in various ways, such as:

- giving a definition and/or a description
- giving examples
- giving lists of points (e.g., arguments or reasons)
- restating the topic sentence in a different way to help clarify it
- giving more information and detail on the topic sentence to clarify it

Often – but not always – the type of sentence is shown by a 'discourse marker' – e.g., *for example, firstly, however, even so, finally, in conclusion*, etc. This helps to signal to the reader how the writer sees the link between the sentences and is therefore a good clue as to the purpose of the sentences following the topic sentence.

Exercise D

Students can work individually (for homework) or in pairs (in class). Ask them to write a summary of about 150 words. They should use their own words as far as possible, but they should also try to incorporate the vocabulary they have practised so far. Refer students to the *Skills bank – Using topic sentences to summarize*.

Methodology note

There are two reasons for students to use their own words in written work (except when quoting and acknowledging sources):

1 The work involved in rewording information and ideas helps us to mentally process them and to retain them in memory.

2 Copying whole sentences from the work of other writers is plagiarism (unless the quotation is acknowledged). Universities disapprove of plagiarism and may mark down students who plagiarize. In the commercial world, an accusation of plagiarism can cause legal problems, and in the academic world it can severely damage a teacher's reputation and career.

Closure

Tell students to define some of the economics words from the text on page 17. Alternatively, give definitions of some of the words and tell students to identify the words. For example, *a higher level or branch of economics* (macroeconomics); *a regular change or development in economics* (pattern); *analyzing or studying something using experiments* (empirically).

2.4 Extending skills

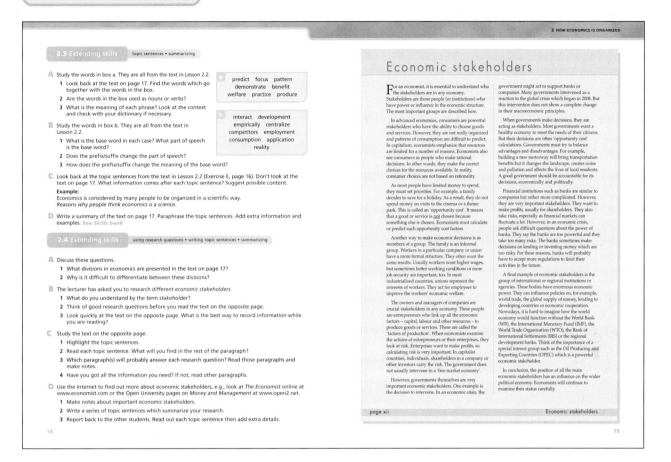

Lesson aims

- use research questions to structure reading research
- write topic sentences for a short research report/summary

Introduction

Give a word from the text in Lesson 2.2 which is part of a) a verb + preposition phrase, b) a noun + preposition phrase, or c) other collocations. Ask students to try to complete the phrase. It's probably better if you give the first word in the phrase, but you might also try giving the second word at times or at the end of the exercise.

Possible phrases:

(Elicit the answers in CAPITALS.)

		Category
reason	FOR	B
is/are based	ON	A
focus	ON	A
relate	TO	A
competitors	FOR	B
decline	IN	A
deal	WITH	A
human	NEEDS/BEHAVIOUR	C
division	INTO/BETWEEN	B
policies	ON	B
effect	ON	B
change	IN	B
taxation	POLICY	C
pay	SUBSIDIES	C
serious	CONSEQUENCES	C
produce	GOODS/CROPS	C
dividing lines	DRAW	C

Exercise A

Group discussion. Build up the list on the board, students' books closed.

Answers

1 Macroeconomics and microeconomics

   Theoretical and applied economics

   National and global economics

   Development economics

   Monetary economics

   Business economics

   Remind students of *econometrics* and mention that most of the branches listed above also have an analytical, statistical focus.

2 It is difficult to differentiate because there is often a connection between the apparent divisions as the text illustrates.

Exercise B

1 This question relates to the reading text on page 19 and acts as a pre-question. Set for pairwork. Feed back orally.

2 Remind students of the importance of research questions – reading for a purpose. Set for pairwork. Feed back, writing up suitable questions on the board.

   For example: *What is the meaning of the term 'stakeholder'? Are stakeholders all of equal importance? How do stakeholders show they are powerful? Do some have limited power? What are some key examples of economic stakeholders?*

3 Elicit the different kinds of notes you can use – see Unit 1 *Skills bank*. Remind students to think about the best kind of notes before and while they are reading.

Methodology note

It is good for students to get into the habit of thinking about the form of their notes before they read a text in detail. If they don't do this, they will tend to be drawn into narrative notes rather than notes which are specifically designed to help them answer their research questions.

Answers

Possible answers:

1 Person or group that has an economic 'stake' or interest in an activity or enterprise.

2 Questions such as those above or:

   How are stakeholders defined? What types of stakeholder are there? Are all stakeholders of equal importance in an economy? Which stakeholders can be considered most important?

3 See Unit 1 *Skills bank*. A spidergram would be an appropriate form of notes.

Exercise C

1/2 Remind students of the importance of topic sentences. Set for individual work and pairwork checking. Encourage students not to read ahead. Perhaps you should ask students to cover the text and only reveal each topic sentence in turn; then discuss possible contents of the paragraph. Remind them that this is a technique for previewing a text and at this point they do not need to read every part of the text. This will come later. If you have an OHP or other visual display, you can tell students to close their books and just display the topic sentences (additional resources section, Resource 2C), or you can give them out on a handout.

3 Set the choice of paragraphs for pairwork. Students then read individually, make notes and compare them. Monitor and assist.

4 Give students time to read other paragraphs if they need to.

Answers

Possible answers:

1/2 See table on opposite page.

3 The appropriate paragraphs to read depend on the research questions you and your students decide on.

Discourse note

It is good to be aware (though you may not feel it is appropriate to discuss with students at this point) that in real academic texts, the topic sentence may not be as obvious as in the texts in this unit. Sometimes there is not an explicit topic sentence, so the overall topic of the paragraph must be inferred. Or the actual topic sentence for the paragraph can be *near* rather than *at* the beginning of the paragraph. Sometimes, also, the first sentence of a paragraph acts as a topic statement for a succession of paragraphs.

Exercise D

1 Set the task for homework and feed back in the next lesson. Encourage students to make notes on various stakeholder groups mentioned in the text.

   The following websites are useful starting points for research on, for example, the major economic stakeholders such as IMF, WB, BIS, etc. Students could also visit the specific sites of these institutions:

   www.bized.co.uk

   www.economist.com/printedition

   www.open2.net

   www.bbc.co.uk/news/business/economy

Topic sentence	Possible paragraph content
For an economist, it is essential to understand who the stakeholders are in any economy.	paragraph will provide a definition and begin to exemplify
In advanced economies, consumers are powerful stakeholders who have the ability to choose goods and services.	illustration of the power of consumers in order to support this statement
As most people have limited money to spend, they must set priorities.	what it means to set priorities; examples of choice
Another way to make economic decisions is as members of a group.	outline of how stakeholders act to achieve group objectives
The owners and managers of companies are crucial stakeholders in any economy.	outline of the importance of these stakeholders; 'factors of production'; risk; entrepreneurship
However, governments themselves are very important economic stakeholders.	the specific stakeholder status of governments
When governments make decisions, they are acting as stakeholders.	what governments do to demonstrate their stakeholder role
Financial institutions such as banks are similar to companies but rather more complicated.	why financial institutions are seen as more complex stakeholders
A final example of economic stakeholders is the group of international or regional institutions or agencies.	global economic stakeholders; some useful institutions
In conclusion, the position of all the main economic stakeholders has an influence on the wider political economy.	conclusion; phrase 'political economy' is important

2/3 If this is set for homework, students, on the basis of the topic sentences, should present their information to fellow students. Make sure students realize that they only have to write the topic sentences. They can add the details in orally.

Closure

1 Focus on some of the vocabulary from the text, including:

stakeholder

power (powerful)

resources

set priorities

opportunity costs

job security

economic welfare

entrepreneur ⎱ (N.B. draw attention to the spelling
enterprise ⎰ of these two related words)

factors of production

intervene

accountable

fluctuate

2 You may also want to redo the text as a jigsaw, as before – the text is reproduced in the additional resources section (Resource 2D) to facilitate this.

Extra activities

1 Work through the *Vocabulary bank* and *Skills bank* if you have not already done so, or as a revision of previous study.

2 Use the *Activity bank* (Teacher's Book additional resources section, Resource 2A).

A Set the wordsearch for individual work (including homework) or pairwork.

Answers

B Do the quiz as a whole class, or in teams, or set for homework – students can reread the texts to get the answers if necessary.

Answers

1 economist
2 applied economics
3 leverage
4 subsidies
5 commodity
6 assets
7 International Monetary Fund
8 capitalism
9 1989
10 oil
11 intervene
12 entrepreneurs

3 Ask students to work in small groups to research and feed back to the group on the other branches or divisions of economics. The three research questions are the same as in Lesson 2.2.

If students are going to do research on the Internet, suggest that they type in terms such as *economic stakeholders* or *political economics* then their topic to get some potential texts. Alternatively, you can do this research before the lesson and print off some pages for students to work from.

Remind students that they can't possibly read everything they find, so they must use the topic sentences to decide if a paragraph is worth reading.

4 You can get students to practise their reading aloud – a skill which is not vital but is sometimes useful – by following this approach.

Photocopy and cut up one of the jigsaw texts in the additional resources section (Resources 2B and 2D). Give topic sentences to Student A and the corresponding paragraphs to Student B.

Student A reads out a topic sentence.

Student B finds the corresponding paragraph and reads it out.

An alternative is to give Student A the topic sentences and Student B a set of sentences chosen from each paragraph (one sentence per paragraph). Student A reads out the topic sentences one by one. Student B decides which of his/her sentences is likely to appear in the same paragraph as the topic sentence. Both students have to agree that the paragraph sentence matches the topic sentence.

5 Have a competition to practise finding words in a monolingual dictionary. Requirements:

● an English–English dictionary for each student (or pair of students if necessary)
● Unit 2 key vocabulary list

Put students in teams with their dictionaries closed. Select a word from the Unit 2 key vocabulary list and instruct students to open their dictionaries and find the word. The first student to find the word is awarded a point for their team. Additional points can be awarded if the student can give the correct pronunciation and meaning.

3 MARKET ECONOMIES

Unit 3 looks at markets and how the basic principles of a free market economy apply in theory and practice. This unit is probably the most theoretical in the book but merely touches upon fundamental concepts and notions such as demand and demand shifts.

The first lecture examines some of these concepts. The second lecture concentrates on the factors which may produce market shifts in demand and considers the UK housing market as an illustration of demand factors.

Skills focus

Listening

- preparing for a lecture
- predicting lecture content
- making lecture notes
- using different information sources

Speaking

- reporting research findings
- asking for information
- formulating questions

Vocabulary focus

- stress patterns in multi-syllable words
- prefixes

Key vocabulary

allocate	disposable	fluctuation	stimulate
availability	downgrade	marginality	substitute
capacity	downturn	outline	supply
complementary	downward	output	undervalue
composite	efficiency	outweigh	unstable
contraction	equilibrium	productivity	upward
conversion	excess	recession	variation
derive	expansion	reduce	
disequilibrium	extension	reliability	

3.1 Vocabulary

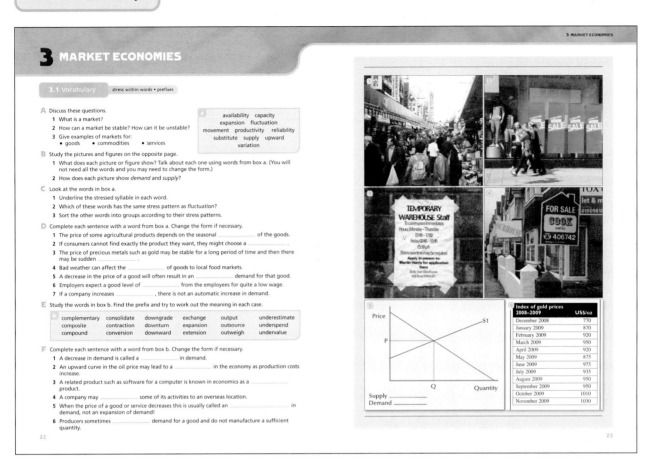

General note

Read the *Vocabulary bank* at the end of the Course Book unit. Decide when, if at all, to refer your students to it. The best time is probably at the very end of the lesson or the beginning of the next lesson, as a summary/revision.

Dictionaries will be useful in this lesson.

Lesson aims

- gain a greater understanding of the importance of stress within words and some of the common patterns
- extend knowledge of words which contain prefixes
- gain fluency in the target vocabulary

Introduction

Revise the vocabulary from the first two units. Check:

- meaning
- pronunciation
- spelling

Exercise A

Tell students that the answers to these questions should involve the ideas related to supply and demand. The students should remember examples of markets from Unit 1. Encourage students, even at this stage, to use the more technical language of economics rather than everyday expressions: *an increase or decrease in demand*; *a fluctuation in market prices*; *a downward movement*; *the index of commodity prices*, etc.

Answers

Possible answers:

1 A market is where goods (or services) are traded. That is, the seller offers goods at a certain price and the buyer (or consumer) decides that he/she wants to purchase the goods, commodity or service. The price of these items can fluctuate, depending on demand and supply.

2 A market can be stable when the prices match the buyers' and sellers' expectations and where supply and demand are satisfactorily maintained. A market can fluctuate, as mentioned, but the supply–demand criteria will be maintained. In an unstable market, there is an imbalance in one or more of the market factors which will lead to more noticeable variations and fluctuations.

3 Accept all reasonable suggestions.

Exercise B

1 Refer students to the pictures and figures on page 23 of the Course Book. Ask students what they can see in the first picture. Elicit *It's a (street) market*. Ask which word(s) from box a could be used to say something *more* about the picture. Accept any suggestions which use the words: *supply, variation, fluctuation, decision*. Encourage students to formulate their ideas as completely as possible, for example:

> *There's a lot of variation in prices according to supply.*
>
> *Prices vary according to supply.*
>
> *Supply can vary according to the time of year for many products.*
>
> *Traders may change prices according to the availability of products.*

Set the remaining pictures for pairwork. Students should make two statements: first what they can see and then a further comment about each picture, using at least one word from box a. If necessary, they should check the meanings of the words in their dictionaries. Not all the words are relevant. Feed back with the whole class. Accept any reasonable suggestions. Check/correct pronunciation, especially the stress patterns.

2 Set for pairwork. All the pictures reflect demand and supply. Students should consider how the words they have used in question 1 relate to demand and supply. Feed back orally, but do not confirm or correct at this stage.

Answers

Possible answers:

1 1 It's a street market where goods are traded. The prices are usually fixed according to the **availability** of **supply** but reduced demand can force sellers to reduce prices to sell the goods.

2 The sign suggests that the demand for the goods was not sufficient, the asking price was too high or consumers found a **substitute** at a lower price.

3 The demand for casual work, especially in services industries, does **fluctuate** according to the strength of the economy. Often, the minimum wage is paid for less skilled labour.

4 The UK has a bouyant housing market. In recent years, there has been a rapid **expansion** of home ownership. Many people try to get mortgages to buy a house. But mortgage rates **fluctuate** and buying a house is expensive. If people cannot afford to buy, they will rent a house. The estate agents put up signs showing 'FOR SALE' or 'TO LET', so a sign with 'LET' indicates that someone has already rented that property.

5 The curve shows the relationships between demand, **supply**, price and quantity on the same figure. The point of equilibrium is shown. If there is an **upward movement** in price, you can observe the impact on the other axis and factors in the curve.

6 The list of prices is an index (a word introduced in Unit 1). Gold is a **reliable** commodity and is considered a safe choice in times of recession.

2 Accept all reasonable suggestions but reinforce the ideas of supply and demand.

Methodology note

From now on, whenever you present a group of words in a box, as here, ask students for the part of speech of each word. This is good practice and also good preparation for changing the form of the word if a different part of speech is required in the associated exercise(s).

Exercise C

Write *fluctuation* on the board. Ask students to say how many syllables there are in the word (there are four). Draw vertical lines to divide the syllables. Then ask students to say where the main stress is and to draw a line under that syllable:

fluc | tu | <u>a</u> | tion

Point out the importance of stressed syllables in words – see *Language note* on opposite page.

1 Set for pairwork. Tell students to identify the syllables first, then to underline the strongest stress. Feed back.

2 Ask students to find a word which has the same stress pattern as fluctuation. Write it on the board like this:

fluc | tu | <u>a</u> | tion

va | ri | <u>a</u> | tion

3 Set for pairwork. Students should match words with the same number of syllables and with main stresses in the same place.

Language note

In English, speakers emphasize the stressed syllable in a multi-syllable word. Sometimes listeners may not even hear the unstressed syllables. Vowels, in any case, often change to *schwa* or a reduced form in unstressed syllables. Therefore it is essential that students can recognize key words from the stressed syllable alone when they hear them in context. Multi-syllable words may seem to have more than one stressed syllable. This is a secondary stress, e.g., ˌproducˈtivity. For the present purposes, students should identify only the primary, or strongest, stress in the word.

Stress sometimes moves to fit common patterns when you add a suffix, e.g., ˈcapable, capaˈbility. Other suffixes, such as ~ment or ~al, don't affect the stress of the root word, e.g., emˈploy, emˈployment; ˈperson, ˈpersonal.

Sometimes it is difficult to be sure exactly how a word should be divided into syllables. Use vowel sounds as a guide to the number of syllables. If in doubt, consult a dictionary.

Answers

1 a|vail|a|<u>bil</u>|it|y
   ca|<u>pa</u>|cit|y
   ex|<u>pan</u>|sion
   fluc|tu|<u>a</u>|tion
   <u>move</u>|ment
   pro|duc|<u>tiv</u>|it|y
   re|li|a|<u>bil</u>|it|y
   <u>sub</u>|sti|tute
   su|<u>pply</u>
   <u>up</u>|ward
   va|ri|<u>a</u>|tion

2 variation

3 See table below.

Exercise D

Set for individual work and pairwork checking. Not all the words are needed. Feed back orally.

Answers

1 The price of some agricultural products depends on the seasonal <u>availability</u> of the goods.

2 If consumers cannot find exactly the product they want, they might choose a <u>substitute</u>.

3 The price of precious metals such as gold may be stable for a long period of time and then there may be sudden <u>fluctuations</u>.

4 Bad weather can affect the <u>supply</u> of goods to local food markets.

5 A decrease in the price of a good will often result in an <u>upward</u> demand for that good.

6 Employers expect a good level of <u>reliability</u> from the employees for quite a low wage.

7 If a company increases <u>productivity</u>, there is not an automatic increase in demand.

Exercise E

Set for pairwork. Students should look at all three words in each column to find and then deduce the meaning of a prefix. Encourage them to use a phrase as a definition rather than a single word translation. They need to develop a sense of the broader meaning of the prefix. Feed back, putting the meanings on the board.

Answers

Model answers:

com = in a joint relationship; together

con = to go together with or accompany, often reducing or summarizing that activity

down = in a downward direction; assess less or lower than before

ex = out from; going further

out = bigger, better or longer than; outside or away/distant from; to illustrate that something is 'out', e.g., *put out* = produced → output (that which is produced)

under = below or less than

Methodology note

With some of these words it is difficult to work out the base word, e.g., *posite*. However, you can point out that you can sometimes understand roughly what a word means if you understand the prefix, e.g., composite must be something to do with being *joined* or *together*, so context will help you to guess the rough meaning.

first syllable	final syllable	second syllable from beginning	third syllable from beginning	fourth syllable from beginning
<u>up</u>ward <u>move</u>ment <u>sub</u>stitute	su<u>pply</u>	ex<u>pan</u>sion ca<u>pa</u>city	fluctu<u>a</u>tion produc<u>tiv</u>ity vari<u>a</u>tion	availa<u>bil</u>ity relia<u>bil</u>ity

Exercise F

This is further practice in using words with prefixes. If students are struggling, point out that all the missing words are from the top row of the box. Feed back, checking pronunciation and stress patterns.

Answers

Model answers:

1 A decrease in demand is called a <u>contraction</u> in demand.

2 An upward curve in the oil price may lead to a <u>downturn</u> in the economy as production costs increase.

3 A related product such as software for a computer is known in economics as a <u>complementary</u> product.

4 A company may <u>outsource</u> some of its activities to an overseas location.

5 When the price for a good or service decreases, this is usually called an <u>extension</u> in demand, not an expansion of demand!

6 Producers sometimes <u>underestimate</u> demand for a good and do not manufacture a sufficient quantity.

Closure

1 Ask students to decide which sentences in Exercise F show some uncertainty or doubt (2, 4, 5, 6) and which are more definite, certain ideas (1, 3).

2 If you have not already done so, refer students to the *Vocabulary bank* at the end of Unit 3. Work through some or all of the stress patterns.

Language note

The patterns shown in the *Vocabulary bank* in Unit 3 are productive, i.e., they enable you to make more words or apply the rules accurately to other words. The words with unusual patterns tend to be the more common ones, so if students come across a new multi-syllable word at this level, it is likely to conform to the patterns shown. Native speakers recognize the patterns and will naturally apply them to unusual words, e.g., proper nouns. How, for example, would you pronounce these nonsense words?

felacom

bornessity

shimafy

emtonology

scolobility

nemponary

cagoral

andimakinise

ortepanimation

3.2 Listening

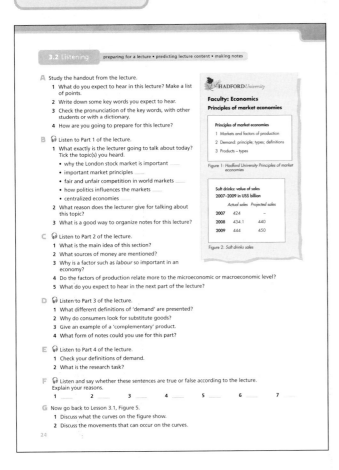

3.2 Listening preparing for a lecture • predicting lecture content • making notes

A Study the handout from the lecture.
  1 What do you expect to hear in this lecture? Make a list of points.
  2 Write down some key words you expect to hear.
  3 Check the pronunciation of the key words, with other students or with a dictionary.
  4 How are you going to prepare for this lecture?

B Listen to Part 1 of the lecture.
  1 What exactly is the lecturer going to talk about today? Tick the topic(s) you heard.
     • why the London stock market is important
     • important market principles
     • fair and unfair competition in world markets
     • how politics influences the markets
     • centralized economies
  2 What reason does the lecturer give for talking about this topic?
  3 What is a good way to organize notes for this lecture?

C Listen to Part 2 of the lecture.
  1 What is the main idea of this section?
  2 What sources of money are mentioned?
  3 Why is a factor such as *labour* so important in an economy?
  4 Do the factors of production relate more to the microeconomic or macroeconomic level?
  5 What do you expect to hear in the next part of the lecture?

D Listen to Part 3 of the lecture.
  1 What different definitions of 'demand' are presented?
  2 Why do consumers look for substitute goods?
  3 Give an example of a 'complementary' product.
  4 What form of notes could you use for this part?

E Listen to Part 4 of the lecture.
  1 Check your definitions of demand.
  2 What is the research task?

F Listen and say whether these sentences are true or false according to the lecture. Explain your reasons.
  1 ___ 2 ___ 3 ___ 4 ___ 5 ___ 6 ___ 7 ___

G Now go back to Lesson 3.1, Figure 5.
  1 Discuss what the curves on the figure show.
  2 Discuss the movements that can occur on the curves.

HADFORD *University*

Faculty: Economics
Principles of market economies

Principles of market economies
  1 Markets and factors of production
  2 Demand: principle; types; definitions
  3 Products – types

Figure 1: Hadford University Principles of market economies

Soft drinks: value of sales
2007–2009 in US$ billion

	Actual sales	Projected sales
2007	424	
2008	434.1	440
2009	444	450

Figure 2: Soft drinks sales

24

Lesson aims

Further practice in:

- planning and preparing for a lecture
- predicting lecture content
- choosing the best form of notes
- making notes

Introduction

Review key vocabulary by:

- using flashcards
- playing the alphabet game in the extra activities section at the end of this unit

Exercise A

Refer students to the handout with Figures 1 and 2. Write the title *Principles of market economies* on the board.

1 Set for individual work and pairwork checking. Feed back, eliciting some ideas.

2 Set for pairwork.

3 Brainstorm to elicit key words. Allow the class to decide if a word should be included.

4 Elicit some points – the four Ps (Plan, Prepare, Predict, Produce). If necessary, refer students to Unit 1 *Skills bank* to review the preparation for a lecture. One way to help the students to make provisional notes is to:

- brainstorm what they would include
- organize their topics into a logical sequence

Answers

Answers depend on the students.

🎧 Exercise B

1 Tell students they are only going to hear the introduction to the lecture. Ask what information they expect to get from the introduction (i.e., the outline of the lecture).

Give students time to read the choices of topics. Check that they understand the meaning and relevance. Remind them they will only hear the introduction once, as in a lecture. Play Part 1. Allow them to compare answers.

Feed back. Ask them to justify their choice by saying what they heard related to it. Confirm the correct answer.

2 Elicit ideas. Confirm or correct.

3 Elicit ideas.

Answers

Model answers:

1 important market principles

2 It is essential for all economists to understand the theory behind markets.

3 These theories and principles will need to be understood at the level of language through diagrammatical representation. So, a spidergram might work, or diagrams with headings and bullet points plus figures (curves) might be combined to produce notes. For example:

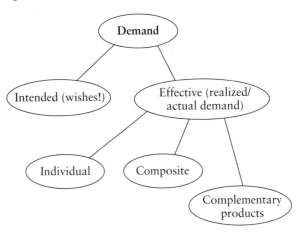

Transcript 🎧 1.11

Part 1

The objective of today's lecture is to outline briefly some of the basic principles which are applied in market economics. Some of you may already be familiar with these, but my lecture will be a reminder for you and will also ensure that all students understand and can apply these principles or concepts. A concept is an abstract idea. It cannot be seen or measured, but a concept is generally accepted by specialists in that discipline. In our case, some basic economic concepts form the focus of my lecture.

Many of you have also studied mathematics but don't worry too much if there are a few gaps in your knowledge. Just to reassure you, you will have a lot of opportunities to improve your understanding of mathematics for economics.

So, today I will talk a little about markets and introduce you to some principles and terminology. I will outline particularly concepts related to demand and you will look at 'supply' later in the course. So, let's start off with the market factors!

🎧 Exercise C

Before playing Part 2, refer students to Figure 1. Ask students what they expect to hear. Give them time to read questions 1–4. Tell them to write only brief notes. The main task is to absorb the meaning.

Play Part 2. Give them time to answer questions 1–4. Allow them to compare their answers. Feed back.

When they thoroughly understand the concepts outlined in this part of the lecture, *Principles of market economies*, ask them what they expect to hear about in the next part of the lecture (question 5). Elicit ideas but do not confirm or correct.

Answers

Model answers:

1 Main idea = that markets depend on the interaction of a number of factors: supply and demand for goods, services, labour and capital.

2 Money as a resource is mentioned, related to wages, interest, rent and profits.

3 Because labour has a direct relationship to the cost of production both in terms of its cost and of its availability.

4 The principles apply mostly to microeconomics but, obviously, macroeconomic decisions involve allocation of resources and must take supply and demand into account.

5 Students will probably predict that the principle of 'demand' forms the next part of the lecture.

Transcript 🎧 1.12

Part 2

We know that humans have certain basic needs. For example, we need food, clothes, somewhere to live, etc. But we also have 'wants'. In economics, 'wants' are things that we would like to buy. These are goods and services. By the way, in economics, we can talk about a good, as well as goods. In other words, *good* is a countable noun. We need a resource to buy goods or services and, in the modern world, the resource is money.

Money can come from a number of sources. Firstly, it can come from wages, as a reward for working. In economics, we call this source 'labour'. Secondly, it can come from interest. This is a payment made for investing money or capital in a business. Thirdly, it can come from rent, which is a payment for land or property. Finally, it can come from profit, which is the extra money that a business makes. We call these sources the 'factors of production'. Each of these factors will have a value and we can sell or lend them and receive payments. So, we have what is known as a factor market. The market for labour, for example, puts a value on wages. In some countries there is a minimum wage, which means that no employee earns less than a certain amount. That is quite an advanced or progressive concept, but obviously it has an effect on production costs. It is important for productivity that we do not overvalue, or undervalue, the costs of labour. Similarly, there is, as you know, a market for capital, where products such as bonds or shares can be traded. In business, entrepreneurs bring together labour, capital and materials to provide the goods and services.

In a free market economy, the markets themselves decide how economic resources – the factors of production – will be used or, to use a more technical word, allocated. Later in your course, you will consider the allocation of resources at different levels of the economy. What I have mentioned so far applies more at the *micro*economic level. It is a bit different at the *macro*economic level where the government must decide how to raise money and how to allocate the resources.

🎧 Exercise D

Play the first four sentences of Part 3. Ask the first question. Set questions 2–4 for individual work and pairwork checking. Play the rest of the recording. Tell students to take notes. Allow students to compare their answers. Don't, at this stage, confirm the answers.

Answers

1 See Exercise E.

2 Substitute products are usually chosen because they are offered at a cheaper price with little or no difference in quality.

3 Complementary products: petrol/cars; computer software/hardware; land prices/houses, DVD players/sales of DVDs.

4 A note-making format with headings and bullet points, but a spidergram might be appropriate for the first part of this section.

Transcript 🎧 1.13

Part 3

Now, let's turn our attention to demand. Economists have many different names for types of demand. But, don't worry, you'll soon see the differences. In a free market economy, the markets are allowed to function according to supply and demand. For example, producers estimate the quantity of a product which consumers will buy at a specific price level to make the maximum profit. Producers understand market and consumer behaviour and make careful calculations, but sometimes they overestimate demand.

So, a good start is, firstly, to mention 'effective' demand, which means the real ability or capacity of consumers to buy something. Lots of people plan to buy something or use a service but then they cannot afford it! So, secondly, we talk about 'realized' or 'actual' demand. This relates to what people actually buy.

You should also remember a third important definition for 'composite' demand. This is where a product may have more than one use and so the demand for the products is seen as composite, or linked. A recent example has been where cereals or other crops have been used in some countries to produce biofuels. This has increased the price of these crops around the world. A fourth type is 'derived' demand where, for example, higher income results in increased demand for better health services or a greater consumption of energy.

When prices increase, there is a movement along the demand curve. This is known as a contraction in demand. The opposite is called an extension if prices decrease. I will talk more about the reasons for these shifts later.
Now, let's think of the products consumers buy. Firstly, we know that if the price increases, consumers often change their minds about a good or a service and choose a substitute at a cheaper price. A further type is the complementary product, where the demand for one product is very closely related to the price and demand for another. A good example is the relationship between the price of petrol and the demand for cars. People buy more

economical cars if the price of petrol increases and less economical cars if petrol prices fall. Another example ... to build houses you need land. If there is a shortage of land, then land prices go up. This will inevitably mean the cost of houses on that land will increase, which might lead to a fall in demand for houses.

🎧 Exercise E

Part 4 summarizes the definition of demand. Tell students that this is the last part of the lecture. What do they expect to hear? Confirm that it is a summary. Play Part 4.

1 Students should check their definitions as they listen. After the summary has finished, they should correct their definitions and complete their notes. Guide them to the correct answer: that is, the correct meaning, not necessarily the words given here.

2 Elicit ideas. (If you wish, you could ask your students to do some research on this topic themselves. However, it is not essential at this stage. Students are asked to do a separate research task at the end of Lesson 3.3 and feed back on that in Lesson 3.4.)

Answers

1 The different definitions are 'effective' demand which relates to the potential capacity or the intention to buy, 'actual' demand which means what people really buy. (Another name for this type is 'realized' demand.) The third definition is 'composite' demand, usually when a good may have more than one use as exemplified with cereals used for bio-fuels. Then the lecturer talks about 'derived' demand where higher income makes people demand more or a better product.

2 To do some research on shifts in demand.

Simple curves are available at:

www.netmba.com/econ/micro/demand/curve/

or

www.bized.co.uk/learn/economics/markets/mechanism/interactive/part1.htm

Transcript 🎧 1.14

Part 4

So, let's summarize quickly. Demand is not a single concept, but has a number of variations – firstly, 'effective' demand, which talks about ability to buy, then 'realized' or 'actual' demand, what we do in fact buy! Goods and services can be related to each other, so we have the third definition of 'composite' demand. Remember our example with cereals and biofuels! Now, definition number four – 'derived' demand comes from a change in economic circumstances; for example, a pay rise for workers might lead to an increased demand for certain goods. I also mentioned what happens to demand – yes, it goes up and it goes down! Or to be more technical, we observe an extension or increase in demand, or a contraction, or a decrease, in the demand curve. So, what are people demanding? Well, goods and services, of course! But what happens when consumers decide that a good or service is too expensive? Well, they choose a substitute, don't they? And finally, don't forget complementary goods, where the interrelationship between goods is very strong and can influence each other. So, that's enough for now. Next time, we'll look at shifts in demand, so please do some research on this topic.

🎧 Exercise F

These are sentences about the ideas in the lecture.

Set for pairwork. Say or play the sentences. Give time for students to discuss and then respond. Students must justify their answers.

Answers

1	true	Employees may be happy to have a minimum wage and may be motivated to increase productivity but higher production costs will occur
2	true	This is a fundamental principle in economics. However, students should be reminded that demand may shift for one or more of the reasons given in the lecture.
3	false	Effective demand reflects what might be bought – consumer capacity, in other words. But what is, in fact, bought is 'actual' or 'realized' demand.
4	false	Consumers generally choose a complementary product because of price decreases in the related product. It is more than likely that demand for both products increases.
5	true	A fundamental principle, but the terminology (*extension*) is important.
6	true	However, a curve is an idealized theoretical representation. Demand or supply do not usually follow straight lines of development. Refer to the figures if necessary.
7	false	House prices doubled in the years 1998–2008.

Transcript 🎧 1.15

1 A minimum wage for employees means higher production costs.

2 If production costs for a good increase, demand is likely to decrease.

3 Effective demand is an indication of what consumers actually buy.

4 Consumers choose a complementary product because demand is less for the related product.

5 An extension of demand occurs when more of a product is consumed.

6 To show relationships in figures in economics, curves are usually straight lines.

7 Demand in the UK housing market contracted in the ten years 1998–2008.

Exercise G

This exercise practises making questions and using the information in the curve diagram shown in Lesson 3.1.

Ask students to think of three questions they could ask about the figure.

Wh~ questions using *Where …?, Which …?, What …?, How …?, Why …?, In which direction …?*, etc. Elicit some examples. Write these on the board:

What does the figure show?

Which is the x-axis?

What is shown on the x-axis?

Which is the demand curve?

Where do the supply and demand lines intersect?

How do you show contraction or extension in demand?

Put students in pairs to ask each other their questions, making sure they include the questions above. Check and provide clarification if necessary.

Answers

1 The figure shows equilibrium in a free market where demand and supply coincide or are equal. The market is stable. (Students should learn about this in the early part of any economics course and they may already know these concepts from their previous studies.)

The curves on the figure are straight, showing demand and supply and where they intersect at the point of equilibrium.

2 Assuming the price stays stable, demand might increase (extension of demand) and this would produce a shift in demand to the right. If supply could not match this, there would be excess demand. This would be a sign of disequilibrium in the market.

Closure

Ask students to give definitions and examples of *market factors, demand, shifts*.

Where necessary, remind students of specific terminology – *market demand, effective demand, substitute goods, composite/derived demand*, etc.

Note: Students will need their lecture notes from Lesson 3.2 in the next lesson.

3.3 Extending skills

3.3 Extending skills   stress within words • using information sources • reporting research findings

A 🎧 Listen to some stressed syllables. Identify the word below in each case. Number each word.

Example:
You hear: 1 *sten* /sten/   You write:

allocate	....	environmental	....
composite	....	equilibrium	....
conversion	....	extension	...1...
disposable	....	improvement	....
entrepreneur	....	marginality	....

productivity	....
recession	....
subsidy	....
undervalue	....
variation	....

B Where is the stress in each multi-syllable word in Exercise A?
  1 Mark the stress.
  2 Practise saying each word.

C Work in pairs or groups. Define one of the words in Exercise A. The other student(s) must find and say the correct word.

D Look at the spidergram on the right.
  1 For each effect of a recession, give some details.
  2 Try to think of other effects.
  3 What action can be taken to overcome the effects?

Spidergram: recession — decrease in demand, low interest rates, price of gold, low business investment, unemployment

Effect	Details	Possible action
low interest rates	encourage consumers to spend	banks must lend for investment

E Before you attend a lecture you should do some research.
  1 How could you research the lecture topics on the right?
  2 What information should you record?
  3 How could you record the information?

F You are going to do some research on a particular lecture topic. You must find:
  1 a dictionary definition
  2 an encyclopedia or textbook explanation
  3 a useful Internet site

🍁 HADFORD *University*

Faculty: Economics
Lecture topics:
  1 Stimulating demand: government scrappage schemes
  2 The UK housing market from 2009
  3 Oil prices rises: factors and implications
  4 Demand in the energy market

Student A
• Do some research on **demand in the UK housing market.**
• Tell your partner about your findings.

Student B
• Do some research on **demand in the energy market.**
• Tell your partner about your findings.

25

General note

Read the *Skills bank* at the end of the Course Book unit. Decide when, if at all, to refer students to it. The best time is probably at the beginning of this lesson or the end of the next lesson, as a summary/revision.

Lesson aim

This lesson is the first in a series about writing an assignment or giving a presentation based on research. The principal aim of this lesson is to introduce students to sources of information.

Introduction

1 Tell students to ask you questions about the information in the lecture in Lesson 3.2 as if you were the lecturer. Refer them to the *Skills bank* for typical language if you wish.

2 Put students in pairs. Student A must ask Student B about the information in the lecture in Lesson 3.2 to help him/her complete the notes from the lecture. Then they reverse roles. Go round, helping students to identify gaps in their notes and to think of good questions to get the missing information. Refer

them to the *Skills bank* for language they can use in the pairwork.

Pairs then compare notes and decide what other information would be useful and where they could get it from. For example, more technical definitions of the words used to describe various forms of demand might be obtained from a specialist dictionary of economics, from an appropriate textbook, or from a good Internet source such as www.economist.com which includes an 'Economics A-Z' as one of its research tools.

In the feedback, write a list of research sources on the board, at least including specialist dictionaries, encyclopedia, specialist reference books (about economics, marketing or business generally) and the Internet.

Point out that dictionaries are good for definitions, although you may need to go to a specialist dictionary for a technical word. Otherwise, try an encyclopedia, because technical words are often defined in articles when they are first used.

You could also try Google's 'define' feature, i.e., type *define: demand*

But remember you will get definitions from other disciplines, not just your own, so you need to scan to check the relevant one.

When doing an Internet search it is also useful to try both American and British English spellings. British spelling: *globalisation* or *globalization*; US: *globalization*.

🎧 Exercise A

Point out the importance of stressed syllables in words – see *Language note* below.

In this exercise, students will hear each word with the stressed syllable emphasized, and the rest of the syllables underspoken.

Play the recording, pausing after the first few to check that students understand the task. Feed back, perhaps playing the recording again for each word before checking. Ideally, mark up an OHT or other visual medium of the words.

Language note

In English, speakers emphasize the stressed syllable in a multi-syllable word. Sometimes listeners may not even hear the unstressed syllables. Vowels, in any case, often change to *schwa* or a reduced form in unstressed syllables. Therefore it is essential that students can recognize key words from the stressed syllable alone when they hear them in context.

57

Answers

allocate	15
composite	3
conversion	2
disposable	11
entrepreneur	9
environmental	6
equilibrium	12
extension	1
improvement	8
marginality	10
productivity	5
recession	7
subsidy	14
undervalue	4
variation	13

Transcript 🎧 1.16

1 ex'tension
2 con'version
3 'composite
4 under'value
5 produc'tivity
6 environ'mental
7 re'cession
8 im'provement
9 entrpre'neur
10 margin'ality
11 di'sposable
12 equi'librium
13 vari'ation
14 'subsidy
15 'allocate

Exercise B

Erase the words or turn off the OHP or other visual medium. Ask students to guess or remember where the stressed syllable is on each word. Tell them to mark their idea with a light vertical stroke in pencil. Elicit and drill. Refer students to the *Vocabulary bank* at this stage if you wish.

Answers

See transcript for 1.16.

Exercise C

Set for pair or group work. Go round and assist/correct.

Exercise D

1/2 Refer students to the spidergram and the table. Elicit question forms for this discussion such as:

Who sets the interest rates?

What is the objective of such a step?

Why do banks and other institutions (decrease/raise) …?

What does this mean for …?

When do they (raise, adjust) the rates?

Why does this happen?

What groups gain by …ing interest rates?

Put students in small groups or pairs to discuss the questions.

Feed back, building up a table in the Answers section on the board. The more details (for each effect) the students can give, the better.

3 Discuss with the whole class. Accept any reasonable suggestions.

Answers

Model answers:

See table on opposite page.

Many elements are interwoven and students should be encouraged to make these observations. The list is not completely comprehensive but covers most of the main impacts that a student might be expected to know at this stage.

Other effects might be *increased government borrowing, spending cuts, postponement of major policy implementation* (e.g., *reforms of the health service or benefits system*), *increasing indirect taxation* (e.g., *value added tax*).

This may be an opportunity to remind students of the macroeconomic and microeconomic 'overlaps', where major issues involving growth (or the lack of it!) overlap with individual or business spending and investment plans.

Effect of recession	Details	Possible action
Decrease in demand	Usually as a result of less disposable income for consumers; a disadvantage for production industries and can lead to short-time working.	Low interest rates will make saving unattractive; sellers can encourage consumers to take advantage of bargains, buy new items or upgrade; price increases for services might be delayed; government schemes such as 'car scrappage'. Lowering direct taxation is unlikely!
Low interest rates	Usually to encourage consumers to spend not to save; can be a benefit to business if banks willing to lend.	Banks must lend to business for investment purposes; supply of goods and services must be attractive.
Unemployment	Consequence of a recession; low-paid, unskilled or part-time workers are most vulnerable; expensive for the government if welfare benefits must be paid; makes labour market very competitive and keeps wage rates low.	Schemes to give unemployed new skills or extend education; encourage companies to take on unemployed through incentives (reduced tax rates for a certain period of time); capital schemes such as road or house-building but these are more risky for governments.
Low business investment	Understandable with weak economy and decrease in demand; efficiency to gain advantage over competition is important.	Keep credit rates for business low; reduce business taxes; do not increase costs of insurance for those in employment; encourage people to work even at lower wage rates rather than receive benefits.
Price of gold	Usually the price of gold increases during a recession as it is seen as a stable, less risky investment; this can mean currencies weaken and governments may have to intervene to support their own currency, especially if export revenues decrease as a result.	Do nothing; intervene as mentioned; see this as a market force which is self-regulating; companies do not usually invest in gold; some mixed investment funds have gold in their portfolios; companies can take advantage of lower currency prices for export or import purposes.

Exercise E

Remind students again about the four Ps. Refer students to the lecture topics and the questions. Make sure they understand that all three questions relate to before, rather than during, the lecture. Work through as a whole class if you wish.

Answers

Model answers:

1 Look up key words in a dictionary/encyclopedia/on the Internet. Check pronunciation so you will recognize words in the lecture.

2 Lecture 1: meaning/definition of key concept; examples/how to record on curves.

   Lecture 2: current resources; predicted needs; supply and demand issues; control – risks and opportunities

   Lecture 3: interpretation/analysis of graphs; impact on economies; predictions based on demand/supply shifts.

   Lecture 4: students might be able to anticipate some of the more simple factors which might cause price elasticity; how to show this on demand/supply curves.

3 Lecture 1: headings, definition, figures/curves as illustrations on the principle and possibly asking questions for clarification.

   Lecture 2: headings plus bullet points or a table with two columns, e.g., advantages/disadvantages; a spidergram might also be appropriate.

Lecture 3: interpretation of tables or graphs; using a two-column table to record discussion of factors and implications.

Lecture 4: identifying key terms; clarifying definitions and using curves to illustrate the concepts of *elasticity* and *inelasticity*.

Perhaps do a spidergram so that it is easier to brainstorm with fellow students and cover all the possible areas that the lecturer might focus on.

Exercise F

Set for pairwork, giving each member of the pair a different research task. If students have access in class to reference material, allow them to at least start the activity in class. Otherwise, set for homework. Before the feed back to partner stage, refer students to the *Skills bank – Reporting information to other people*.

Closure

Dictate sentences with words from Exercise A in context for students to identify the words again.

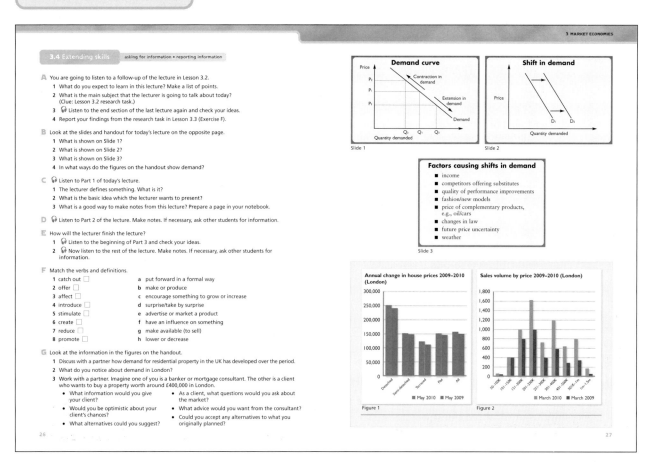

Lesson aims

- ask other people for information

Further practice in:

- choosing the best form of notes
- making notes
- reporting information

Introduction

1 Elicit some information from the lecture in Lesson 3.2. If necessary, prompt students by reading parts of the transcript and pausing for students to complete in their own words. Don't spend too long on this, however.

2 Remind students of the language involved in asking for information from other people – see *Skills bank*. Drill some of the sentences if you wish.

🎧 Exercise A

1/2 Set for pairwork. Encourage students to ask each other for information.

3 Play Part 4 of the lecture from Lesson 3.2 to enable students to check their answers. Feed back.

4 Elicit information from the students' research (Lesson 3.3). Do not confirm or correct at this stage except pronunciation mistakes on key words.

Answers

Model answers:

1 Students should learn more about demand and the factors which cause shifts. They might anticipate examples to illustrate the concepts.

2 Shifts in demand and why they occur.

3/4 As students should have read something about the topic, it is likely they will mention some of the factors mentioned in the lecture.

Transcript 🎧 1.14

Part 4

So, let's summarize quickly. Demand is not a single concept but has a number of variations – firstly, 'effective' demand which talks about ability to buy, then 'realized' or 'actual' demand, what we do in fact buy! Goods and services can be related to each other, so we have the third definition of 'composite' demand. Remember our example with cereals and biofuels! Now, definition number four – 'derived' demand comes from a change in economic circumstances; for example, a pay rise for workers might lead to an increased demand for certain goods. I also mentioned what happens to demand – yes, it goes up and it goes down! Or to be more technical, we observe an extension or an increase in demand, or a contraction, or a decrease, in the demand curve. So, what are people demanding? Well, goods and services, of course! But what happens when consumers decide that a good or service is too expensive? Well, they choose a substitute, don't they? And finally, don't forget complementary goods, where the interrelationship between goods is very strong and can influence each other. So, that's enough for now. Next time, we'll look at shifts in demand, so please do some research on this topic.

Exercise B

Refer students to the lecture slides. Set for pairwork discussion. Feed back. Don't try to explain slides 1 and 2 as they form the focus of the first part of the lecture.

Answers

Model answers:

1 A figure showing how demand changes in response to price.
2 A figure illustrating shift in demand.
3 An outline of reasons for shifts in demand.
4 Both figures from the handout give detailed information about demand in the UK housing market.

🎧 Exercise C

Set for individual work, then pair or group discussion. Play Part 1 of the lecture.

Methodology note

Don't tell students words they can't remember. It would be quite normal in a lecture that they can't write all of them down. If they don't remember them all this time, they should at least put the key words they remember in order. They can then listen for the other key words as the text develops.

Answers

Model answers:

1 The lecturer defines shifts in economics as movements along the respective demand (or supply) curve.
2 The lecturer wants to emphasize that shifts in demand occur when more or less of a good or a

service is bought when it is at the same price. It is not the price of the product itself which is driving demand.

3 Suitable ways of making notes for this lecture would be:
- headings plus bullet points, expanding the outline given by the lecturers' slides
- a table such as that constructed for Part 2 (see next page)

There is no hierarchy in these shift factors, so a spidergram would also be quite appropriate but more difficult. Either of the other two systems would be useful. Remind students that they would be expected to copy curves used as illustration of the concepts during the lecture and improve/refine them later.

Transcript 🎧 1.17

Part 1

Now, today I want to talk specifically about what causes 'shifts' in demand. I hope you have done some research on this topic. Well, a shift is basically a movement in one direction. But here we need to ask the question 'Why would people want to buy more of a good *at the same price*?' Remember, we are not talking about price fluctuations which cause contractions or extensions in demand, but we are talking about a movement of the whole demand curve. It isn't really a straight line, but this is how it is shown in economics.

So Slide 1 reminds us of how prices influence demand. That is, when prices change, these changes cause extension or contraction of demand. Have a good look.

Now, let's have a look at the shift in demand on Slide 2 when prices don't change. What has happened is that the whole demand curve has shifted. We can see that demand is greater in curve D2 at the same price. So, what might the reasons be for this shift?

🎧 Exercise D

Play Part 2 of the lecture. Students should recognize the rhetorical structure of the lecture. They will get some details or examples but they need to complete the rest of the information for themselves. Slide 2 has given students an outline of key points and the lecture fills in some of the gaps but not all. After students have completed note-making, put the following table on the board with the factors listed and one or two of the other columns completed. Ask students to complete the table individually and then compare in pairs.

Answers

Model answers:

Factor	Effect on demand	Example(s)
Disposable income	Shift to right (higher wages) Shift to left (reduction in earnings, unemployment)	None given. Elicit from students – holidays; update of home equipment; non-essentials
Substitute products	Shift to left (as lower price for substitutes)	None given. Elicit from students, e.g., trainers; mobile technology items
Promotion/advertising fashion	If advertising is successful, likely to increase demand. Shift to right	None given. Elicit from students, e.g., computer games, technology; perfumes, cosmetics; food products, etc.
Quality improvements	Shift to right	None given. Computer software; consumer items such as toothpaste, washing products
Complementary products	Depends on price movement	Alternative energy items; oil: cars; cheap flights → car hire, hotel, holiday services
Changes in law	Depends on whether changes result in stricter legislation or not. Could be shift to right – not so many restrictions.	Tobacco, DVDs
Future prices	Shift to right – bulk or panic buying; generally of short duration!	Petrol 'shortages'; food products
Weather	Depends on weather!	None given; garden furniture; food products; theme parks and other tourist services

Transcript 🎧 1.18

Part 2

So I will now move on to talk about the possible reasons for such shifts in demand which are shown on Slide 3.

Firstly, income is perhaps the most important. If people have more disposable income, they are likely to spend more, often on better goods.

The second reason is that competitors might reduce prices for substitute products. That should increase demand for their product, but this could reduce demand for your product.

Thirdly, good advertising or promotion of a product stimulates confidence among consumers who are likely to buy more.

Very often, the performance or quality of a product is improved and, usually as a result of increased efficiency or lower costs for materials, producers can offer the good at the same price.

In many consumer sectors, it is important to have new models, updates or new applications. Just think of mobile communications technology. Producers can create a fashion or a trend for a product to stimulate demand.

Now, I have mentioned complementary products before. So, if the price for one product changes, then demand for the other product will shift. Again, oil and cars provide a good example, but think, too, of the increased demand for alternative energy items such as domestic solar heating systems or small wind turbines when energy prices are high.

Think, too, of the cheap flights offered by airlines and the impact on complementary services.

Changes in the law can affect demand. In many countries, there are special laws to protect young people and prevent them from buying certain products such as tobacco, certain video or computer games, or DVDs. Now, if the law changes – for example, if an age limit is raised, let's say from 18 to 21, it will have an impact on demand for these goods and services.

Two final factors which may cause demand shifts relate to consumer behaviour and the weather! Firstly, consumers sometimes believe that there will be a shortage of some food products or petrol and become worried. So, they buy much more than usual, sometimes called 'panic-buying'!

Finally, we should not forget the weather. It often influences demand for certain products and this can sometimes catch out producers who have not provided enough or have produced too much!

🎧 Exercise E

Ask the initial question and elicit ideas, but do not confirm or correct at this stage.

1 Play the first three sentences of Part 3. Feed back.

2 Play the rest of Part 3. Give students time to do their own work, then set for pair or group completion.

Answers

Model answers:

1 The lecturer will provide an example of market demand. The lecturer suggests that he/she will talk about the demand for oil. But he/she provides reasons why oil is not the best example to use.

2 The lecturer talks about demand in the UK housing market in the years 1998–2008.

Transcript 🎧 1.19

Part 3

Right, to complete our examination of demand, we need an example. Now, the demand for oil is interesting and *might* be useful. But as you know, oil prices can fluctuate quite sharply, almost daily, for many reasons. Demand might be affected, but oil is so essential for industry, transport and energy production that there is no substitute for many consumers. Therefore, oil is not the best example! So, we will consider the UK housing market, but focus mostly on the demand side.

British people could tell you that house prices doubled in the years 1998–2008. That is a huge increase. For most goods or services, a 10% increase every year would mean that demand would fall dramatically. But demand in the housing market remained strong. So, why was demand consistently high? There are several important factors which give us an answer. Firstly, employment was high and people earned more. Secondly, lots of people came to work in the UK. Thirdly, these workers often rented property, affecting the availability of places to rent. Point number four is that the banks offered low interest rates for mortgages, you know, credit to buy a house. Finally, property was seen as an attractive investment by some very large investors. So, you can see that housing is an example of an economic sector where demand is rather special. Now take some time to look at the statistics on your handout and think about what is involved. I'm sure you will learn much more about demand in the future.

Exercise F

Set for pairwork. Monitor and assist. Feed back, writing the words on the board as students identify them correctly. Check pronunciation and stress patterns.

Answers

1	catch out	d	surprise/take by surprise
2	offer	g	make available (to sell)
3	affect	f	have an influence on something
4	introduce	a	put forward in a formal way
5	stimulate	c	encourage something to grow or increase
6	create	b	make or produce
7	reduce	h	lower or decrease
8	promote	e	advertise or market a product

Exercise G

Refer students to the handout items Figures 1 and 2.

Tell students to consider especially the demand factors in the housing market and discuss the questions.

1 Encourage the students to write a few notes about the information so they will improve their fluency when reporting back to each other.

2 Students should observe that demand in London has grown extremely rapidly, even for the more expensive homes. Actual numbers of sales seem quite low in some categories but this relates to just one year.

3 Put students in different pairs to do the role-play. They could both prepare both roles and then decide their preference or even play both roles.

Remind students of the need to ask politely for information (refer to the *Skills bank* if necessary).

Answers

Will depend on the students. You might want to compare the advice given by one 'consultant' and a 'consultant' from a different pair. Similarly, you could compare questions from different 'clients'.

Methodology note

End all listening lessons by referring students to the transcript at the back of the Course Book, so they can read the text while the aural memory is still clear. You could set this as standard homework after a listening lesson. You can also get students to highlight key sections and underline key sentences.

Closure

Ask students in pairs to test each other on the vocabulary items related to demand and supply, ensuring that students practise giving definitions and talk about market relationships accurately.

Alternatively, have some flashcards with key vocabulary items to remind students of the terminology. Encourage them to discuss the various curves that have been used in the lessons and what more they expect they will learn. Possible answers here might be how the markets behave in other, more complex, circumstances, for example, *elasticity of price* (mentioned in the lecture), *excess demand* where demand is greater than supply, or *excess supply*.

Extra activities

1 Work through the *Vocabulary bank* and *Skills bank* if you have not already done so, or as a revision of previous study.

2 Use the *Activity bank* (Teacher's Book, additional resources section, Resource 3A).

A Set the crossword for individual work (including homework).

Answers

B This game practises pronunciation and meaning recognition. It can be played in groups in class.

Students must think of one word for each of the categories on the bingo card. Allow them to use any of the vocabulary from this unit. They should write their words on card 1, or copy the bingo grid into their notebooks.

Each student says one of their own words at random, once only, concentrating on the pronunciation. The others must identify the category and cross it out on card 2.

The winner is the first student to identify the correct category for all the words. If the teacher keeps a record of all the words which have been said, he/she can say when a successful card could have been completed.

3 Students can play an alphabet game by themselves or as a group/class. The aim is to think of a word related to economics for each letter of the alphabet. For example:

Student 1: *allocate*

Student 2: *allocate, bargain*

Student 3: *allocate, bargain, curve*

Each student adds something for the next letter of the alphabet. They should try to use words from the unit if possible. A student misses a turn if he/she can't remember the items or can't add another word for the next letter.

4 Tell students to do some Internet research on one or two of these topics:

- Inflation and recession in Europe in the 1920s
- The Great Depression in the USA, 1929–1940
- The oil crisis of 1973
- The importance of North Sea oil to the UK
- Norway: an interesting approach to oil revenues
- Supply and demand in the US automobile industry

Note that a lot of the information will be in very complex English, but students should be able to record the basic details and report back in the next lesson.

4 ECONOMICS AND TECHNOLOGY

In this unit, one type of external influence on economics is covered: technology. Lesson 4.2 looks at how technology plays a vital role in computer-based applications, management of statistical data, access to financial transactions, and in various forms of economic planning and communication. At the same time, the use of computers in education is covered: Lessons 4.1, 4.3 and 4.4 guide students to a more efficient use of the Internet and computers in research.

Note that students will need access to a computer with an Internet connection for some exercises in this unit.

Skills focus

Reading
- identifying topic development within a paragraph
- using the Internet effectively
- evaluating Internet search results

Writing
- reporting research findings

Vocabulary focus
- computer jargon
- abbreviations and acronyms
- discourse and stance markers
- verb and noun suffixes

Key vocabulary

access (n and v)	exit (v)	media	software
auction	hyperlink	menu	spreadsheet
browse	index	mortgage	surplus
compile	Intranet	password	technology
data	keyword	portfolio	transaction
database	laundering	revenue	username/ID
default	ledger	revolutionize	web page
document	log in/log on (v)	scam	
drawback	login (n)	search (n and v)	
electronic	log off	search engine	

Abbreviations and acronyms

The *Jargon Buster* on page 31 of the Course Book gives the meanings of all of these.

CAL	JPEG	USB
DVD	LCD	WAN
HTML	PIN	WWW
HTTP	ROM	
ISP	URL	

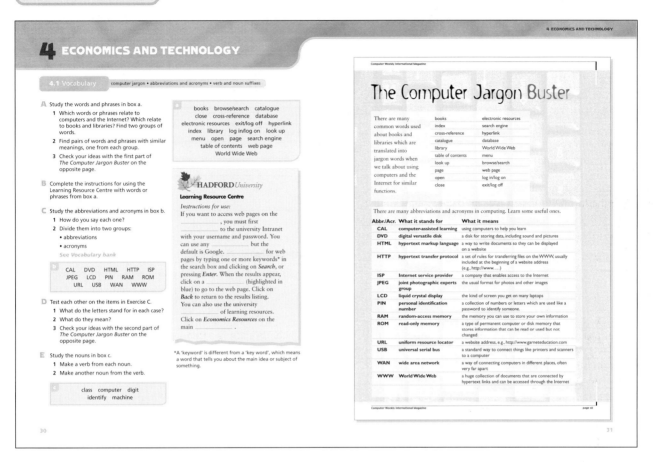

General note

If possible, hold this lesson in a room where there is a computer, or bring in a computer.

Read the *Vocabulary bank* at the end of the Course Book unit. Decide when, if at all, to refer your students to it. The best point is probably Exercise C, or at the very end of the lesson or the beginning of the next lesson, as a summary/revision.

PC	CPU *(central*	USB port
laptop	*processing unit)*	accessory
monitor	hard disk	printer
screen	USB stick	scanner
desktop	program	CD burner
icon	database	Internet
keyboard	slot	e-mail
keys	CD	the Web
mouse	DVD	Wi-Fi

Lesson aims

- gain fluency in the meaning, pronunciation and spelling of key computing terms, abbreviations and acronyms
- understand how verbs can be formed from nouns, and nouns from verbs, through the addition of suffixes

Introduction

Familiarize students with English terms for computer terminology using some or all of the following activities.

1 Using a computer or a picture of a computer as a starting point, elicit some or all of the following:

2 Ask students to suggest verbs used in computing. Elicit some or all of the following. A good way to do this is to open a program such as Word (in English) and look at the words and symbols on the toolbars.

switch on	exit
start up	save
shut down	select
log on/log off	copy
click	paste
double-click	enter
hold	delete
press	insert
open	highlight
close	undo

3 Ask students whether they normally use the library or the Internet to find information. Elicit the advantages and disadvantages of both. (There is so much emphasis on using computers nowadays, students often forget that there is a lot of information readily to hand in the library.)

Answers

Possible answers:

Library

Advantages	Disadvantages
easy to look things up in a dictionary or an encyclopedia	books can be out of date
you can find information in your own language	the book may not be in the library when you want it
information is usually correct	most books can't be accessed from home (though this is now starting to change)

Internet

Advantages	Disadvantages
a lot of information from different sources	difficult to find the right keywords*
information is usually more up-to-date than books	difficult to know which results are the best
can be accessed from home	information is often not correct
you can quickly and easily get copies of books or journal articles not in your library	you may have to pay for the books/articles/information

*Point out to students that a 'keyword' is different from a 'key word', which means a word that tells one about the main idea or subject of something.

Exercise A

Ask students to study the words in box a and elicit that they all relate to research.

Set for pairwork. Tell students to decide *and justify* the pairs they choose. If necessary, give an example: *index, search engine.*

To help students understand what a database is, refer to ones they are familiar with in your college, e.g., student records, exam results, library catalogues, etc.

Students may argue that some terms are not exact equivalents, e.g., *catalogue/database.* Discuss any objections as they arise.

Answers

Model answers:

Common word or phrase for books and libraries	Word or phrase for Internet and electronic information
books	electronic resources
index	search engine
cross-reference	hyperlink
catalogue	database
library	World Wide Web
table of contents	menu
look up	browse/search
page	web page
open	log in/log on
close	exit/log off

Language note

Log in and *log on*: these two verbs are used a little differently. *Log in* is used when accessing a closed system such as a college Intranet. *Log on* is used for open systems such as the Internet in general, as in *You can log on to the Internet with a laptop.* Note also that the related noun has now become one word (*login*). The opposite of *log in* is *log out*, while the opposite of *log on* is *log off*.

Exercise B

Set for individual work and pairwork checking. Ensure that students read *all* the text and have a general understanding of it before they insert the missing words.

Feed back by reading the paragraph or by using an OHT or other visual display of the text. Discuss alternative ideas and decide whether they are acceptable. Verify whether errors are due to using new words or to misunderstanding the text.

Answers

Model answers:

If you want to access web pages on the World Wide Web, you must first log in to the university Intranet with your username and password. You can use any search engine but the default is Google. Browse/Search for web pages by typing one or more keywords in the search box and clicking on *Search*, or pressing *Enter*. When the results appear, click on a hyperlink (highlighted in blue) to go to the web page. Click on *Back* to return to the results listing.

You can also use the university database of learning resources. Click on *Economics Resources* on the main menu.

Exercise C

Set for pairwork. Feed back, eliciting ideas on pronunciation and confirming or correcting. Build up the two lists on the board. Establish that one group are acronyms, i.e., they can be pronounced as words: PIN = /pɪn/. The other group are abbreviations, i.e., they are pronounced as letters: HTTP = H-T-T-P. Drill all the abbreviations and acronyms. Make sure students can say letter names and vowel sounds correctly.

Elicit that words with normal consonant/vowel patterns are *normally* pronounced as a word and those with unusual patterns are *normally* pronounced with single letters. Refer to the *Vocabulary bank* at this stage if you wish.

Methodology note

Don't discuss the meaning at this point. This is covered in the next activity.

Answers

Acronyms: CAL /kæl/, JPEG /dʒeɪpeg/, PIN /pɪn/, ROM /rɒm/, WAN /wæn/.

Abbreviations: DVD, HTML, HTTP, ISP, LCD, URL (not pronounced /ɜːl/), USB, WWW.

Exercise D

1 Introduce the verb *stand for*. Elicit examples of common abbreviations and ask what they stand for. Set for pairwork. Tell students to pick out the ones they already know first. Next, they pick out the ones they are familiar with but don't know what they stand for – and guess.

2 Elicit the meanings without reference to the *Jargon Buster* if possible.

3 Refer students to the *Jargon Buster* to verify their answers. As a follow-up, elicit other common abbreviations from IT or economics.

Language note

If students don't use acronyms or initial abbreviations in their language, a discussion about the reasons for using them is useful. They will then know how to find the meaning of new ones when they meet them. You might point out that abbreviations can sometimes be longer than the thing they abbreviate! For example, World Wide Web is three syllables, whereas WWW is six. It evolved because it is quicker to write, but it is longer, and harder, to say. Note that WWW is frequently written in lower case letters (www), presumably because it is lower case in URLs.

It is also possible to mix acronyms with abbreviations: for example, JPEG – J /peg/.

Point out the field of ICT is developing at an incredible speed and new acronyms and abbreviations are constantly being created.

Exercise E

Set for individual work and pairwork checking. Feed back, highlighting the changes from noun form to verb in the case of *identity/identify* and *machine/mechanize*.

Answers

Model answers:

Noun 1	Verb	Noun 2
class	classify	classification
computer	computerize	computerization
digit	digitize	digitization
identity	identify	identification
machine	mechanize	mechanization

Language note

Both *~ise/~ize* (*~isation/~ization*) forms are acceptable in British English. American English usage is *~ize* (*~ization*).

Closure

Ask students whether they agree with the following statements.

1 Every college student must have a computer.

2 The college library uses a computer to help students find information.

3 College departments use computers to store research data.

4 Students can't do research without a computer.

5 College computers can access research data from other colleges and universities.

6 College computers can access research data from businesses and the media.

7 A personal computer can store information students think is important.

8 Computers can help us to talk with students from other colleges and universities.

9 Computers can help students access data from anywhere in the world.

10 A computer we can carry in our pocket can access worldwide data.

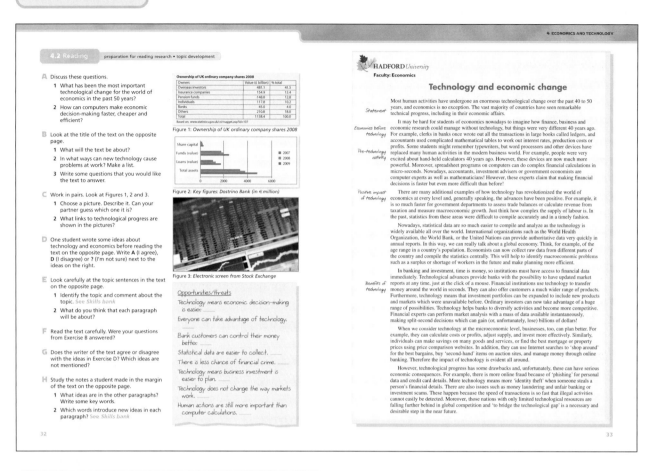

General note

Read the *Skills bank – Developing ideas in a paragraph* at the end of the Course Book unit. Decide when, if at all, to refer students to it. The best time is probably Exercise E, or at the very end of the lesson or the beginning of the next lesson, as a summary/revision.

Lesson aims

- prepare to read a text by looking at the title and topic sentences
- understand the purpose of discourse markers and stance markers in the development of a topic

Introduction

Ask students how, where and why they use computers. They should answer in some detail with examples. Encourage them to use the vocabulary, abbreviations and acronyms from Lesson 4.1.

Exercise A

Set for general discussion. Allow students to debate differences of opinion. Encourage them to give examples if they can.

Answers

Possible answers:

1 Probably information technology, i.e., the use of computers in all aspects of economic activities. For example, storing data and keeping records, electronic transfers and other aspects of Internet banking, economic planning processes, communicating with customers and the general public are all important.

2 Economic decision-making relies on fast responses to global markets and events. A computer can reduce the number of employees needed. It can make analysis quicker and more efficient; it can make data access much quicker and more complete.

70

Exercise B

1 Write the title of the reading text on the board. Discuss with the whole class, eliciting suggestions.

2 Set for pairwork and whole class feedback. Tell students to think of four or five possible problem areas. Do not confirm or correct at this point.

3 Set for pairwork. Tell students to think of four or five questions with different *Wh~* question words:

What ...?

Where ...?

When ...?

Why ...?

How ...?

If you want, you could choose some questions to write on one side of the board.

Answers

Possible answers:

1 The different ways in which computers and technology have changed the way economists and other specialists work.

2 Possible disadvantages of new technology in an area of economic activity. (You might prompt students with suggestions such as Internet banking, government record-keeping, economic planning, world economic forecasts.)

- cost: it may be expensive to introduce
- people may resist new technology if it threatens their jobs
- skills: people may need to learn new skills
- reliability: the new technology may not work well
- clients and customers may not like the switch to new technology
- people may criticize specialists such as bankers or economists more as there are so many economics and business websites which analyze decisions made by so-called specialists
- it may be difficult to decide how certain information might affect the financial markets
- people will notice more when forecasts are incorrect
- there are new opportunities for hiding illegal financial actions as money and other securities such as bonds can be traded so rapidly that it is difficult to track them
- there are chances financial information or personal identity details may be stolen
- databases become huge, but people are worried about removing information in case it is needed again

3 Possible questions:

What are the current challenges of new technology?

What were the results of new technology in the past?

Where has there been the most change from new technology?

When has there been the most change from new technology?

Why does new technology mean change?

What groups of people benefit most from technology?

What groups of people benefit least from technology?

Exercise C

1 Set for pairwork.

2 Set for pairwork and whole class feedback. Write the answers on the board.

Answers

Model answers:

1 A government table providing statistical data. Even this small table shows the way that technology permits governments to compile statistics involving huge sums of money and several variables. Government statistics need to be updated regularly. This table was published in 2010 but applies to 2008. This underlines how some statistics (such as ownership of shares in UK companies) are difficult to compile. Without computer technology, such statistics would be almost impossible to collate. The UK statistics office, www.statistics.gov.uk, usually gives information about the computer methodology used to compile data. Students who are really keen on computer programs may want to look at such details.

2 Part of a bank balance sheet. Again, technology permits the institution to present data in order to show the performance of the bank over a certain period. Students will notice that this (fictitious) bank has performed well year on year.

3 An electronic screen from a stock exchange. Transactions are recorded instantaneously on such screens for the companies which are listed on a stock exchange, for example, LSE. The screen-based trading has replaced face-to-face trading and information is updated every few seconds. Dealers can buy and sell shares electronically and these transactions are then shown on such screens.

Exercise D

Set for individual work and pairwork checking. Feed back, trying to get consensus on each point, but do not actually confirm or correct. Preface your remarks with phrases like: *So most of you think … You all agree/disagree that …*

Point out that the statements are very strong. Draw students' attention to words like *everyone*. Point out also that the use of plurals with countable nouns when making a generalizing statement implies *all*, e.g., *governments* means *all governments*. The truth may actually be better expressed with a limiting word, e.g., *most/some/many*, or with words which express possibility such as *may* or *seem*, or adverbs such as *sometimes*, *usually*, *often*.

Remind students to look back at these predictions while they are reading the text (Exercise F).

Exercise E

Review paragraph structure – i.e., paragraphs usually begin with a topic sentence which makes a statement that is then expanded in the following sentences. Thus, topic sentences give an indication of the contents of the paragraph. You may wish to refer students to the *Skills bank* at this point.

1 Write the topic sentences from the text on an OHT or other visual medium, or use Resource 4B from the additional resources section. Take the first

sentence and identify the subject of the main clause with a box. This is the **topic**. For example:

> There are many additional examples of how technology has revolutionized the world of economics at every level and, generally speaking, the advances have been positive.

What is the sentence saying about *the impact of new technology on the world of economics*? The answer is: *the advances have been positive*. Underline these words. These words constitute the comment which the sentence is making about the topic. Note that the subordinate clause simply provides more information about the topic: it is not the focus of the sentence. The focus of the sentence is on the **comment** being made. Thus a topic sentence consists of both a topic and a comment about the topic which is explained and expanded on in the rest of the paragraph.

Set the remaining sentences for individual work and pairwork checking.

2 Set for pairwork. Tell students that their analysis of the topic sentences may help them. Feed back with the whole class. Point out any language features which led them to draw their conclusions.

Answers

Possible answers:

1 See table below.

2 See table at top of opposite page.

	Topic	Comment
Para 1	Most human activities have undergone an enormous technological change over the past 40 to 50 years,	and economics is no exception.
Para 2	It may be hard for students of economics nowadays to imagine how finance, business and economic research could manage without technology,	but things were very different 40 years ago.
Para 3	There are many additional examples of how technology has revolutionized the world of economics at every level	and, generally speaking, the advances have been positive.
Para 4	Nowadays, statistical data are so much easier to compile and analyze	as the technology is widely available all over the world.
Para 5	In banking and investment, time is money,	so institutions must have access to financial data immediately.
Para 6	When we consider technology at the microeconomic level,	businesses, too, can plan better.
Para 7	However, technological progress has some drawbacks	and, unfortunately, these can have serious economic consequences.

	Predicted content	Notes
Para 1	a historical view of technology and economics	the words *and economics is no exception* point to the idea of a generalized development
Para 2	a contrastive historical view of how technology has impacted on economics	the use of the modal form *may be hard* and the verb *to imagine* invites students to reflect on the present and past contrasts
Para 3	examples of the various technological revolutions in economics	the word *additional* links this paragraph with the previous one in which some examples are outlined
Para 4	focus on statistical data	students may suggest that all of the changes relate to statistics, which, in a way, is true; however, the speed of access, response to change, range of choices, etc., are more than simply numbers
Para 5	specific examples of areas of economics which have benefitted from the technological revolution	students will begin to think about the impact of technology on banking
Para 6	technology at a microeconomic level	switching focus to microeconomics
Para 7	disadvantages of technological progress in this field	reminding students to develop critical awareness

Exercise F

Set the reading. Tell students to read for good understanding. When everyone has read the text, discuss any vocabulary items that may have caused difficulties.

If you have previously written questions on the board, ask students to say which were answered. Then tell the same pairs as in Exercise B to discuss which of their questions were answered. Feed back with the whole class, asking a few pairs to say which of their questions were answered and which were not.

Exercise G

Set for individual work and pairwork checking. Feed back with the whole class, asking students to say which parts of the text discuss the ideas. Ask students to say how the sentences in Exercise D could be better worded to reflect the ideas in the text.

Answers

Possible answers:

See table below.

Idea	Agree/disagree/no mention	Possible rewording
Technology means economic decision-making is easier.	disagree – para 2, last sentence (N.B. Decisions can be made faster but the decisions themselves are even more difficult!)	Technology means economic decision-making *can be faster* but *not necessarily* easier.
Everyone can take advantage of technology.	disagree – para 7, sentence 6	*Most people* can take advantage of technology.
Bank customers can control their money better.	agree – para 6, sentence 3 disagree – para 7, sentence 2	Bank customers can *usually* control their money *more effectively*.
Statistical data are easier to collect.	agree – para 4, sentence 1 (N.B. Suggestion that skills are more computer-based than mathematically-based in paragraph 2, final sentences!)	Statistical data *become* easier to collect *when people have the necessary expertise or training*.
There is less chance of financial crime.	disagree – para 7, sentence 2	There is, *however, some chance/risk* of financial crime.
Technology means business investment is easier to plan.	agree – para 6, sentence 1 (But there are many aspects to business investment, not just the financial data!)	Technology means *some aspects of* business planning *are* easier.
Technology does not change the way markets work.	not mentioned	(But it can have an impact on speed of information and response to it.)
Human actions are still more important than computer calculations.	not mentioned	(An interesting point for students to discuss, if time allows.)

Exercise H

The purpose of this exercise is for students to try to identify the information structure of each paragraph and to see how a new step in the progression of ideas may be signalled by a rhetorical marker or phrase. Direct students' attention to the handwritten notes in the left margin of the text. Explain that the notes are key words which summarize (in the reader's own words) the ideas in the text. The notes are written next to the relevant parts of the text. A good idea is to make an OHT or other visual medium of the text and use a highlighter to indicate which are the relevant parts of the text. Point out that often (but not always) a new step in the development of ideas is shown by a rhetorical marker or a phrase. The writer may introduce more information: in paragraph 2 we have *for example*, and *moreover* (which reinforce an idea) and in paragraph 5 we have *furthermore*. Or the writer may introduce a contrast: in paragraph 7 we have *however* and in paragraph 2 *nevertheless*, which is also a contrastive marker.

1 Set for pairwork. Tell students to decide on some similar key words for the ideas in the remaining paragraphs and to write these words next to the appropriate part of the text. Feed back with the whole class, eliciting suitable key words for the left margin and using a highlighter or OHT pen to indicate the phrases or sentences in the text which correspond to the key words.

2 Set for individual work and pairwork checking. Feed back with the whole class, identifying the discourse and stance markers.

Answers

Possible answers:

1 Para 4: quicker to compile statistics

Para 6: implications at microeconomic level + examples for businesses and individuals

Para 7: drawbacks of technology in economic areas of activity + examples

2 Para 1: the vast majority/remarkable (stance of author)

Para 2: it may be hard ... to imagine (stance), for example, moreover

Para 3: for example

Para 4: in this way (stance), really (stance)

Para 5: furthermore

Para 6: for example, similarly, in addition, therefore

Para 7: however, unfortunately (stance), for example, moreover

Language note

The relation of one sentence to the previous sentence is not always made explicit by rhetorical markers or phrases. In fact, overuse of markers is to be avoided.

If there is no marker or phrase, the relationship can be deduced usually by the position of the sentence in the paragraph, or by the meaning. For example, in the first paragraph the second sentence expands on the first sentence.

Closure

1 Divide the class into groups. Write the seven topic sentences on strips, or photocopy them from the additional resources section (Resource 4B). Make a copy for each group. Students must put them into the correct order.

Alternatively, divide the class into two teams. One team chooses a topic sentence and reads it aloud. The other team must give the information triggered by that topic sentence. Accept a prediction or the actual paragraph content. However, ask students which it is – prediction or actual.

Language note

There is no universal logic to the structuring of information in a text. The order of information is language-specific. For example, oriental languages tend to have a topic sentence or paragraph summary at the end, not the beginning, of the paragraph. Or students whose first language is Arabic might structure a particular type of discourse in a different way from native English speakers. So it is important for students to see what a native speaker writer would consider to be a 'logical' ordering.

2 Refer students back to the sentences in Exercise D. Students should find it easier to comment on these now that they have read the text.

3 Focus on some of the vocabulary from the text, including:

adjust

authoritative (+ *collocations ... report, ... information, ... source*)

claim (v)

compile

fraud

identity theft

money laundering

portfolio

raw

scam

4.3 Extending skills

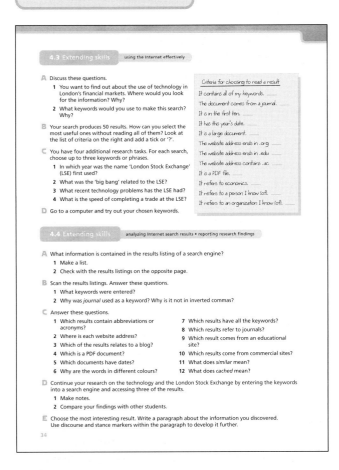

General note

Students will need access to a computer with an Internet connection. If computers are not available during the lesson, part of the lesson can be set for private study.

Lesson aim

● learn or practise how to use the Internet efficiently for research

Introduction

Brainstorm the uses of the Internet. Then brainstorm what the important factors are when using the Internet. These should include:

● the search engines students use and why. Note that there is now a large number of search engines to suit different purposes. It is not necessarily a good idea to use Google exclusively.

● how to choose *and write* keywords in their preferred search engine

● how they extract the information they want from the results

Put students in groups and ask them to compare how they normally use a computer to find information. Ask each group to produce a set of advice for using the Internet. Then, as a class, produce an accepted set of advice.

Key words to elicit: *search engine, keyword, website, web page, website address, search result, subject directory*

Note: Where the subject is a new one or a fairly general topic, it is a good idea to start first with a **subject directory** which evaluates sites related to the topic and collects them in one place. Some examples are: Academic Info or INFOMINE:

www.academicinfo.net

http://infomine.ucr.edu/ (Scholarly Internet Resource Collections)

A very useful academic database is provided at www.intute.ac.uk but there are many specialized sites such as:

http://epp.eurostat.ec.europa.eu/portal/page/portal/eurostat/home/

http://ec.europa.eu/eclas/F (European Commission Libraries catalogue)

www.bis.org (Bank for International Settlements)

www.bankofengland.co.uk

www.ft.com (*Financial Times*)

http://data.worldbank.org

www.uktradeinfo.com/index.cfm?task=Home (UK
www.bized.co.uk/index.htm (A site for general information in economics and business)

www.finweb.com/ (An independent financial site)

www.statistics.gov.uk/hub (UK national statistics)

http://unstats.un.org/unsd/default.htm (United Nations statistics database)

www.oecd-ilibrary.org/finance (OECD online resources for economic issues)

Other online databases which offer open access include:

www.helsinki.fi/WebEc/ (This was – until 2007 – the site for the WWW Virtual Library, but is no longer updated. However, a lot of economics information and links are still available.)

http://bubl.ac.uk/index.html (This is a catalogue of Internet resources and provides links to a large number of resources in economics, including some of the specialist sites mentioned here. However, since April 2011, it is no longer being updated.)

www.oxfordreference.com/pub/views/home.html
(Provides subscription-based access to all Oxford University Press reference resources but students may have free access through their institution or sign up for a free 30-day trial.)

Exercise A

Write *London financial markets* on the board.

1 Set for class discussion. Make sure students give reasons for their answers. Accept their answers at this stage.

2 Remind students that words in English often have more than one meaning, so care must be taken to get the desired result.

Answers

Possible answers:

1 On the Internet. Students can get a lot of information from Wikipedia. Other online reference books and encyclopedia are available.

On the Internet, information will be good if the correct keywords are used and a careful selection of results is made. Students should be aware of the commercial sites.

In a textbook – useful if there is an up-to-date one, but books take time to publish, so even the latest may be out of date, especially in these technologically fast-moving times.

For any historical topic, a good encyclopedia in the university library is an option.

2 In this list of possible keywords, the first three are obvious starting points; others may also be useful.

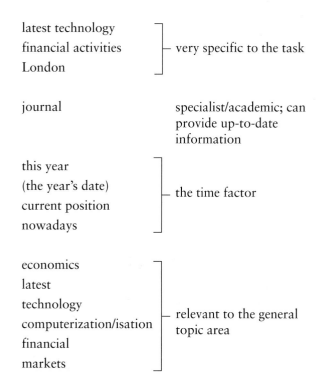

Exercise B

Set for pairwork. Remind students of the research topic.

Feed back, encouraging students to give reasons for their decisions. Emphasize that we only know what *might* be useful at this stage.

Establish that company sites often end in *.com*.

Answers

Model answers:

✓ It contains all of my keywords. (*but check that the meaning is the same*)

✓ The document comes from a journal. (*current information*)

? It is in the first ten. (*a web page can have codes attached to put it high in the list*)

✓ It has this year's date. (*current information*)

? It is a large document. (*size is no indication of quality*)

✓ The website address ends in .org (*because it is a non-profit organization*)

✓ The website address ends in .edu (*because it is an educational establishment*)

✓ The website address contains .ac (*because it is an educational establishment*)

? It is a PDF file. (*file type is no indication of quality*)

? It refers to economics. (*may not be relevant*)

✓ It refers to an organization I know (of). (*reliable*)

? It refers to a person I don't know. (*may not be reliable*)

Language note

PDF stands for *portable document format*. PDF documents look exactly like the original documents, and can be viewed and printed on most computers, without the need for each computer to have the same software, fonts, etc. They are created with Adobe Acrobat software.

Exercise C

Set for individual work and pairwork checking. Ask students to compare their choice of keywords with their partner, and justify their choice. In Google, you can, for example, exclude commercial and other sites. In the *Search* or *Advanced Search* box, you put a minus sign in front of addresses you want to exclude.

For example, -.com -.co means you want to exclude commercial sites. However, students should be aware that even the big database resources which search for academic journal articles (such as Science Direct) have .com sites, e.g., www.sciencedirect.com

Such an exclusion could mean students miss possible useful material.

Answers

Possible answers:

1 In 1773. The following combinations will produce results provided the word(s) in bold are included: **History + "London Stock Exchange"**, e.g., www.londonstockexchange.com/about-the-exchange/company-overview/our-history/our-history.htm

2 This refers not to a 'crash' in share prices but to deregulation of the LSE in 1986 and the introduction of computer-based trading rather than face-to-face. Keywords would be **"London Stock Exchange" + big bang.**

   www.londonstockexchange.com/about-the-exchange/company-overview/our-history.htm

3 A serious breakdown in the computer system occurred in September 2009 when the LSE had to close for a whole day because the system collapsed. As a result, the LSE switched computer software suppliers. A lot of information about the LSE and technology may be found at: www.cio.co.uk/news/

   To get information about these problems, students need to use **"London Stock Exchange" + "computer problems"** or **"London Stock Exchange" + "latest technology"**.

4 Plans to reduce the trading speed to under a millisecond were announced in February 2010 but, according to the LSE's online site FAQ, the speed is around 6 milliseconds!

   www.londonstockexchange.com/traders-and-brokers/membership/faqs/rulebook-faq/rulebook-faqs.htm

   "London Stock Exchange" + "speed of trading" will obtain this answer.

   You might like to mention that LSE is also the abbreviation for the London School of Economics, which is part of the University of London! Students might find this site worth a visit, too.

   www2.lse.ac.uk/home.aspx

Exercise D

Students should try out different combinations to discover for themselves which give the best results.

Closure

Tell students to think of their own question for research, as in Exercise C, and find the best web page for the data by entering appropriate keywords.

Ask students to write their question on a piece of paper and sign it. Put all the questions in a box. Students pick out one of the questions at random and go online to find the best page of search results. From those results they can find the most useful web page. They should ask the questioner for verification.

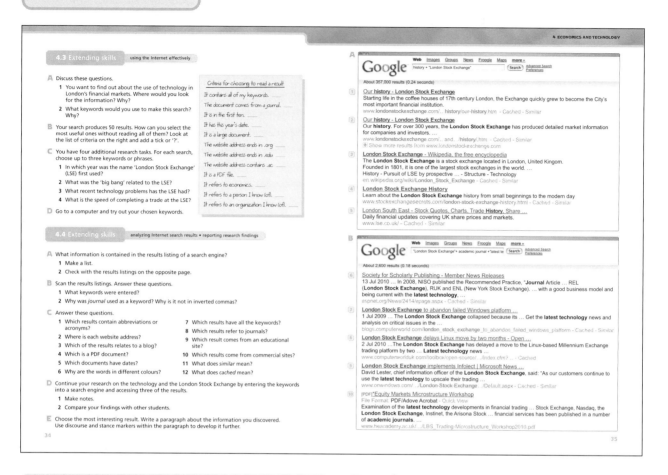

General note

Students will need access to a computer with an Internet connection. If computers are not available during the lesson, part of the lesson can be set for private study.

Lesson aims

- examine a page of Internet search results critically
- report Internet search findings in a short written summary

Introduction

Ask students what problems they had, what lessons they have learnt and what advice they can give from their Internet search experience in Lesson 4.3. Brainstorm the important factors when searching for information on the Internet and put them in order of importance.

Exercise A

Set for pairwork. Students should first make a list of information they expect to find in search engine results. (They should do this before they look at the search engine results on the opposite page.) They should then look at the page of results and identify any other information that is there.

Answers

Possible answers:

number of results

keywords used

time taken

title of document

type of document

quotations from the text with keywords highlighted

date

web address/URL

Exercise B

This is further reinforcement on keywords. Set for pairwork or whole class discussion.

Answers

Model answers:

1. 1 history + "London stock exchange"
   2 "London stock exchange"+ academic journal + "latest technology"

2. Because journals give specialist/academic information which (in a recent issue) is up to date. Inverted commas are put round a phrase to indicate that it is all a meaningful lexical item. In Google, *academic journal* might also be put in inverted commas; however, results are the same.

Exercise C

This detailed examination of the results page should make students aware of the content, so that they can make an educated selection of a web page with useful information. Set for pairwork.

Make sure in feedback that students are aware of what the following abbreviations stand for: PDF (portable document format). They may also encounter PPT (PowerPoint), RTF (rich text format). A search specifically for PowerPoint items can sometimes be quite useful. In their Google search, students need only specify the topic and write PowerPoint, for example: "financial trading" powerpoint.

Answers

Possible answers:

1. Acronyms/abbreviations:
   Result A1: .com/.htm
   Result A2: .com/.htm
   Result A3: en./.org (LSE = London Stock Exchange)
   Result A4: .com/.html
   Result A5: .co.uk
   Result B6: .org/.aspx (aspx = active server page extended file)

   Abbreviations in the result could be followed up by students)

   NISO = www.niso.org/publications (National Information Standards Organization)

The other abbreviations are interesting and may be found in the search result document by using CONTROL + f (to find within a document).

They relate to the 'ticker signals' on different stock exchanges for the publisher Reed Elsevier. Students might want to get a definition of 'ticker symbol' from Google. However, it relates to quite advanced communications and display technology!

Definition:

A series of letters that are used to identify a stock in a corporation whose shares are traded on an exchange. Also known as the "ticker".
www.scag.gov/wp-content/uploads/2011/03/glossary.html

The text is as follows:

The company is part of <u>Reed Elsevier Group PLC</u>, a world-leading publisher and information provider, which is jointly owned by Reed Elsevier PLC and Reed Elsevier NV. The ticker symbols are REN (Euronext Amsterdam), REL (London Stock Exchange), RUK and ENL (New York Stock Exchange).

Result B7: .com

Result B8: .com/.cfm

Result B9: .com/.aspx

Result B10: .ac.uk/.pdf/PDF (Nasdaq is not capitalized but could be followed up by students – NASDAQ is basically the biggest stock exchange in the world!)

2. At the end.

3. B7

4. B10

5. None of the A search results have specific dates. Dates seem more prominent in the + academic journal search. Specific publication dates are included as part of the reference in B6, B7 and B8.

6. Blue = titles and viewing information; green = website address; black = keywords.

7. All the A results (history + "London stock exchange"). The B results ("London stock exchange" + academic journal + "latest technology") produce only 2 mentions of academic journals but all have the other search terms.

8. B6 (although following up the search, it is a reference to the *Wall Street Journal*, which is a newspaper!). B10 only mentions the words *academic journals* as part of the result.

9. Result B10.

10. Results A1, A2, A4 and A5; B7, B8 and B9.

11. There were other very similar results, so the search engine ignored them. They are available if you click on the words.

12. It is a more efficient way of storing information. (It means that you can go to a copy of the page stored by Google, in case the actual website happens to be down at the time of the search; of course, it could be a little out of date.)

Exercise D

1 Set for individual work. Students should input the keywords again. They will not get exactly the same results page as here, but the results should be comparable. Tell them to take notes.

2 Set for pairwork. Feed back, getting students to tell the rest of the class about their most interesting findings. Encourage other students to ask questions.

Exercise E

Set for individual work. Students can complete it in class or for homework.

Closure

1 Focus on some of the vocabulary connected with using the Internet, including:

website

web address/URL

search engine

search results

input

keyword

key in

log in/log on

username

password

access

2 The importance of the care needed when selecting keywords can be demonstrated by a simple classroom activity. Tell the class you are thinking of a particular student who you want to stand up. Say (for example):

It's a man. (all the men stand up and remain standing)

He has dark hair. (only those with dark hair remain standing)

He has a beard.

He has glasses.

He's tall.

His name begins with A.

When only one student remains, ask the class to list the minimum number of keywords necessary to identify only that student. Make sure they discard unnecessary ones. For example, if all students have dark hair, that is unnecessary.

3 Finding the keywords for familiar topics is another activity, done in groups. For example, they could:

- find their own college record (name, ID number or date of entry)
- find their last exam results (name, class, subject, date)
- find a book in the library about technology in economics

Extra activities

1 Work through the *Vocabulary bank* and *Skills bank* if you have not already done so, or as a revision of previous study.

2 Use the *Activity bank* (Teacher's Book additional resources section, Resource 4A).

A Set the wordsearch for individual work (including homework) or pairwork.

Answers

B Set for pairwork. Teach students how to play noughts and crosses if they don't know – they take it in turns to say the abbreviation or acronym, and what it stands for. If they succeed, they can put their symbol – a nought 0 or a cross X – in that box. If a person gets three of their own symbols in a line, they win.

3 Write the acronyms and abbreviations from the unit on cards, or photocopy them from the additional resources section (Resource 4C). Divide the class into two teams. A student selects a card and reads it correctly. (Speed is of the essence.) Alternatively, one team picks a card with an acronym or abbreviation; the other team gives the actual words.

You can follow this up by eliciting other acronyms and abbreviations from the students – in particular, common/useful ones from the field of economics.

4 Have a class debate: 'If an economy, for example in the developing world, does not have the latest technology, it cannot possibly compete successfully.' Ask two students to prepare an opening argument for and against.

Some points: remind students of the points in Lesson 4.2 Exercises A and B2.

Arguments for might be:

● technology gives governments more information to compete for trade and development

● technology can help develop literacy

● it provides access to the wider world

● it helps coordination of employment and investment opportunities

● it can encourage small businesses to develop or expand

● it helps academics and specialists exchange information and ideas

Arguments against might be:

● the introduction of new technology may be expensive to introduce

● some technology is simply dumped onto developing countries; it is not state of the art and may be outdated very quickly

● people may resist new technology if it threatens their jobs

● the skills gap becomes wider when only some people learn new skills

● reliability: the new technology may not work well if the infrastructure is poor

● the availability of more information to the people can be a threat to some governments

● people can take advantage of others' lack of knowledge in financial transactions

● corrupt government officials can 'hide' money more easily

● it is possible to make progress by improving general levels of efficiency and more basic communication

5 Ask students to work in small groups to research and feed back to the group on some inventions which have helped economics during the 20th century. Three research questions could be:

   1 *What problem did people face in this area?*

   2 *Was there a specific turning point in solving the problem or was it a gradual evolution?*

   3 *How did the solution change economic activities?*

These inventions might include the telephone, telex (explain if students are not familiar with it), the fax machine (for exchange of information or contracts, etc.), computer software (using economic models for analysis and prediction), the mobile telephone and satellite technology (for speed of information gathering and sharing).

If students are going to do research on the Internet, suggest that they type in *History* then their topic to get some potential texts. Alternatively, you can do this research before the lesson and print off some pages for students to work from.

Remind students that they can't possibly read everything they find, so they must use the topic sentences to decide if a paragraph is worth reading.

6 Use the *Activity bank* (Teacher's Book additional resources section, Resource 4D). Abbreviations are important in financial trading, especially to refer to major currencies in foreign exchange (FOREX) markets. Other acronyms do not seem to be used.

Students work in pairs. Each has a card with six abbreviations and six currency names. They take it in turns to ask their partner for <u>either</u> the respective country or the <u>abbreviation of its currency and what it stands for</u>. Whoever gets the most correct answers wins. If students disagree about the pronunciation of the abbreviation, the teacher may need to intervene and award points accordingly.

Example:

Card 1 holder asks

   '*What is the abbreviation for the Hong Kong Dollar?*'

OR

   '*What is the name of the currency and country using the abbreviation JPY?*'

5 ECONOMICS, GLOBALIZATION AND SUSTAINABILITY

Economic factors related to globalization are presented in this unit. The relationship between globalization, sustainability and environmental issues is considered in the first lecture. It takes a rather critical stance, without being overly negative about the globalization process itself. The suggested research task for students from this first lecture relates to the status of developing countries, referred to during the main lecture. The second listening extract is from a seminar about foreign direct investment (FDI) and provides students with some useful perspectives on this economic activity. This leads into possible further research on various features of sustainable development and FDI, using information provided.

Skills focus

🎧 Listening

- understanding 'signpost language' in lectures
- using symbols and abbreviations in note-taking

Speaking

- making effective contributions to a seminar

Vocabulary focus

- word sets: synonyms, antonyms, etc.
- the language of trends
- common lecture language

Key vocabulary

affluence	extractive	partnership	stimulate
debt	finite	pharmaceutical	substitution
debt relief	globalization	raw materials	surplus
degradation	improvement	recipient	transfer (v)
diversify	migration	renewable	wasteful
donor	misuse	replaceable	wealth
enterprise	mobility	replacement	
exploitation	non-renewable	self-sufficient	
extraction	outsourcing	small-scale	

5.1 Vocabulary

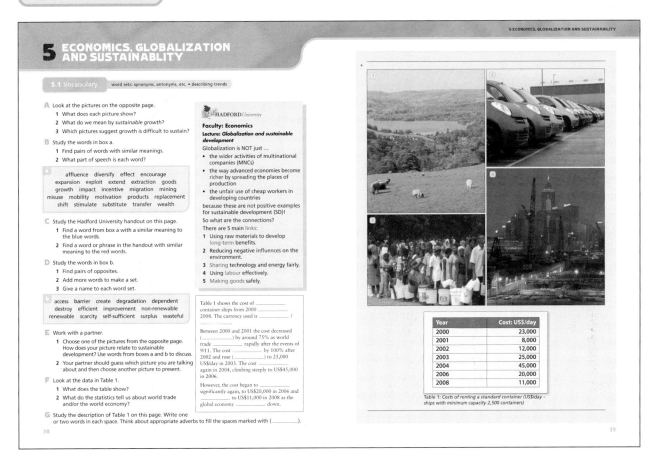

General note

Read the *Vocabulary bank – Vocabulary sets* and *Describing trends* at the end of the Course Book unit. Decide when, if at all, to refer your students to it. The best time is probably at the very end of the lesson or the beginning of the next lesson, as a summary/revision.

Lesson aims

- gain an understanding of lexical cohesion in texts through building word sets, synonyms and opposites/converses
- use appropriate language for describing trends

Introduction

Do some vocabulary revision from the previous units. For example:

1 Choose some words with different meanings in general English or English for economics (see Units 1 and 2). Ask students to say or write two sentences using each word with a different meaning. Some examples are: *interest, resources, liquid, welfare, labour, enterprise, shares, capital, access*, etc. If necessary, students can work with their dictionaries.

2 Choose some prefixes and suffixes (see Units 1 and 4). Write them on the board. Ask students to give the meaning of the affix and an example of a word.

3 Dictate some of the key vocabulary from Unit 3. Ask students to check their spellings (with a dictionary) and group the words according to their stress patterns.

Exercise A

Set both questions for pairwork discussion and whole class feedback. Do not comment or correct at this point. Students should identify that successful development of agriculture is crucial to world growth. They may be familiar with the increase in agricultural production during the so-called 'green revolution'. Do not go into too much detail on this, as there is a later unit on the economics of agriculture. Students should also observe that resources such as water or land are very important. They should see that consumption plays a vital role in economic development and that the rapid economic growth such as in China or India has been strongly linked to production and consumption where there is a large population. Students should, ideally, observe that not all countries experience growth and globalization can have negative as well as positive impacts.

85

Answers

Model answers:

1 1 Successful agriculture; ability to grow food; need to retain a healthy agricultural environment.

   2 A large number of new cars, waiting to be exported or transported; consumer spending; exports; more cars = more pollution + more expenditure on infrastructure.

   3 People queuing for water; risk of water shortages; threat to growth and life itself.

   4 A scene showing economic expansion, reflecting construction and consumption, e.g., building activity in Asia or Europe; construction can be linked to speculation, e.g., many office blocks only partially occupied; property sales affected by economic downturn.

2 Accept all reasonable answers.

   Students are probably aware of the nature of globalization at the basic level. They should know that MNCs (multinational companies/corporations) or MNEs (multinational enterprises) are now an economic reality and this pattern of development will continue.

   Try to remind students that it not just at the level of McDonald's, Starbucks, Nokia, Microsoft, etc. Globalization is a complex economic process.

   Activities such as banking, insurance, shipping, air transport and various forms of communication are important global activities. The energy production and supply sector has become much more multinational. Similarly, mining for various metals and minerals is multinational and globalized, with the oil industry as a prime example. Pharmaceutical companies are also fully international with production, research and marketing taking place in many different countries for worldwide consumption of medications or agricultural chemicals.

   Ask students, for example, if they can trace the 'global' nature of Middle Eastern oil – extracted in one country, transported in ships which are registered in another, stored in Rotterdam, refined there or in another destination country, sold in petrol stations which may be American, Middle Eastern or Russian-owned.

   On the production side, students probably know that Japanese cars are assembled in the UK (and elsewhere), that German cars may be manufactured or assembled in Brazil, that Finnish mobile phones are made in South Korea, British shoes in Vietnam, American computers in China or German washing-machines made in Slovenia. They may also know about developments in the steel industry with Indian companies having taken over British or Romanian steel-making plants.

   Students should be encouraged to do research on the globalization process in order to understand how international financial markets, multinational oil, pharmaceutical or mining companies operate and how globalization brings serious challenges for sustainable development.

3 Picture 3 depicting people queuing for water should be mentioned. Some students may want to discuss how economic growth in a single country (e.g., Picture 4) might be sustained. Encourage students to think of globalized sustainability.

Exercise B

The purpose of this exercise is to build sets of synonyms. This not only helps in understanding textual cohesion, but is useful for paraphrasing.

Set both questions for pairwork. Students should look for pairs of words/items. Tell them to use their dictionaries if necessary to check the grammatical information, and to note if they find other words with similar meanings.

Feed back with the whole class, building up a table on the board, and eliciting other words which can be used with the same meaning.

Answers

1/2 Model answers:

See table at top of opposite page.

Word 1	Part of speech	Word 2	Part of speech	Words with similar meanings/notes
affluence	n (U)	wealth	n (U)	prosperity
diversify	v (T)	extend	v (T)	expand (v, T)
effect	n (C)	impact	n (C)	influence (n, C)
encourage	v (T)	stimulate	v (T)	motivate (v, T)
expansion	n (usually U)	growth	n (U)	development, extension, spread (n, usually U)
exploit	v (T)	misuse	v (T)	useful here to tell students that 'exploit' can be used to talk about *exploiting resources* in a generally positive context. The idea of *exploit* as 'misuse' or 'abuse' is important in issues such as child labour.
extraction	n (C usually singular)	mining	n (U)	exploitation (n, C, usually singular) is a more general word for using natural resources
goods	n (C usually plural)	products	n (C)	remind students of possible collocations – *manufactured …*; *consumer …*; remind them also of *items* as a general term
incentive	n (C)	motivation	n (usually singular)	encouragement, stimulus
migration	n (C usually singular)	mobility	n (U)	movement; remind students of *immigration* and *emigration*
replacement	n (C)	substitute	n (C)	alternative (n, C)
shift	v (T)	transfer	v (T)	share

Exercise C

Set for individual work and pairwork checking. Feed back with the whole class. Discuss alternative ideas and decide whether they are acceptable. Check the meaning of any unknown words in the text (e.g., *long-term*). Note that the blue words are general purpose words frequent in academic contexts.

Answers

1/2 Model answers:

Word/phrase (blue) in handout	Words from box
wider	extended; expanded
richer	wealthier; more affluent
spreading	expanding; extending; transferring
unfair use	exploitation; misuse
influences	impacts; effects
Word/phrase (red) in handout	Another word from handout
links	connections
long-term	sustainable
sharing	spreading
labour	workers
making goods	production

Exercise D

1 Set for pairwork. Feed back. Start the first column of the table as shown in the Answers section.

2 Do the first pair of words with the whole class as an example. Set the remainder for pairwork. Feed back, completing the second column of the table on the board.

3 Discuss with the whole class. Elicit a word or phrase which describes the whole set of words and add this to the table.

Answers

Possible answers:

Opposites	Other words	Name for set
access; barrier	openings; restrictions; opportunities; limitations	trading conditions (situation)
create; destroy	build; degrade; construct; devastate; produce; eliminate	changing environments
degradation; improvement	destruction; enhancement; misuse; exploitation; utilization; advancement; ruin; damage; devastation	making better or worse
dependent; self-sufficient	reliant on; independent; obligated to; self-reliant; autonomous	dependence (status)
efficient; wasteful	effective; ineffective; competent; misused; well-organized; uneconomical	efficiency
non-renewable; renewable	non-recyclable; non-regenerative; generative	energy sources
scarcity; surplus	shortage; excess; lack; abundance; under-production; over-production	quantity required or available

Language note

The designation of word-sets is quite difficult and students should be encouraged to use their dictionaries to differentiate between items, their precise meaning and use.

Exercise E

Remind students that the topic is not simply globalization. Ensure students have a good understanding of the words from the boxes and can focus on the idea of sustainable development (SD).

You might suggest to students that they use the word-set concepts below to discuss the pictures. So, for example, you might do the first item in the table together (*trading conditions/situation*) using note forms and abbreviations. Then leave students to complete notes in the table, referring to the pictures as required. You could put up the model version below as a transparency or as a data-show text for the beginning of the next lesson.

Answers

Possible answers:
See table below.

Exercise F

Discuss what is involved in container transportation. Encourage students to think of as many aspects of containerization as possible, including the advantages and disadvantages, before looking at Table 1 and the accompanying text.

For example:

Advantages

- goods can be transported safely, quickly, easily and in large quantities
- containers are standardized to make transportation easier
- countries can build up their container-handling facilities (at docks)
- movement of containers can be made more efficient
- improves communication between different countries

Disadvantages

- only wealthier nations can afford large container ships
- only certain harbours are really big enough to handle a lot of container traffic (elicit examples – Hamburg, Rotterdam, Aden, Shanghai, Yokohama or others)
- increases dependence of some countries on ship owners/transporting companies
- cost of containers can fluctuate
- the infrastructure of a country must be good to get goods to the docks

Concept	Notes	Picture
trading conditions	**Example** ● *important for all countries* → *access to trade opportunities* ● *break down trade barriers* ● *create incentives to share resources & encourage growth*	2
changing environments	● *people should learn – impact of change on environments* ● *make sustainable improvements to way of life* ● *use labour efficiently* ● *use renewable resources where possible* ● *be efficient & not wasteful with energy*	1, 2, 4
making better or worse	● *development* → *expansion & growth, not destruction of way of life*	All
dependence (status)	● *SD = more interdependence, e.g., agric. + environment* ● *agric. + chemicals (risks/benefits)* ● *exploitation can be avoided* ● *communities* → *self-sufficiency & independence*	1, 3
efficiency	● *learn not to be wasteful & use resources well* ● *use substitutes* ● *reduce negative impact of industrialization*	1, 3
energy sources	● *world needs to expand renewable energy sources* ● *improve recycling* ● *control of harmful activities, e.g., extractive industries* → *pollution & degradation of the environment*	1, 2, 4
quantity required or available	● *use only necessities* ● *global economy should concentrate on a fair distribution* ● *transfer of surpluses to countries where there is a shortage*	All

- some products cannot be easily transported in containers
- fluctuations in the world economic situation can affect the cost of containers and can lead to shortages of shipping (during economic growth) or surplus (during economic downturn).

With the whole class, discuss what Table 1 shows. Elicit some of the expressions, especially verbs and adverbs which students may need in order to discuss question 1. For example:

Go up	No change	Go down	Adverbs
rise	stay the same	fall	slightly
increase	remain at	decrease	gradually
grow	doesn't change	decline	steadily
improve	is unchanged	worsen	significantly
		drop	sharply
			dramatically

Note: These verbs are generally used in an intransitive sense when describing trends.

1 Discuss with the whole class. The answer to this question should be one sentence giving the topic of the table.

2 Set for pairwork. Students should write sentences to describe the trends and information shown in the table. Feed back, by eliciting sentences from the students. Write correct sentences on the board or display the model answers on an OHT or other visual medium. Make sure that students give details appropriately and pay attention to the prepositions used with the numbers and dates.

Answers

Model answers:

1 The table shows changes in the cost of renting containers during the period 2000 to 2008.

Specific descriptions might include, for example:

- The cost of renting containers fell dramatically between 2000 and 2001.
- After 2001, the cost rose slightly to US$12,000 in 2002.
- In 2003, the cost increased significantly and then rose very sharply until 2004.
- The cost stayed very high at US$45,000 during 2004 but then fell rapidly to US$20,000 in 2006.
- The cost dropped significantly to US$11,000 in 2008. This was the lowest point since 2001.

2 This is a difficult question but it should encourage students to think about a particular aspect of globalization. If the teacher thinks that it will be helpful to students to explain this table in a detailed way, such a task could be set as homework.

Students should be able to identify at least two or three features from among the following:

- The comparative cost has fallen significantly over the whole period. Not many trends in economic costs would show the same pattern!
- The cost has fluctuated quite dramatically during the period, sometimes doubling year-on-year.
- The events on September 11, 2001 had a significant influence on world trade generally.
- The cost recovered very quickly when the world economy began to grow, especially reflecting the dramatic growth in China.
- The highest cost (in 2004) reflects the demand/supply relationship during a boom in the world economy. If students simply compare 2004 with 2003, it meant that an exporter, for example, had to pay US$20,000/day more for each container than in the previous year. What does this mean in terms of prices for consumers?
- The weakest countries (from a production/export point of view) suffer most when costs increase. The question is whether they can take advantage during periods when costs are lower. This is because there may be less traffic overall, activities at the big ports may be partly reduced (high labour costs; uneconomical shipping).
- Students should start to see how this is an issue of globalization and be able to explain it!

Exercise G

First ask students to look again at Table 1 and the gapped text related to it. Ask them to identify in pairs the adverbs which are to be found in the text (*rapidly*, *steeply*, *significantly*). Feed back briefly and check students understand the meaning of the adverbs and elicit different options for them. Remind students that it is good idea to try to vary adverb use in a text if possible.

Again, make sure that students notice how percentage increases and decreases are expressed, especially the use of *by* to show the size of the changes. Ask them to find the examples in the text (*by around 75%*, *by 100%*).

Set the text completion for individual work and pairwork checking.

Answers

Model answer:

Table 1 shows the cost of <u>renting</u> container ships from 2000 <u>to</u> 2008. The currency used is <u>US$/day</u>.

Between 2000 and 2001 the cost decreased (<u>sharply</u>) by around 75% as world trade <u>declined</u> rapidly after the events of 9/11. The cost <u>increased</u> by 100% after 2002 and rose (<u>dramatically</u>) to 25,000 US$/day in 2003. The cost <u>rose</u> again in 2004, climbing steeply to US$ 45,000 in 2006.

However, the cost began to <u>decline</u> significantly again, to US$20,000 in 2006 and <u>fell</u> to US$11,000 in 2008 as the global economy <u>turned/slowed</u> down.

Closure

Put the following list on a PowerPoint slide or write it on the board. In groups, ask students to:

- rank the features from most to least important;
- discuss how the richest and poorest nations compare in these areas;
- discuss which should be a priority area for global sustainable development;
- suggest other features which might be important.

Feed back briefly with the whole class.

Important features of everyday life for people all over the world.

Wide range of consumer goods. ____

Clean and safe living environment. ____

Access to clean water and acceptable housing. ____

Access to health care. ____

Good transportation systems. ____

Good universities and research. ____

Good range of media and communications. ____

Fair export trading opportunities. ____

5.2 Listening

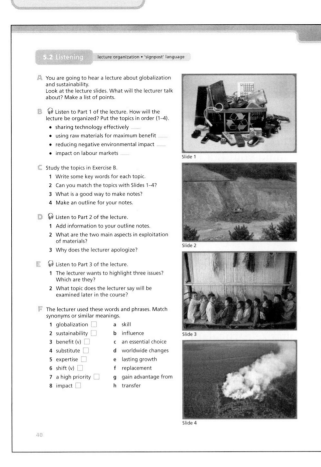

General note

Read the *Skills bank – Signpost language in a lecture* at the end of the Course Book unit. Decide when, if at all, to refer students to it. The best time is probably at the very end of the lesson or the beginning of the next lesson, as a summary/revision.

Lesson aims

- improve comprehension through understanding of signposts and lexical cohesion
- deal with disorganization in lectures/fractured text

Further practice in:

- predicting content from own background knowledge and from the lecture introduction
- using the introduction to decide the best form of notes to use

Introduction

1 Review key vocabulary by writing a selection of words from Lesson 5.1 on the board and asking students to put the words in groups, giving reasons for their decisions.

2 Remind students about preparing for a lecture. If you wish, review Unit 1 *Skills bank – Making the most of lectures*.

Exercise A

Remind students that when lecturers begin their talks, they usually provide their listeners with an outline. Remind/tell students about the *signpost language* which speakers use at the beginning to list the areas they will cover. On the board, build the table below, eliciting suggestions from the students. Alternatively (or in addition), you could refer to the *Skills bank* at this point.

Sequencing words		Verbs
To start with, Firstly,		begin/start by …ing discuss examine
Secondly, Then … After that,	I'll	consider mention talk about look at
Finally,		define give a(n) outline/overview/definition/ summary of … end/finish/conclude by …ing

Language note

Speakers will usually avoid repeating words. So they would be unlikely to say *To start with, I'll start by …*.

Refer students to the lecture images. Set the exercise for pairwork.

Ask students to feed back their possible lecture ideas to the whole class using the signpost language on the board to order their points. Accept any reasonable ideas. One possibility is given in the following.

Answers

Possible answer:

To start with, the lecturer will define 'globalization'. After that he/she will talk about the relationship of globalization and sustainability. Then he/she will discuss exploiting raw materials, labour issues and, finally, the environmental challenges.

Methodology note

Students may not be too familiar with the 'sustainability' aspect of globalization and only be able to make simple points about the images. If they already know something about the subject, they may realize that the images illustrate the concepts which the lecturer will discuss, i.e., Slide 1 hints at technology; Slide 2 at extractive industries and exploitation of raw materials; Slide 3 at labour issues and Slide 4 at environmental issues. These ideas will appear in the exercises that follow.

🎧 Exercise B

Tell students they are only going to hear the introduction to the lecture. Give students time to read the topics. Check that they understand the meaning. Remind them they will only hear the introduction once, as in a lecture. Tell them to listen out for the signpost language on the board. While they listen, they should number the topics from 1–4 in the order in which the lecturer will talk about them.

Play Part 1. Allow students to compare answers. Feed back. Ask students to say what signpost language they heard related to each topic. Confirm the correct answers.

Answers

- sharing technology effectively (2) (*Then, I will consider technology transfer, i.e., sharing technology effectively.*)
- using raw materials for maximum benefit (1) (*So, the first topic I will examine …*)
- reducing negative environmental impact (3) (*After that, I will emphasize particular environmental issues, especially related to industrial expansion and pollution.*)
- impact on labour markets (4) (*Finally, my lecture concentrates on how globalization affects labour market conditions …*)

Transcript 🎧 1.20

Part 1

Good afternoon everybody. Today's lecture has the title 'Globalization and sustainable development'. So, we have two separate concepts which are closely related. As you know from other lectures, globalization depends on multinational activities, including manufacturing, finance and services. You have heard about multinational companies or multinational enterprises, so I'm sure I don't need to remind you! But today, I want to focus on how globalization can be sustainable. To illustrate this, I have four main topics. Of course, the environment affects all sustainability issues … in one way or another, but, I must point out, today I'm not going to discuss the specific topic of climate change! That will come later.

So, the first topic I *will* examine refers to the raw materials which the world needs and uses, or exploits. Then, I will consider technology transfer, i.e., sharing technology effectively. After that, I will emphasize particular environmental issues, especially related to industrial expansion and pollution. Finally, my lecture concentrates on how globalization affects labour market conditions, especially in the developing world.

Exercise C

1 Set for pairwork. Divide the topics up among the pairs so that each pair concentrates on one topic. Feed back. Accept any reasonable suggestions.

2 Refer students to the lecture slides. Students should try to guess which of the topics each slide could refer to. Set for individual work and pairwork checking. Feed back, but do not confirm or correct yet.

3 Elicit suggestions from the whole class. If you wish, refer students to Unit 1 *Skills bank*.

4 Set for individual work. Students should prepare an outline on a sheet of paper preferably using either numbered points (with enough space between the points to allow for notes to be added) or a mind map/spidergram (see example on opposite page).

Answers

Possible answers:

1 Some key words are:

   raw materials – deposits; rare minerals; exploit; technology; environment

   sharing technology and energy – gap; growth; transfer

   reducing negative environmental impact – protection; laws; pollution; resources

   impact on labour markets – opportunities; migration; working conditions; workers' rights

2 Accept any reasonable answers with good justifications.

3/4 Example of a spidergram:

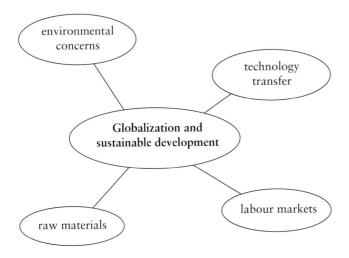

Methodology note

There is no need to teach all the words given in the model answers for question 1. However, if students suggest words that others do not know, it would of course be reasonable to check/clarify meanings of such words at this point.

🎧 Exercise D

Tell students to use their outline from Exercise C to take notes. Which topics do they expect to hear in this section?

Play Part 2. Put students in pairs to compare their notes and discuss the questions.

Feed back. When it becomes clear that the lecturer did not actually stick to the plan in the introduction, say that this happens very often in lectures. Lecturers are human! Although it is a good idea to prepare outline notes, students need to be ready to alter and amend these. Discuss how best to do this. One obvious way is to use a non-linear approach such as a mind map or spidergram, where new topics can easily be added.

After checking answers to questions 2 and 3, build a complete set of notes on the board as a spidergram, as in the example in the Answers section.

Answers

Possible answers:

1

accidents
- e.g., BP (2010)
- MNCs extraction of resources can be harmful to environ.
- MNCs must not ignore environ. regulations

environmental concerns

raw materials

exploitation of resources
- N.B. finite
- e.g., rare deposits (China, Africa)
- oil industry needs W. expertise

regulations
- less strict in developing world, e.g., gold mining in W. Africa
- computer recycling

2 a) the finite nature of raw materials

  b) recycling

3 The lecturer starts to talk about the environment which he/she planned to do as the final or fourth part of the lecture.

Transcript 🎧 1.21

Part 2

Nowadays, most people see globalization as an incentive to improve. But it is also a challenge because the real motivation must be sustainability. This will make sure that the majority of people benefit from global activities such as the exploitation of raw materials. There are two main aspects to this discussion: resources and regulations! Now, first of all, remember we are talking about finite resources. What do I mean by this? Well, everything we take from the ground – such as oil, copper, and coal, zinc, bauxite – that's B-A-U-X-I-T-E, for manufacturing aluminium – will, one day, be used up, at an end! We cannot replace many raw materials so substitutes must be found. Economists can construct models to show the exploitation of resources, but they must build in the finite aspect. Many MNCs extract metals or minerals such as gold, copper, platinum, aluminium or cement. Other countries, especially in Africa, possess the only deposits of certain raw materials. China, for example, has many rare deposits. But, unfortunately for the developing countries, they do not always have the technology to exploit resources. Even now, the oil-refining capacity of Middle Eastern countries is much less than its production capacity. So, developing countries need the expertise of more advanced economies. The commercial extraction of oil is only about 150 years old but ... er ... we all know how powerful the oil MNCs are, don't we? Even today, we see how harmful oil extraction can be for the environment. You remember how BP had to pay huge amounts of compensation for the Gulf of Mexico environmental accident in 2010? Well, things have improved ... a little.

This is the second key aspect to consider ... regulations. If MNCs want to exploit gold in Ghana or oil in Nigeria, for example, they must not ignore environmental regulations or take advantage of laws there which seem less strict. We can see one example of how some MNCs ignore regulations in Ghana where recycling of bits from computers is big business and dangerous for the workers! So some MNCs have shifted these recycling processes to the developing world where labour is cheaper and regulations less strict. I think most people agree that international environmental laws should protect all regions and all workers. Global standards should be as similar as possible ... Oh dear, I am sorry. I think I have already started to talk specifically about the environment ... which I wanted to mention later. Never mind, let's just carry on!

🎧 Exercise E

Ask students what they expect to hear about in the next part. Refer students to their outline again. Give them time to read the questions. Note that the final part of the lecture will be heard in Lesson 5.3, but there is no need to tell them that at this point. Play Part 3. Set the questions for pairwork. Students should use their notes to help them answer the questions.

Feed back. Note that there is no need to build a set of notes on the board at this point – this will be done in Lesson 5.3.

Answers

Model answers:

1 Priorities, pollution and poverty
2 CSR – Corporate Social Responsibility

Transcript 🎧 1.22

Part 3

Now turning to the next topic, technology transfer. Here I want to mention 3Ps – priorities, pollution and poverty! Well, basically, technology should not just be shifted to a developing country. It must be appropriate and safe technology for industrial and agricultural purposes. Of course, a high priority must be technology which will benefit most people. That is to say, it is necessary to think of the welfare of the people. Computers are extremely useful and can bring a lot of benefits, but will they improve the welfare of the majority of people in the developing world? One important element is CSR, that is corporate social responsibility. But we'll look at CSR later in the course.

Returning to the main idea now, a factory with modern technology will manufacture cheaper products, for example, plastic goods. So, a new factory will definitely have a positive impact on local employment. But such production will probably cause pollution. Furthermore, if there are small-scale metal enterprises or workshops, which manufacture products such as pots, pans or buckets, a plastics factory will have a negative impact on local employment. What I mean is, there are some very important decisions to be made. Some people argue that all technology transfer decisions will, inevitably, have negative consequences. They maintain that only the rich will gain from it and the poor will not benefit. Perhaps that is too pessimistic, but clean water and basic sanitation do not need advanced technology!

Exercise F

This gives further practice in identifying words and phrases used synonymously in a particular context. Set for individual work and pairwork checking.

The lecturer used these words and phrases. Match synonyms or similar meanings.

Answers

1	globalization	d	worldwide changes
2	sustainability	e	lasting growth
3	benefit (v)	g	gain advantage from
4	substitute	f	replacement
5	expertise	a	skill
6	shift (v)	h	transfer
7	a high priority	c	an essential choice
8	impact	b	influence

Closure

Check that students understand some of the key concepts and vocabulary in the unit so far, including:

cheap labour

economic self-sufficiency

environmental protection

exploitation of resources

exploitation of people

globalization

outsourcing

sustainability

technology transfer

Note: Students will need their lecture notes from this lesson in Lesson 5.3.

Lesson aims

- use symbols in note-taking
- understand and use lecture language such as stance adverbials (*obviously*, *arguably*), restatement (*in other words* ...) and other commentary-type phrases

Further practice in:

- stress within words
- asking for information
- formulating polite questions

Introduction

As in Unit 3, encourage students to ask you questions about the information in the lecture in Lesson 5.2 as if you were the lecturer. Remind them about asking for information politely. If they can't remember how to do this, you could tell them to revise the *Skills bank* for Unit 3.

Put students in pairs. Student A must ask Student B about the information in the lecture in Lesson 5.2 to help him/her complete the notes from the lecture. Then they reverse roles. Again, they can revise language for this in the *Skills bank* for Unit 3.

Exercise A

1 Revise/introduce the idea of using symbols and abbreviations when making notes. Ask students to look at the example notes and find the symbols and abbreviated forms. Do they know what these mean? If not, they should try to guess.

If you wish, expand the table in the Answers section below with more symbols and abbreviations that will be useful for the students. There is also a list at the back of the Course Book for students' reference.

2 Ask students to tell you what kind of notes these are (linear and numbered). Set the question for pairwork. Students will need to agree what the notes are saying and then make the corrections.

3 Set for individual work. Feed back with the whole class and build the spidergram in the Answers section on the board.

Answers

Model answers:

1

Symbol/abbreviation	Meaning
=	equals, the same as, is which means/definition
&	and
→	leads to, causes, results in
e.g.	(for) example
∴	therefore
(+) / (−)	advantage/disadvantage
esp.	especially
W.	West
+	in addition to/and
approx.	approximately/about/around
y.o.	years old
↗	increased/more/additional

2 Suggested corrections shown in capitals.

Exploitation of raw materials

globalization = incentive & challenge → sustainability

2 aspects: i) resources ii) regulations

i) resources are FINITE = will run out, e.g., oil (no replacement ∴ substitutes needed)

China has A NUMBER OF rare deposits

(+) developing countries, esp. in Africa many raw materials

(−) need expertise from W. + technology to exploit, e.g., oil industry (approx. 150 YEARS OLD)

Mid East refining capacity LESS THAN production; risk to environment e.g., BP (2010) in Gulf of Mexico

ii) <u>regulations</u> some improvements but problems with LESS STRICT laws in W. Africa. ∴ environmental laws to protect all workers

3 Example notes:
See spidergram below.

Language note

Some abbreviations are universal and some are personal. People often develop their own personal system of symbols and abbreviations. For example, *bn* for *billion* is used by many people, but *esp.* for *especially* is an example of a longer word abbreviated by the individual who wrote these notes.

🎧 Exercise B

Tell students they will hear the final part of the lecture. Give them time to read the questions. They should complete the final leg of the spidergram.

Play Part 4. Put students in pairs to compare their notes and discuss the questions. Feed back. For question 2, ask students if they can remember the exact words used by the lecturer (*Oh dear, unfortunately I've run out of time and we'll have to stop here.*)

Answers

2 Because there is no more time.

3 To find out economic and environmental information about four developing countries.

Transcript 🎧 1.23
Part 4

I now want to turn to the topic of labour market issues. I will highlight three main issues: workers' rights, child labour and outsourcing. Often workers in the developing world move to urban, industrial areas to work in production, construction or assembly processes. Unfortunately, there is a danger of serious exploitation of these workers, meaning the *misuse* of their labour. They often have to work for low wages, work very long hours and live in poor conditions, usually paying a high proportion of their wages for their bed in a hostel. In addition, any downturn in the economy or in the particular industry means unemployment and real hardship.

Now let's consider the second issue. A very serious form of exploitation is child labour. An estimated 30 million children, globally, are working full-time. Children are used for dirty or dangerous jobs, but their wages are much lower than for adults. These children must live away from their families. Moreover, they receive little or no education or training and they face unemployment and poverty in a recession.

Moving on now to the third labour issue – outsourcing. Many first-world companies and financial institutions have shifted the location of some customer services to other countries. So many UK banks, insurance companies, utilities and communications companies have outsourced to India, for example. Often, workers there have less job security and fewer rights. Oh dear, unfortunately I've run out of time and we'll have to stop here. I haven't discussed everything so I'd like you to do some research. Please find out and evaluate what the main economic and environmental issues are in Ghana, Indonesia, Brazil and Rwanda, which is in Central Africa. We'll discuss your information next time.

environmental concerns

accidents
- e.g., BP (2010)
- MNCs extraction of resources can be harmful to environ.
- MNCs must not ignore environ. regulations

Globalization and sustainable development

raw materials

exploitation of resources
- N.B. finite
- e.g., rare deposits (China, Africa)
- oil industry needs W. expertise

regulations
- less strict in developing world, e.g., gold mining in W. Africa
- computer recycling

labour markets

workers' rights
- exploitation
- low wages
- poor conditions

child labour
- dirty, dangerous jobs
- no education
- face unemployment

outsourcing
- W. companies → developing world
- cheap labour
- less job security

technology transfer

priorities
- benefit to people
- need for technology?

pollution
- impact of new industries

poverty
- impact on local employment

🎧 Exercise C

Remind students of the importance of stressed syllables in words (see the teaching notes for Unit 3.3, Exercise A). Play the recording, pausing after the first few to check that students understand the task.

Feed back, perhaps playing the recording again for each word before checking. Ideally, mark up an OHT or other visual medium of the words.

Answers

appropriate	3
assemble	1
efficient	5
environment	2
expertise	4
exploit	6
extractive	10
manufacture	7
pharmaceutical	11
replaceable	12
substitution	8
sustainable	9

Transcript 🎧 1.24

1 a'ssemble
2 en'vironment
3 a'ppropriate
4 exper'tise
5 e'fficient
6 ex'ploit
7 manu'facture
8 substi'tution
9 su'stainable
10 ex'tractive
11 pharma'ceutical
12 re'placeable

🎧 Exercise D

This exercise gives students a chance to focus on some typical lecture language.

1 Set for pairwork. Students should try to think of a word for each of the blank spaces.

   Note that they should *not* try to use the words from the box for this. Do not feed back at this point.

2 Tell students they will hear sentences from the lecture and should fill in the missing words as they listen. There will be pauses at the end of each sentence but you will play the recording straight through without stopping (as a kind of dictation).

Feed back with the whole class, playing the section again if necessary. Check the meanings and functions of the words and phrases. Point out the fixed phrases and encourage students to learn these. Ask students to repeat the sentences for pronunciation practice, making sure that the stress and intonation are copied from the model.

3 Set for individual work and pairwork checking. Students should check in their dictionaries for meanings or pronunciations of words from the box that they don't know. Feed back, building the first two columns of the table in the Answers section on the board.

4 Elicit suggestions from the whole class for a third column: 'Other similar words'.

   If you wish, students can practise saying the sentences in question 2 but this time with words from questions 3 and 4.

   After completing Exercise D, students can be referred to the *Vocabulary bank – Stance* and the *Skills bank – Signpost language in a lecture* for consolidation.

Answers

Model answers:

1/2 Now <u>turning to</u> the next topic, technology transfer. Here I want to mention 3Ps – priorities, pollution and poverty! Well, <u>basically</u>, technology should not just be shifted to a developing country. <u>Of course</u>, a high priority must be technology which will benefit most people. <u>Returning to the main idea</u>, a factory with modern technology will manufacture cheaper products, for example, plastic goods. So, a new factory will <u>definitely</u> have a positive impact on local employment. But it will <u>probably</u> cause pollution. <u>What I mean is</u> there are some <u>very important</u> decisions to be made. Some people <u>argue</u> that all technology transfer will, <u>inevitably</u>, have negative consequences. They <u>maintain</u> that only the rich will gain from it and the poor will not benefit.

3/4 See table at top of opposite page.

Transcript 🎧 1.25

Now turning to the next topic, technology transfer. Here I want to mention 3Ps – priorities, pollution and poverty!

Well, basically, technology should not just be shifted to a developing country.

Of course, a high priority must be technology which will benefit most people.

Returning to the main idea, a factory with modern technology will manufacture cheaper products, for example, plastic goods.

So, a new factory will definitely have a positive impact on local employment.

Word/phrase from the lecture	Words/phrases from the box	Other similar words/phrases
turning to	moving on	dealing (now) with
basically	fundamentally	essentially
Of course	naturally	without doubt
Returning to the main idea	As I was saying	to return to …; to get back to the main point
definitely	certainly	undoubtedly
probably	most likely	as you would expect
What I mean is	in other words	expressed differently
very important	crucial	vital, essential
(Some people) argue	Some people say	It is argued that …/It is claimed that …
inevitably	without doubt	obviously; clearly; in all probability
maintain	claim	assert; argue

But it will probably cause pollution.

What I mean is, there are some very important decisions to be made.

Some people argue that all technology transfer will, inevitably, have negative consequences.

They maintain that only the rich will gain from it and the poor will not benefit.

Language note

There are three main categories of language here:

1 Stance markers. These are words or phrases that speakers use to show what they feel or think about what they are saying. Adverbs used like this are generally (though not always) positioned at the beginning of the sentence.

2 Phrases used to indicate a restatement. It is very important for students both to understand and to be able to use these, since speakers frequently need to repeat and explain their points.

3 Phrases used to show that the speaker has deviated from the main point and is now about to return to it. Again, this type of phrase is very common in lectures and discussions.

Exercise E

Remind students of the task set by the lecturer at the end of Part 4. Set the questions for pairwork discussion. Students should first list the sort of information they will need to find, then discuss and make notes on what they already know. Then they should compile a list of possible sources of information.

Feed back on all three questions with the whole class. Do not discuss further at this point, as the topic will be extended in the next lesson.

Answers

Possible answers:

1 Statistical, economic, social and environmental data.

2 Answers depend on the students.

3 Internet, library, subject textbooks, encyclopedias, etc.

Closure

Play a version of the game 'Just a minute'. Put students in groups of four. Give them an envelope in which they will find topics written on slips of paper. Students take turns to take a slip of paper from the envelope and then have a minute or two for preparation of the topic and the language they might use. Then they talk for one minute on the topic. Encourage them to use as many of the words and phrases from Exercises C and D as they can. Each person should talk for up to a minute without stopping. If they can talk for one minute they get a point. If they deviate from their topic or can't think of anything more to say, they have to stop. The person who has the most points is the winner.

Suggestions for topics:

child labour

raw materials

technology transfer

unacceptable products for developing countries

extractive industries and environmental risk

positive sides of globalization

job security

the future of shipping

official development assistance (ODA)

foreign direct investment (FDI)

finding new consumers in the developing world

5.4 Extending skills

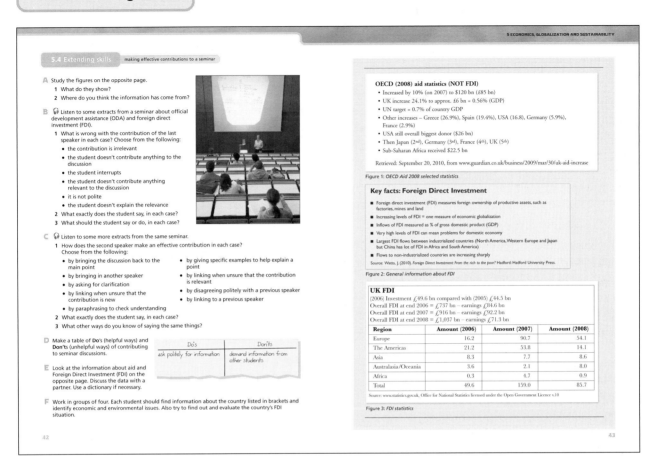

5.4 Extending skills making effective contributions to a seminar

A Study the figures on the opposite page.
  1 What do they show?
  2 Where do you think the information has come from?

B Listen to some extracts from a seminar about official development assistance (ODA) and foreign direct investment (FDI).
  1 What is wrong with the contribution of the last speaker in each case? Choose from the following:
  - the contribution is irrelevant
  - the student doesn't contribute anything to the discussion
  - the student interrupts
  - the student doesn't contribute anything relevant to the discussion
  - it is not polite
  - the student doesn't explain the relevance
  2 What exactly does the student say, in each case?
  3 What should the student say or do, in each case?

C Listen to some more extracts from the same seminar.
  1 How does the second speaker make an effective contribution in each case? Choose from the following:
  - by bringing the discussion back to the main point
  - by bringing in another speaker
  - by asking for clarification
  - by linking when unsure that the contribution is new
  - by paraphrasing to check understanding
  - by giving specific examples to help explain a point
  - by linking when unsure that the contribution is relevant
  - by disagreeing politely with a previous speaker
  - by linking to a previous speaker
  2 What exactly does the student say, in each case?
  3 What other ways do you know of saying the same things?

D Make a table of **Do's** (helpful ways) and **Don'ts** (unhelpful ways) of contributing to seminar discussions.

Do's	Don'ts
ask politely for information	demand information from other students

E Look at the information about aid and Foreign Direct Investment (FDI) on the opposite page. Discuss the data with a partner. Use a dictionary if necessary.

F Work in groups of four. Each student should find information about the country listed in brackets and identify economic and environmental issues. Also try to find out and evaluate the country's FDI situation.

42

OECD (2008) aid statistics (NOT FDI)
- Increased by 10% (on 2007) to $120 bn ($85 bn)
- UK increase 24.1% to approx. £6 bn = 0.56% (GDP)
- UN target = 0.7% of country GDP
- Other increases – Greece (26.9%), Spain (19.4%), USA (16.8), Germany (5.9%), France (2.9%)
- USA still overall biggest donor ($26 bn)
- Then Japan (2nd), Germany (3rd), France (4th), UK (5th)
- Sub-Saharan Africa received $22.5 bn

Retrieved: September 20, 2010, from www.guardian.co.uk/business/2009/mar/30/uk-aid-increase

Figure 1: OECD Aid 2008 selected statistics

Key facts: Foreign Direct Investment
- Foreign direct investment (FDI) measures foreign ownership of productive assets, such as factories, mines and land
- Increasing levels of FDI = one measure of economic globalization
- Inflows of FDI measured as % of gross domestic product (GDP)
- Very high levels of FDI can mean problems for domestic economy
- Largest FDI flows between industrialized countries (North America, Western Europe and Japan but China has lot of FDI in Africa and South America)
- Flows to non-industrialized countries are increasing sharply

Source: Watts, J. (2010). *Foreign Direct Investment: From the rich to the poor?* Hadford: Hadford University Press.

Figure 2: General information about FDI

UK FDI
(2006) Investment £49.6 bn compared with (2005) £44.5 bn
Overall FDI at end 2006 = £737 bn – earnings £84.6 bn
Overall FDI at end 2007 = £916 bn – earnings £92.2 bn
Overall FDI at end 2008 = £1,037 bn – earnings £71.3 bn

Region	Amount (2006)	Amount (2007)	Amount (2008)
Europe	16.2	90.7	54.1
The Americas	21.2	53.8	14.1
Asia	8.3	7.7	8.6
Australasia/Oceania	3.6	2.1	8.0
Africa	0.3	4.7	0.9
Total	49.6	159.0	85.7

Source: www.statistics.gov.uk, Office for National Statistics licensed under the Open Government Licence v.10

Figure 3: FDI statistics

43

Lesson aims

- make effective and appropriate contributions to a seminar

Further practice in:

- speaking from notes
- reporting information

Introduction

Revise stance words and restatement/deviation phrases from the previous lesson. Give a word or phrase and ask students to give one with a similar meaning. Alternatively, give a sentence or phrase from the lecture in Lessons 5.2 and 5.3 and ask students to tell you the accompanying stance word or restatement phrase, e.g.,

Returning to the main idea, we can accept that, for example, a plastics factory will probably bring advantages.

Exercise A

1 Tell students to look at the information in the figures. Set for pairwork discussion.

2 As the figures have references on them, students should observe this. It is useful to remind students that providing reference sources is accepted practice for lectures/presentations. Feed back, accepting any reasonable suggestions.

Answers

Possible answers:

1 Figure 1 is from a newspaper article and summarizes the OECD – make sure students research what the Organisation for Economic Cooperation and Development is.

  If students want more information, they can go to the OECD website:

  www.oecd.org/home/0,2987,en_2649_201185_1
  _1_1_1_1,00.html

2 Figure 2 has come from an academic source.

3 Figure 3 has come from the official UK government statistics website and shows UK FDI over a number of years.

Subject and methodology note

Students should be encouraged to research the concepts of Foreign Direct Investment (FDI) and Official Development Assistance (ODA). Students can find adequate definitions and information from the OECD or United Nations, CIA or World Bank websites. They should *not* be misled into thinking it is OVERSEAS Development Assistance, even though this is what it often amounts to! This is highlighted in one of the mini-dialogues in the seminar extracts (Lesson 5.4, Exercise B, Extract 3). The research task in Exercise G is quite challenging but provides an opportunity for students to do some research on a developing country and its FDI position.

🎧 Exercise B

In this exercise, students will hear examples of how *not* to contribute to a group discussion.

1/2 Allow students time to read the questions. Tell them they will hear five extracts. They should choose a different answer for each one. Set for individual work and pairwork checking. Play all the extracts through once.

Play the extracts a second time, pausing after each one. Students should write down the actual words, as in a dictation, then check in pairs. When students have completed questions 1 and 2, feed back with the whole class, maybe building up columns 1 and 2 of the table in the Answers section on the board.

3 Set for pairwork discussion. Feed back, adding a third column to the table on the board.

Transcript 🎧 1.26

Extract 1

LECTURER: Right, Leila and Majed, what did you find out about UK aid and foreign direct investment?

LEILA: Well, first we looked at the official government websites to see what information is accessible.

MAJED: You can find everything there – statistics on children's pocket money, the music industry, how many cars there are …! All sorts of topics!

Extract 2

LECTURER: Right, so what else did you do?

LEILA: We spoke to some of the students from Africa to see what their experiences were. It was very useful.

MAJED: That's nonsense. They couldn't tell us anything specific at all.

Extract 3

LECTURER: Leila, can you give us a working definition of FDI?

LEILA: Well, basically it's not about governments giving aid to a developing country. That's ODA – official development assistance. FDI is about private investment.

LECTURER: That's a good start. What can the rest of you add to what Leila has said? Jack, what about you?

JACK: Well, erm … I'm not really sure.

Answers

Model answers:

	Contribution is poor because	Exact words	How to improve
Extract 1	it is irrelevant	Majed: You can find everything there – statistics on children's pocket money, the music industry, how many cars there are …! All sorts of topics!	support other speakers and add useful comments, e.g., *And it's quite user-friendly. It's very well-organized.*
Extract 2	it is not polite	Majed: That's nonsense. They couldn't tell us anything specific at all.	use polite (tentative) language when disagreeing, e.g., *Actually, that's not quite right. I don't think they really wanted to talk to us.*
Extract 3	the student doesn't contribute anything to the discussion	Jack: Well, erm … I'm not really sure.	be ready to contribute something when brought into the discussion by the lecturer or other students
Extract 4	the student doesn't explain the relevance	Evie: Well, debt is a much bigger amount than debt relief.	the comment is relevant to the topic but she doesn't explain why. She should try to give a clear definition or make a clear differentiation, e.g., *Well, debt relief is when interest payments on the original debt don't have to be paid.*
Extract 5	the student interrupts	Majed: No, in fact, it might have to pay back part of the debt.	he should wait until the speaker has finished.

Extract 4

LECTURER: Evie, can you explain the difference between debt and debt relief?

EVIE: Well, debt is a much bigger amount than debt relief.

Extract 5

LECTURER: Yes, but what do we actually mean by debt relief, Leila?

LEILA: It's when an aid-giving government or institution says a recipient country doesn't have to …

MAJED: No, in fact, it might have to pay back part of the debt.

🎧 Exercise C

1/2 This time students will hear good ways of contributing to a discussion. Follow the same procedure as for 1 and 2 in Exercise B above. This time they need to listen for the second speaker.

Again, when students have completed 1 and 2, feed back with the whole class, maybe building up a table on the board. If you wish, students can look at the transcript at the back of the Course Book (page 123).

3 Ask the whole class for other words or phrases that can be used for the strategy and add a third column to the table as below.

Transcript 🎧 1.27

Extract 6

LECTURER: Let's go back to the third diagram for a minute and see how we can interpret it. First of all, tell us about the distribution of UK FDI over the past few years.

LEILA: Well, it's obvious that most FDI was in the already developed world. Wouldn't you say so, Majed?

MAJED: Yes, and the earnings from FDI reflect that, too.

Extract 7

EVIE: Yes, in 2006 there was more investment in South-East Asia than in Africa and Oceania combined.

MAJED: Sorry, I'm not quite sure I follow … Could you explain what you mean, please?

EVIE: Yes. It's the growing importance of China and other so-called 'Tiger economies'. That shows how FDI takes advantage of economic trends.

Extract 8

MAJED: I'm sorry, I don't see why FDI is criticized. It's business investment.

EVIE: Yes, but there are many advantages to the investing company such as expanding markets, lower labour costs, tax benefits and government guarantees.

Answers

Model answers:

	Helpful strategy	Exact words	Other ways to say it
Extract 6	brings in another speaker	Leila: Wouldn't you say so, Majed?	What do you think, Majed? What do you make of this, Majed?
Extract 7	asks for clarification	Majed: Sorry, I'm not quite sure I follow … Could you explain what you mean, please?	I don't quite understand. Could you say a bit more about …?
Extract 8	gives specific examples to explain a point	Evie: Yes, but there are many advantages to the investing company such as …	For instance, …
Extract 9	paraphrases to check understanding	Jack: So, what you're saying is that governments provide less than private companies?	So, in other words … So, expressed differently, …
Extract 10	brings the discussion back to the main point	Majed: Yes, so if we go back to the basic principles, FDI involves …	Thinking about … If we can go back to … for a moment …
Extract 11	disagrees politely with a previous speaker	Jack: No, I'm not sure that's completely true.	I don't think I agree with that. In my opinion …
Extract 12	links to a previous speaker	Evie: Well, it's what Leila mentioned earlier.	Going back to what Leila said a while ago … I think Majed brought this point up before…
Extract 13	links when not sure the contribution is new	Jack: I'm sorry. Has anyone actually mentioned that FDI is like a sort of multilateral partnership?	I don't know if this has been said already, but … I'm not sure if someone has already mentioned that …
Extract 14	links when not sure the contribution is relevant	Leila: Well, I don't know if this is quite relevant but …	I'm not sure if this is a little off the point, but …

Extract 9

LEILA: Yes, there is a big difference between government ODA and the private companies' FDI. You can see how little ODA is in comparison.

JACK: So, what you're saying is that governments provide less than private companies?

Extract 10

LECTURER: This is all very useful to understand FDI, isn't it?

MAJED: Yes, so if we go back to the basic principles, FDI involves connections between private investment, governments, and credit agencies. And don't forget the banks!

Extract 11

EVIE: Well, this just shows that FDI is all about making profit for private enterprise.

JACK: No, I'm not sure that's completely true. A lot of FDI really tries to help the people of the recipient country. Think of job opportunities and technology transfer!

Extract 12

LECTURER: So what do you think is really behind the statistics in the figures?

EVIE: Well, it's what Leila mentioned earlier. UK FDI goes mostly to the already developed world because there is less investment risk.

Extract 13

LECTURER: Any other ideas?

JACK: I'm sorry. Has anyone actually mentioned that FDI is like a sort of multilateral partnership?

LECTURER: Yes, in fact Majed and Leila made that point earlier. But your choice of expression is very appropriate.

Extract 14

LECTURER: So, what should we consider when we are talking about UK FDI in Africa?

LEILA: Well, I don't know if this is quite relevant but South Africa receives so much more FDI because of its advanced economy compared to other countries. But they often have much bigger populations with less advanced economies!

LECTURER: Yes, that's certainly a relevant point. FDI does not depend on population size.

Exercise D

Set for group work. Tell students to brainstorm suggestions for more good and bad seminar strategies. They should think about what helps a seminar discussion to be successful. It may help to think about having seminar discussions in their own language, but they should also think about what is involved in having a seminar discussion in English. Aspects to consider include language, how to contribute to discussions and how to behave. Feed back, making a list on the board.

Answers

Possible answers:

Do's	Don'ts
ask politely for information	demand information from other students
try to use correct language	
speak clearly	mumble, whisper or shout
say when you agree with someone	get angry if someone disagrees with you
link correctly with previous speakers	
build on points made by other speakers	
make a contribution, even if you are not sure if it is new or relevant	stay silent, waiting for 'the perfect moment'
be constructive	be negative
give specific examples to help explain a point	be vague
listen carefully to what others say	start a side conversation
allow others to speak	dominate the discussion
paraphrase to check understanding	
prepare the topic beforehand	

Exercise E

Set students to work in groups of five or six. Groups should appoint one person to take notes on the discussion and two others to observe the discussion. Groups should discuss some key questions, which you can put on the board:

1 How important is it to have ODA and FDI?

2 How does each contribute to sustainable development?

3 Should countries give more ODA? Under what circumstances?

4 What would happen if wealthier countries reduced ODA and/or FDI?

While students are talking, you can listen in and note where they may need help with language, and where particularly good examples of language are used.

The students acting as observers for the discussion should use a checklist of things to watch for. One observer can concentrate on poor contributions and the other on good contributions. Sample checklists are provided in the additional resources section (Resource 5C) – students simply mark in each cell whenever the behaviour occurs.

Exercise F

This is a genuine (if challenging) research task which could lead to a presentation, poster presentation or wallchart project for a later lesson. The results will be similar but groups will probably approach the task differently. Encourage students to meet together outside class to share information and to plan their (poster) presentation. If you limit the presentation/poster presentation time, e.g., to 12 minutes per group plus 3 minutes for questions, all group members can be involved and contribute. The preparation period should encourage students to discuss their findings and the focus of their presentations. The presentations themselves should encourage students to use the seminar discussion type of language as in Lesson 5.4. The *discussion task* cards, Resource 5D, are quite informative but teachers can add other sources, ideas, etc. Some are provided below.

UK ODA

To obtain the official UK government position on development aid, students should go to:

www.hm-treasury.gov.uk/development_aid_budget.htm

DFID is the Department of International Development and has a very user-friendly site.

www.dfid.gov.uk/About-DFID/Quick-guide-to-DFID/how-aid-is-spent

www.dfid.gov.uk/About-DFID/Your-Questions-Answered1/

www.dfid.gov.uk/Where-we-work/

For a more critical view on development aid, students could consult the OXFAM site:

www.oxfam.org/

As a starting point for the World Bank position on development, students might use:

www.worldbank.org/

or the OECD

www.oecd.org/home/0,2987,en_2649_201185_1_1_1_1_1,00.html

The following tables contain the type of information which the students may find. The CIA Factbook uses 266 'entities' (countries). The comparison statistics are based on this number. Please note that this information was researched in September 2010 and new statistics are likely to be available. The CIA changes its website quite regularly so the home page content may vary. It is unlikely that the basic format will change, however. The students' task cards give guidelines but some students may want to include more. Remind them of time constraints for presentation purposes!

Example data

BRAZIL

https://www.cia.gov/library/publications/the-world-factbook/index.html

GDP/per capita:

$10,100 (2009 est.)

country comparison to the world: 107

$10,300 (2008 est.)

$9,900 (2007 est.)

Note: data are in 2009 US dollars

Labour force:

101.7 million (2009 est.)

country comparison to the world: 6

Labour force – by occupation:

agriculture: 20%

industry: 14%

services: 66% (2003 est.)

Unemployment rate:

8.1% (2009 est.)

country comparison to the world: 89

7.9% (2008 est.)

Population below poverty line:

26% (2008)

Exports:

$153 billion (2009 est.)

country comparison to the world: 26

$197.9 billion (2008 est.)

Exports – commodities:

transport equipment, iron ore, soybeans, footwear, coffee, autos

Exports – partners:

China 12.49%, US 10.5%, Argentina 8.4%, Netherlands 5.39%, Germany 4.05% (2009)

Imports:

$127.7 billion (2009 est.)

country comparison to the world: 26

$173.1 billion (2008 est.)

Imports – commodities:

machinery, electrical and transport equipment, chemical products, oil, automotive parts, electronics

Imports – partners:

US 16.12%, China 12.61%, Argentina 8.77%, Germany 7.65%, Japan 4.3% (2009)

Environmental problems:

deforestation in the Amazon Basin destroys the habitat and endangers a multitude of plant and animal species indigenous to the area; there is a lucrative illegal wildlife trade; air and water pollution in Rio de Janeiro, Sao Paulo, and several other large cities; land degradation and water pollution caused by improper mining activities; wetland degradation; severe oil spills

Direct foreign investment – domestic:

$319.9 billion (31 December 2009 est.)

country comparison to the world: 13

$294 billion (31 December 2008 est.)

Stock of direct foreign investment – abroad:

$117.4 billion (31 December 2009 est.)

country comparison to the world: 24

$127.5 billion (31 December 2008 est.)

GHANA

www.cia.gov/library/publications/the-world-factbook/index.html

www.unctad.org/sections/dite_dir/docs/wir10_fs_gh_en.pdf

GDP/per capita:

$1,500 (2009 est.)

country comparison to the world: 199

$1,500 (2008 est.)

$1,400 (2007 est.)

Note: data are in 2009 US dollars

Exports

$5.715 billion (2009 est.)

country comparison to the world: 100

$5.27 billion (2008 est.)

Exports – commodities:

gold, cocoa, timber, tuna, bauxite, aluminum, manganese ore, diamonds, horticulture

Exports – partners:

Netherlands 13.45%, UK 7.87%, France 5.85%, Ukraine 5.84%, Malaysia 3.97% (2009)

Imports:

$8.437 billion (2009 est.)

country comparison to the world: 93

$10.27 billion (2008 est.)

Imports – commodities:

capital equipment, petroleum, foodstuffs

Imports – partners:

China 16.8%, Nigeria 11.88%, US 6.63%, Cote d'Ivoire 5.99%, India 5.57%, France 5.09%, UK 4.23% (2009)

Labour force by occupation:

agriculture: 56%

industry: 15%

services: 29% (2005 est.)

Unemployment rate:

11% (2000 est.)

country comparison to the world: 123

Population below poverty line:

28.5% (2007 est.)

Environmental problems:

recurrent drought in north severely affects agricultural activities; deforestation; overgrazing; soil erosion; poaching and habitat destruction threatens wildlife populations; water pollution; inadequate supplies of potable water

FDI information at:

www.unctad.org/sections/dite_dir/docs/wir10_fs_gh_en.pdf

INDONESIA

https://www.cia.gov/library/publications/the-world-factbook/index.html

GDP/per capita:

4,000 (2009 est.)

country comparison to the world: 155

$3,900 (2008 est.)

$3,700 (2007 est.)

Note: data are in 2009 US dollars

Labour force:

113.3 million (2009 est.)

country comparison to the world: 5

Labour force – by occupation:

agriculture: 42.1%

industry: 18.6%

services: 39.3% (2006 est.)

Unemployment rate:

7.7% (2009 est.)

country comparison to the world: 77

8.4% (2008 est.)

Population below poverty line:

17.8% (2006)

Exports:

$119.5 billion (2009 est.)

country comparison to the world: 31

$139.6 billion (2008 est.)

Exports – commodities:

oil and gas, electrical appliances, plywood, textiles, rubber

Exports – partners:

Japan 17.28%, Singapore 11.29%, US 10.81%, China 7.62%, South Korea 5.53%, India 4.35%, Taiwan 4.11%, Malaysia 4.07% (2009)

Imports:

$84.32 billion (2009 est.)

country comparison to the world: 32

$116.7 billion (2008 est.)

Imports – commodities:

machinery and equipment, chemicals, fuels, foodstuffs

Imports – partners:

Singapore 24.96%, China 12.52%, Japan 8.92%, Malaysia 5.88%, South Korea 5.64%, US 4.88%, Thailand 4.45% (2009)

Environmental problems:

deforestation; water pollution from industrial wastes, sewage; air pollution in urban areas; smoke and haze from forest fires

Stock of Foreign Direct Investment (domestic):

$73.57 billion (31 December 2009 est.)

country comparison to the world: 44

$68.27 billion (31 December 2008 est.)

Stock of direct foreign investment – abroad:

$9.681 billion (31 December 2009 est.)

country comparison to the world: 51

$6.694 billion (31 December 2008 est.)

RWANDA

https://www.cia.gov/library/publications/the-world-factbook/index.html

GDP/per capita:

$1,000 (2009 est.)

country comparison to the world: 212

$1,000 (2008 est.)

$900 (2007 est.)

Note: data are in 2009 US dollars

Labour force:

4.446 million (2007)

country comparison to the world: 79

Labour force – by occupation:

agriculture: 90%

industry and services: 10% (2000)

Unemployment rate:

NA%

Population below poverty line:

60% (2001 est.)

Exports:

$191 million (2009 est.)

country comparison to the world: 181

$257 million (2008 est.)

Exports – commodities:

coffee, tea, hides, tin ore

Exports – partners:

Kenya 33.88%, Democratic Republic of the Congo 13.56%, Thailand 6.22%, China 5.49%, US 5.47%, Swaziland 5.43%, Belgium 5.19% (2009)

Imports:

$867 million (2009 est.)

country comparison to the world: 174

$880 million (2008 est.)

Imports – commodities:

foodstuffs, machinery and equipment, steel, petroleum products, cement and construction material

Imports – partners:

Kenya 16.53%, Uganda 14.92%, China 7.92%, UAE 6.89%, Belgium 5.54%, Germany 5.19%, Tanzania 4.81%, Sweden 4% (2009)

Environmental problems:

deforestation results from uncontrolled cutting of trees for fuel; overgrazing; soil exhaustion; soil erosion; widespread poaching

FDI information at:

www.unctad.org/sections/dite_dir/docs/wir10_fs_rw_en.pdf

Closure

1 If you wish, refer students to the *Skills bank –
Seminar language* for consolidation.

2 Focus on some of the vocabulary connected with
research from Lessons 5.2 and 5.4. For example:

analyze (v)

analysis

attitudes

concept

data

define

definition

evaluate

examine

find out

focus

identify

interpret

make notes

methods

observation

overview

paraphrase

priority

resources

statistical

statistics

topic

trend

view

You could ask students to work together in pairs
and discuss where/how the words relate to a
research task.

1 Work through the *Vocabulary bank* and *Skills bank* if you have not already done so, or as a revision of previous study.

2 Use the *Activity bank* (Teacher's Book additional resources section, Resource 5A).

A Set the crossword for individual work (including homework) or pairwork.

Answers

B Students choose six words or phrases from the box and write one in each square of their bingo card.

You call out some words or phrases. If students have the **opposite** word or phrase on their card, they cross it out.

The first person to cross out all the items on their card is the winner.

You call out:

revenue (expenditure)

unemployment (job security)

advantage (drawback)

approximately (exactly)

self-sufficient (dependent)

national (multinational)

surplus (shortage)

barrier (access)

producer (consumer)

improvement (degradation)

speed up (slow down)

create (destroy)

debts (assets)

poverty (affluence)

urban (rural)

loss (profit)

localization (globalization)

decline (growth)

safe (dangerous)

wasteful (efficient)

3 Use the *Activity bank* (Teacher's Book additional resources section, Resource 5B).

Answers

Possible answers:

Verbs	Nouns	Adverbs	Adjectives
rise	a rise	gradually	gradual
increase	an increase	sharply	sharp
grow	growth*	slightly	slight
improve	improvement	markedly	marked
fall	a fall	significantly	significant
decrease	a decrease	rapidly	rapid
drop	a drop	steeply, sharply	steep, sharp
decline	a decline	steadily, dramatically	steady, dramatic
climb	a climb	rapidly, steadily, sharply	rapid, steady, sharp

*usually (but not always) uncountable in this sense

6 MACROECONOMICS ... BUT MICROFINANCE!

Unit 6 highlights some of the large-scale features of macroeconomics alongside smaller-scale alternative economic strategies, specifically microfinance and fair trade. In Lesson 6.1, students are encouraged to analyze macroeconomic growth through paraphrasing activities. The notion of microfinance is introduced in Lesson 6.1 and expanded in the reading text of Lesson 6.2. A further microeconomic focus is provided in Lesson 6.2 by discussion of the growing fair-trade movement. Lesson 6.3 reinforces student awareness of more complex sentences types, leading in to a microfinance case study in Lesson 6.4 to consolidate writing skills.

Skills focus

Reading
- locating key information in complex sentences
- identifying sentence structure

Writing
- reporting findings from other sources: paraphrasing
- writing complex sentences

Vocabulary focus
- synonyms, replacement subjects, etc., for sentence-level paraphrasing

Key vocabulary

assess	finance (v)	match (n and v)	procedure
availability	founder	measure (n and v)	proceed
borrower	fund (v)	microcredit	referral
commitment	grant (n)	microfinance	reject
contract (v)	guarantee (n and v)	mission	saturated
craft	homeowners	negotiate	security
credit (n and v)	imbalance	overheads	self-sufficient
cycle	imply	perform	term
effectiveness	initiative	performance	underserved
entrepreneurial	lasting	pioneer (n and v)	unserved
ethical	loan (n and v)	prediction	weapons
expectations	maintain	premises	

6.1 Vocabulary

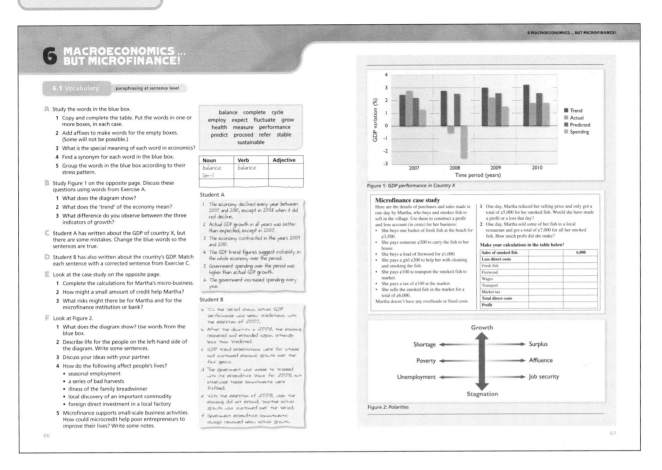

6 MACROECONOMICS ... BUT MICROFINANCE!

General note

Read the *Vocabulary bank* at the end of the Course Book unit. Decide when, if at all, to refer students to it. The best time is probably at the very end of the lesson or the beginning of the next lesson, as a summary/revision.

Lesson aims

- paraphrase at sentence level using synonyms, negatives, replacement subjects

Further practice in:

- affixes
- words with different meanings in general English
- stress within words
- word sets – synonyms, antonyms

Introduction

1 Revise affixes, e.g., *re~*, *un~*, *in~*, *out~*, *~ize*, *~al*, *~ty*, *~ly*, *~ion*, *~ive*. Do this by dividing the class into small groups. Give each group one affix. Allow three or four minutes. The group which can list the most words is the winner.

2 Revise some of the words relating to trends (from Unit 5) to enable students to discuss the bar graph with some confidence. It is not necessary to revisit all of the vocabulary as students only need terms such as *rose*, *fell*, *grew*, *declined*, *cut* but emphasize and reinforce expressions such as *... by 0.5%, ... reached 3.5%, ... grew as predicted, did not grow as predicted, grew more than predicted.*

Exercise A

1 Tell students to make a table with three columns and 15 rows in their notebooks. Go through the example in the Course Book. Set the exercise for individual work and pairwork checking. Tell students to use their dictionaries if they need to check meanings, grammatical category, etc. Feed back with the whole class, building the first three columns of the table in the Answers section on the board. Ask students to say what general meanings they can give for the words.

2 Refer to the example (*balance*) in the Course Book. Ask students to suggest a form of *balance* which is an adjective (*balanced*). Note that it is possible to use the past participle of a verb as an adjective if there is no other possibility. Elicit/point out that the verb form is identical to the noun (*to balance*). Ask

111

what the opposite of the noun *balance* is. Students might say IN-balance, which is not correct. Point out *IM-balance* as an antonym to *balance*. Ask what the opposite of the adjective might be. The correct answer is *UNbalanced*, not *IMbalanced*!

Set for pairwork. Students should try to fill as many empty boxes as possible with words with appropriate affixes. They should continue to use their dictionaries to check meanings and spellings. To extend the activity a little, students should think of other affixes to make new words or antonyms. Feed back with the whole class, checking meanings of the words added to the table.

3 Add a fourth column on the board and give it the heading *Meaning in economics*. Underline or highlight the words as shown in the table below, and with the whole class, ask students to suggest (or find in their dictionaries) meanings specific to economics for these words.

4 Work in a similar way with the fifth column, *Synonym from economics*. Limit the synonyms to those for the underlined words.

5 Set for pairwork. Feed back with the whole class, checking pronunciation.

Answers

Model answers:

1–4 See table below.

5

one syllable	grow, health
Oo	measure, cycle
oO	complete, employ, expect, predict, proceed, refer
oOo	performance
Ooo	fluctuate

> **Language note**
>
> Some grammatical forms of the words may have particular meanings that are extremely unlikely in an economic context, e.g., *unbalanced* (adj), *cycle* (v), *stable* (n). Point this out if necessary but don't spend much time on these words.

Noun	Verb	Adjective	Meaning in economics	Synonym from economics
balance (im~)	balance	balanced (un~)	(n) an acceptable relationship between two elements, e.g., exports and imports	(n) equilibrium
completion	complete	1 complete (in~), 2 completed (un~)	as in general English 1 total, 2 finished	as in general English (adj) whole; entire
cycle	cycle (re~)	cyclical	(n) a regular economic pattern	(n) trend
employment (un~) (under~)	employ (re~)	employed (un~) (under~)	(v) to provide work for	(v) to hire labour
expectation (over~) (under~)	expect	expected (un~)	as anticipated, e.g., in the growth of the economy or anticipation of risk	predict
fluctuation	fluctuate	fluctuated	(v) when the economy performs in a series of downturns or upturns	(v) change; move; surge; collapse; swing
growth	grow	grown (over~) (out~)	(v intr.) increase economic performance	(v) expand
health	(heal) N.B. verb usage is not immediately obvious	healthy (un~)	(n) state of the economy	(n) strength (or weakness); viability
1 measurement 2 (take) measures	measure	measured	(v) to quantify; to fix a standard or point	(v) calculate; evaluate
performance (over~) (under~)	perform (over~) (out~) (under~)	performed	(n) amount of growth in the economy	(n) trend; behaviour
prediction	predict	predictable (un~)	(v) to expect statistically	(v) forecast; anticipate
procedure	proceed	procedural	(v) to move forward as part of a planned process	(v) to continue with
1 reference 2 referral	refer (to)	referred	(v) 1 relate to standard or point of measurement, 2 transfer responsibility	(v) consult; delegate
stability (in~) (un~)	stabilize (re~) (de~)	stable (un~)	(adj) level, without large fluctuations	(adj) balanced
sustainability	sustain	sustainable (un~)	(adj) long-term; can be repeated	(adj) lasting

Language note

Rules in language are made to be broken. The suffix *~ly* normally makes an adjective into an adverb, but there are some interesting exceptions and anomalies. For example, it is the noun *cost* which creates the adjective *costly* by the addition of *~ly*. However, *likely* is usually used as an adjective but can also have adverbial usage, whereas *lively* or *lonely* can only be adjectives! Students might use their dictionaries to check the use and restrictions of, for example:

> *late* (adjective and adverb) compared with *lately* = recently
>
> *hard* (adjective and adverb) compared with *hardly* = scarcely
>
> *fast* (adjective and adverb)
>
> *poor/poorly* (both can be adjectives with rather different meanings but *poorly* is usually used as an adverb)
>
> *kind/kindly* (both can be adjectives with similar meanings but *kindly* is usually used as an adverb)

Of course, many adjectives do not have an accompanying adverb! Adjectives derived from the present participle *~ing* (*developing*, *lasting*, *growing*, *booming*, *expanding*) are common in economics. Interestingly, *~ed* participles will not usually generate adverbs but there are a few exceptions, usually with a more specific meaning, e.g., *admittedly*, *advisedly*, *decidedly*, *determinedly*, *markedly*, *unexpectedly*.

Exercise B

1 Set for pairwork discussion. Students should refer to the words they have looked at in Exercise A to help describe the statistical data in Figure 1. Monitor but don't assist. Feed back with the whole class, checking that students can give the basic information from the figure. Elicit words which can be used from Exercise A (underlined below, including synonyms).

2 Set for pairwork discussion. Remind students about words they have already studied for describing trends in graphs. Feed back with the whole class, asking one or two students to describe main features of the bar graph. Make sure that students use the past simple tense to talk about the GDP/expenditure figures.

Answers

Model answers:

It is unlikely that students will be able to use all the words from box a. Some may be elicited through appropriate questions.

1 Figure 1 shows the Gross Domestic Product (GDP) development of the economy of a country over a four-year period. Very simply expressed, the GDP of an economy <u>refers</u> to the output of goods and services that the whole economy generates over a 12-month period. It is <u>measured</u> as a positive percentage or as zero or minus <u>growth</u> if the economy stagnates or declines. There are four indicators on the bar graph to show trend, <u>predicted</u> and actual GDP growth as well as government spending. Students may already be familiar with these concepts.

2/3 **Trend** shows the average <u>performance</u> of an economy over a period of time (e.g., over four years) and shows the <u>sustainable</u> nature of growth (or not!) In other words, trend growth indicates whether the country has the capacity to expand or if it is likely to contract. In this graph, the trend growth is shown as quite <u>stable</u> (at approximately 0.25% year on year, i.e., between 2.5% and 3.25% per annum). This would be considered a very <u>healthy</u> trend growth rate for an advanced economy.

Predicted growth relates to how economic experts from the government, the World Bank, or other well-informed institutions anticipate the economy will perform. These predictions indicate how economists <u>expect</u> the country to perform. Because economists use long-term statistics to assess the trends, they can recognize <u>fluctuations</u> and economic <u>cycles</u> more easily. The diagram does not show a cyclical pattern but does show a severe fluctuation in actual growth between 2007 and 2008. However, the economy recovered well, almost reaching the predicted growth level in the following year. In such situations, the government has to make some difficult decisions whether to cut spending or to <u>proceed</u> with their expenditure plans. As shown in the figure, the government cut spending by 2.5% in 2008.

Actual growth is the performance of an economy at a specific point in time (rather than the 'average' used for trend growth). Quarterly growth figures are common for most advanced economies. Obviously factors such as <u>employment</u> depend on the real output of the economy. <u>Balanced</u> economic growth, from a GDP perspective, also includes factors such as prices because a healthy economy will not simply increase its GDP by increasing prices. Therefore, economists have developed a more <u>complete</u> measure known as REAL GDP which takes inflation into account.

Exercise C

As well as requiring the use of antonyms, this exercise checks that students have understood the figure in Exercise B. Set for individual work and pairwork checking. Feed back with the whole class. A good way to do this is to use an OHT, or other visual medium, with blanks for the blue words (see additional resources section, Resource 6B).

Answers

Model answers:

1 The economy <u>grew</u> every year between 2007 and 2010 except in 2008 when it <u>contracted</u>.
2 Actual GDP growth in all years was <u>worse</u> than expected except in 2007.
3 The economy <u>expanded</u> in the years 2009 and 2010.
4 The GDP trend figures suggest <u>stability</u> in the whole economy over the period.
5 Government spending over the period was <u>lower</u> than actual GDP growth.
6 The government increased spending <u>every year except for 2008</u>.

Exercise D

Introduce the idea of paraphrasing – or restating. Elicit from the students the main ways to do this at sentence level, namely:

● using different grammar
● using different words
● reordering the information

Write these points on the board. Also make the point very strongly that a paraphrase is not a paraphrase unless 90% of the language is different. There are some words which must remain the same, but these are very few, and are likely to be words specific to the subject, such as *growth predictions*. It is best to try to use all three of the above strategies, if possible.

Students should look carefully at the corrected sentences from Exercise C and then compare them with the paraphrases. The first step is to identify which sentences match. Set for individual work and pairwork checking. It may be helpful for the students if you reproduce the corrected sentences from Exercise C and the sentences in Exercise D on strips of paper so that they can move them around. Both sets of sentences are reproduced in the additional resources section (Resource 6C) to facilitate this.

Feed back with the whole class. A good way to do this is to reproduce the sentences on datashows with each sentence appearing as a separate item. Make the sentences appear one at a time, as you agree what is the correct match.

Once the sentences are correctly paired, ask students to locate the parts of each sentence which seem to match. They will need to look at the overall meaning of each phrase, using what they know about the subject, to make sure that the phrases are similar. Set for pairwork. Feed back with the whole group.

Answers

Model answers:

1	The economy grew every year between 2007 and 2010 except in 2008 when it contracted.	e	With the exception of 2008, when the economy did not expand, positive actual growth was sustained over the period.
2	Actual GDP growth in all years was worse than expected except in 2007.	a	In the period shown, actual GDP performance was below predictions with the exception of 2007.
3	The economy expanded in the years 2009 and 2010.	b	After the downturn in 2008, the economy recovered and expanded again, although less than predicted.
4	The GDP trend figures suggest stability in the whole economy over the period.	c	GDP trend expectations were for stable and sustained economic growth over the four years.
5	Government spending over the period was lower than actual GDP growth.	f	Government expenditure commitments always remained below actual growth.
6	The government increased spending every year except for 2008.	d	The government was unable to proceed with its expenditure plans for 2008 but otherwise these commitments were fulfilled.

A final step is to discuss the changes that have been made in detail. Students should refer to the list of types of changes you have written on the board. Look at each paraphrase with the class and ask students what changes have been made. Be specific about the types of vocabulary or grammar changes. For example, in the first answer above, the paraphrase reorders the information, uses time clause/passive, uses replacement subject *growth* (derived from the verb form in the original) and changes key vocabulary.

Exercise E

Put students in pairs to complete the table and answer the questions. Feed back with the whole group.

Answers

1 Model answer:

Sales of smoked fish	6,000
Less direct costs	
Fresh fish	3,500
Firewood	1,000
Wages	400
Transport	100
Market tax	100
Total direct costs	**5,100**
Profit	**900**

Other scenarios:

1 Martha makes a loss of 100 cents.

2 Martha makes a profit of 1,900 cents.

2 Encourage students to be imaginative, realistic and serious about the discussion.

Martha could be helped by microcredit in a number of ways, e.g.:

- to buy a refrigerator to keep fish fresh (if the electricity supply is reliable)
- opportunity to buy firewood in larger quantities at a cheaper rate
- to buy a cart to transport her fish
- to buy a bicycle to take fish to other locations
- to rent a little room for preparing the fish
- to employ two people to clean and prepare a larger quantity of fish
- to form a partnership with another person to share the responsibility

3 The microcredit institution would expect a simple business plan from Martha, outlining her plans to expand.

The risks for the bank *and* for Martha relate mainly to:

Martha's health: What happens if she is ill?

Natural environment: Is the fishing itself sustainable? What if weather conditions are bad for a longer period?

Competition: Are there many other fish-sellers? Is the market saturated, i.e., is there room for expansion? Could the price for smoked fish fall?

The microfinance institution would have to make a decision based on predicted profits and Martha's capacity to repay the loan.

This scenario is based on information for small entrepreneurs in agriculture and fishing, available from:

Rural Infrastructure and Agro-Industries Division, Food and Agriculture Organization of the United Nations (FAO), Rome, Italy.

Students might want to look at the FAO website: www.fao.org

Exercise F

1/2 Set for individual work. Words from box a may be used (underlined below) but this activity gives students the chance to discuss global imbalance.

3/4 Set for pairwork. Feed back with the whole class.

5 Students work individually and then exchange ideas with a partner. Students might write notes such as these. The teacher could put these notes on an OHT or other visual medium to consolidate further.

Answers

Possible answers with key vocabulary underlined.

1–3 The diagram shows the lack of balance in the global economy. On the left-hand side, there are negative factors which many hundreds of millions of people have to deal with daily.

They face poverty and a good way of life is difficult or impossible to sustain. Even if the economy grows, it is impossible to predict if there are benefits for the poorest. Their income fluctuates, usually dependent on their employment situation. Their health is often unstable as they cannot buy healthy food. Government measures to help the poorest are often incomplete or inadequate.

4 *Seasonal employment* – instability; shortages at times of unemployment, uncertainty, migration, family problems, stagnation (very little flexibility in the economy)

Series of bad harvests – food shortages, unemployment, poverty, food price increases, migration

Illness of the family breadwinner – shortages, cost of medicines/doctors, lack of financial stability, poverty

Local discovery of an important commodity – employment, price rises, cultural change, (in)stability

*Foreign direct investment in a local facto*ry – employment, more stability, growth

5 availability of microcredit ➔ entrepreneurial activities not day-to-day existence

microfinance (m/f) = support but people need ideas and initiative, incl. better education

m/f banks ➔ fair profit ↓ risk and sustainable projects

poverty ➔ low expectations BUT also ↓ initiative/entrepreneurial ideas

m/f ➔ stability of income/employment

m/f ➔ personal growth (confidence, family stability, happiness)

m/f ≠ solution to all poverty BUT important measure

Closure

Discussion:

1 Can students think of other polarities (opposites) to add to the diagram in Figure 2?

2 How important is growth in the macroeconomic sense?

3 Can students do a SWOT analysis of microfinance?

4 If students can access a library, refer them to the article 'A partial marvel: Microcredit may not work wonders but it does help the entrepreneurial poor' in *The Economist* (July 18–24, 2009). *The Economist* only has subscription access for older archive items. The students' institution may have access. An alternative version is available via a Google search, for example:

http://creationinvestments.com/news/microcredit-may-not-work-wonders-but-it-does-help-the-entrepreneurial-poor-economist/ [Retrieved: September 22, 2010]

6.2 Reading

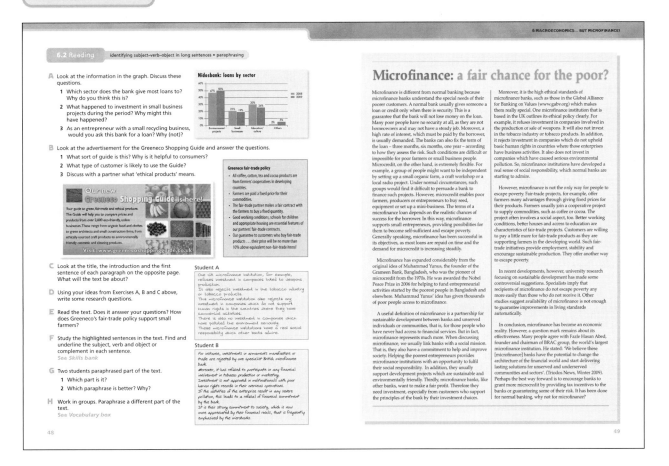

Lesson aims

- identify the kernel SVC/O of a long sentence

Further practice in:

- research questions
- topic sentences
- paraphrasing

Introduction

Remind the class about techniques when using written texts for research. Ask:

What is it a good idea to do:

- *before reading?* (think of research questions)
- *while you are reading?* (look for topic sentences)
- *after reading?* (check answers to the research questions)

What words in a text signal the development of a topic in a new direction? (Markers showing contrast such as *but, however, at the same time, on the other hand,* etc.) If you wish, refer students to Unit 4 *Skills bank.*

Exercise A

Set for general discussion. Allow students to debate differences of opinion. Encourage them to give examples if they can. Do not correct or give information at this point, as these topics will be dealt with in the text.

Answers

1 The bank gives more loans to projects in the environmental sector. This sector is generally expanding and more finance is available from governments, groups such as the EU or financial institutions such as the World Bank.

2 The number of loans actually declined. The likely reason was the general recession worldwide and fewer enterprises which were seeking loans.

3 The bank clearly is keen to invest in such activities but its small business lending declined. However, it seems a good option for an entrepreneur.

117

Exercise B

1/2 Set for pairwork discussion. Feed back with the whole class. If students don't know, don't tell them too much as the reading text will provide more information.

3 Set for pairwork. Feed back with the whole class.

Answers

Possible answers:

1/2 Accept any reasonable answers.

3 Students may find it hard to define 'ethical products' depending on their background, culture and general knowledge. They may equate 'ethical' with religious factors but try to help them make a distinction. Ethical consumers try to avoid buying products related to, for example, corporate bad practice, especially in the developing world. This might be a pharmaceutical company which makes dangerous pesticides for agriculture, or a tobacco company which tries to win customers by selling cigarettes very cheaply, marketing very strongly with lots of little free gifts for the people who buy their products. It might be a company marketing medications which are unsuitable for the developing world or too expensive for the poor.

Ethical decisions may also relate to weapons and military equipment, as many armaments companies also make non-military products, too. People are concerned that weapons get into the hands of criminals, drug lords, terrorists, dictators or unofficial militia, who may use child soldiers.

Many ethical consumers are concerned about animal welfare and protecting species such as the orang-utan in the jungles of Borneo and Indonesia. They are also interested in promoting good standards of animal welfare for meat production.

Most students will know about child labour. Ethical consumers try to avoid products from child-labour sources or 'sweatshops' where workers have to suffer very bad conditions, low pay and poor living standards although the products may be sold for a high price in Western shops.

Environmental awareness also forms part of ethical consumer decisions. People try to avoid buying products which have come from protected rainforests (furniture, wood, etc.) or products grown on cleared rainforests. Some companies have a bad pollution record and so are avoided by ethical consumers.

Exercise C

Set for individual work. Elicit ideas, but do not confirm or correct.

The students will see that the text focuses on microfinance, its origins and definition. They should identify that ethical issues are discussed and fair trade is also presented.

They might recognize that there is some academic debate about microfinance.

Exercise D

Students might write down such questions as:

What is microfinance?

Where did the idea come from?

Who can apply for it?

Why do microfinance banks have a social and ethical mission?

How do fair-trade agreements work?

Is fair trade effective?

Exercise E

Answers depend on the students.

Encourage students to search further on the Internet outside class. For example, they might want to find out more about the organization in the text, Global Alliance for Banking on Values (www.gabv.org) or about a couple of leading British-based institutions (www.triodos.co.uk and www.icof.co.uk), as well as the pioneering bank of Muhammad Yunus (www.grameen.com).

For more information about BRAC and Sir Fazle Hasan Abed go to:

www.microfinancefocus.com

They might want to find out more about fair trade. The UK organization is:

www.fairtrade.org.uk

Exercise F

Draw a table with the headings from the Answers section on the board. If you wish, students can also draw a similar table in their notebooks. Explain that in academic writing, sentences can seem very complex. This is often not so much because the sentence structure is highly complex in itself, but that the subjects and objects/complements may consist of clauses or complex noun phrases. Often the verb is quite simple. But in order to fully understand a text, the grammar of a sentence must be understood. Subject + verb + object or complement is the basic sentence structure of English. Students need to be able to locate the subjects, main verbs and their objects or complements.

Elicit from the students the subject, main verb and object for the fourth sentence. Ask students for the *head word* of each subject, main verb and object (underlined in the table in the Answers section). Write them in the table on the board. Using high-speed questioning, get students to build the whole phrase that constitutes the subject/main verb/object/complement.

Example 1:

Helping the poorest entrepreneurs provides microfinance institutions with an opportunity to fulfil their social responsibility.

> *What is this sentence about?* = helping
>
> *What does helping do?* = it provides an opportunity
>
> *Who does it provide the opportunity to?* = microfinance institutions
>
> *What opportunity does it provide?* = to fulfil their social responsibility

Write these head words in the table on the board.

Then elicit the remaining words and add to the table:

> *Helping who exactly?* = the poorest entrepreneurs
>
> *Give me more information about how this will help microfinance institutions* = (it will help them) to fulfil their social responsibility

Example 2:

This example shows how to deal with *is* + complement.

A useful <u>definition</u> of microfinance <u>is a partnership</u> for sustainable development between banks and unserved individuals or communities ...

> *What is this sentence about in general?* = microfinance
>
> *More particularly?* = a definition of microfinance
>
> *What's the main verb in this sentence?* = is
>
> *So what is microfinance?* = a partnership between banks and communities
>
> *A partnership for what?* = for sustainable development

The idea is that students should be able to extract something which contains the kernel even if it does not make complete sense without the full phrase.

Ask students to identify the leading prepositional/adverbial phrase in the third sentence in paragraph three. (*When discussing microfinance, ...*). Point out that this part contains information which is extra to the main part of the sentence. The sentence can be understood quite easily without it.

Set the remainder of the exercise for individual work followed by pairwork checking. Finally, feed back with the whole class.

You may wish to refer students to the *Skills bank – Finding the main information*.

Answers

Model answers:

Subject	Verb	Object/complement
... <u>such groups</u>	<u>would find</u>	<u>it difficult</u> to persuade a bank to finance such projects.
A useful <u>definition</u> of microfinance	<u>is</u>	<u>a partnership</u> for sustainable development between banks and unserved individuals or communities ...
... <u>we</u> ...	(usually) <u>link</u>	<u>banks</u> with a social mission.
<u>Helping</u> the poorest entrepreneurs	<u>provides</u>	<u>microfinance institutions</u> with an opportunity to fulfil their social responsibility.
In addition, <u>they</u>	(usually) <u>support</u>	<u>development projects</u> which are sustainable and environmentally friendly.
One microfinance <u>institution</u> that is based in the UK	<u>outlines</u>	<u>its</u> ethical <u>policy</u> clearly.

N.B. The first sentence is tricky as the sentence pattern is SVO (*it*) C (*difficult ...*).

Exercise G

Set for individual work and pairwork checking. Make sure that students identify the original phrases in the text first (the final five sentences of paragraph 4) before looking at the paraphrases.

Feed back with the whole class. A good way to demonstrate how Student A's text contains too many words from the original is to use an OHT or other visual medium and highlight the common words in colour. (A table giving the sentences plus commentary is included in the additional resources section – Resources 6D and 6E.) Check that students are able to say which parts of the paraphrase match with the original, and which structures have been used.

Answers

1 The last part of paragraph 4.

2 Student A's sentences are, in fact, instances of plagiarism or near plagiarism. Student B's paraphrase is better, because it uses fewer words from the original text and uses different sentence structures.

Exercise H

Refer students to the *Vocabulary bank* at this stage. Review paraphrasing skills with the whole class before starting this exercise. You might want to take Paragraph 4 (first sentence) and work through it as an example, e.g.:

Some microfinance institutions have formed the Global Alliance for Banking on Values which emphasizes the need for strict ethical practices. It is such measures which make these banks different. A leading British microfinance bank provides strong ethical guidelines.

Divide the text into parts. For example, the text might be divided so that there are four different sections:

Paragraph 1

Paragraph 2 and first part of Paragraph 3

Paragraph 4 (remainder) and 5

Paragraph 6 and 7

Give each section to different students to work on. Alternatively, you could choose one part of the text for all students to work on, e.g., the remainder of paragraph 4. This can be done in class or if you prefer as individual work/homework.

If students are doing the work in class in groups or pairs, a good way to provide feedback is to get them to write their paraphrase on an OHT or other visual medium. Show each paraphrase (or a selection) to the class and ask for comments. Say what is good about the work. Point out where there are errors and ask for suggestions on how to improve it. Make any corrections on the OHT with a different coloured pen.

Closure

1 Divide the class into two teams. Write the seven topic sentences from the reading text on strips, or photocopy them from the additional resources section (Resource 6F). One team chooses a topic sentence and reads it aloud. The other team must give the information triggered by that topic sentence. Accept only the actual paragraph content.

2 Ask students to complete the SWOT grid for microfinance.

(If you did the SWOT analysis for fair trade, then this SWOT analysis might be omitted). Some ideas are given in the table.

(S) The strengths of microfinance are that it …	(W) The weaknesses of microfinance are that it …
<ul><li>can change lives.</li><li>can help the poorest escape poverty.</li><li>emphasizes that no project is too small.</li><li>establishes links within communities.</li><li>challenges other banks to re-think ideas.</li></ul>	<ul><li>is available only to those with most initiative.</li><li>relies on education and confidence (poor people do not always have this!)</li><li>could lead to unrealistic expectations.</li><li>could lead to jealousy, envy, fraud, exploitation.</li></ul>
(O) Opportunities created by microfinance include …	(T) Threats to the success of microfinance might be …
<ul><li>provision of employment possibilities.</li><li>encouragement of others to apply for microfinance when they see it works.</li><li>expansion of communities.</li><li>establishment of contacts between different social groups.</li></ul>	<ul><li>the general economic downturn in a country.</li><li>the failure of a large microfinance institution or of a major project.</li><li>the lack of government support for m/f.</li><li>the competitive behaviour of other non m/f banks.</li><li>the lack of individuals such as Muhammad Yunus or Fazle Hasan Abed.</li></ul>

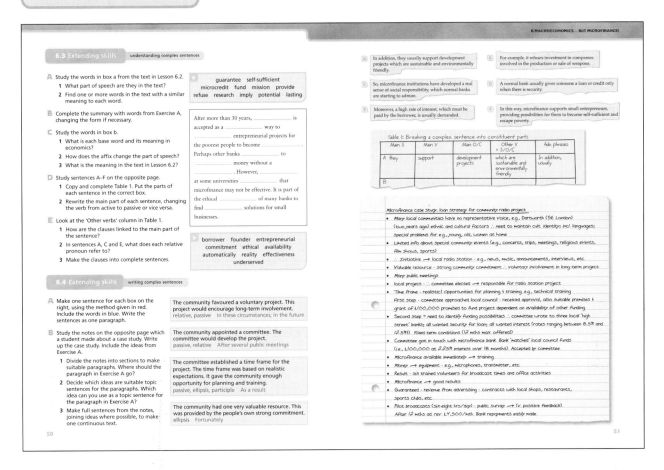

Lesson aims

- study sentence structure in more detail
- identify the main information in:

  an active sentence

  a passive sentence

  a complex sentence with participles

  a complex sentence with embedded clauses

Further practice in:

- vocabulary from Lesson 6.2

Introduction

Ask students to see how many phrases or compound nouns they can make with the word *sustainable*. Tell students to brainstorm a list in pairs. If necessary, start them off with *sustainable development*. Feed back with the whole class.

Possible answers: *sustainable growth, sustainable production, sustainable output, sustainable income, sustainable expenditure, sustainable market, sustainable prices, sustainable benefits, sustainable resources, sustainable energy, sustainable investment, sustainable performance, sustainable revenue,* etc.

You might like to ask about more abstract ideas which need additional details or information, for example: *sustainable policies, sustainable measures, sustainable commitments.*

Exercise A

Ask students to study the words in the box and to find the words in the text. Set for individual work and pairwork checking. Tell students not to use their dictionaries to begin with but to use what they know to guess meanings and parts of speech. If necessary, they should use dictionaries when checking in pairs. Deal with any common problems with the whole class.

Answers

Model answers (paragraph numbers are given in brackets):

Word	Part of speech	Similar meaning
guarantee (1)	n (C)	security (1)
self-sufficient (1)	adj	independent (1)
microcredit (1)	n (U)	microfinance (title and throughout)
fund (2)	v (T)	finance (1)
mission (3)	n (C)	commitment (3) responsibility (3)
provide (3)	v (T)	give (1), grant (7)
refuse (4)	v (T)	reject (4) N.B. because of meaning, verbs are not always interchangeable
research (6)	n (U) N.B. explain that *research* is usually singular in British English. To specify further, use: *piece of research* or *research study*	studies (6)
imply (6)	v (T but usually with *that*)	suggest (6)
potential (7)	n (U)	possibilities (1), opportunity (3)
lasting (7)	adj	sustainable (3)

Exercise B

Set for individual work and pairwork checking. Students should make use of all the words they have discussed in Exercise A (i.e., the synonyms as well as the words in the box). Feed back with the whole class.

Answers

Model answers:

After more than 30 years, microcredit/microfinance is accepted as a potential/possible way to fund/finance entrepreneurial projects for the poorest people to become self-sufficient/independent. Perhaps other banks have refused to provide/grant money without a guarantee (N.B. without security). However, research/studies at some universities implies/imply/suggests/suggest that microfinance may not be effective. It is part of the ethical mission/responsibility/commitment of many banks to find lasting/sustainable solutions for small businesses.

Language note

The use of words as synonyms often depends on the context. For example, although the base meanings of *imply* and *suggest* are not exactly synonymous, they could both be used in the third sentence of the summary text with very little difference in meaning. Similarly, *mission* is not entirely synonymous with *commitment* but both could be used in the final sentence.

Exercise C

Set for pairwork. Feed back with the whole class. Note that not all the base words have specific meanings in economics. Tell students to explain the meaning in terms of economics as far as possible.

Answers

Model answers:

See table at top of opposite page (paragraph numbers are given in brackets).

Exercise D

1 Copy the table headings from the Answers section onto the board and complete the example with the students. Tell them that when they look at the 'Other verbs' column they may well find several, and should number each verb and subject/object/complement section separately. Point out that the order of each part of the sentence is not reflected in the table: the table is just a way to analyze the sentences.

Set the rest of the sentences for individual work and pairwork checking. Feed back with the whole class. Draw their attention to the 'main' parts of the sentence: it is very important in reading that they should be able to identify these. Notice also that the main parts can stand on their own and make complete sentences.

2 Set for individual work. If the clause is active it should be changed to passive, and vice versa.

Word	Base and meaning	Effect of affix	Meaning in text
borrower (1)	borrow (v, T or I) N.B. If students are not clear about *borrow* and *lend* in English, remind them of their specific usage.	~*er* = very common way to focus on the person who carries out the action of that verb: *employer, banker, stockbroker*	person who is granted or given a loan
founder (2)	found (v, T) – establish or set up a business or organization N.B. Students should be made aware of this quite important verb in a business context	~*er* = common nominal suffix added to verb	person who established the first [microfinance] institution
entrepreneurial (2)	entrepreneur (n, C) from French	~*ial* = not so common suffix to form adjective: *industrial, trivial, menial, colloquial, dictatorial*	associated with activities of running a business
commitment (3)	commit (v, T) – to say or promise something will be used; a financial commitment is a promise to spend money at a future date	~*ment* = nominal ending, i.e., to make a noun (not very common but ... *movement, improvement, nourishment, confinement, government*)	promise to take responsibility; (pledge); accept as a mission
ethical (4)	ethics (n, C but commonly pl.)	~*al* = adjective ending	following a high moral standard; agreeing with the ethics of the specific context
availability (6)	available (adj)	~*ity* = common nominal suffix	when there is access to something
automatically (6)	automatic (adj) natural; spontaneous; as a natural event	~*ally* = adverb ending; when adjective ends in –*ic* (*pragmatic, dogmatic, systematic*)	when something does (or does not) happen as a completely natural outcome
reality (7)	real (adj) true; authentic; accepted	~*ity* = common nominal ending	a situation which really exists (and is not imagined)
effectiveness (7)	effective (adj) working well; producing good results	~*ness* = nominal ending	how good or successful the results of an action are
underserved (7) N.B. used in the text as an adjective but could be used (in rare cases) as a collective, generic noun: *the underserved*, cf. *the poor, the innocent, the unemployed*	serve (v, T) to provide services for someone	1 *under*~ = quite common prefix to show idea of *less than* 2 ~*(e)d* past participle ending to make adjective	applied to those people who do not receive the services to which they are entitled

Answers

1 Model answers:

	Main subject	Main verb	Main object/complement	Other verbs + their subjects + objects/complements	Adverbial phrases
A	they	support	development projects	which* are sustainable and environmentally friendly.	In addition usually
B	it	refuses	investment	in companies involved in the production or sale of weapons.	For example,
C	microfinance institutions	have developed	a real sense of social responsibility,	which normal banks are starting to admire.	So,
D	A normal bank	gives	1 someone (indirect object) 2 a loan or credit (direct object)	only when there is security.	usually
E	a high rate of interest,	is demanded.	–	which must be paid by the borrower,	Moreover, usually
F	microfinance	supports	small entrepreneurs,	providing possibilities for them to become self-sufficient and escape poverty.	In this way,

*underlined text = means by which dependent clause is joined to main clause

2 Possible answers:

A Development projects which are sustainable and environmentally friendly are usually supported by (microfinance/microcredit/microfinance institutions).

(N.B. Discourage students from simply writing *… by them*, in sentences where the meaning is not completely clear).

B For example, investment is refused in companies involved in the production and sale of weapons.

C A real sense of social responsibility has been developed by microfinance institutions, which normal banks are starting to admire.

D 1 Someone is usually given a loan or credit by a normal bank only when there is security.

2 A loan or credit is usually given (to someone) by a normal bank only when there is security.

E Moreover, [banks] usually demand a high rate of interest which the borrower must pay.

F In this way, small entrepreneurs are supported by microfinance, providing possibilities for them to become self-sufficient and escape poverty.

(N.B. Students should, ideally, *not* attempt to change the last part of sentence F. A partial change into the passive (*businesses to be started up*) would make it necessary to rephrase the rest of the sentence.)

Exercise E

This exercise involves looking carefully at the dependent clauses in sentences A–F.

1 Say that these clauses have special ways to link them to the main part of the sentence. Do this exercise with the whole class, using an OHT or other visual medium of the table in Exercise D, and a highlighter pen to mark the relevant words. (A version of the table without underlining is included in the additional resources section – Resource 6G.) Go through the clauses asking students what words or other ways are used to link the clauses to the main part of the sentence.

2 Set for individual work and pairwork checking. Students should look at each sentence and identify the antecedents of the relative pronouns. You could ask them to use a highlighter pen or to draw circles and arrows linking the words.

Language note

Make sure that students observe what any participle refers to and that they are aware of some of the risks with participles! *If you have time*, you might want to illustrate this to students. Ask students about these sentences.

What is wrong with those marked (!)?

Providing poor clients with microcredit has given many banks a new group of customers.

Repaying microcredit loans is difficult (for people) without job security.

(!) *Losing their job can make microcredit difficult to repay.*

(!) *Providing money to poor borrowers, many small enterprises can be supported.*

(!) *Having rejected investment in tobacco companies, a strong ethical policy is maintained.*

Answer: The participle clauses in the examples marked (!) do not match the subject or content of the main clause. You might like to ask students how to solve the problems.

Examples:

Losing their job can make it difficult *for borrowers* to repay microcredit.

By providing money to poor borrowers, many small enterprises can be supported.

Having rejected investment in tobacco companies, a strong ethical policy is maintained *by microfinance institutions*.

3 Students must be able to get the basic or kernel meaning of the clause. Take sentence A as an example and write it on the board. Point out that the relative pronouns and other ways of linking these clauses to the main clause will need to be changed or got rid of. Students should aim to write something that makes good sense as a complete sentence. They can break a sentence into shorter sentences if necessary.

Set the remaining clauses for individual work. Feed back with the whole class. Accept anything that makes good sense.

Answers

1 See table in Exercise D. Sentences A, B, C and E use relative clauses. Sentence D uses an adverbial clause (*only when …*) and F uses a participle clause (*providing possibilities*, etc.).

2 A *which* = the development projects

C *which* = a real sense of social responsibility

E *which* = a high rate of interest

N.B. There is a 'reduced relative' form in Sentence B, i.e., *companies* (which are) *involved in …*

3 Possible answers:

A In addition, microfinance institutions usually support development projects. These should be sustainable and environmentally friendly.

B Some companies are involved in the production and sale of weapons. However, microfinance institutions refuse investment in such enterprises.

C So, microfinance institutions have developed a real sense of social responsibility. Normal banks are starting to admire this.

D A normal bank has strict conditions. For example, a person must provide a guarantee or security before he/she is granted a loan.

E Moreover, a normal bank demands a high rate of interest. This must be paid by the borrower.

F In this way, microfinance supports small entrepreneurs. Such banks (N.B. not simply *they*) provide possibilities for individuals and small groups to start up business and escape poverty.

Language note

A dependent clause contains a verb and a subject and is a secondary part of a sentence. It is dependent because it 'depends' on the main clause. A main clause can stand by itself as a complete sentence in its own right (usually). A dependent clause always goes with a main clause and cannot stand by itself as a sentence in its own right.

Dependent clauses are typically joined to main clauses with certain types of words: for example, relative pronouns (e.g., *who*, *which*, etc.), linking adverbials (e.g., *if*, *when*, *before*, *although*, *whereas*, etc.), words associated with reporting speech (e.g., *that*, a *Wh~* word such as *what* or *why*), and so on.

Some dependent clauses are non-finite, that is, they don't have a 'full verb' but a participle form (e.g., *having finished*, *opening*) and the subject may not be stated.

For more on this, see a good grammar reference book.

Closure

Write the following underlined beginnings and endings of words on the board or dictate them. Ask students to give the complete word. Accept alternatives and other parts of speech.

bene(fit)

fin(ance)

supp(ort)

eth(ical)

(*recip*)*ient*

(*entrepren*)*eur*

(*meas*)*ure*

(*pov*)*erty*

(*wea*)*pon*

(*up*)*hold*

(*stag*)*nation*

(*expendit*)*ure*

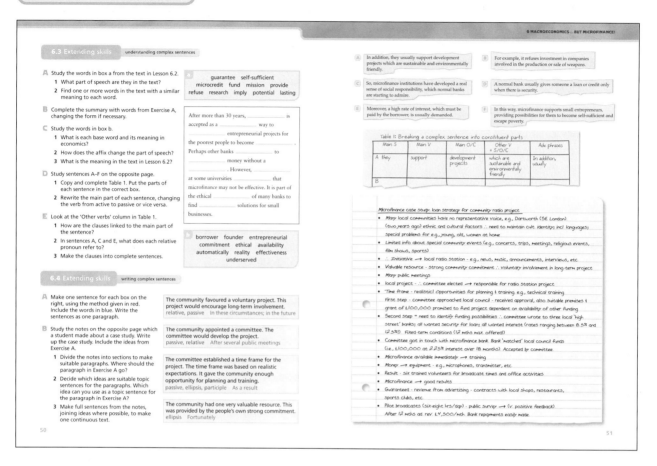

6.4 Extending skills

Lesson aims

- write complex sentences:

  with passives

  joining with participles

  embedding clauses

  adding prepositional phrases

Further practice in:

- writing topic sentences
- expanding a topic sentence into a paragraph

Introduction

As students have seen a practical example of a microbusiness in Lesson 6.1 and of fair-trade practice in Lesson 6.2, it is more than likely that they will have satisfactorily understood the concepts. Some students, however, may be questioning the economic basis of such alternative approaches. Others may want to know how microfinance banks can raise capital through investment in order to provide microcredits. There may also be questions about the link between economic growth and environmental protection.

Ask students to think about and discuss the following questions, attempting to consider both sides of the question. You may put just key words on the board.

1 Is **microcredit** the **best way** forward for **poorer, developing countries**?

2 Should **FDI** (remind students of what they discussed in Unit 5) have a specific **social role**? For example, should **a proportion of profits** from its activities be paid into a **social fund** to help **infrastructure** (schools, hospitals, transport, water supply) for everyone not just as taxation paid to the government?

3 Should **investors** pay a **special global tax** to support the **development activities** of, for example, the **United Nations**?

4 How can people be encouraged to **support** the idea of **fair trade**?

5 Is it **acceptable** for a **bank** to **support non-governmental** (**environmental**) **organizations** (**NGOs**) with **donations**?

Answer

Possible answers:

1 Students will probably recognize that microcredit depends on money being available to lend to small-scale entrepreneurs. This means that there must be investment in the products that the bank offers to investors.

2 Most multinational corporations have a Corporate Social Responsibility policy which relates to their social role in the country. It is difficult to force a company to pay a proportion of its profits. Taxation revenue is often incorrectly used by recipient governments.

3 This idea sounds very unlikely but may be adopted by even the biggest banks to raise their environmental and social profile.

4 Basically, people must make up their own mind. They need to recognize that, in a global economy, they can make a small difference to other people's lives. Schools, universities and the media should also take part in providing information and teaching people about fair trade.

5 Some microfinance institutions work together with environmental-protection groups to fund sustainable projects. Others give direct donations to NGOs.

Some people may argue that banks should think about their own customers, profits and not give funding to other organizations unless there is a direct benefit. Economists always consider 'Opportunity Costs' when discussing allocation of resources and the potential of any economy. In an expanding economy, if the costs of pollution of the environment match or outweigh GDP growth, then perhaps the government should rethink its policies.

Exercise A

Set for individual work and pairwork checking. If necessary, do the first box with the whole class. Make sure students understand that they should write the four sentences as a continuous paragraph. Help the students to scan the sentences in order to identify the likely topic sentence. As the students do not know the topic, they can only use the information given. Sentences 1 and 4 talk about 'the community' and its resources. Sentences 2 and 3 refer to a 'committee'. So the best order for the sentences is:

4 – quite general information about the community

1 – specific information about the type of project

2 – information about the election of a committee by the community

3 – details of action by the committee to establish a time frame

Feed back with the whole class. Accept any answers that make good sense. Point out where the phrases in blue act as linkers between the sentences to make a continuous paragraph.

Answers

Possible answer:

Fortunately the community had one very valuable resource provided by the people's own strong commitment. In these circumstances, a voluntary project was favoured by the community, which would encourage long-term involvement in the future. After several public meetings, a committee which would develop the project was appointed by the community. As a result, a time frame for the project based on realistic expectations was established (by the committee), giving the community enough opportunity for planning and technical training.

Exercise B

In this exercise, students are required to use all they have practised about sentence structure as well as revise what they know about topic sentences and paragraphing.

Set for pairwork. Do not feed back after each question but allow students to work through the questions, proceeding to write up the whole text. They will need to decide the best place for the paragraph in Exercise A, and should also add this to their text. Students can change the wording and add extra phrases to help the flow of the text, as long as the sense remains the same.

If possible, pairs should write their text on an OHT or other visual medium. Select two or three OHTs for display and comment by the whole class. Make any corrections on the text yourself with a coloured pen. Alternatively, circulate the transparencies to other pairs to correct and comment on. These pairs then display the corrected work and explain why they have made the corrections.

Answers

Possible answers:

1/2 See table on next page.

Paragraph divisions are given, with the possible topic sentences underlined. Note that other answers may be possible.

Many local communities have no representative voice, e.g. Dartworth (SE London)

- (Two years ago) ethnic and cultural factors ∴ need to maintain cult. identity; incl. languages; special problems for, e.g., young, old, women at home
- Limited info about special community events (e.g., concerts, trips, meetings, religious events, film shows, sports, etc.)
- ∴ Initiative → local radio station – e.g., news, music, announcements, interviews, etc.

Valuable resource – strong community commitment ∴ voluntary involvement in long-term project

- Many public meetings
- Local project – ∴ committee elected → responsible for radio station project
- Time frame – realistic! Opportunities for planning and training, e.g., technical training

First step

- Committee approached local council – received approval, also suitable premises & grant of £100,000 promised to fund project dependent on availability of other funding

Second step = need to identify funding possibilities

- ∴ committee wrote to three local 'high street' banks; all wanted security for loan; all wanted interest (rates ranging between 8.5% and 12.5%!) Fixed-term conditions (12 mths max. offered!)
- Committee got in touch with microfinance bank. Bank 'matched' local council funds (i.e., £100,000 at 2.25% interest over 18 months). Accepted by committee.
- Microfinance available immediately → training
- Money → equipment – e.g., microphones, transmitter, etc.
- Result – six trained volunteers for broadcast times and office activities

Microfinance → good results

- Guaranteed – revenue from advertising – contracts with local shops, restaurants, sports clubs, etc.
- Pilot broadcasts (six–eight hrs/day) – public survey → (v. positive feedback)
- After 12 mths ad. rev. £4,500/mth. Bank repayments easily made.

3   Many local communities have no representative voice, for example, Dartworth in South-East London. Two years ago, as a result of ethnic and cultural factors, there was a need to maintain cultural identity, including languages. In addition, there were special problems for certain members of the community, for example, young or old people and women at home. There was a lack of information about special community events such as concerts, trips, meetings, religious events, film shows and sports activities. Therefore there was an initiative to start a local radio station with news,

music, announcements and interviews on the programmes.

Fortunately the community had one very valuable resource provided by the people's own strong commitment. In these circumstances, a voluntary project was favoured by the community, which would encourage long-term involvement in the future. After several public meetings, a committee which would develop the project was appointed by the community. As a result, a time frame for the project based on realistic expectations was established (by the committee), giving the community enough opportunity for planning and training.

The first step for the committee was to approach the local council. They received approval for the project and they were allocated suitable premises for the radio station. In addition, the committee was promised a grant of £100,000 to fund the project if the community could identify availability of a similar amount of funding.

The second step for the committee was to identify other funding possibilities. Therefore, the committee wrote to three local 'high street' banks. All wanted security for the loan and required interest at rates ranging between 8.5% and 12.5%. Moreover, they demanded fixed-term conditions for the loan and a maximum period of 12 months was offered. Consequently, the committee contacted a microfinance bank which matched the local council funds, offering £100,000 at 2.25% interest over a period of 18 months. This offer was accepted by the committee. As the microfinance was available immediately, training began. In addition, money was used for equipment for local radio broadcasts such as microphones, transmitters and other items. As a result, six volunteers were trained for broadcast times and office administration.

The availability of microfinance funding produced some successful results. Revenue from advertising was guaranteed through contracts with, for example, local shops, restaurants and sports clubs. There were some pilot broadcasts for 6–8 hours per day and a public survey provided very positive feedback on the radio station. After 12 months, advertising revenue had increased to £4,500 per month and the committee could easily make the repayments to the microfinance bank.

Closure

Give students some very simple three- or four-word SVO/C sentences from the unit (or make some yourself) and ask them to add as many phrases and clauses as they can to make a long complex sentence. Who can make the longest sentence?

For example:

Microfinance helps small-scale enterprises.

By providing funding to poorer farmers or producers who have the initiative to start or develop sustainable businesses, **microfinance helps small-scale enterprises** which are not supported by normal banks because these institutions demand security or a guarantee for loans, which are usually impossible for such customers to provide. (48 words)

Extra activities

1 Work through the *Vocabulary bank* and *Skills bank* if you have not already done so, or as a revision of previous study.

2 Use the *Activity bank* (Teacher's Book additional resources section, Resource 6A).

   A Set the wordsearch for individual work (including homework) or pairwork.

   Answers

Verb	Noun
approach	approach
approve	approval
assess	assessment
borrow	(loan) (credit)
broadcast	broadcast
commit	commitment
contract	contraction
escape	escape
evaluate	evaluation
fund	fund
grow	growth
imply	implication
maintain	maintenance
predict	prediction
preserve	preservation
provide	provision
refuse	refusal
reject	rejection
saturate	saturation
succeed	success

B Students work in pairs or small groups and try to think of word pairs. They should be able to explain the meaning.

Alternatively, photocopy (enlarged) the words from the additional resources section (Resource 6H) and cut up into cards. Put the A and B words into separate envelopes. Put students into groups of four. Make one set of A and one set of B words for each group. Give one pair in each group the A words and the other pair the B words. Each pair takes it in turns to pick a word from their envelope. The other pair must try to find a word from their own envelope which can go with it.

Accept all reasonable word pairs. Possible pairs are:

A	B
actual	growth
agricultural	sector
craft	enterprise
customer	choice
economic	cycle
entrepreneurial	initiative
environmentally	sustainable
ethical	standards
expenditure	plans
fair-trade	product
fixed-term	loan
human rights	policy
market	prices
microfinance	institution/bank
minimum	price
predicted	growth
seasonal	employment
social	commitment
sustainable	development
underserved	individuals/groups

7 SAVING, SPENDING ... BORROWING AND LENDING!

This unit looks at a number of macroeconomic issues, especially government expenditure and debt, as well as considering personal and government saving. The first listening extract, from a lecture, looks at the concept of aggregate demand and discusses the importance of investment. It also describes notions of consumer and business expectation and interest rate fluctuations. Finally, the significance of debt in macroeconomic planning is highlighted through the seminar topic. The second listening extract is from a seminar discussion on deficits and debt. Additional materials require students to make realistic budget decisions to reduce borrowing.

Skills focus

 Listening
- understanding speaker emphasis

Speaking
- asking for clarification
- responding to queries and requests for clarification

Vocabulary focus
- compound nouns
- fixed phrases from economics
- fixed phrases from academic English
- common lecture language

Key vocabulary

See also the list of fixed phrases from academic English in the *Vocabulary bank* (Course Book page 60).

accelerator effect	designate	inject	rightward
afford	exceed	injection of capital	spread (v)
aggregate	fiscal	leftward	variation
assessment	forecast	mortgage	willing
basis point	gross	privatization	withdrawal
bond	idealization	procurement	yield (n)
borrowing	implement	raise (taxes)	
cautious	impose (taxes)	rating	
competitive	indices (pl)	relevance	

7.1 Vocabulary

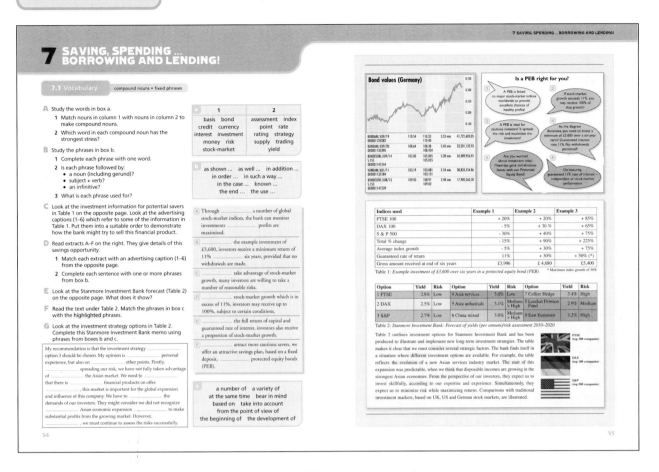

General note

Read the *Vocabulary bank* at the end of the Course Book unit. Decide when, if at all, to refer your students to it. The best time is probably at the very end of the lesson or the beginning of the next lesson, as a summary/revision.

Lesson aims

- understand and use some general academic fixed phrases
- understand and use fixed phrases and compound nouns from the discipline

Introduction

1 Revise some noun phrases (noun + noun, adjective + noun) from previous units. Give students two or three minutes to make word stars with a base word, trying to find as many possible combinations as they can (preferably without having to look at dictionaries).

For example:

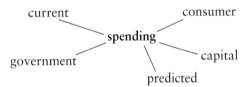

Other base words which could be used are *budget, debt, growth, investment*. If they are stuck for ideas, tell them to look back at previous units.

2 Introduce the topic of the lesson by looking at the advertising captions. Discuss what financial product is on offer. Discuss where such advertisements appear and how banks try to attract investors.

Exercise A

Set for individual work and pairwork checking. Feed back with the whole class, making sure that the stress pattern is correct. Ask students to suggest other fixed phrases which could be made using the words in column 2.

Answers

Model answers. Other possible combinations exist but these are most appropriate:

'stock-market index

'risk assessment

'currency trading

'credit rating

'bond yield

'interest rate

in'vestment strategy

'money supply

'basis point

Exercise B

1/2 Set for individual work and pairwork checking. Feed back with the whole class, building the first three columns of the table in the Answers section on the board.

3 Add the fourth column with the heading 'Use to …'. Give an example of the kind of thing you are looking for, i.e., a phrase which can describe why you would choose to use this fixed phrase. Elicit suggestions from the students to complete the table, supplying the information yourself if students don't know the answer. If students are not sure about the meaning of some of the phrases, give them some example sentences and tell them that you will look further at how they are used shortly. Leave the table on the board as you will return to it.

Answers

Model answers:

Phrase		Followed by …	Use to …
as shown	in/by	noun/gerund	indicate a diagram or table
as well	as	noun/gerund	add information
in addition	to	noun/gerund	add information
in order	to	infinitive	give the purpose for doing something
in such a way	that*	subject + verb	give the result of doing something
in the case	of	noun/gerund	mention something
known	as	noun	give the special name for something
the end	of	noun	refer to the end of something
the use	of	noun	refer to the use of something

*as to is also possible after in such a way, although in this exercise, one word is required

Exercise C

Set for pairwork. Students should try to identify what the general content of each caption entails. On the board, build up as many key words to describe the investment opportunity as students can come up with. If students don't know some important words, tell them they will meet them shortly. Remember the captions should be sequenced as part of this exercise. Discuss each caption before ordering.

Answers

Key ideas/**words** from each caption:

1 Location of investment – **stock-market indices/** advantages

2 **Return (yield)/maturity/term/**details of profits

3 Saver attitude/**cautious** or **willing** to **take a risk/** type of product, i.e., bond

4 Investment details

5 Investor attitude – maximize **returns (gains)** minimize risk

6 More details of the product; **rate of interest/ maturity/stock-market performance**

The best caption order is probably 5, 3, 1, 4, 2, 6.

Exercise D

Explain that the information from the leaflet goes with the captions they have just discussed. Each extract (A–F) goes with one caption although this is not the main objective of the exercise and there may be slightly differing views. Students should first read the extracts, checking words they can't guess in the dictionary. They should not pay attention to the spaces at this point.

1 Set for pairwork. Feed back with the whole class. Add any key words which might have been useful in Exercise C to the board.

2 Set for individual work. Refer back to the table in Exercise B, which will help students to choose the correct phrase. Feed back with the whole class.

Answers:

Model answers:

See table at top of opposite page.

If you wish, ask students to return to the table in Exercise B and write one sentence for each of the fixed phrases to show their meaning. This may utilize contexts such as banking, savings or investments, which students may be familiar with, for the purposes of advertising or marketing financial products.

Exercise E

Set for pairwork discussion. Feed back with the whole group, making sure that students understand the concept behind the chart. Do not correct or confirm students' views of the content at this point.

Caption		Extracts (model sequence)
5	C	In order to take advantage of stock-market growth, many investors are willing to take a number of reasonable risks.
3	F	In order to attract more cautious savers, we offer an attractive savings plan, based on a fixed deposit, known as protected equity bonds (PEB).
1	A	Through the use of a number of global stock-market indices, the bank can monitor investments in such a way that profits are maximized.
4	B	As shown in the example investment of £3,600, investors receive a minimum return of 11% at the end of six years, provided that no withdrawals are made.
2	E	In addition to the full return of capital and guaranteed rate of interest, investors also receive a proportion of stock-market growth.
6	D	In the case of stock-market growth which is in excess of 11%, investors may receive up to 100%, subject to certain conditions.

Subject note

This is a highly simplified investment strategy chart but it serves to illustrate the factors of yield and risk assessment in investment banking. Students might be asked which is the best option for a long-term (10-year) investment with cautious investors in mind! Students will probably recognize that Asia Services is the most suitable option.

Exercise F

Set for individual work and pairwork checking. Students should use their dictionaries if they are not sure of the meaning of the phrases. Note that some phrases can be used for the same thing – it is a good idea to use a different word to avoid repetition.

Answers

Model answers:

Table 2 outlines investment options for Stanmore Investment Bank and has been produced to illustrate and implement new long-term investment strategies. The table makes it clear that we must (consider) take into account (several) a number of strategic factors. The bank finds itself in a situation where (different) a variety of investment options are available. For example, the table reflects (the evolution of) the development of a new Asian services industry market. (The start of) The beginning of this expansion was predictable, when we (think) bear in mind that disposable incomes are growing in the strongest Asian economies. (From the perspective of) From the point of view of our investors, they expect us to invest skillfully, (according to) based on our expertise and experience.

(Simultaneously) At the same time, they expect us to minimize risk while maximizing returns. Comparisons with traditional investment markets, based on UK, US and German stock markets, are illustrated.

Language note

The fixed phrases here are often used in situations which describe a series of chronological stages. In this short memo, the phrases are used in a more general way to make comments on a prevailing situation and to assess options. The same words can also be used when writing or talking in more general abstract academic terms, for example when introducing an essay, lecture or piece of research. This use of these words will be covered later in the unit.

Exercise G

Set for pairwork. Feed back with the whole class.

Answers

Model answers:

My recommendation is that the investment strategy as shown in option 3 should be chosen. My opinion is based on personal experience but also on a number of other points. Firstly, from the point of view of spreading our risk, we have not fully taken advantage of the development of the Asian market. We need to bear in mind that there is a variety of financial products on offer. In addition, this market is important for the global expansion and influence of this company. We have to take into account the demands of our investors. They might consider we did not recognize the beginning of Asian economic expansion in such a way as/in order to make substantial profits from the growing market. However, at the same time, we must continue to assess the risks successfully.

Closure

Put the following key ideas on the board

Investment amount (currency)

Term (period)

Risk level

Minimum expected return (% annum)

Indices to be used

Other conditions

Students should interview each other to verify their partner's investment expectations.

Encourage them to consider their options seriously!

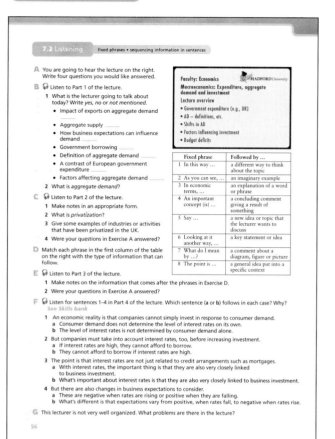

7.2 Listening

Lesson aims

- improve comprehension through recognition of fixed phrases and what follows them in terms of words/type of information
- understand how information can be sequenced in different ways within a sentence, e.g., for emphasis (see *Skills bank*)

Further practice in:

- understanding fractured text

General note

Read the *Skills bank – 'Given' and 'new' information in sentences* at the end of the Course Book unit. Decide when, if at all, to refer students to it. The best time, as before, is probably at the very end of the lesson or the beginning of the next lesson, as a summary/revision. Alternatively, use the *Skills bank* in conjunction with Exercise F.

Introduction

Review key vocabulary by writing a selection of words from Lesson 7.1 on the board and asking students to put them into phrases of two or more words.

Exercise A

Remind students about preparing for a lecture. If you wish, review Unit 1 *Skills bank – Making the most of lectures*. Remind students that, when they begin their talks, lecturers usually provide their listeners with an outline in order to aid comprehension. Elicit from the students the kinds of signpost words lecturers might use (e.g., *To start with, … , Firstly, … , I'll begin/start by …ing*, etc.). If necessary, refer students to Unit 5.

Refer students to the lecture slide. Tell them to look at the title and bullet points and to list ideas/make questions for each bullet point. At this stage do not explain any words from the slide, or allow students to check in their dictionaries, as the meanings will be dealt with in the lecture. Set the exercise for pairwork.

Feed back with the whole class: ask several students to read out their questions. Write some of the questions on the board.

Answers

If students suggest questions which are inappropriate, draw their attention to the focus on government (or macroeconomic) factors compared with microeconomic (personal, household, individual business) issues. They might recall the discussion of 'shifts' in microeconomic supply and demand from Unit 3.

🎧 Exercise B

Tell students they are going to hear the introduction to the lecture – not the whole thing. Give students time to read questions 1 and 2. Remind them they will only hear the recording once. Play Part 1. Allow students to compare their answers.

Feed back. Confirm the correct answers.

Answers

Model answers:

1

impact of exports on aggregate demand	no
aggregate supply	no
how business expectations can influence demand	yes
government borrowing	no
definition of aggregate demand	yes
a contrast of European government expenditure	not mentioned
factors affecting aggregate demand	yes

136

2 Aggregate demand is a concept which relates to the total demand in any economy. It comprises a number of factors: consumption + investment + government expenditure + net exports (i.e., value of exports minus imports).

The formula (NOT used in the lecture) is:

$$AD = C + I + G + (X - M)$$

Transcript 🎧 1.28

Part 1

Good morning everybody. What I'm going to talk about today is a variation on earlier themes – demand and supply – which you learnt about when applied to the microeconomy – individuals, households or a single business enterprise. You should already be familiar with these concepts at the micro level, but today I want to discuss their relevance to the macroeconomy. In other words, how do governments deal with the *total* amount of demand and the *total* supply of goods and services in the economy at the same time? Please bear in mind that this is, in fact, an ideal view, based on a number of theories and models, but not always a reflection of macroeconomic reality. For this reason, economists talk of an 'idealization'.

So today, I'll start by giving you a little background based on the UK expenditure situation. Then I will continue by providing a definition and discussion of the concept known as aggregate demand, or AD. After that, I'll outline how AD shifts. In addition, I will concentrate on those factors which influence investment, and finally I will deal briefly with budget deficits. Now, today I won't consider how the government borrows money, i.e., government borrowing, nor will I talk about the role played by the balance of trade. They will all be discussed in a later lecture in order to make things a bit easier to understand. Oh, yes, sorry, I forgot to say, I will deal with aggregate supply in the next lecture, too. So, just to remind you, today's focus is on expenditure, aggregate demand as well as some associated topics.

🎧 Exercise C

Refer students to the first point on the lecture slide ('government expenditure'). Ask students to suggest an appropriate type of notes. The most likely form of making notes is a spidergram. This is because the lecture topic explores aspects of expenditure at a more abstract level while assuming that students know, from Units 1, 2 and 3, how governments raise money. Students might, quite rightly, suggest that a pie chart or (bar) graph would show statistical data clearly but the lecture does not, in fact, include statistics. These figures are used later in the unit.

Give students time to read the questions. Ask them how governments raise money (considered in earlier units).

Can they suggest key words to associate with fiscal measures, i.e., revenue and expenditure issues? Write these on the board.

Examples: *taxes*, *revenue*, *budget*, *balance*, *deficit*, *surplus*, *allocation*, *prioritize*

Play Part 2.

Put students in pairs to compare their diagrams and discuss the questions. With the whole class, ask students how many answers to their questions in Exercise A they heard.

Answers

Model answers:

1

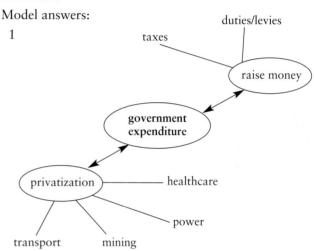

2 Privatization is when an industry or service activity was previously under government control but is then privatized by the formation of private companies to continue that industry or activity. So, for example, in Germany where there are large private-sector production and service industries, control of the post and railways still remains in government hands and the government is quite reluctant to privatize.

3 Transport, production and extractive industries, power generation.

In fact, in the UK, the electricity industry, railways, water supply, steel production, coal mining, shipyards, even the oil industry, have all been put into private hands (in different ways).

4 Answers depend on students' questions.

Transcript 🎧 1.29

Part 2

Governments all over the world have to spend money! So let's try to ask and answer some simple questions. Firstly, how is money raised? Do all economies have similar spending opportunities? Does government spending always increase? What is the difference between public and private spending? And finally, how does government spending influence aggregate demand?

Governments can raise money by taxes and invest money in infrastructure, public goods and welfare, etc., as well as spending that money carefully and usefully. In the case of developing countries, governments' fiscal policy, that is, the way taxes are imposed, is often quite limited. Perhaps the government is in the early stages of the development of a national income tax structure or at the beginning of the introduction of a national insurance programme. This means governments impose taxes or duties on goods – tobacco, petrol, luxury goods or imported items, etc. From the point of view of expenditure, governments in developing countries rely on less revenue from income taxation and more from those consumer taxes, known as duties or levies.

In Britain, people talk about the increase in UK public sector spending. But, in fact, government spending – as a proportion of all investment expenditure – has fallen over the past 50 years or so. This is partly because of privatization. Expenditure on transport, mining, power generation and even areas of health care or education have been taken away from the public sector and shifted to the private sector.

Moreover, privatization of a variety of industries and economic activities in the 1980s, and later, has resulted in a shift of investment responsibility. But bear in mind that government expenditure is crucial in advanced economies. If public sector spending increases, then aggregate demand shifts, as I will now outline.

Exercise D

Explain that these are common phrases in an academic context such as a lecture. Knowing the meaning of the phrases will help a lot with comprehension. Make sure students understand that the items in the second column are not in the correct order.

Set for individual work and pairwork checking. Tell students to check the meaning of any words they don't know in a dictionary. They should be able to guess the meanings of the phrases, even if they don't actually know the phrases.

Feed back with the whole class, completing the first two columns of the chart in the Answers section for Exercise E on the board. (Alternatively, make a datashow from Resource 7B in the additional resources section.) Once the 'Followed by …' column is completed, this will act as a predictive support for Part 3 of the lecture.

Methodology note

Two-column activities are good for pair checking and practice. Once students have got the correct answers they can test each other in pairs. Student A covers the first column and tries to remember the phrases, then B covers the second column and tries to remember the purpose of each phrase.

You can then check memory by getting students to close their books and giving a phrase; students (as a group or individually) must give its purpose. Then change roles.

🎧 Exercise E

1 Tell students that in Part 3 of the lecture they will hear the phrases in Exercise D. They know now what *type* of information is likely to follow. Now they must try to hear what *actual* information is given. If you wish, photocopy the table in the additional resources section (Resource 7B) for students to write their answers on.

Do the first one as an example. Play the first part of the recording and stop after '*common understandings of economic principles*'. Ask students: *What is referred to by the expression 'In this way …'?* (Answer: *Use/Value of figures and models for economists*).

N.B. If you wish, refer the students to the aggregate demand diagram (Figure 2) in Lesson 4. This might help students as they listen.

Play the rest of the recording, pausing briefly at the points indicated by a // to allow students to make notes. Put students in pairs to check their answers.

Feed back with the whole class, asking questions based on the words in the 'Followed by …' column. For example:

After phrase number 2, what is the word or phrase that is explained?

After phrase number 3, what is the diagram that is commented on?

2 Refer back to students' questions in Exercise A. Discuss with the whole class whether they heard any answers to their questions.

Answers

1 Model answers: See table on opposite page.
2 Answers depend on students' questions.

	Fixed phrase	Followed by ...	Actual information (suggested answers)
1	In this way ...	a concluding comment, giving a result of something	justifying the use of figures by economists
2	As you can see, ...	a comment about a diagram, figure or picture	pointing out the x-axis and the y-axis on the figure
3	In economic terms, ...	a general idea put into a specific context	to introduce the notion of 'the wealth effect'
4	An important concept (is) ...	a new idea or topic that the lecturer wants to discuss	to introduce the idea of 'consumer expectation'
5	Say ...	an imaginary example	talking about price decreases
6	Looking at it another way, ...	a different way to think about the topic	focus on the macroeconomic factors behind aggregate demand
7	What do I mean by ...?	an explanation of a word or phrase	explanation of AD shift
8	The point is ...	a key statement or idea	changes in macroeconomic factors can cause AD shifts

Transcript 🎧 1.30

Part 3

Economics relies on diagrams and models to show a variety of relationships. This figure represents an idealization of the concept of aggregate demand. In this way, economists can represent economic conditions and describe changes in diagrams, figures or models, etc., based on common understandings of economic principles. // So, let's look at a diagram of aggregate demand. As you can see, the y-axis has the label 'price level', while the x-axis is designated 'real output'. // The curve has the label AD and slopes downwards from left to right. Let's examine it more closely. You can see that a fall in price levels means that real output increases. In economic terms, consumers notice what is generally called a 'wealth effect'. They find themselves with more money to spend on consumer goods or services because prices are lower. //

An important concept is a factor known as consumer expectation. // Consumers might expect prices to rise in the future and therefore they increase their consumption at the present time. When prices rise, real output falls as a reaction to a fall in demand. Say that prices fall nationally, then exports will be cheaper, imports will become more expensive and that will lead to ... // Oh, I'm sorry, I forgot that I intended to talk about exports in a later lecture!

Looking at it another way, aggregate demand involves those factors which influence the macroeconomy. // This form of demand is made up of consumption, investment, government expenditure and the balance of trade, otherwise known as net exports.

Now, moving on to AD shifts. What do I mean by a shift of the AD curve? Well, basically it is a movement of the curve to the right, a rightward shift, based on an increase in AD or a movement to the left, a leftward shift, based on a decline in AD. //

The point is that changes in any of the factors I have mentioned can result in a shift of the AD curve. // I have mentioned price levels already, so let's focus on investment, government expenditure and exports ... Oh dear. I did it again! Exports will be dealt with in the next lecture! I am sorry.

🎧 Exercise F

The purpose of this exercise is to look at how information tends to be structured in sentences. It also requires very close attention to the listening text.

Before listening, allow students time to read through the sentences. In pairs, set them to discuss which sentence (**a** or **b**) they think will follow the numbered sentences.

Play Part 4 all the way through. Students should choose sentence **a** or **b**. Put them in pairs to check and discuss why **a** or **b** was the sentence they heard.

Feed back with the whole class. Deal with sentences 1 and 2 first. Tell students that all the sentences are correct, but sentence **a** 'sounds better' when it comes after the first sentence. This is because of the way that sentences go together and the way in which information is organized in a sentence. Draw the table on the next page on the board. Show how the underlined words in the second sentence have been mentioned in the first sentence. In the second sentence the underlined words are 'old' or 'given' information. When sentences follow each other in a conversation (or a piece of writing), usually the 'given' information comes in the first part of a sentence.

Now look at sentences 3 and 4. These are different. The normal choice would be the **a** sentences. However, here the speaker wanted to emphasize the idea of 'important' and 'different'. So a *Wh~* cleft sentence structure was used, which changes the usual order of information. Show this on the table. This 'fronting' of information has the effect of special focus for emphasis.

Answers

First sentence			Second sentence	
			Given information	New information
1 An economic reality is that companies cannot simply invest in response to <u>consumer demand</u>.			a <u>Consumer demand</u> …	… does not determine the level of interest rates on its own.
2 But companies must take into account <u>interest rates</u>, too, before increasing investment.			a If <u>interest rates</u> are …	… they cannot afford to borrow.
3 The point is that <u>interest rates</u> are not just related to credit arrangements such as mortgages.	Normal order		a With <u>interest rates</u>,	… the important thing is that they are also very closely linked to business investment.
	Special focus		b What's <u>important</u> about interest rates is …	… that they are also very closely linked to business investment.
4 But there are also <u>changes in business expectations</u> to consider.	Normal order		a <u>These</u>	… are negative when rates are rising or positive when they are falling.
	Special focus		b <u>What's different</u> is …	… that expectations vary from positive, when rates fall, to negative when rates rise.

Further examples of different ways to 'front' information and more practice will be given in Lesson 7.3.

Language note

In English, important information can be placed at the beginning or at the end of a sentence. There are two types of important information. The first part of the sentence contains the topic and the second part contains some kind of information or comment about the topic. Usually the comment is the more syntactically complicated part of the sentence.

Once a piece of text or a piece of conversation (i.e., a piece of discourse) has gone beyond the first sentence, a 'given'/'new' principle operates. Information which is 'given', in other words that has already been mentioned, goes at the beginning of the sentence. Normally speaking, information which is new goes at the end of the sentence. So in the second sentence of a piece of discourse, an aspect of the comment from the previous sentence may become the topic. Thus the topic of the second sentence, if it has already been mentioned in the previous sentence, is also 'given'. Of course, the given information may not be referred to with exactly the same words in the second sentence. Other ways to refer to the given information include reference words (*it, he, she, this, that, these, those,* etc.) or vocabulary items with similar meanings.

Information structure is covered in the *Skills bank* in the Course Book unit.

Transcript 🎧 2.1

Part 4

As I mentioned, investment is a key factor in macroeconomic terms. If there is increased consumer demand, businesses will want to cater for this. Perhaps you remember the definition of investment. It's really defined as the amount that entrepreneurs are willing to invest in new machinery or equipment, or expanding their premises to increase output. So any capital investment of this type will inject a lot of money into the economy. This injection of capital that is to say, investment, will result in a rightward shift of the AD curve. Another important concept is called the accelerator effect. This is when investment responds to changes in consumer income.

So, as I said, if people have more wealth, the aggregate demand increases. At the same time, increased investment usually follows. So, factors which influence business investment are very important in our discussion of aggregate demand. An economic reality is that companies cannot simply invest in response to consumer demand. Consumer demand does not determine the level of interest rates on its own. In other words, if consumers have disposable income, they are likely to demand more. But companies must take into account interest rates, too, before increasing investment. If interest rates are high, they cannot afford to borrow. But, if interest rates are low or there is a falling trend, borrowing becomes cheaper for businesses. In order to meet any increased demand, businesses can borrow so that they can invest. If they invest in capital equipment, there is a good chance they will retain their competitive position. This increase in investment results in a rightward shift of the AD curve. On the other hand, a leftward shift occurs if interest rates increase. The point is that interest rates are not just related to credit arrangements such as mortgages. What's important about interest rates is that they are also very closely linked to business investment. Now, earlier I mentioned the concept of consumer expectations. But there are also changes in business expectations to consider. What's different is that expectations vary from positive, when rates fall, to negative when rates rise.

But I can see that I am running short of time and I still need to talk about what happens when governments spend too much!

Exercise G

Set for pairwork discussion. Feed back with the whole class. Note that the lecture has not yet finished. The last part will be heard in Lesson 7.3.

Answers

Model answers:

The lecturer has started to talk about the impact of exports on aggregate demand even though this was specifically excluded from his/her lecture content.

The lecturer is running out of time.

Closure

It would be helpful for students to consider AD shifts in more detail. They will learn about this in their economics classes but a little practice and opportunity for group work discussion would be appropriate. Some simple suggestions are given.

Students might discuss the following scenarios in groups:

What happens to the AD curve if:

- interest rates fall (AD shifts to the right – borrowing is cheaper for business leading to new investment)
- foreign investment increases into Country X (AD shifts to the right as output is likely to increase UNLESS there is direct competition with X's own firms, in which case there could even be a slight shift to the left)
- a new government is elected which is committed to reductions in public expenditure (AD shifts to the left as government investment is likely to be reduced)

7.3 Extending skills

Reproduction of the student book page 57, showing:

7 SAVING, SPENDING ... BORROWING AND LENDING

7.3 Extending skills — stress within words • fixed phrases • giving sentences a special focus

A 🎧 Listen to some stressed syllables. Identify the word below in each case. Number each word.

Example:
You hear: *1 tane* /teɪn/   You write:

accelerator ___	financial ___	privatization ___
aggregate ___	injection ___	procurement ___
competitive ___	maximize ___	resource ___
expectation ___	mortgage ___	simultaneously _1_

B 🎧 Listen to the final part of the lecture from Lesson 2.
1 Complete the notes on the right by adding a symbol in each space.
2 What research task(s) are you asked to do?

C Study the phrases from the lecture in the blue box. For which of the following purposes did the lecturer use each phrase?
- to introduce a new topic
- to emphasize a major point
- to add a point
- to finish a list
- to give an example
- to restate

D Rewrite these sentences to give a special focus. Begin with the words in brackets.
1 Spending less than you earn or receive is a much better idea rather than the opposite. *(It)*
2 Immediately after the Second World War, the Labour government established the pattern of government spending. *(It)*
3 The government prioritized social expenditure because so much infrastructure had been destroyed in the war. *(Two sentences. First = 'It'; second = 'The reason')*
4 It is really important to bear in mind this division of expenditure when discussing public sector budgets. *(What)*
5 These three categories enable the government to decide spending priorities. *(The advantage)* *See Skills bank*

E Choose one section of the lecture. Refer to your notes and give a spoken summary. Use the fixed phrases and ways of giving special focus that you have looked at.

F Work with a partner.
1 Make expenditure and revenue charts for a country, explaining your priorities. Use the UK government expenditure chart on the next page as a model.
2 Present your charts to another pair. Practise using fixed phrases and ways of giving special focus. *See Vocabulary bank and Skills bank*

Budget planning = v. complex ___
1 range of factors, e.g., previous year, predictions, guesswork!
+ borrowing ___ deficit
2 modern UK macroeconomics
When? Post-SWW
Who? Labour government
What? Established pattern of gov. spending
infrastructure destroyed in war ___
social priorities
i.e., welfare, social benefits ___
3 expenditure categories
1 transfer payments, e.g., unemployment/ social benefits, etc.
2 current e., e.g., day-to-day public sector/wages
3 capital e., e.g., infrastructure
N.B. (+) gov. can prioritize e.
(+) allocate public sector resources

etc.
i.e./that is to say
In other words, ...
Let's take ...
Let me put it another way.
I almost forgot to mention ...
Not to mention the fact that ...
Plus there's the fact that ...
The fact of the matter is, ...
You've probably heard of ...

57

Lesson aims

- extend knowledge of fixed phrases commonly used in lectures
- give sentences a special focus (see *Skills bank*)

Further practice in:

- stress within words

Introduction

As in Units 3 and 5, tell students to ask you questions about the information in the lecture in Lesson 7.2 as if you were the lecturer. Remind them about asking for information politely. If they need to revise how to do this, tell them to look back at the *Skills bank* for Unit 3.

🎧 Exercise A

Remind students of the importance of stressed syllables in words (see the teaching notes for Unit 3, Lesson 3, Exercise A). Play the recording, pausing after the first few to check that students understand the task.

Feed back, perhaps playing the recording again for each word before checking. Ideally, highlight the words in a datashow. Finally, check students' pronunciation of the words.

Answers

accelerator	7
aggregate	10
competitive	3
expectation	8
financial	11
injection	2
maximize	12
mortgage	5
privatization	9
procurement	6
resource	4
simultaneously	1

Transcript 🎧 2.2

1 simul'taneously
2 in'jection
3 com'petitive
4 re'source*
5 'mortgage
6 pro'curement
7 ac'celerator
8 expec'tation
9 privati'zation
10 'aggregate
11 fi'nancial
12 'maximize

Note

*Word stress differs between British and American speakers for certain words, such as resource (in American English) from the list above. Other examples include 'research (Am E) compared with re'search (Br E); 'garage (Br E) compared with ga'rage (Am E) is quite well known as is 'ballet (Br E) compared with ba'llet (Am E) or 'debris (Br E) compared with de'bris (Am E).

As you may observe, there is a connection with French words in a number of these items. Commonly, American speakers give more vowel length to some words beginning with re- (*retire, retreat, rewind*) which makes the word stress seem a little different.

🎧 Exercise B

Write these words on the board and ask students to say what symbols you can use for them when taking notes. Put the symbols on the board.

is, means	=
because	∵
numbers or bullet points	a list
causes, leads to*	→
for example	e.g.
increase(d), more	↗
and	& +
that is, that is to say	i.e.
and so on, and others	etc.
therefore, so	∴
or	/
take note of/remember	N.B.
advantage/disadvantage	(+) (−)

*the arrow has a wide range of possible meanings, including *makes/made*, *produces*, *did*, *results in*, etc.

Tell students they will hear the final part of the lecture. Ask them to read the notes through. Remind them also to listen for their research task. Play Part 5.

Put students in pairs to compare their symbols. Feed back with the whole class, if possible using an OHT or other visual medium of the notes. Discuss acceptable alternatives, e.g., *start & finish* instead of *start/finish*.

Answers

Model answers:

1 Budget planning = v. complex ∵
  1) range of factors, e.g., previous year, predictions, guesswork!
     + borrowing ↗ deficit
  2) modern UK macroeconomics
     When? Post-SWW
     Who? Labour government
     What? Established pattern of gov. spending ∵ infrastructure destroyed in war ∴ social priorities, i.e., welfare, social benefits →
  3) expenditure categories
     1 transfer payments, e.g., unemployment/social benefits, etc.
     2 current e., e.g., day-to-day public sector/wages
     3 capital e., e.g., infrastructure
        N.B. (+) gov. can prioritize e.
        (+) allocate public sector resources

2 They must research forecasts for UK income (i.e., revenue) and expenditure for this current year and check the IMF website for information on government debt.

Transcript 🎧 2.3

Part 5

Now, let's move on to budget deficits, that is to say, the situation when a government spends more than it receives. Think of someone who earns £600 a month. If he spends £700, then he is asking for trouble! In other words, it is a much better idea to spend less than you earn or receive, rather than the opposite! Yes, that's true, but the fact of the matter is, for governments, a balanced budget where receipts equal spending is extremely difficult to achieve. And a government surplus, when receipts exceed expenditure, is a very rare event indeed! Let me put it another way, governments learn to live with deficits. It is a complex process to plan the budget. The reason for this is that expenditure decisions are based on a range of important factors. These include previous years' figures, predictions and careful guesswork! Plus there is the fact that borrowing adds to deficits, but I will talk about that in a later lecture.

Now, let's take a brief look at the growth of macroeconomics in the UK. You've probably heard of the welfare state – health, education, social housing, etc. Well, it was immediately after the Second World War that the Labour government established the pattern of public sector spending. By that I mean the systematic allocation of funding. It was social expenditure that the government prioritized. The reason was that so much infrastructure had been destroyed in the war.

So over the past 60 years or so, UK government spending has generally consisted of three main categories. These are transfer payments, current spending and capital spending. What is really important to bear in mind when discussing public sector budgets is this division of expenditure. Let's take transfer payments first. These usually include payments to unemployed people, child benefits, housing benefits, and other social welfare commitments. *Current* spending includes all the everyday costs of the things that the public sector needs, in schools and hospitals, for police or transport, etc., not to mention the fact that wages in the public sector have to be paid, too. *Capital* spending relates to expenditure to improve existing schools, hospitals and roads or to construct new ones – infrastructure, in fact. The advantage of these three categories, transfer payments, current spending and capital spending, is that they enable the government to decide spending priorities. The government can then allocate appropriate resources to the public sector.

Oh dear, I seem to have run out of time and I really haven't covered everything I wanted to! So I will leave you with a fairly simple research topic. For the next seminar, I would like you to find out from the UK government website – HM Treasury – what the forecasts for income, or revenue, and expenditure were for this current year.

Exercise C

Set for pairwork. Feed back with the whole class. If necessary, play the relevant sections again. Ask for other phrases which have similar meanings, particularly from Lesson 7.2, and also from Unit 5. Build the table in the Answers section on the board. Accept any suitable words or phrases for the third column.

Answers

Model answers:
See table below.

Language note

The phrases below are appropriate in speaking. Many are not suitable for written language, for which different phrases should be used.

Exercise D

Students need to decide which word(s) should receive the particular focus and then try to rewrite the sentences. Depending on the class, they can work in pairs or individually first.

Feed back with the whole class. Take each sentence in turn. Ask for suggestions as to which aspect could receive special emphasis (actual words are underlined below). Accept any reasonable answers. If you wish, replay Part 5 of the lecture for students to check their answers. Note that:

- sentences 1, 2 and the first part of 3 use an *It* construction to give the special focus

- sentence 4 uses a *Wh~* cleft sentence already seen in Lesson 7.2
- sentences 3 (second part) and 5 introduce new, general words (often found in academic contexts) followed by *is* plus a *that* clause

Answers

Model answers:

1 <u>Spending</u> less than you earn or receive is a much better idea rather than the opposite. (*It*)

It is a much better idea to spend less than you earn or receive rather than the opposite!

2 Immediately after <u>the Second World War</u>, the Labour government established the pattern of public sector spending. (*It*)

It was immediately after the Second World War that the Labour government established the pattern of public sector spending.

3 The government prioritized <u>social expenditure</u> because so much infrastructure had been destroyed in the war. (*Two sentences. First = 'It'; second = 'The reason'*)

It was social expenditure that the government prioritized. The reason was that so much infrastructure had been destroyed in the war.

4 It is really important to bear in mind this <u>division of expenditure</u> when discussing public sector budgets. (*What*)

What is really important to bear in mind when discussing public sector budgets is this division of expenditure.

5 These <u>three categories</u> enable the government to decide spending priorities. (*The advantage*)

The advantage of these three categories is that they enable the government to decide spending priorities.

Use	Fixed phrase	Other phrases
to introduce a new topic	You've probably heard of …	Now, an important concept is … Now you may be familiar with …
to make a major point	The fact of the matter is, …	Actually, … In fact, … The point is that …
to add points	Not to mention the fact that … Plus there's the fact that …	also, and, too, In addition, …
to finish a list	etc.	and so on
to give an example	Let's take …	For example, … e.g., … Let's look at an example of this. For instance, …
to restate	Let me put it another way. In other words, …	What I mean is … That is to say, … By that I mean … To put it another way, …

After completing Exercises C and D, students can be referred to the *Vocabulary bank* and the *Skills bank* for consolidation and preparation for Exercise E.

Exercise E

Set the initial preparation for individual work. Students can refer to their notes in Lesson 7.2 (Exercises C and E) or the notes for completion in Lesson 7.3 (Exercise B). They should think about how they can use the phrases they have looked at, and ways of giving special focus/emphasis. (Note: They should not write out exactly what they are going to say in complete sentences and then read!)

Put students in pairs to give their oral summaries to each other, preferably pairing students who have chosen different sections to summarize.

Go around the class noting any problems or especially good examples of language use. You may wish to choose one or two individuals to give their summary to the whole class.

With the whole class, feed back any language or other difficulties which you noticed.

Exercise F

1 Ask students to look at the UK expenditure pie chart. They should not copy it but use it as a model only. Encourage students to explain or justify their allocation of resources. In this way, they are likely to use the fixed phrases quite a lot.

2 Put the pairs in groups of four to present their charts to each other.

Closure

Dictate some words for which students have learnt note-taking symbols or abbreviations such as *and, results in, therefore, because, remember, that is to say, for example.*

Students should write the symbol or abbreviation.

Remind them of the list of symbols and abbreviations at the back of the Course Book.

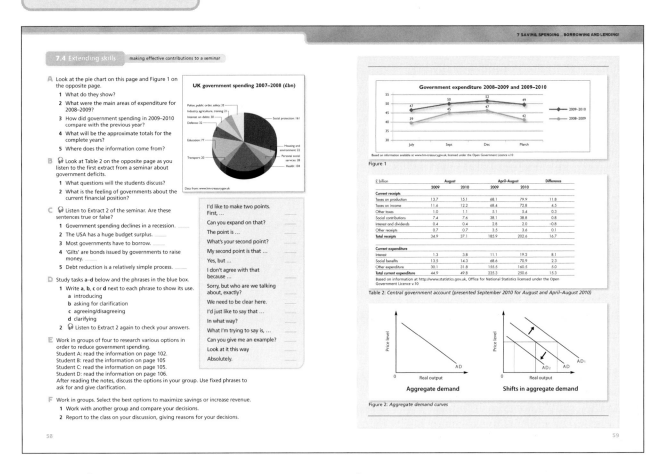

Lesson aims

- make effective contributions to a seminar:

  using pre-organizers – *I'd like to make two points*; *My second point is that …*

  responding to queries by clarifying – *What I'm trying to say is …*; *We need to be clear here …*

Introduction

Revise phrases from the previous lessons. Give a word or phrase and ask students to give one with a similar meaning. Ask for phrases from the previous lesson which can be used to:

- introduce a new topic
- emphasize a major point
- add a point
- finish a list
- give an example

Exercise A

Set for pairwork discussion. Feed back.

Answers

Possible answers:

1 The pie chart shows the division of UK government expenditure in 2007–2008. Figure 1 (on the opposite page) shows UK government spending, comparing the period July–March in two different years, 2008–2009 and 2009–2010.

2 The pie chart shows that social protection, health and education were the three main areas of public sector expenditure in 2007–2008.

3 It was higher in every month shown in the figure.

4 2008–2009 <u>approximately</u> (43.5 average/month x 12) = £522 bn
   2009–2010 <u>approximately</u> (49.5 average/month x 12) = £594 bn

5 Students can find out more exact figures from HM Treasury website:

   www.hm-treasury.gov.uk

   and they may want to look at the UK government budget as shown in, for example:

   www.hm-treasury.gov.uk/d/Budget2009/bud09_econfinances_968.pdf

   www.statistics.gov.uk/pdfdir/psf0910.pdf (for August 2010)

🎧 Exercise B

Allow students time to read the two questions. Play Part 1 once only. Check answers in pairs. Feed back with the whole class.

Answers

Model answers:

1 They will discuss budget deficits and debt.

2 Governments are very worried about deficits and especially debt levels. Table 2 is a (slightly) simplified version of the real *receipts: expenditure* situation but is adequate for the purposes of students' awareness at this stage.

If students look closely at Table 2, they will see from the UK government figures for August 2010 (including the period April–August as the new financial year so far) that:

- Total receipts were higher for August 2010 compared with August 2009 (£37.1 bn/£34.9 bn).

- Total receipts for the period April–August 2010 were higher than for the equivalent period in 2009 (£202.6 bn compared with £185.9 bn, i.e., receipts for the 2010 period were £16.7 bn higher). This means people paid more taxes and social contributions, businesses paid more taxes and there was a higher taxation on production (mostly based on increased VAT).

- Expenditure for August 2010 was £49.8 bn compared with £44.9 bn in 2009 (i.e., expenditure was higher for that month).

- Expenditure was also higher for the April–August period (2010, £250.6 bn compared with 2009, £235.3 bn).

- Deficit for August 2010 was £49.8 bn – £37.1 bn = £12.7 billion for that one month!

- Deficit for the period April–August 2010 was £250.6 bn – £202.6 bn = £48 bn for the period.

- Deficit for August 2009 was £10 bn, compared with £12.7 bn in 2010.

- Deficit for April–August 2009 was £49.4 bn, compared with £48 bn in 2010.

- If the pattern for August 2010 was repeated over 12 months, this would mean a total annual deficit for 2010 of £152.4 bn.

- If the pattern for April–August 2010 was repeated over 12 months, the total deficit would be around £115.2 bn.

- The August (single month) pattern figure was closer to the reality!

Transcript 🎧 2.4

Extract 1

Well, as I outlined in the lecture, most governments, including the UK, are very worried about the imbalance in their current accounts, that is, the deficits that most of them have. But they are even more worried about levels of debt following the global economic crisis beginning in 2008. Before that, government and private debt had been considered a natural and almost healthy feature of the economy. Now debt is seen as an economic weakness and dealing with high levels of debt is difficult. Governments need to borrow money, but 2008–2009 showed how quickly the investors disappear! Here, I mean all those institutions such as banks, finance and investment companies, pension funds, even other governments, etc., which were the main lenders to governments before 2008. They have lost confidence since the global economic crisis. So, I hope you have done some research on deficits and debt so we can discuss these issues together.

🎧 Exercise C

Allow students time to read the questions. Play Extract 2 straight through once while they mark the answers true or false. Check in pairs and/or with the whole class. Check any unknown vocabulary, such as *expand on*, *untapped potential*.

Answers

1	true	
2	false	The USA has a huge budget deficit, a huge trade deficit and very high levels of debt.
3	true	
4	true	(This is generally true but corporate bonds issued by a very strong company such as VW, Allianz, Toyota or Honda might also be designated gilts.)
5	false	Debt reduction is a very complex process.

Transcript 🎧 2.5

Extract 2

JACK: OK, well, we all agree that annual government spending generally increases ...

LEILA: No, sorry, I don't agree with that because in a recession, there is often a reduction in government spending ...

JACK: Hmm, maybe. What I'm trying to say is that over the long term, that's to say, 20 years or so, expenditure grows.

LEILA: Alright. We need to be clear here about what a government budget really is. The point is that it's almost impossible for government revenue to increase to match expenditure. Very few governments have a true budget surplus.

MAJED: Can you expand on that a little, please?

LEILA: Yes. For example, Saudi Arabia has a budget surplus. It receives enormous revenues from its oil production compared to expenditure. Or South Korea frequently has a budget surplus because it has such good productivity of consumer goods. But, most countries have a budget deficit – with the USA having the biggest of all!

EVIE: OK. Let's consider that. I'd like to make two points. First, Jack is right about long-term spending and Leila is also right about the difficulty in balancing budgets. That's the first point!

MAJED: So, what's your second point?

EVIE: My second point is that nowadays it is not enough just to talk about government spending and revenue in an isolated way.

MAJED: In what way?

EVIE: Well, the point is that most governments cannot survive without borrowing and that increases their debts. So having debts becomes a fact of economic life!

MAJED: Sorry, I'd just like to say that I'm not sure I fully understand the difference between budget deficit and debt.

EVIE: OK. Look at it this way, if government spending exceeds revenue – that's a deficit! To pay for the spending, the government has to borrow money. That's when it has debts. Usually governments in advanced economies issue bonds, known as 'gilts', to raise money – but they have to pay interest on what they have borrowed, of course!

MAJED: OK, thanks. Now I understand, but can you give me an example of countries with large debts?

EVIE: Absolutely. Let's talk about deficits first. Erm … Consider the European Union. It has regulations that the budget deficits of the member countries should not exceed, I think, about -3%. Now, that's the approved or accepted deficit! But a strong economy will have a smaller deficit …

MAJED: Sorry, but who are we talking about exactly?

EVIE: Well, Germany, for example, had a budget deficit of only -0.1% in 2008, but Britain's was about -5.5%. In 2009, Britain's budget deficit had increased to -11.5% and even Germany's had increased to -4.6%.

JACK: So, if the deficit increases, then borrowing increases to enable the government to fulfil its spending commitments.

LEILA: Yes, exactly. Or the government cuts back on its spending commitments.

EVIE: Yes, but reducing the amount of debt is a complex process. We must think about macroeconomies in a global financial environment. But earlier, Majed asked for examples – well in Europe, Portugal, Ireland, Greece, Spain, and Italy, have high levels of debt, but the problem is how to help such countries to make real reductions.

LECTURER: Well done, everyone! I think we've really made a lot of progress!

Note: The underlining relates to Exercise D.

🎧 Exercise D

Check the meaning of 'introducing' phrases. This means a phrase to use before your main statement to announce that you are going to say something. It may also signal how much you are going to say, or how important you think what you are going to say is.

1 Set for individual work and pairwork checking. Feed back.

2 Play Part 2 from Exercise C. Ask students to tell you to stop when they hear each phrase (underlined in the transcript above). Check what kind of phrase they think it is. Get students to repeat the phrase to copy the intonation.

   If you wish, ask students to suggest other phrases that could be used in the same way.

Answers

Model answers:

I'd like to make two points. First, …	a
Can you expand on that?	b
The point is …	d
What's your second point?	b
My second point is that …	a
Yes, but …	c
I don't agree with that because …	c
Sorry, but who are we talking about, exactly?	b
We need to be clear here.	d
I'd just like to say that …	a
In what way?	b
What I'm trying to say is, …	d
Can you give me an example?	b
Look at it this way.	d
Absolutely.	c

Exercise E

With the whole class, revise asking for information. Remind students of the questions used by the lecturer in Unit 5, Lesson 3 (see Unit 5 *Skills bank*). Remind students also about reporting information to people (see Unit 3 *Skills bank*).

Set students to work in groups of four. Each student is provided with the background to the task and various options to try to reduce budget deficits/debt. Students should turn to the relevant page to make notes on the information. When everyone is ready they should feed back to their group, giving an oral report on the information. It's important that they do not simply read aloud the information, but use it to inform their speaking. The group should then discuss the various options, considering the economic, political and social impact of their decisions.

Alternatively, the research activity might be done as a 'wall dictation' as follows. Use Resource 7C in the additional resources section. Make large A3 (or A4) size copies of the information (one set of options per page) and pin the sheets on the classroom walls. Each student (designated A, B, C or D) should leave his/her seat and go to the wall to find the information he/she needs. Students should not write anything down: instead they should read and try to remember the information. Then they return to their group and tell them the information. If they forget something they can go back to the wall to have another look.

Circulate, encouraging students to ask for clarification and to use the appropriate phrases when giving clarification. Note where students are having difficulty with language and where things are going well. When everyone has finished, feed back to the class on points you have noticed while listening in to the discussions.

Exercise F

After a group of four students has made its decisions, make sure that everyone in the group is familiar with the outcome (even if they did not necessarily agree with the choices!)

It is probably best to allow just two groups to compare and reach a new consensus.

So, for example, groups 1 and 3 might work together and groups 2 and 4 likewise.

Then students should try and reach a compromise in these combined groups.

One or two people from each group of eight should then present the decision and the reasons for the decision to the class. It will help their presentation if they use visual aids such as a list of savings. Finally, the whole class should try to reach agreement on the site decision, taking a vote if necessary.

Remind students about agreeing and disagreeing, and about good and bad ways to contribute to seminar discussions (refer to Unit 5 if necessary).

While the representatives are presenting their group decisions, you should occasionally interrupt with a wrong interpretation so that students are forced to clarify their statements. Or you could ask for clarification.

Closure

Prepare the table as a datashow. Ask students in groups of four to think about combinations. Each student should take it in turns to suggest a three-part combination. The other students may accept or challenge his/her choice! Each acceptable combination gains one point. The student who has made the most combinations wins. The teacher should be ready to adjudicate where necessary!

Draw students' attention to the adjective + noun + noun combinations that are common in economic contexts.

adjective	noun	noun
fixed	interest rate	assessment
long-term	benefit	strategy
aggregate	demand	prospect
fiscal	deficit	lending
current	debt	fluctuation
social	account	expansion
maximized	budget	reduction
minimized	risk	forecast
annual	revenue	injection
major	capital	investment
cautious	growth	spending
global	credit	prediction
guaranteed	rate	return
competitive		policy
increased		payment
reduced		

1 Work through the *Vocabulary bank* and *Skills bank* if you have not already done so, or as a revision of previous study.

2 Use the *Activity bank* (*Teacher's Book* additional resources section, Resources 7A).

A Set the crossword for individual work (including homework) or pairwork.

Answers

B Ask students to consider the topic '*Studying effectively*'. Ask them to make a few bullet points related to what students *have to/must/should* do. For example:

- *make good notes*
- *buy a good dictionary*
- *revise carefully*
- *practise listening*

Then ask students in pairs to transform them into *Wh~* cleft sentences. For example:

Student A: *I have to revise my notes regularly*

Student B: *What you have to do is to revise …*

Student B: *I have to listen more to native speakers.*

Student A: *What you have to do is to listen …*

If there is time, you could ask students to make similar transformations related to other topics such as *Relaxing outside class* or even *How the X government should improve the economic situation!*

8 THE ECONOMICS OF AGRICULTURE

This unit looks at the special market relationship between economics and agriculture. The provision of food is essential for human well-being but global hunger is a serious obstacle to a decent standard of living for hundreds of millions of people. Not surprisingly, economists feel a high level of responsibility to improve this situation. They try to understand the markets for agricultural products and find suitable methods of description and analysis. This can be used to improve policy and planning.

The unit will reinforce students' awareness of the trade in agricultural products. It will help students to understand the importance of commodity prices. Certain concepts from the discipline are briefly considered in order to illustrate the potential role of economics. The reading text discusses various aspects of economics in global agricultural policy. It highlights a number of debates on production, consumption, protection and supply. Students are encouraged to engage critically with the topic through the approaches to essay writing.

Skills focus

Reading
- understanding dependent clauses with passives

Writing
- paraphrasing
- expanding notes into complex sentences
- recognizing different essay types/structures:
  descriptive
  analytical
  comparison/evaluation
  argument
- writing essay plans
- writing essays

Vocabulary focus
- synonyms
- nouns from verbs
- definitions
- common 'direction' verbs in essay titles (*discuss, analyze, evaluate*, etc.)

Key vocabulary

alleviate	elasticity	mechanism	starvation
arise	facility	minimal	storage
aware	fluctuation	perishability	subject (to)
barrier	inelasticity	proportionately	subsistence
biofuel	infrastructure	release	surplus
buffer stocks	justification	replace	tariff
consistent	long-term (adj)	soar	variable
deprivation	magnitude	staple	wastage

8.1 Vocabulary

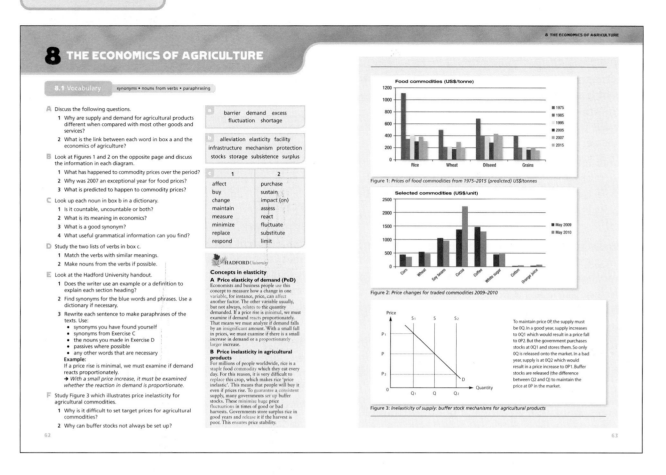

Lesson aims

- extend knowledge of synonyms and word sets (enables paraphrasing at word level)
- make nouns and noun phrases from verbs (enables paraphrasing at sentence level)

Further practice in paraphrasing at sentence level with:

- passives
- synonymous phrases
- negatives
- replacement subjects

Introduction

Revise ways of paraphrasing sentences. Write the following sentences based on Unit 6 Lesson 2 on the board and ask students to say what changes have been made to the paraphrased sentences.

Original sentence: *The minimum fair-trade price covers the cost of sustainable production for the farmer.*

Paraphrase: *For the producer, the everyday expenses of growing the crop are balanced by the guaranteed fair-trade price.*

(answer: change in word order, active to passive, use of synonyms)

Original sentence: *Farmers can negotiate a higher minimum price for better quality or organic products.*

Paraphrase: *For superior or organic commodities, negotiations for a raised guaranteed price can be carried out.*

(answer: change in word order, use of synonyms, replacement subject, active to passive)

Exercise A

Set for pairwork or class discussion. Accept any reasonable answers.

Answers

Possible answers:

1 Supply and demand for agricultural products: different because 1. food is essential to life (especially demand for staple foods, e.g., rice, flour, cooking oil, etc.) 2. supply can be unpredictable because of weather conditions, natural disasters, crop diseases and political circumstances.

Note: Students may know that the trading in agricultural commodities relates to 'futures', that is

153

to future prices of the items. The 'buyer' of such futures may not keep them or need them (as food commodities) but is trying to make a profit on the sale. This speculation is sometimes responsible for higher food prices than the actual supply or demand situation would justify.

2 **barrier**: agricultural products are subject to various kinds of trade barriers, usually to protect the agricultural industry. Developing countries often point out the unfairness of closing major markets to their agricultural products.

demand: more urgent demand for agricultural products than for other consumer goods. For most people around the world, demand for agricultural products is based on necessity and so supply is crucial.

excess: there can be an excess of agricultural products in good years which will ensure supply (and probably keep prices down). Note: the developing world in particular does not always have the facilities to store surplus food products.

fluctuation: prices for food commodities have fluctuated a lot (see graphs in the Course Book, page 63). Note: at a subsistence level, a small fluctuation in food prices can cause serious, life-threatening problems.

shortage: population growth and poor distribution of food cause shortages. The dramatic failures of harvests or absence of rain in many areas cause severe shortages and require massive food aid from the World Food Programme.

Exercise B

Set for pairwork discussion. Check that students understand the vocabulary shown in the figures (*grains, soy beans, wheat* and *corn*). Remind students that interpreting such figures is very important for an economist. Tell students to bear in mind the points they have just discussed. Feed back with the whole class.

Answers
Possible answers:

1 Staple commodity prices are lower than 30 years ago. In some cases, particularly for rice, the current price is approximately 70% less than in 1975. However, in the past 25 years, price levels have remained relatively stable.

2 2007 was an exceptional year for food prices as all commodities shown on the graph increased in price.

3 Commodity prices are predicted to remain relatively stable.

Exercise C

Set for pairwork. You may wish to divide the work up between different pairs. For question 4 (useful grammatical information), tell students to look out for words that can have the same form when used as a noun or verb, nouns that can be only singular or only plural, nouns that change their meaning when used as U or C, etc.

Feed back, building up the table in the Answers section on the board.

Answers
Model answers:

See table at top of next page.

Exercise D

Set for individual work and pairwork checking. Make sure students understand that they should find a verb in column 2 with a similar meaning to one of the verbs in column 1.

Feed back with the whole class, discussing the extent to which the verbs are exact synonyms, and if not, identifying any differences in meaning.

Answers
Model answers:

See table below.

Verb	Noun	Verb	Noun
affect	effect (N.B. spelling)	impact (on)	impact
buy	in everyday language, *buy* may be used in the collocation *a good buy*, but generally not noun	purchase	purchase
change	change	fluctuate	fluctuation
maintain	maintenance	sustain	sustainability
measure	measurement	assess	assessment
minimize	usually not noun but *minimization* = making the computer screen smaller	limit	limitation
replace	replacement	substitute	substitution; substitute
respond	response	react	reaction

Word	C/U	Meaning in economics	Synonym	Useful grammatical information
alleviation	U	reduction, diminishing, lessening	*improvement*; used to show a qualitative change, usually from a poor situation to a slightly better condition; *improvement in the patient's condition; alleviation of hunger through the World Food Programme*	*alleviation* is usually followed by the preposition *of*, whereas *improvement* is usually followed by the preposition *in*
elasticity	U	concept related to effect of a variable, such as price, on another variable, such as demand	*flexibility*; usually used to indicate the capacity of something to change dependent on other factors	
facility	C	provision of service	*service*	usually used in plural form to describe suitability of amenities or premises, e.g., *modern facilities*
infrastructure	U	system or network of communications and transport	*network*; usually used to cover transport, communications and utilities such as electricity, etc.	
mechanism	C	method or process to get a specific result	*measure; process*	
protection	U	barrier or tariff measure to protect, for example, against cheap imports	*restriction; barrier*	
stocks	C	1 goods kept in depot or storage (as used in text) 2 alternative word for shares in company	*supplies*	used in singular with prepositions; *in stock* but *out of stock*
storage	U	process of storing commodities	*depot; warehouse* (place for storage)	used as prepositional phrase: *in storage*
subsistence	U	standard of life with just enough food/money to stay alive	*survival*; also *very low standard of living*	used in collocations – *subsistence farming; subsistence level*
surplus	C/U	extra or additional goods; commodities, money, etc. which are more than needed	*excess*	usually singular

Exercise E

This is an exercise in paraphrasing based on word and sentence level techniques. As well as finding their own synonyms from memory and using the synonyms already discussed in Exercises C and D, students will use noun phrases in place of verb phrases as a technique in paraphrasing. Students should also make passive sentences wherever they can.

1 Set for individual work. Feed back with the whole class.

2 Set for individual work and pairwork checking. Remind students that they might need to change the grammar of a sentence depending on which synonym(s) they choose.

3 Set for pairwork; pairs then check with other pairs. Alternatively, tell some students to write their answers on an OHT or other visual medium, for discussion by the whole class.

Answers

Model answers:

1 A A technical definition is provided.

B A context with an example (rice) is provided; a further explanation follows before a more exact definition.

2 Possible synonyms (including synonyms from Exercises C and D). Students may require some help with rephrasing for some sentences.

A **Price elasticity of demand (PeD)**

Economists and business people (*use*) <u>utilize</u> this concept to measure how a change in one (*variable*) <u>factor</u>, for instance, price, can (*affect*) <u>impact on</u> another factor. The other variable usually, but not always, (*relates to*) <u>refers to/affects</u> the quantity demanded. If a price rise is (*minimal*) <u>insignificant/small/minor</u>, we must examine if demand (*reacts*) <u>responds</u> proportionately. That means we must analyze if demand falls by (*an insignificant*) <u>a tiny/a small/an insubstantial</u> amount. With a small fall in prices, we must examine if there is a small increase in demand or a (*proportionately larger increase*) <u>an increase to a greater degree/an increase to a proportionately larger extent</u>.

B **Price inelasticity in agricultural products**

For millions of people worldwide, rice is a (*staple*) basic/essential food (*commodity*) product/item which they eat every day. For this reason, it is very difficult to (*replace*) substitute this crop which makes rice 'price inelastic'. This means that people will buy it even if prices rise. To (*guarantee*) ensure/be sure of a (*consistent*) regular/reliable supply, many governments (*set up*) establish buffer stocks. These (*minimize*) limit/reduce/avoid (*huge*) large/significant price (*fluctuations*) changes/alterations in times of good or bad harvests. Governments store surplus rice in good years and (*release*) it distribute/make (it) available if the harvest is poor. This (*ensures*) guarantees price stability.

3 Possible paraphrases:

A **Price elasticity of demand (PeD)**

This concept is utilized by economists and entrepreneurs to assess how, for example, variation in one factor such as price can impact on another variable.*

The factor 'quantity', i.e., how much is demanded, is most commonly referred to.

With a small price increase, it must be examined whether the reaction in demand is proportionate.

That is, it is necessary to analyze whether demand is reduced insignificantly.

In case of a minor reduction in prices, it must be examined whether demand increases in proportion by an equally small or by a larger amount.

*The term *variable* is an accepted technical designation and does not need a paraphrased version.

B **Price inelasticity in agricultural products**

For a large proportion of the global population, a staple food element is provided by rice, which is their main daily food item.

Price inelasticity of this commodity occurs because it cannot be easily substituted.

It is purchased even in times of price increases.

To ensure regular availability of the crop, buffer stocks are established by numerous governments.

In this way, large price changes are limited when crop supplies are reduced.

Excess produce is stored after good harvests and (it is)* made available by governments if harvests are bad.

In this way, stable prices are guaranteed.

*These words may be omitted to make a 'reduced passive' form.

Exercise F

Set for pair or small group discussion. Feed back with the whole class. Accept any reasonable suggestions. This is quite a challenging task but encourage students to focus on the price-fixing aspect, as well as thinking about the overall difficulty.

Answers

Possible answers:

1 (*Why is it difficult to set target prices for agricultural commodities?*)
   - basic human needs
   - risk of starvation/severe shortage if miscalculated
   - products subject to weather conditions
   - fluctuations in supply
   - harvests are difficult to predict
   - crops may be for home consumption or export
   - price may be fixed for home consumption but then bad harvest → hunger
   - prices may be fixed for export then surplus → importers unhappy → new contracts
   - guaranteed price (remind students of fair trade) may not be at market price level
   - farmers want to benefit from production in good and bad years

2 (*Why can buffer stocks not always be set up?*)
   - crops are not necessarily suitable
   - lack of capital to buy up surplus stocks
   - lack of storage facilities
   - lack of infrastructure for distribution in bad years
   - dissatisfied farmers want to benefit from higher prices in poor years

Closure

Ask students to work in pairs and discuss in what ways the oil industry and oil, as a commodity, are similar to food commodities markets and in what ways they are different. Ask students to concentrate on:

supply

demand

prices

control

Possible ideas:

Supply can fluctuate (political factors; natural factors; accidents; price factors; new fields discovered; more efficiency).

Demand is consistent and increasing (substitutes are difficult to find in many cases).

Demand can, however, fluctuate according to economic

activity or in a global/local crisis.

Demand can be affected by macroeconomic factors, e.g., increases in petrol taxes (duties) which are imposed by governments. Most governments try to avoid taxing food products for consumers.

Prices fluctuate because oil is traded internationally but OPEC will intervene if prices fall too low. During such interventions, production is usually reduced.

Control is different than for agricultural products because OPEC is a powerful global body that can make decisions on cutting or increasing production dependent on world market price. Profit is all-important to this industry. The food industry is also driven by profit motives but governments will often intervene to protect their citizens if food prices increase dramatically. Governments will not usually intervene when oil prices increase.

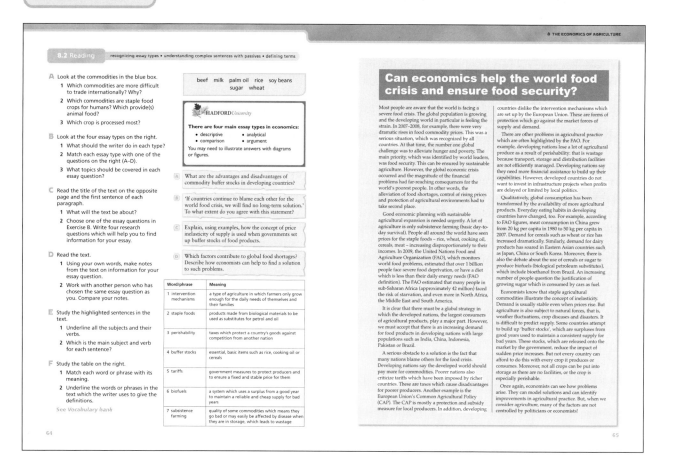

General note

Read the *Vocabulary bank* and *Skills bank* at the end of the Course Book unit. Decide when, if at all, to refer students to them. The *Vocabulary bank* section *Understanding new words: using definitions* is relevant to Lesson 8.2; the *Skills bank* will be more relevant to Lessons 3 and 4.

Lesson aims

- understand essay types
- interpret essay titles
- find the main information in a passive clause
- understand internal definitions (see *Vocabulary bank*)

Further practice in:

- reading research
- finding the kernel of a long sentence

Introduction

With the whole class, discuss how to use written texts as sources of information when writing an answer for an essay question. Ask students:

1 *How can you choose useful sources?* (to get an idea of whether a text might be useful, survey the text, i.e., look at the title, look at the beginning and the end and the first line of each paragraph; in other words, skim-read to get an approximate idea of the text contents)

2 *If you decide that a text is going to be useful, what is it a good idea to do …*

… before reading? (think of questions related to the essay question to which you would like to find some answers)

… while reading? (identify useful parts of the text; make notes **in your own words**)

… after reading? (check answers to the questions)

Exercise A

Set the three questions for pairwork discussion with whole class feedback.

Answers

Possible answers:

1 Rice and milk. Only rice and milk are not traded internationally. Rice may be traded in some national South East Asian markets. Milk is virtually impossible to trade internationally as so many production factors are involved. It is perishable. Some milk is sold directly on local markets but it is also produced in huge quantities and then processed. Some is stored in the form of milk powder. Some countries have high technology for pasteurizing or homogenizing milk, others do not.

2 Human staple foods include milk, wheat, rice, meat (beef) and, for developed countries, sugar. The others are not really staple foods. Very large quantities of soy beans are fed to animals.

3 Students might say 'milk' but in fact it is almost certainly palm oil which is used in thousands of hygiene products (soaps, creams, shampoos, cosmetics), food products (margarine, biscuits, chocolate) and many more.

Exercise B

1 Refer students to the lecture slide. Discuss this question with the whole class. Build up the table in the Answers section on the board.

2 Set for pairwork. Feed back with the whole class. Ask the class to identify the key words in each title which indicate what type of writing it is.

3 Set for pairwork. Feed back using the second table in the Answers section, discussing with the whole class which topics will need to be included in each essay. Add the notes in the third column.

Answers

Possible answers:

1

	What the writer should do
Descriptive writing	describe or summarize key ideas/key events/key points. Give the plain facts. Could involve writing about: a narrative description (a history of something); a process (how something happens); key ideas in a theory; main points of an article (answers the question *What is/are …?*)
Analytical writing	try to analyze (= go behind the plain facts) or explain something or give reasons for a situation; may also question accepted ideas and assumptions (answers the question *Why/how …?*)
Comparison	compare two or more aspects/ideas/things/people, etc.; usually also evaluate, i.e., say which is better/bigger, etc.
Argument writing	give an opinion and support the opinion with evidence/reasons, etc.; may also give opposing opinions (= counter-arguments) and show how they are wrong

2/3 See table below. Key words are underlined:

Type of writing	Question	Topics
Descriptive writing	D <u>Which factors</u> contribute to global food shortages? <u>Describe</u> how economists can help to find a solution to such problems.	• how serious is the global food shortage? • factors which contribute to it • role of economists to find solution
Analytical writing	C <u>Explain</u>, using examples, <u>how the concept of</u> price inelasticity of supply is used when governments set up buffer stocks of food products.	• what is price inelasticity of supply? • how the concept works for agricultural commodities • examples of buffer stock commodities
Comparison	A <u>What are the advantages and disadvantages of</u> commodity buffer stocks in developing countries?	• 'buffer stocks', what are they? • commodities which are (not) stored • special status of developing countries • advantages • disadvantages
Argument writing	B 'If countries continue to blame each other for the world food crisis, we will find no long-term solution'. <u>To what extent do you agree</u> with this statement?	• definition of 'world food crisis' • type of 'blame' linked to problem • who blames who? • how justified is this blame? • meaning of a 'long-term solution'

Exercise C

1 Set for individual work. Feed back with the whole class.

2 If necessary, remind students of the purpose of research questions and do one or two examples as a class. Set for individual work and pairwork checking. Feed back, getting good research questions for each essay topic on the board.

Answers

Possible answers:

1 The title suggests that the text will consider the link between economics and global hunger and whether a solution can be found. The question format implies that economics may only be a partial answer as the topic is extremely complex. The world food crisis is commonly analyzed from many perspectives – climate change, environmental concerns, food production, patterns of consumption, farming methods, genetically modified crops, development aid and others. These perspectives are sometimes affected by subjective, political or emotional views. Economics provides a way of analyzing the issues in order to provide more objective answers.

The topic sentence for each paragraph is reproduced here.

Paragraph 1: *Most people are aware that the world is facing a severe food crisis.*
This paragraph is going to give details of the global situation.

Paragraph 2: *Good economic planning with sustainable agricultural expansion is needed urgently.*
This paragraph provides a statement of how economics and global agricultural strategy must cooperate, especially to develop sustainability.

Paragraph 3: *It is clear that there must be a global strategy in which the developed nations, the largest consumers of agricultural products, play a major part.*
This paragraph reminds us that the division of the world into developing and developed countries is at the heart of the problem. The richer nations have a responsibility to cooperate and a key interest in helping.

Paragraph 4: *A serious obstacle to a solution is the fact that many nations blame others for the food crisis.*
Here there is an emphasis on blame and what the nature of this criticism is.

Paragraph 5: *There are other problems in agricultural practice which are often highlighted by the FAO.*
The emphasis in this paragraph is on practical issues in farming, related to efficiency, management, production and distribution methods.

Paragraph 6: *Qualitatively, global consumption has been transformed by the availability of more agricultural products.*
This paragraph switches attention to changing consumption patterns.

Paragraph 7: *Economists know that staple agricultural commodities illustrate the concept of inelasticity.*
This paragraph focuses on the concept in economics which is widely used to explain, analyze and enlighten thinking about supply and demand in a very special area of consumption. The reader anticipates a definition and the text provides a brief explanation.

Paragraph 8: *Once again, economists can see how problems arise.*
The final paragraph relates back to the title. It points to a realistic assessment of the situation but without being over-optimistic.

2 Answers depend on the students.

Exercise D

Set for individual work then pairwork comparison/ checking. If you wish, students can make notes under the headings in the 'Topics' column of the table in Exercise B. Encourage students to make notes in their own words. Teachers might like to follow up further on the points which are underlined or visit the websites given. Alternatively, teachers might like to suggest that the students do this.

Answers

Possible notes:

A *What are the advantages and disadvantages of commodity buffer stocks in developing countries?*

- definition of buffer stocks; surplus agricultural commodities purchased and stored by governments to ensure stable prices for essential (staple) food products
- outline of the process for release of buffer stocks (in times of bad harvest)
- commodities which are (not) stored – usually non-perishable items which can be stored without wastage (e.g., cereals, rice, cooking oil)
- why do developing countries come into a special category? Obviously they are developing, i.e., infrastructure may be incomplete; problems of wastage, etc.
- advantages – price stability; no unfair price rises in bad years; people recognize government intervention helps people
- disadvantages – farmers may not be happy with buffer price level anyway; needs a lot of money to store goods; needs good distribution and organization

B *'If countries continue to blame each other for the world food crisis, we will find no long-term solution.' To what extent do you agree with this statement?*

- definition of 'world food crisis'; details about world food deprivation; <u>use FAO statistics; point out rising food prices especially in 2007–2008, www.fao.org</u>

- why is 'blame' linked to problem? Not productive but understandable; many areas of the world have very large numbers of hungry people because only subsistence farming; lack of investment in infrastructure in developing countries; developed world only interested in own food security

- who blames who? Developing world mentions tariffs and other forms of protection <u>(details of these at FAO or www.eubusiness.com for CAP)</u>

- blame from developed countries about lack of infrastructure – storage, transport, distribution, etc.

- how justified is this blame? Tariffs certainly limit sale of produce; intervention mechanisms protect local (European) farmers – <u>also check US Department of Agriculture at www.usda.gov)</u>

- developed world argument about lack of infrastructure is rather weak; investment in agriculture or infrastructure is not profitable enough for investors!

- meaning of a 'long-term solution' – sustainable results both in food production for rising population and more freedom for developing world to export

C *Explain, using examples, <u>how the concept of</u> price inelasticity of supply is used when governments set up buffer stocks of food products.*

- definition and explanation of elasticity and price inelasticity of supply

- explain why the concept is important and why food products are different from most other goods (compare oil?)

- how the concept works for agricultural commodities; illustrate using diagram

- definition of buffer stocks and the process – surplus agricultural commodities purchased and stored by governments to ensure stable prices for essential (staple) food products

- examples of buffer stock commodities; discussion of problems – type of crops, cost, infrastructure

- concept is part of economists' analysis; real world is often different

D <u>*Which factors*</u> *contribute to global food shortages? <u>Describe</u> how economists can help to find a solution to such problems.*

- definition and examples of global food shortages – systemic/natural disasters/farming methods/developing world vs developed world

- outline of how serious food deprivation is

- factors contributing to problems – natural (disease, weather, food, crop failure) but also human factors – changes in demand and consumption patterns; price increases for staple foods; lack of infrastructure; protection (tariffs); use of crops for biofuels

- what economists can do to analyze world agriculture – data gathering; develop models; focus on inelasticity; advise on buffer stocks; suggest fair practice

- big issues: is there a long-term solution? Can the FAO extend its work/influence? Will the developed world accept more responsibility? Economists have an important role to play.

Exercise E

Set for individual work and pairwork checking. Students could copy out the sentences in their notebooks and then underline all the verbs and subjects.

Feed back with the whole class, building up the table in the Answers section on the board. Point out that each sentence has two verbs, which means that each sentence has at least two *clauses*. This means that the sentences are complex. (A simple sentence has only one main verb and subject.) To enable students to identify which is the 'main' part of the sentence (in bold in the table on the next page), ask how the other clauses are 'joined' and add the joining words (here: a time word and relative pronouns). The main part of the sentence is linked to the *dependent* part with these words.

Check understanding of the passives in each case by asking how each clause or sentence could be rephrased with an active verb. Provide assistance if sentence structure causes problems for some students.

Answers

Possible answers:

See table at top of next page.

Language note

The choice of whether to use an active or a passive construction often depends on how the writer wants to structure the information. Refer to Unit 7 *Skills bank* for a note on information structure.

	Joining word	Subject	Verb	Object/complement
1		a serious <u>situation</u>*		
	which		was recognized	by all countries
2		Poorer <u>nations</u>	criticize	tariffs
	which		have been imposed	by richer countries
3		developing <u>countries</u>	dislike	**intervention mechanisms**
	which		are set up	by the European Union
4		developed <u>countries</u>	do not want	to invest in infrastructure projects
	when	<u>profits</u>	are delayed or limited	by local politics

*the underlined noun is the head word of the noun phrase

Exercise F

Set for individual work and pairwork checking. In question 2, tell students to look for the actual words used and the punctuation, grammatical and vocabulary devices which are used to indicate meanings.

Feed back with the whole class, pointing out the structures given in the third column of the table for question 2 in the Answers section. If you wish, refer students to the *Vocabulary bank – Understanding new words: using definitions*.

Answers

1

Word/phrase	Meaning
1 intervention mechanisms	government measures to protect producers and to ensure a fixed and stable price for them
2 staple foods	essential, basic items such as rice, cooking oil or cereals
3 perishability	quality of some commodities which means they go bad or may easily be affected by disease when they are in storage, which leads to wastage
4 buffer stocks	a system which uses a surplus from a good year to maintain a reliable and cheap supply for bad years
5 tariffs	taxes which protect a country's goods against competition from another nation
6 biofuels	products made from biological materials to be used as substitutes for petrol or oil
7 subsistence farming	a type of agriculture in which farmers only grow enough for the daily needs of themselves and their families

Closure

Put this list of everyday products with an agricultural connection on the board.

Ask students to look at the list before considering the questions below.

Shampoo

Biscuits

Margarine

Packet soup

Frozen meat (e.g., chicken)

Fresh vegetables

Frozen vegetables

Bread

Soap

Cooking oil

Chocolate

Processed meat (e.g. hot dogs, hamburgers)

Breakfast cereals such as corn flakes

Students should work in small groups and choose two or three items. Then they should discuss the following:

1 What agricultural products are involved?

2 Can there be shortages of the main items? What happens in such situations?

3 Can producers build up buffer stocks of the main items?

4 What divisions between the developing and developed world are represented by these items?

2 Model answers:

Word/phrase	Actual words giving the meaning	Punctuation/vocab/structure
subsistence farming	(basic day-to-day survival)	word/phrase followed by definition in brackets
staple foods	– rice, wheat, cooking oil, cereals, meat –	word/phrase followed by a dash + examples then another dash
tariffs	These are taxes which cause disadvantages for poorer producers.	demonstrative pronoun (plural) + verb *be* + noun phrase + *which* (relative clause) + verb
intervention mechanisms	These are forms of protection which go against the market forces of supply and demand.	demonstrative pronoun (plural) + verb *be* + noun phrase + *which* (relative clause) + verb
perishability	: that is wastage because transport, storage and distribution facilities are not efficiently managed.	colon + *that is* + noun phrase + reason
biofuels	(biological petroleum substitutes)	word/phrase followed by definition in brackets
buffer stocks	, which are surpluses from good years used to maintain a consistent supply for bad years.	word/phrase followed by a comma + *which* (relative clause, including here, a reduced relative, *used*)

8.3 Extending skills

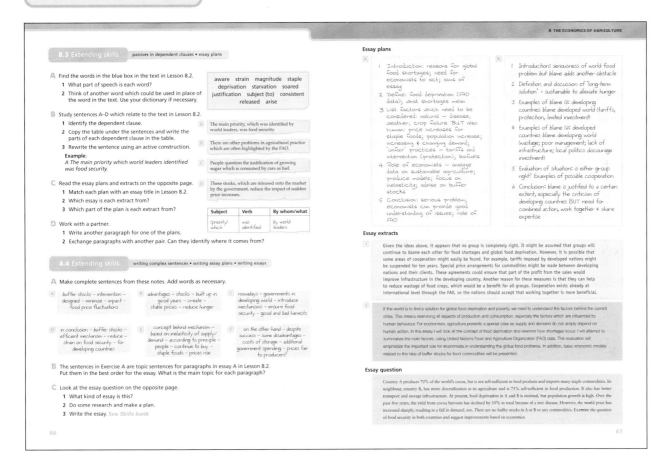

Lesson aims

- find the main information in a passive dependent clause
- recognize appropriate writing plans for essay types

Further practice in:

- vocabulary from Lesson 8.2

Introduction

Choose about 10–15 words from the previous unit which you think that students should revise. Write them in a random arrangement and at different angles (i.e., not in a vertical list) on an OHT, other visual medium, or on the board. Allow students two minutes to look at and remember the words, and then take them away. Students should write down all the words they can remember.

Exercise A

Set for individual work and pairwork checking. Feed back with the whole class.

Answers

Model answers (paragraph numbers are given in brackets):

Word	Part of speech	Another word
aware (1)	adj. N.B. with prep. *of*	informed (about); familiar (with); knowledgeable (about); conscious (of)
strain (1)	n (C)	difficulty; pressure; stress
magnitude (1)	n (U)	size; dimension
staple (2)	adj	basic; essential
deprivation (2)	n (C)	lack; absence; shortage
starvation (2)	n (U)	hunger
soared (6)	v (past participle)	rose/increased (but with idea of *rapidly* or *sharply*)
justification (6)	n (C)	reason; rationale
subject (to) (7)	adj + prep	dependent (on); influenced (by)
consistent (7)	adj	regular; stable
released (7)	v (past participle)	made available; distributed; circulated
arise (8)	v (I)	occur; happen (N.B. these verbs are also intransitive)

Exercise B

Set for individual work and pairwork checking. Make sure that students can correctly identify the main clause, the dependent clause and the linking word. Do the first transformation with the class to check that they know what to do. Note that they do not need to rewrite the main clauses. Also, if no agent is given they will need to supply one themselves.

Answers

Model answers:

1/2 See table below.

3 A The main priority which world leaders identified was food security.

B There are other problems in agricultural practice which the FAO often highlights.

C People question the justification of growing sugar which cars consume as fuel.

D These stocks, which the government releases onto the market, reduce the impact of sudden price increases.

Exercise C

Tell students to look back at the essay questions in Lesson 8.2. You may also need to remind them of the topics which you decided are suitable for the essay.

Set all three questions for individual work and pairwork checking. Feed back with the whole class. Ask students to say what aspects of the plans and the extracts enabled them to be identified. Check that students can match the parts of the extracts with the corresponding parts of the essay plan.

Answers

Model answers:

1 Essay plan A = essay title D (Essay type: Descriptive)

Which factors contribute to global food shortages? Describe how economists can help to find a solution to such problems.

Essay plan B = essay title B (Essay type: Argument)

'If countries continue to blame each other for the world food crisis, we will find no long-term solution.' To what extent do you agree with this statement?

2 Extract 1 = essay plan B

Extract 2 = essay plan A

3 Extract 1 = Plan B, point 5: *Evaluation of situation: is either group right? Examples of possible cooperation.*

Extract 2 = Plan A, point 1: *Introduction: reasons for global food shortages; need for economists to act; aims of essay.*

Language note

Sometimes topic sentences are not the first sentence of a paragraph. As can be seen in point 5 of essay B, the first sentence of the paragraph links with the previous paragraph. The topic is given in the second sentence.

Exercise D

Remind students about writing topic sentences. Set for pairwork. Even students who chose one of these two essay questions in Lesson 8.2 should refer to the model essay plans/notes in the Course Book. In all cases, students should write using their own words, i.e., paraphrase the ideas in the text.

If you wish, you could ask some students – perhaps those who finish early – to write their paragraphs on an OHT, or other visual medium; for all the class to look at. Comment on the extent to which students have managed to paraphrase, whether they have successfully covered the point in the plan, and whether their topic sentence is supported well by the sentences that follow.

Closure

Ask students to finish the following sentences as quickly as possible.

The basic objective of buffer stocks is …

'Subsistence farming' is …

'Sustainable agriculture' means …

'Futures' are … which …

The CAP is …

'Price inelasticity of demand' means …

An example of a staple food commodity is …

An international organization which oversees farming issues is …

	Main clause	Linking word	Dependent clause		
			Subject	Verb	By whom/what
A	The main priority	which	–	was identified	by world leaders …
B	There are other problems in agricultural practice	which	–	are highlighted	by the FAO.
C	People question the justification of growing sugar	which	–	is consumed	by cars …
D	These stocks …	which	–	are released …	by the government …

8.4 Extending skills

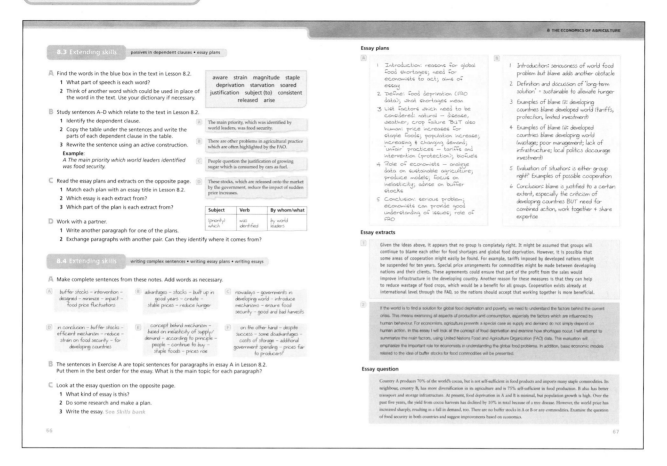

Lesson aims

- expand notes into complex sentences
- make an essay plan
- write an essay

Further practice in:

- writing topic sentences
- expanding a topic sentence into a paragraph
- writing complex sentences with passives
- identifying required essay type

Introduction

Remind students about complex and compound sentences – that is, sentences with more than one clause. Remind students that academic texts typically consist of sentences with several clauses. Give the following simple sentences (or make your own) and ask students to add some more clauses to them:

The global financial crisis means changing priorities.

Sustainable agriculture means food security.

The FAO must monitor the global food situation.

Food deprivation is a very serious issue.

Food consumption habits are changing.

Supplies of basic foods can be affected by bad weather.

Exercise A

Set for individual work and pairwork checking. Remind students that they should try to make sentences in a good 'academic' style. Also remind them to use passives where necessary/possible, and to look out for ways of making dependent clauses, such as relative pronouns, linking words, etc. They will also need to pay attention to making correct verb tenses.

Feed back with the whole class.

Answers

Possible answers:

A Buffer stocks are a type of intervention which is designed to minimize the impact of food price fluctuations.

B The advantages are that stocks are built up in good years to create stable prices and reduce hunger.

C Nowadays, governments in the developing world can introduce mechanisms which ensure food security in times of good and bad harvests.

D In conclusion, buffer stocks are an efficient mechanism to reduce the strain on food security for developing countries.

E The concept behind the mechanism is based on the principle of inelasticity of supply and demand, according to which people continue to buy staple foods even when prices rise.

F On the other hand, despite the success of buffer stocks, there are some disadvantages such as the costs of storage, the additional government spending and the question of whether prices are fair to producers.

Exercise B

Set for individual work. Feed back with the whole class. Point out how this comparison essay is organized by discussing all the advantages first and then all the disadvantages. (See *Skills bank* for an alternative approach to comparison.)

If you wish, you could take this exercise further, asking students to build on the topic sentences by suggesting what ideas could follow the topic sentence in each paragraph. For this they will need to refer to ideas in the text.

Answers

Model answers:

See table below.

Exercise C

Discuss question 1 with the whole class. Set the research and planning (question 2) for group work, and the writing for individual work (this could be done at home). Students can do web searches on buffer stocks, commodities and cooperation agreements for agricultural commodities.

Answers

1 Model answer:

This essay is largely analytical since it requires careful analysis of a number of factors in each country, identifying reasons (possibly using a SWOT approach) for the current situation. It also asks students to think critically about the economics of the situation and make appropriate suggestions based on these principles.

2 Possible essay plan:

Introduction: definition of food security; analysis of situation; typical single crop agriculture situation in A; country B is apparently in better situation but needs to maximize revenue from food production; aims of essay.

Most important points

Country A:

- world cocoa price has increased but demand has fallen
- yield has been reduced because of tree disease
- need for more diverse agriculture
- reduction in food deprivation is required; population growth
- need to maximize revenue from cocoa
- infrastructure problems
- lack of food self-sufficiency

Country B:

- self-sufficiency in food
- diversity in agriculture
- good infrastructure
- population growth

Next points

Options for both countries

- continue in isolation – discuss, e.g., both have growing populations; food security issues; global cocoa market; infrastructure factors

	Topic sentences	Paragraph topic
C	Nowadays, governments in the developing world can introduce mechanisms which ensure food security in times of good and bad harvests.	introduction
A	Buffer stocks are a type of intervention which is designed to minimize the impact of food price fluctuations.	definition
E	The concept behind the mechanism is based on the principle of inelasticity of supply and demand, according to which people continue to buy staple foods even when prices rise.	explanation of how the mechanism works
B	The advantages are that stocks are built up in good years to create stable prices and reduce hunger.	advantages of buffer stocks
F	On the other hand, despite the success of buffer stocks, there are some disadvantages such as the costs of storage, the additional government spending and the question of whether prices are fair to producers.	disadvantages of buffer stocks
D	In conclusion, buffer stocks are an efficient mechanism to reduce the strain on food security for developing countries.	conclusion

- cooperate and make agreements – discuss, e.g., benefit to both countries; opportunity to start new relationship; buffer stocks for cocoa to stabilize world prices and maximize revenue; maximize B's storage and infrastructure facilities; identify staple food crops from B for storage and distribution to both countries

Conclusion: cooperation agreement is the way forward; provide model for other countries; encourage regional cooperation rather than rivalry and competition; make progress towards fairer prices for major traded commodities such as coffee, cocoa, sugar from the developing world.

Closure

Ask students if they can remember a word or words from the unit ...

	Example(s)
beginning with *sub*	subsistence, substitute
beginning with *in*	inelasticity, infrastructure
ending with *ity*	perishability/inelasticity/facility
ending with *age*	wastage, storage
with two syllables	aware, surplus/affect
with three syllables	consistent, magnitude, variable, protection
with four syllables	economy, infrastructure, fluctuation
with five syllables	alleviation, proportionately
a verb beginning with *re*	react, respond, replace
which is an uncountable noun	perishability, subsistence, storage, wastage
which is an adverb	proportionately, qualitatively
which goes together with another word	(buffer) stocks, (subsistence) farming, (staple) foods, food (security)
which is difficult to pronounce	inelasticity, proportionately, mechanism (students' answers will vary)

Accept all reasonable answers.

1 Work through the *Vocabulary bank* and *Skills bank* if you have not already done so, or as a revision of previous study.

2 Use the *Activity bank* (Teacher's Book additional resources section, Resource 8A).

   A Set the wordsearch for individual work (including homework) or pairwork. Establish that the words are uncountable in the context in which they are used in the unit, although some can be countable in other contexts.

   Answers

   B Set the spelling exercise for individual work and pairwork checking. If students are having difficulty, give them the first letter of the word.

   Answers

Jumbled word	Correct spelling
lfubeoi	biofuel
naatssubeli	sustainable
elspat	staple
atrffi	tariff
ybusisd	subsidy
chsanmemi	mechanism
iiiflcatse	facilities
tyovpre	poverty
ncotissnte	consistent
tskcos	stocks

3 Check word stress by writing the following words on the board *without* stress markings. Students have to mark the stress and pronounce the words correctly.

con'sumption	'concept
'maximize	'surplus
sur'vival	e'conomy
'mechanism	'subsidize
a'lleviate	agri'cultural

4 Remind students of how to give definitions (see Lesson 8.2). Then select five or six familiar items (e.g., iPod, laptop, sunglasses, pen, mobile phone) and ask students to think of definitions (e.g., *it's something that you use to listen to music, you need these when it is sunny*, etc.).

This can also be done the other way round by giving the definitions and asking students to guess the word or phrase; once they get the idea students can come up with items, questions and definitions from this unit. Other forms for definitions can include:

   (tariff) *This is a trade protection mechanism which …*

   (FAO) *This is an organization which …*

   (Washington) *The main location of the IMF*

   (buffer stocks) *If you want to stabilize food commodity prices, you need to build up …*

   (biofuels) *These are substitutes for petrol made from biological materials*

Other categories which can be used to practise both the language of definition as well as general economics and cultural knowledge include:

- organizations or institutions such as FAO, WTO, WB, CAP, EU, IMF, OPEC
- familiar international currencies
- important personalities in politics and economics

Or, if you prefer, use sports personalities, famous people or familiar places for the students. An alternative is to use the typical quiz show format, e.g.,

   What 'R' is an important staple food? (Rice)

   What 'I' is an important concept in supply and demand economics? (Inelasticity)

   What 'V' refers to a value or factor in mathematical formulae? (Variable)

9 THE ECONOMICS OF HEALTH CARE

This unit focuses on welfare economics and one related sector, health care. It is designed to present a balance between the underlying economic theory and some practical applications in authentic health care contexts. The skills focus for the unit reinforces the importance of effective listening and note-taking from a lecture and also the need to make appropriate contributions to seminars. The theoretical perspectives are addressed in sufficient depth to support the content of the unit, while providing a useful framework for the skills practised. Some of the most frequent fixed phrases from the discipline are practised in context, as well as language items frequently encountered in academic lectures.

The unit considers how economics and the provision of a service such as health care are considered in advanced economies. Earlier units have raised students' awareness of issues such as poverty, hunger, exploitation, fair trade and development aid in a world where many forms of inequality exist. Through this unit, students will gain a better understanding of the role played by welfare economics in decision-making on health matters to achieve greater fairness.

Skills focus

🎧 Listening
- using the Cornell note-taking system
- recognizing digressions in lectures

Speaking
- making effective contributions to a seminar
- referring to other people's ideas in a seminar

Vocabulary focus

- fixed phrases from economics
- fixed phrases from academic English

Key vocabulary

allocate	entitle	medication	self-reliant
allocative	equality	needy	suffer
classify	equalize	norm	treat
competitiveness	equity	Pareto-efficient	treatment
coverage	ethnic	pharmaceutical	unskilled
designate	exempt	prescription	utility
discrimination	gender	redistribution	value (n and v)
distort	GP (general	referral	variable
distortion	practitioner)	reimburse	welfare
drugs	judgement	relative (adj)	workload

9.1 Vocabulary

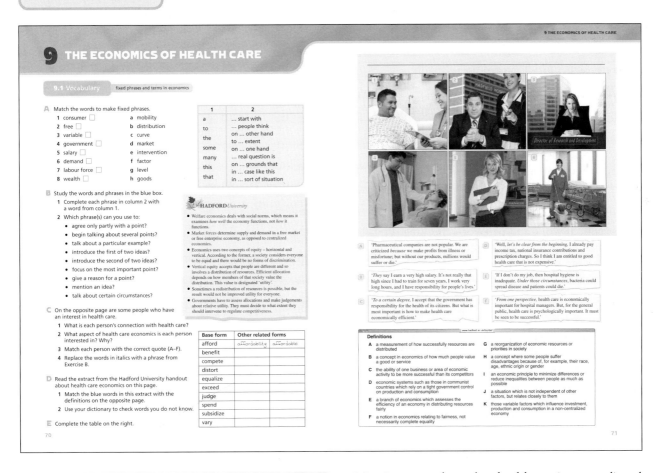

General note

Read the *Vocabulary bank* at the end of the Course Book unit. Decide when, if at all, to refer your students to it. The best time is probably at the very end of the lesson or the beginning of the next lesson, as a summary/revision.

Lesson aims

- understand and use some fixed phrases/compound nouns from economics
- understand and use some fixed phrases from academic English

Introduction

Introduce the topic for the unit. Ask students to say what *health care* is and arrive at a definition on the board, such as:

Health care is the prevention, treatment and management of illness and the maintenance of mental and physical well-being using services provided by state or private medical facilities.

(Adapted from http://medical-dictionary. thefreedictionary.com)

Mention to students that *healthcare* (one word) and *health care* (two words) mean the same. *Healthcare* is often used in noun–noun compounds, for example, *healthcare issues*, *healthcare policies*, *healthcare politics*, etc.

Exercise A

This gives revision of some compound noun phrases (noun + noun, adjective + noun) connected with economics from previous units.

Set for individual work or pairwork. Check that students remember the meanings and that they can pronounce the compounds with the main stress on the correct word. Accept any reasonable alternatives which apply to the topic of economics. Ask students to make sentences with the compounds.

Answers

Model answers:

1	'consumer	goods	n + n
2	free	'market	adj + n
3	variable	'factor	adj + n
4	government*	'intervention	n + n
5	'salary	level	n + n
6	'demand	curve	n + n
7	'labour force	mobility	n + n
8	'wealth	distribution	n + n

*here the noun *government* often gives contrastive information and so stress shifts to the second noun

Exercise B

Set for individual work and pairwork checking. Point out that some of the words in the first column of the box must be used more than once. Feed back with the whole class.

Answers

Model answers:

to start with	to begin talking about several points
many/some people think	to mention an idea
on the other hand	to introduce the second of two ideas
to some extent	to agree only partly with a point
on the one hand	to introduce the first of two ideas
the real question is	to focus on the point which the writer/speaker thinks is the most important
on the grounds that	to give a reason for a point
in a case like this	to talk about a particular example
in this/that sort of situation	to talk about certain circumstances

Exercise C

1/2 Set for pairwork discussion.

 3 Set for individual work and pairwork checking.

 4 Set for individual work. Check with the whole class, asking students to read out the quotation with the alternative phrase inserted in place of the original words in italics.

Answers

Model answers:

1/2 1 is a patient – likely to be interested in the care he/she receives, and whether it is value for money, especially in a national health insurance system.

 2 is a government minister – likely to be interested in how to fund health care effectively.

 3 is a manager or director of a pharmaceutical company which supplies drugs (medications) to hospitals.

 4 is a public sector doctor – likely to be interested in whether his/her salary is appropriate for the training and responsibility.

 5 is a hospital manager – likely to be interested in how to spend the resources allocated most efficiently.

 6 is an employee of the hospital (a cleaner) – likely to be concerned about the low level of payment for a job that has responsibility (especially hygiene issues).

3 (patient): quote D

 (government minister): quote C

 (pharmaceutical company manager/director): quote A

 (public sector doctor): quote B

 (hospital manager): quote F

 (hospital employee): quote E

4

A	*because*	We are criticized *on the grounds that* we make profits from illness or misfortune; but without our products, millions would suffer or die.
B	*They say*	*Many/some people think* I earn a very high salary.
C	*To a certain degree*	*To some extent*, I accept that the government has responsibility for the health of its citizens.
D	*let's be clear from the beginning*	*To start with*, I already pay income tax, national insurance contributions and prescription charges.
E	*Under those circumstances*	*In that sort of situation*, bacteria could spread diseases and patients could die.
F	*From one perspective*	*On the one hand*, health care is economically important for hospital managers.

Exercise D

This exercise gives some terms in a special branch of economics – and so is rather technical.

Set students to read the handout extract first and ask them to discuss in pairs which of the blue words they know and which are new for them. Feed back with the whole class, to establish how much is known. Where students give correct explanations tell them they are right, and where they are wrong also tell them, but do not give the right answer at this point.

Set questions 1 and 2 for individual work and pairwork checking. Feed back with the whole class, checking the meaning of other possibly unknown words. The words will be used throughout the next two units, so don't worry too much about practice at this point. However, for extra practice at this point if you wish, set students to work in pairs. One student should shut the book.

The other student should say one of the words for the first student to explain. Then change over.

Answers

Model answers:

welfare economics	E	a branch of economics which assesses the efficiency of an economy in distributing resources fairly
market forces	K	those variable factors which influence investment, production and consumption in a non-centralized economy
centralized economies	D	economic systems such as those in communist countries which rely on a tight government control on production and consumption
equity	F	a notion in economics relating to fairness, not necessarily complete equality
discrimination	H	a concept where some people suffer disadvantages because of, for example, their race, age, ethnic origin or gender
vertical equity	I	an economic principle to minimize differences or reduce inequalities between people as much as possible
efficient allocation	A	a measurement of how successfully resources are distributed
utility	B	a concept in economics of how much people value a good or service
redistribution	G	a reorganization of economic resources or priorities in society
relative	J	a situation which is not independent of other factors, but relates closely to them
competitiveness	C	the ability of one business or area of economic activity to be more successful than its competitors

Exercise E

Set for individual work. Tell students to use their dictionaries to check on the meanings and grammatical categories of the words if they are not sure. Point out that some verbs will have more than one noun derived from them.

Feed back with the whole class, pointing out that most of the words have a particular use in the area of economics. Check students can pronounce all the words correctly, particularly those where the word stress shifts.

Answers

Model answers: See table below.

Language note

With a good class, you can spend plenty of time on the issue of whether each noun is used as countable or uncountable or both, i.e., can the word be made plural, and if so, does that change the meaning?

Closure

It is important that students are familiar with the terminology from this lesson. On the board write some terms from the lesson and ask students to give a definition; choose items from Exercises A and D. Or read out a definition and ask students to tell you the appropriate word or phrase. Check the pronunciation. This exercise can also be done as a dictation.

Alternatively, write the words and definitions on different cards and give a card to each student. The student then reads out the word or the definition and the rest of the class must produce the correct answer.

Base form	Other related forms	
afford (v, I)	affordability	affordable
benefit (n, C), (v, T)	benefit (n, C)	beneficial
compete (v, I used with 'with')	competition (n, C but usually U in an economics/business context)	competitive
distort (v, T)	distortion (n, C)	distorted (adj)
equalize (v, T)	equality (n, usually U); equalization (n, U)	
exceed (v, T)	excess (n, C but plural meaning is somewhat different)	excessive
judge (v, T)	judge (n, C), judgement (n, C)	
spend (v, T)	spending (n, U), expenditure (n, U)	
subsidize (v, T)	subsidy (n, C)	subsidized (adj)
vary (v, I)	variety (n, C), variation (n, C), variable (n, C) (N.B. the noun form is identical to the adj form)	variable (adj)

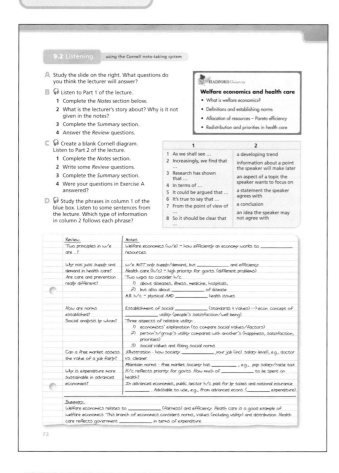

Introduction

1 Review key vocabulary from this unit by writing a selection of words from Lesson 9.1 on the board and asking students to put the words in groups, giving reasons for their decisions. For example:

allocation, distribution, provision = how to use resources

equity, efficiency, utility = concepts in economics with specific meanings

taxation, contributions, charges = methods of obtaining revenue

supply, demand, labour, investment = market forces or variable market factors

2 Revise note-taking symbols and abbreviations by using extra activities 3 and 4 at the end of this unit.

3 Introduce the elements of the Cornell note-taking system. Try to elicit some of the **R** words. Ask students to try to think of five words beginning with *re~* with six or seven letters that are good strategies to use when studying and taking notes. Write the words as follows on the board:

RE _ _ _ _ = *record*

RE _ _ _ _ = *reduce*

RE _ _ _ _ = *recite*

RE _ _ _ _ _ = *reflect*

RE _ _ _ _ = *review*

Discuss with the class what each word might mean when taking notes. Try to elicit the following, helping where needed.

record	Take notes during the lecture.
reduce	After the lecture, turn the notes into one- or two-word questions or 'cues' which help you remember the key information.
recite	Say the questions and answers aloud.
reflect	Decide on the best way to summarize the key information in the lecture.
review	Look again at the key words and the summary (and do this regularly).

Tell students that in this lesson they will be introduced to this system of note-taking – which can be used both for lectures, and also for reading and for revision for exams later. Do not say much more at this point; they will see how the system works as the lesson progresses.

General note

Read the *Skills bank – Using the Cornell note-taking system* at the end of the Course Book unit. Decide when, if at all, to refer students to it. The best time is probably at the very end of the lesson or the beginning of the next lesson, as a summary/revision.

Lesson aims

● use the Cornell note-taking system

Further practice in:

● listening for an established purpose
● understanding fractured text
● recognition of fixed phrases and what type of information comes next
● using abbreviations and symbols in note-taking

Subject note

The Cornell system was developed by Walter Pauk at Cornell University, USA. Pauk advised students to use a large, loose-leaf notebook, with holes punched for filing. This is better than a bound notebook, because you can organize the notes in a file binder. You can also take out notes and rewrite them. Pauk's method, which is now called the Cornell system, is based on a specific page layout.

Pauk told students to divide up the page into three areas. The first area is a column 5 cm wide on the left side of the page. This is the cue area. The main part of the page is the note-taking area. At the bottom of the page is a row 8 cm high, which is the summary area. The basic grid with information on what each section should contain is reproduced in the additional resources section (Resource 9B).

The most recent edition is Pauk, W. and Owens, R. (2010). *How to Study in College* (10th edition). Belmont, CA: Wadsworth Publishing.

The note-taking and learning process involves the Five Rs in the order listed in the introduction to this lesson (and in the *Skills bank*). There are many references on the Internet for this system. Useful ones at the time of writing are:

www.yorku.ca/cdc/lsp/skillbuilding/notetaking.html

http://lsc.sas.cornell.edu/Sidebars/Study_Skills_Resources/Study%20Skills%20PDFs%20for%20LSC%20Website/Cornell%20Note-Taking%20System.pdf

www.montgomerycollege.edu/Departments/enreadtp/Cornell.html (also offers a model)

A Google search using *Pauk + Cornell note-taking system* will get additional items.

Exercise A

Set for pairwork discussion. Refer students to the lecture slide. Tell them to look at the title and bullet points, and for each bullet point to make questions which they expect the lecturer to answer. Do not explain any words from the slide, or allow students to check in their dictionaries at this point, as the meanings of these words will be dealt with in the lecture.

Feed back with the whole class, asking several students to read out their questions. Write some of the questions on the board if you wish.

🎧 Exercise B

1–3 Refer students to the notes at the bottom of the page. Tell them that this student has used the Cornell system to take notes but has not managed to complete everything and so has left some gaps. (Note that this is quite a normal occurrence in note-taking – details may need to be filled in later by checking with other people, for example.)

Allow students time to read the gapped notes. Also make sure they read question 2 and are ready to listen out for a story.

Play Part 1, pausing after each major point if you wish.

Tell students to work in pairs to compare their answers to questions 1 and 2, and to complete the summary in 3. Feed back with the whole class, using an OHT or other visual display of the answers if you wish. The completed notes are reproduced in Resource 9C, in the additional resources section, to facilitate this.

4 Now focus on the *recite* element of the Cornell system. Point out that here the student has completed the *Review* section. Tell students to cover up the *Notes* section of the answer and ask them if they can say anything about the first and second questions in the *Review*. Then put students in pairs to test each other on the remaining notes.

Answers

Model answers:

1/3/4 See table on next page and Resource 9C.

2 The lecturer talks about his/her own experience of difficulties in accessing health care in a developing country. It is not in the notes because it is a digression – that is, as a personal experience it is not essential information for the subject.

Transcript 🎧 2.6

Part 1

Good morning, everyone. Today's lecture provides a general background to welfare economics and a more specific example of health care. First of all, my lecture involves an examination of a number of important principles in welfare economics. This is the branch of economics which considers how efficiently the economy works to manage its resources. Then I will concentrate on the economics of health care itself. As we shall see, welfare economics cannot simply be based on supply and demand. And health care most definitely cannot be based on supply and demand! Welfare economics must also consider equity and efficiency. For the moment, you can think of equity as 'fairness', but we will look at the definitions of these soon.

Right … so our starting point is to think of health care as one important area of welfare economics. Increasingly, we find that the health of their citizens represents a major priority for governments in different ways. We can think of health and health care in two ways. Firstly, responding to illness and disease with medicine, treatments, hospitals and so on. Secondly, we should think of health care as dealing with the

Review	Notes
Two principles in w/e are …?	Welfare economics (w/e) = how efficiently an economy works to <u>manage</u> resources.

Why not just supply and demand in health care?
Are care and prevention really different?
	w/e NOT only supply/demand, but <u>equity</u> and efficiency
	Health care (h/c) = high priority for govts. (different problems)
	Two ways to consider h/c
	  1) about diseases, illness, medicine, hospitals
	  2) but also about <u>prevention</u> of disease
	N.B. h/c = physical AND <u>mental</u> health issues

How are norms established?
 	
Social analysis by whom?
	Establishment of social <u>norms</u> (standards & values) → econ. concept of <u>relative</u> utility (people's satisfaction/well-being).
	Three aspects of relative utility:
	  1) economists' explanation (to compare social values/factors)
	  2) person's/group's utility compared with another's (happiness, satisfaction, priorities)
	  3) social values and fixing social norms

Can a free market assess the value of a job fairly? Why is expenditure more sustainable in advanced economies?	Illustration – how society <u>values</u> your job (incl. salary level), e.g., doctor vs. cleaner. Maintain norms – free market society has <u>mechanisms</u>, e.g., pay salary/raise tax. H/c reflects priority for govts. How much of <u>GDP</u> to be spent on health? In advanced economies, public sector h/c paid for by taxes and national insurance <u>contributions</u>. Advisable to use, e.g., from advanced econs. (<u>sustainable</u> expenditure).

Summary

Welfare economics relates to <u>equity</u> (fairness) and efficiency. Health care is a good example of welfare economics. This branch of economics considers norms, values (including utility) and distribution. Health care reflects government <u>priorities</u> in terms of expenditure.

prevention of disease, providing health education and helping people to stay healthy. Moreover, we must remember that health is not only about *physical* health, but also about *mental* well-being. Research has shown that someone who is physically healthy but unemployed can easily suffer with mental health problems. So welfare resources must be available to help different groups of needy people. And, of course, that means money! So, governments need revenue from taxes and so on for health expenditure. But they must distribute resources equitably, that is to say, fairly, according to the needs of the people and also according to efficiency criteria. More on this in a moment!

But before we begin, I have a little story to tell you. About 20 years ago, I was working in a developing country. I won't say which one! Basic health care was provided for the people by government hospitals, but there were also a few private hospitals. These were better equipped, with many doctors who had trained abroad. Treatment was better, but quite expensive by local standards. Well, I fell and cut my knee quite badly when I was jogging. So after cleaning the injury at home, I thought it was best to go to the nearest hospital, the private one. When I arrived at just before six in the evening, there was a

crowd of people outside the gates but the hospital was closed. People were not happy as they wanted treatment but the gates were closed. There was also a guard with a big stick who was keeping everyone, including me, back. My knee was obviously injured and covered in blood, but there was nothing I could do. So, I just went home, and hoped for the best! The next day I went to the government hospital where I got treatment quickly and cheaply.

Of course, the point of that story was that it illustrates basic principles of supply and demand – and to some extent of equity and efficiency. Let's analyze this from the perspective of economics. The private hospital decided to close at 5.30 every evening, even if there was demand for the services. In terms of allocation of resources, the government provided the *public* sector hospital. Moreover, that evening, when I tried to get treatment at the private hospital, the government hospital had probably been open. So, it could be argued that the government had, in fact, provided a system which was equitable and efficient! The government knew that the private sector hospital could fill in some gaps and so the government could concentrate its spending on the majority of the people who needed cheaper treatment. The private sector hospital, however, was allowed to make its own rules, fix the fees, doctors' salaries and … yes, opening times!

So, to get back to the main topic of the lecture, the next part examines how most advanced economies establish social norms. This means the way society arrives at those standards and values which most people can accept. To begin with, you already know the economic concept of 'utility'. You probably associate it with the idea of a person's well-being or satisfaction, but analyzed from an economic point of view. In welfare economics, we should think of the wider concept of relative utility. So, I will mention three aspects of relative utility to help you understand better. Firstly, relative utility is how economists explain the way that society compares or values various factors. Secondly, relative utility involves comparing how one person's or group's happiness or satisfaction or priorities compare with another person's or group's. Thirdly, it involves social values and how social norms are established. So, just to repeat the three aspects – we have the economist's viewpoint, the social comparison and the establishment of social norms.

If we move on now to an illustration of establishing norms. Think about how society values a person's job and what his or her salary level is. In most societies, for example, a doctor's job is valued higher than a cleaner's. The doctor, who has a higher salary, can buy more, and has more opportunities, economically speaking, than the cleaner. But he or she may also have a lot of stress and responsibility that the cleaner does not have. This can all be calculated – again, economically speaking – as part of the doctor's utility. To maintain such relative norms, a free market society, or a government, usually has a lot of mechanisms. For example, the government determines the level of salaries people receive in the public sector and the tax someone pays. With this money, the government tries to meet the health care priorities for the country and decides how much of GDP is spent on health care compared with other priorities. This is where the concept of equity, or fairness, is important and especially in health care.

In most advanced economies, the government has revenue from taxes and special health insurance contributions to establish a public sector health system. It's true to say that many developing countries often set up a private health care system in parallel with the state system, but today I'm not going to talk about health care in the developing world. From the point of view of welfare economics, it is advisable to use advanced economies as examples, not because they are necessarily better, but because health care

expenditure is usually sustainable there. So it should be clear that we are really talking about the relative importance of health care applied to developed economies.

🎧 Exercise C

1 Tell students to divide up a page of their notebooks into the three sections of the Cornell system. They should try to take notes in the *Notes* section as they listen. Warn them that they may not be able to complete their notes while writing so they should leave spaces which they can fill in later.

Play Part 2 straight through. Then put students in pairs to complete any gaps in their notes. Feed back with the whole class. Build up a set of notes on the board.

2/3 Set students to work in pairs to complete the *Review* questions and the *Summary*. Feed back with the whole class.

4 Discuss with the class the extent to which their pre-questions in Exercise A have been answered.

Answers

Possible answers: See table on next page.

Transcript 🎧 2.7

Part 2

Now, let's return to welfare economics. To begin with, I said earlier that we need to define some important terms to help us understand the allocation and distribution of resources. There are, in fact, six definitions we need to focus on. I will say them slowly. Firstly, we must define equity, where we have two types, so two definitions; then we need a definition of discrimination. Next we have efficiency, and finally utility, which I have already mentioned. So, that's five altogether. In addition, there's a sixth definition which I will give you at the end of this part of the lecture.

Firstly, let's define equity itself. By the way, you may have met this word in another financial context, related to businesses and their capital status. Here, in welfare economics, we define it in a different way to mean 'fairness'. In other words, it means giving people a fair chance in education, health care, employment opportunities and so on.

Let's turn now to the two concepts of equity in welfare economics – horizontal and vertical equity and their definitions. Well, according to the first type of equity, a society considers everyone to be equal. In such situations, everyone receives equal treatment in all ways.

Review	Notes
	w/e has six important definitions for understanding of allocation/distribution of resources

What is business meaning of equity?	Two types of 'equity' (not same as in business context)
	 Here equity = fairness in education, health, jobs, opportunities, etc.
	   (1) horizontal equity = everyone equal/equal treatment
	   (2) vertical equity = distribution acc. to needs/priorities

Can h. equity be applied in practice?	Problem with h. equity • means no (3) discrimination (no disadvantages because of race, sex, age, ethnic group) • equity realistic? Tried by communist countries • unsuccessful because of market forces (influenced by S&D)
How do free mkts influence h/c?	Free markets = initiative, incentive, individual motivation, so free mkts. prefer v. equity principle V. equity = • acceptance of differences + • reduction of consequences by fair redistribution of resources +
Isn't efficiency just making a profit or maximizing production or services?	• (4) efficiency (= efficient allocation according to how society values goods/services) N.B. v. equity also tries to achieve efficiency through efficient allocation of res. acc. to (5) 'utility' (person's economic happiness/well-being)
Can we calculate the costs of 'utility'?	BUT 'utility' is relative, e.g. (choices) • individual choice – in health care – person may choose private system but has already paid for national h/c system • govt. choice – sustain spending (with fewer patients) OR maintain spending to give better service
Why do people oppose v.e.?	N.B. v. equity not always welcomed, e.g., President Obama's attempts to reform in USA (2010)
Does Pareto efficiency include equity principle?	(6) definition of Pareto efficiency (1909 economic theory) to illustrate distribution (Pareto-efficient distrib. = point where it is impossible to reallocate res. so *someone* receives more, but *nobody* gets less)

Summary

Economics looks at distribution and redistribution in a systematic way. Concepts of equity are very useful and the idea of utility is relevant to health care/education/job market, but can a 1909 theory still be applied today?

The second definition relates to vertical equity and I will discuss it more in a moment. But, basically, it means that resources are distributed according to needs and priorities in society.

Now, with the concept of horizontal equity, we can see a few problems. Firstly, horizontal equity means there would be no forms of discrimination – definition number three. Discrimination is when people are at a disadvantage because of their race, age, ethnic origin, social class or gender. So without discrimination everyone would be considered socially and economically equal. You may think that is very unrealistic. Well, it probably is, but centralized economies, such as those in communist countries, wanted to give everyone equal access to health care, education, and welfare payments such as sickness benefit or state pensions when people retired. But it doesn't really work.

Why doesn't horizontal equity work? Well, basically, market forces determine supply and demand – or S&D, as we say – in a free market or free enterprise economy as opposed to a centralized economy. Free markets try to provide incentives, encourage initiative, growth and expansion and make people self-reliant. That means that people are not so dependent on the state.

So most free market economies accept that vertical equity is a more workable principle. Now, when we look at this second form of equity, we can identify the differences. Vertical equity means that society recognizes and accepts differences, but tries to reduce the implications of those differences. Vertical equity involves an equitable allocation of resources, but this should also mean efficiency, which is our fourth definition. Efficiency or efficient allocation relates to how members of that society value the distribution.

This leads us to definition number five. When people in society value something, this value is designated 'utility' as I mentioned before. But remember, we are talking about relative utility, that is how one person's happiness or satisfaction – or how important they think something is – compares with another person's. People will value things differently, especially in free market economies.

Now, you don't need to take notes on this part, but I hope it helps you to understand the concepts better. Let's say that country X has a big problem with kidney disease. Now, there are a number of ways to treat patients with kidney problems. You can use drugs, because relatively cheap forms of medication are available. The second option is dialysis, that's spelt D-I-A-L-Y-S-I-S. Dialysis involves installing expensive machines in hospitals which function – temporarily, of course – like the person's kidneys and, to express it simply, wash the patient's blood. Now, this second option is much more expensive. Moreover, patients have to travel to the hospital and stay there for several hours. So the patient who is rich and lives in the city, where the hospital probably is, has a higher relative utility from this treatment than the poor person who has to travel a long distance to the city from a rural area. For the poor person, the provision of inexpensive drugs would bring a higher utility, but a dialysis machine shows the country has high-tech treatments. I hope this explanation helps a little?

Well, let's take another example … by the way, I think you should take a few notes here. Let's say some people are dissatisfied with the national health service. So, they start using private hospitals and health care, which they must, of course, pay for! If this happens in the UK, where there is a national health service, the government has some choices to make, according to the principles of equity and efficiency. The government may decide to reduce the allocation to the state system because they can see that there are fewer patients who are using the system. That would seem to be efficient. But it is also possible that the expenditure on health will be sustained. Why would that happen? Well, the answer is that even the people who are dissatisfied with the system have already paid taxes and contributions for state health care. They can't avoid paying them, so their contributions support the health care provisions generally. Perhaps they even enable some redistribution within the system.

To some extent, this form of vertical equity is accepted, but it is not always welcomed! For example, as many of you know, President Obama attempted a major reform of the American health care system in 2010, but this was opposed quite strongly by a lot of Americans for a variety of reasons. You may want to do some research on that. I'll provide a couple of references later.

Now, where was I? Oh, yes, I was talking about how important it is for governments to assess allocations and make judgements about relative utility. Moreover, they must decide to what extent they should intervene to regulate competitiveness, for example between government departments, to show that they are reducing costs or providing better service. So, here's our final definition. It's a bit complicated, so listen carefully! In 1909, a very important economic measure or principle called *Pareto efficiency* was developed by Vilfredo Pareto, an influential Italian economist. His name is spelt V-I-L-F-R-E-D-O P-A-R-E-T-O, but you only really need to remember Pareto! The definition states that an allocation of resources is Pareto-efficient if it is impossible to move to any other allocation which would make *some* people receive more, but where *nobody* receives less. I will expect you to read up on this concept, and find the diagrams which illustrate it so you can apply it and identify any limitations.

🎧 Exercise D

Allow students time to read the phrases and the types of information, making sure that they understand any difficult words. Note that they are being asked not for the words that the speaker uses but what *type* of information the words represent. Note also that the information types may be needed more than once.

Play the sentences one at a time allowing time for students to identify the type of information which follows. Check answers after each sentence, making sure that students understand the actual information that follows.

Answers

Model answers: See table on next page.

Fixed phrase	Type of information that follows	Actual words/information
1 As we shall see …	information about a point the speaker will make later	health care economics is not only about supply and demand.
2 Increasingly, we find that …	a developing trend	the health of their citizens represents a major priority for governments in different ways.
3 Research has shown that	a statement the speaker agrees with	someone who is physically healthy but unemployed can easily suffer with mental health problems.
4 In terms of …	an aspect of a topic the speaker wants to focus on	allocation of resources, the government provided the *public* sector hospital.
5 It could be argued that …	an idea the speaker may not agree with	the government had, in fact, provided a system which was equitable and efficient!
6 It's true to say that …	a statement the speaker agrees with	many developing countries often establish a private health care system in parallel with the state system.
7 From the point of view of …	an aspect of a topic the speaker wants to focus on	welfare economics, it is advisable to use advanced economies as examples …
8 So it should be clear that …	a conclusion	we are really talking about the relative importance of health care applied to developed economies.

Transcript 🎧 2.8

1 As we shall see, welfare economics cannot simply be based on supply and demand.

2 Increasingly, we find that the health of their citizens represents a major priority for governments in different ways.

3 Research has shown that someone who is physically healthy but unemployed can easily suffer with mental health problems.

4 In terms of allocation of resources, the government provided the *public* sector hospital.

5 So, it could be argued that the government had, in fact, provided a system which was equitable and efficient!

6 It's true to say that many developing countries often set up a private health care system in parallel with the state system.

7 From the point of view of welfare economics, it is advisable to use advanced economies as examples …

8 So it should be clear that we are really talking about the relative importance of health care applied to developed economies.

Closure

Predicting information: play short sections from the lecture again. Stop the recording just before a word or phrase you want students to produce and ask them what comes next in the lecture. For example:

1 Here, in welfare economics, we define equity in a different way to mean [STOP] … *'fairness'*.

2 Let's turn now to the two concepts of equity in welfare economics [STOP] … *horizontal and vertical*.

3 Market forces determine supply and demand in a free market or free enterprise economy compared with [STOP] … *centralized economies*.

4 The definition states that an allocation of resources is Pareto-efficient if it is impossible to move to any other allocation which would make *some* people receive more, but [STOP] … *where nobody receives less*.

Alternatively, do this exercise by reading out parts of the transcript.

9.3 Extending skills

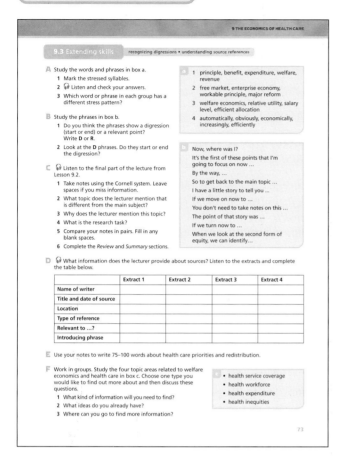

Lesson aims

- recognize digressions: start and end
- understand reference to other people's ideas: source, quotes, relevance

Further practice in:

- stress within words and phrases
- leaving space in notes for missing information

Introduction

Revise the lecture in Lesson 9.2 by asking students to use their Cornell notes. They should cover up the *Notes* section and use the *Review* and *Summary* sections to help recall the contents of the lecture. They could work in pairs to do this.

If time, check that students are clear about the difference between *horizontal* and *vertical equity* and if there seems to be any confusion between *utility* and *equity*. Ask them to think of some of the main factors in (re)distribution of resources by prompting as below:

- *Horizontal equity* involves basically equal distribution of (welfare) resources according to the needs of the majority such as in centralized economies; *vertical equity* involves a

(re)distribution of resources to provide an efficient and equitable provision of services and facilities.

- *Utility* involves the economic welfare of a person or a group to obtain maximum happiness or satisfaction from economic choices; *equity* involves fairness based on evaluation or prioritization according to various norms and values, such as a country believing that expenditure on health services is more important than expenditure on defence.

🎧 Exercise A

1 Set for individual work and pairwork checking. Students can underline the stressed syllables.

2 Play the recording and get students to check their answers.

3 Set for individual work and pairwork checking. Tell students they need to identify the odd one out in terms of stress (not the meanings of the words). Feed back with the whole class, checking students' pronunciation, especially of the compound words, and eliciting the odd ones out.

Answers

Model answers:

1/3 (odd one out in italics)

1 'principle, 'benefit, *ex'penditure* (stress is on second syllable), 'welfare, 'revenue

2 free 'market, *'enterprise economy* (noun + noun; stress on first word), workable 'principle, major re'form

3 welfare eco'nomics, relative u'tility, *'salary level* (stress on first word), efficient allo'cation

4 auto'matically, *'obviously* (stress on first syllable), eco'nomically, in'creasingly, e'fficiently

Transcript 🎧 2.9

1 'principle, 'benefit, *ex'penditure*, 'welfare, 'revenue

2 free 'market, *'enterprise economy*, 'workable principle, major re'form

3 welfare eco'nomics, relative u'tility, *'salary level*, efficient allo'cation

4 auto'matically, *'obviously*, eco'nomically, in'creasingly, e'fficiently

Exercise B

Point out that the phrases in the box are likely to introduce either a digression or a relevant point. The students' task is to identify which is more probable.

Set for individual work and pairwork checking. Feed back with the whole class. Note that most of these phrases occurred in the lecture in Lesson 9.2. Some have occurred in previous units and one or two are new. Note also that the end of a digression is actually a transition back to the main point.

Answers

Model answers:

Now, where was I? D (end)

It's the first of these points that I'm going to focus on now ... R

By the way, ... D (start)

So to get back to the main topic ... D (end)

I have a little story to tell you ... D (start)

If we move on now to ... R

You don't need to take notes on this ... D (start)

The point of that story was ... D (end)

If we turn now to ... R

When we look at the second form of equity, we can identify ... R

🎧 Exercise C

Refer students to the lecture slide in Lesson 9.2. Ask them what they know already about welfare economics and redistribution. What would they like to know?

Tell them to prepare a page to take notes using the Cornell system. Remind them that they may not get all the information. If they miss something, they should leave a space. They can fill it in after the lecture.

Let them read the questions through and tell them to listen out for the answers to questions 2, 3 and 4.

1 Play Part 3 straight through. Students should complete the *Notes* section.

2–4 Set for pairwork. Feed back with the whole class. Ask for suggestions for phrases to use to find out about the importance of digressions, e.g., *Why did the lecturer start talking about ...? I didn't understand the bit about ... Is it important?* and so on (see *Skills bank*). Set question 3 for pairwork.

5/6 Set for pairwork. Students compare their notes, complete any blank spaces and then write the *Review* and *Summary* sections.

Feed back with the whole class, building a set of notes on the board.

Answers

Possible answers:

1 See notes on the opposite page.

2 The Cornell note-taking system.

3 It's important to know how to take good notes.

4 To find out about health care differences around the world.

5/6 See notes.

Transcript 🎧 2.10

Part 3

In any discussion of welfare economics, the topic of redistribution is linked to fairness. This is then linked to the concept of efficiency. But how realistic is this concept anyway? Let's take a hospital, for example. The management team wants it to be efficient. It wants to allocate resources well. It wants to avoid waste in every possible way. So, it works out its efficiency model. Many economists call this an allocative model. In other words, economists argue that if the hospital provides the right resources, it will achieve efficiency and, in the case of a company, maximum profit. However, we know that hospitals and companies are really composed of the people who work there. These people or members of their families have problems such as illnesses. They come to work late. They do not feel motivated and perhaps do not work efficiently themselves! So, do you see the problem? The resources may be efficiently managed, but there are many flaws in the system. I think Krugman and Wells summarized the problem extremely well. This quotation comes from one of your core texts, *Microeconomics*. The second edition was published in 2008. Writing about governments, on page 15, they say, '... there is typically a trade-off between equity and efficiency: policies that promote equity often come at a decreased efficiency in the economy, and vice versa'. Governments have to keep that in mind when providing health care.

In health care economics, a very useful example of this 'trade-off' is the provision of medications or drugs. Many pharmaceutical companies make large profits by manufacturing, for example, heart disease drugs, diabetes management and cancer management and treatment. There you are! Now, this raises three issues in the equity versus efficiency debate. Firstly, the profit motive. The companies do not provide these drugs at the lowest possible price. They are commercial enterprises and want to maximize profits. Secondly, their R&D, or research and development, costs have probably been quite high. So, a government health service must pay the companies for the drugs for the patients. And

Review	Notes
Are hospitals usually non-profit making?	Redistribution – allocative model of efficiency; resources allocated correctly BUT organizations (e.g., hospitals, companies) rely on people – problems/health/motivation/skills, etc. → less efficiency
Does efficiency matter as much as for companies?	Krugman & Wells (2008) equity: efficiency 'trade-off' health care (h/c) = e.g., of this trade-off Specific, e.g., = provision of medication

Cheaper treatments – availability?	Three issues:
	  1 pharma. companies want to make profit
	  2 R&D investment prob. v. high so govt must pay high prices
	  3 Treatment is expensive, e.g., cancer treatment £30–40K/p.a. per patient (heart treatment also expensive)

Isn't horizontal equity impossible? How to find more real examples? N.B. five solutions and five criteria – how to keep separate?	Debate: entitlement vs cost Weeks (1971) – economics does *not* focus enough on inequality! Solutions & strategies – issues of: (1) redistribution (rich pay more taxes) (2) entitlement (who gets treatment) (3) equality (same treatment – age, status factors) (4) priorities (e.g., waiting lists for ops.) (5) standards (which level of care) → discussion of 'discrimination' Useful way to analyze health care systems acc. to five criteria: (i) funding; (ii) coverage; (iii) welfare; (iv) doctors; and (v) facilities Difficult for govts e.g. Davis (2001) said USA lack of health coverage is big problem!

Summary

The allocative model is opposed by some economists. This is because human factors are involved, not just economic considerations, and people have different motivation, can be ill or inefficient in their work. So this means that it is impossible to apply efficiency criteria in health care systems. BUT the idea of a 'trade-off' is important, for example when making decisions about treatment, drugs, and priorities. Weeks' five strategies (which offer possible solutions) are very relevant. So a systematic analysis of any health care system, for example, using the five-criteria model is very useful.

thirdly, the actual cost of treatment. In some cases, for example, cancer treatment, drugs can cost £30–40,000 a year per person. Many heart diseases can be controlled by expensive drugs to ensure a more or less normal life for the person. But you can see where the equity: efficiency debate is going, can't you? It is really a question of 'entitlement' against 'cost'. In simple terms, the person says, 'I am entitled to this treatment. That is the system of a national health service which I have contributed to.' The health care providers say, 'But we can't give everybody the best treatment because it is so expensive. We must be selective.' Now, as John Weeks argued, as long ago as 1971, in an important article in the journal, *Review of Radical Political Economics*, called 'Political Economy and the Politics of Economists', economics does not focus enough on *in*equality. It focuses too much on the positive side – utility, maximization, continued growth, increased consumption and so on. So how do the health care providers solve the problem of inequality?

By the way, I see that some of you are using the Cornell note-taking system. That's very good. Do you all know about this? No? Right, well, if you want to know more about it, I suggest you look at *How to Study in College* by Walter Pauk and Ross Owens, the 10th edition, which was published in 2010. It's very good, and it should be in the university library. I'm sure that you all know the importance of taking good notes – and this system is particularly useful.

Anyway, let's get back to our main topic. The influence of Weeks can be seen in the numerous strategies which health authorities use to balance efficiency and equity. They have five points to consider. So, let's look at them in turn. The five points are: firstly, redistribution; secondly, entitlement; thirdly, equality; fourthly, priority and finally, standards.

I will go through these slowly. Firstly, redistribution is a simple starting point. Rich people must pay more taxes to pay for their own and poor people's health care. Now, the second idea relates to entitlement. Is a rich person only entitled to the same care and treatment as the poorer person? Or the same drugs? If he or she wants something more than the national health service, that is, private health care, the rich person has to pay again! So when does fairness become unfair? This brings us to point three – equality. For example, should people receive the same treatment for the same disease, no matter what their age is or their status in society? Should everybody have the same level of access to all health services? Point four relates to priority and highlights another debate. For example, if someone needs a non-emergency operation, should they simply wait their turn, or should a policeman, soldier, social worker or a doctor have priority over a factory worker or a labourer or an unemployed person? Our fifth consideration is standards. Well, you might think that it should be the best possible care for everyone. But we have another dilemma. For example, many patients will never recover from their disease or illness, but they may live for a long time. What standards or levels of care or medication should they receive? The very best? The most expensive? Or something less than that? These issues are difficult and they are real. Earlier in the lecture, I mentioned the word *discrimination*, and I hope that this brief examination has shown you how discrimination can occur in health care.

In this final section of the lecture, I will give you a useful approach to the analysis of health care. You will be asked to do a research task on different systems around the world, to observe some crucial differences between them.

So let's think about our analysis. Here we also have five ideas or criteria. So to make it easier for you to take notes, organize the information under five headings: firstly, funding – how the government gets money to provide health care. Secondly, coverage. That means who is covered and who is not covered by the system, also the extent of their cover. Thirdly, welfare. Here, I mean questions such as how much help is given by the government to needy people – for example, the elderly, disabled, unemployed, low-income groups and so on? Fourthly, priorities. For example, in staffing, the doctors are arguably the most important group of staff in the system, but what about other staff? And, another example, do you remember the care versus prevention discussion? Which is the higher priority? Finally, criteria number five, we should mention the facilities which are provided in the health care system. When you do the research task, you will be able to evaluate what priorities have been set by different countries and how allocation of resources varies. But it is not

easy for governments. For example, the absence of universal health coverage in the USA is, to quote Karen Davis from an influential article she wrote in 2001 in the *Journal of Urban Health*, '... one of the great unsolved problems facing the United States at the onset of the 21st century.'

Well, I think that's enough background on welfare economics and some of the theories. However, as I have tried to emphasize, this is a human issue as well as an economic one. So, it is important for you to see in practice how governments set health care priorities. So, in the next tutorial, we will consider the national systems you have researched. I will provide you with some information and you can research these more. You should work in groups and report back on your findings.

Note

Source references for lecture:

Krugman, P. and Well, R. (2008). *Microeconomics*. (2nd edition). New York: Worth Publishers.

Weeks, J. (1971). Political economy and the politics of economists. *Review of Radical Political Economics*, 3(2), 75–83.

Pauk, W. and Owens, R. (2010). *How to Study in College* (10th edition). Belmont, CA: Wadsworth Publishing.

Davis, K. (2001). Universal coverage in the United States: Lessons from experience of the 20th century. *Journal of Urban Health*, 78(1), 46–58.

🎧 Exercise D

Tell students that lecturers will often give references while they talk and it is important to note down any references. The kinds of information may differ – they may just be names of books or articles, they may be an exact quotation (a 'direct quote') or they may be a paraphrase (sometimes called an 'indirect quotation'). Refer students to the table and check that they know what each row represents.

Play each extract and allow students time to complete the sections of the table. Check with the whole class.

Answers

Model answers:

	Extract 1	Extract 2	Extract 3	Extract 4
Name of writer(s)	Krugman and Wells	John Weeks	Walter Pauk and Ross Owen	Karen Davis
Title and date of source	*Microeconomics* 2nd edition, 2008	'Political economy and the politics of economists', 1971	*How to Study in College* 10th edition, 2010	2001
Location	core textbook	journal article from *Review of Radical Political Economics*	university library	journal article from *Journal of Urban Health*
Type of reference	direct quotation	paraphrase	name of book	direct quotation
Relevant to …?	'trade-off' between equity and efficiency	issue of inequality	Cornell note-taking	absence of health care coverage in USA
Introducing phrase	I think Krugman and Wells summarized the problem extremely well. This quotation comes from one of your core texts …	Now, as John Weeks argued …	I suggest you look at …	to quote Karen Davis …

Transcript 🎧 2.11

Extract 1

I think Krugman and Wells summarized the problem extremely well. This quotation comes from one of your core texts, *Microeconomics*. The second edition was published in 2008. Writing about governments, on page 15, they say, '… there is typically a trade-off between equity and efficiency: policies that promote equity often come at a decreased efficiency in the economy, and vice versa.'

Extract 2

Now, as John Weeks argued, as long ago as 1971, in an important article in the journal, *Review of Radical Political Economics*, called 'Political Economy and the Politics of Economists', economics does not focus enough on *in*equality. It focuses too much on the positive side – utility, maximization, continued growth, increased consumption and so on.

Extract 3

By the way, I see that some of you are using the Cornell note-taking system. That's very good. Do you all know about this? No? Right, well, if you want to know more about it, I suggest you look at *How to Study in College* by Walter Pauk and Ross Owens, the 10th edition, which was published in 2010. It's very good, and it should be in the university library.

Extract 4

For example, the absence of universal health coverage in the USA is, to quote Karen Davis from an influential article she wrote in 2001 in the *Journal of Urban Health*, '… one of the great unsolved problems facing the United States at the onset of the 21st century.'

Language note

A 'core text' is the main text for the course. Students are usually told they should buy a copy of the core text for their course.

Exercise E

Set for individual work – possibly homework – or else a pair/small group writing task. If the latter, tell students to put their writing on an OHT or other visual medium so that the whole class can see and comment on what has been written. You can then correct the language errors.

Exercise F

Tell students to work in groups of four. Either give each group a welfare economics and health care topic, or allow them to choose.

Feed back on questions 1–3 with the whole class. Tell them that each student should now carry out research into the group's topic, with reference to *two* different countries. They should each look at a different source and so will need to decide who is going to look at which one. Ideally groups should choose a developed and a developing country. Please note that students should be asked *not* to research those countries illustrated in the graph in Exercise E in Lesson 9.4.

You will also need to arrange the date for the feedback and discussion of the information – this is the focus of Exercise D in Lesson 9.4. Tell students that in Lesson

9.4 they will take part in a seminar on this topic. Emphasize that students will be expected to talk about their data. Although there is a lot of focus on statistics, the contrastive side and the implications of the statistics should be central to each group's presentation.

Answers

Possible answers:

1 Information to find: What are these topic areas concerned with? What aspects of health care are involved in each of the four areas?

2 Answers depend on the students. They should know that the criteria for analysis (from the lecture) will help them. They should think about how much is spent on health care; how important private health care is in the system; what specific health problems exist in the country; the ratio of doctors: patients; and issues relating to mortality and children.

3 Use subject course books, the library and the Internet to find out the necessary information. An example website at the time of writing is: www.who.int/whosis/whostat/EN_WHS11_Part2.pdf

The World Health Organization (WHO) statistics for 2011 are easily available and accessible. Direct students to this website. The link above is for Part 2, which includes the four selected topic areas in this exercise. If students wish to include other data (in addition to the four topic areas), they may find it at the WHO site: www.who.int/whosis/whostat/2011/en/index.html

For more general information: www.cia.gov/library/publications/the-world-factbook/

For specific information on the 30 OECD countries: http://stats.oecd.org/Index.aspx?DataSetCode= HEALTH
or
www.globalissues.org/ (individual site for critical analysis of many issues)

The World Bank also has health as one of its main priorities in its mission statements. See, for example: http://data.worldbank.org/topic/health

Closure

Ask students if they can remember the five indicators for analyzing any health care system. These were given in the latter part of the lecture. If they have forgotten, remind them:

funding

coverage

welfare

doctors

facilities

Discuss what each indicator relates to.

Refer students to the Research Resource table at the back of their Course Book. The table follows the analytical criteria given in the last part of the lecture. The table shows students how they might compare systems. Ask them to read through the table quickly (and read more thoroughly for homework) and discuss the contents and differences that they observe. Encourage students to ask questions to clarify content or language.

The information is based on OECD and WHO data, so you might want to remind students of the website addresses.

9.4 Extending skills

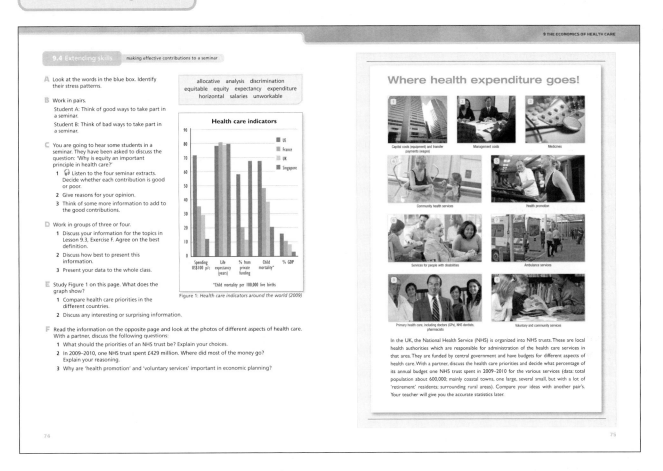

General note

Students will need the information they researched for Lesson 9.3, Exercise F.

Decide how you want students to present their information, e.g.,

- short talk with/without PowerPoint, OHT, or other visual medium
- to the whole class or to another group

Make sure that students understand the options for the presentation types.

Lesson aims

- make effective contributions to a seminar

Further practice in:

- stress within words

Introduction

Use a few of the review cues from the Cornell notes in Lesson 9.3 for students to try to recall the ideas on *equity and efficiency in health care* in the lecture. If students appear to be having difficulty remembering, ask them to look again at their own notes from

Exercise C in Lesson 9.3. Remind students, if necessary, of the five criteria – redistribution, entitlement, equality, priority and standards. Discuss and clarify where necessary.

Exercise A

Set for individual work and pairwork checking.

Answers

Model answers:

Ooo	equity, salaries
Oooo	allocative, equitable
oooOo	discrimination
ooOo	horizontal
oOoo	analysis, expenditure, expectancy, unworkable

Exercise B

This is revision from Unit 5. Set for individual work and pairwork checking. Feed back with the whole class. Give a time limit and see which pair can think of the most Do's and Don'ts in the time. Refer to Unit 5 Lesson 4 for suggestions if you need to.

187

Answers

Possible answers:

Do's	Don'ts
prepare the topic beforehand	
ask politely for information	demand information from other students
try to use correct language	
speak clearly	mumble, whisper or shout
say when you agree with someone	get angry if someone disagrees with you
link correctly with previous speakers	
build on points made by other speakers	simply repeat the same information
make a contribution, even if you are not sure if it is new or relevant	stay silent, waiting for 'the perfect moment'
be constructive	be negative
give specific examples to help explain a point	be vague
listen carefully to what others say	start a side conversation
allow others to speak	dominate the discussion
paraphrase to check understanding	
use clear visuals	

🎧 Exercise C

Check that students understand the topic for the seminar discussion. Ask them what they might expect to hear. Work through these extracts one at a time. Complete questions 1–3 for each extract before moving on to the next.

1　Set for individual work.

2　First check that students have understood the extract as much as possible. Then ask for opinions from the whole class on the contribution.

3　Once everyone has a clear notion of whether the contribution is a good one, ask for suggestions for additional points. Alternatively, set this part for pairwork after you have completed questions 1 and 2.

Transcript 🎧 2.12

Extract 1

It's clear that health care is an area where the government needs to be as fair as possible. I think we all accept that horizontal equity is a good idea, but is really unworkable in practice. So, in fact, we should look at the three basic advantages of equitable allocation of resources rather than just allocative efficiency. Firstly, it tries to avoid discrimination in access to health care; secondly, it is based on redistribution as a realistic policy; and thirdly, it is politically acceptable.

Answers

Model answers:

	✓/✗	Reasons	Possible additional information
Extract 1	✓	speaks clearly explains the point clearly answers correctly uses good fixed phrases	follow up on the three advantages mentioned clarify the efficiency: equity differentiation if required
Extract 2	✗	doesn't speak clearly doesn't answer the question is talking about global health discrimination poor use of terminology poor use of visuals	
Extract 3	✗	speaks clearly, but doesn't answer the question the points are interesting but not relevant to the question is talking about development aid rather than equity in health care	
Extract 4	✓	speaks clearly explains the point clearly answers question with relevant points uses good fixed phrases; has prepared well has a good visual	authentic statistics from Scandinavian countries discussion on the taxation/health care issue role of government borrowing (mentioned particularly in Unit 7) to finance health care

Extract 2

Well … erm, I think equity is obviously important. Yes, it's very important. Erm … it's possible … er … you can see that there is no real fairness in health. It's obvious. You can see from the diagram that … oh, sorry, that's the wrong diagram … er, just a minute … right, so you can see that the … erm … figures are different between the countries … er … you can see this difference which the WHI, that's the World Health Institute, … no, sorry, I mean the WHO, the World Health Organization … Erm … anyway, the WHO says that health care is a global problem.

Extract 3

Everybody has the right to good health. That's a basic humanitarian principle. But many countries are so poor that people can't get proper treatment because the health system is underdeveloped or resources are badly allocated. The richer countries should give more in development aid so the poorer countries can improve their health infrastructure.

Extract 4

We need to ask the question, 'How does a country get the best possible and most equitable health care?' On the one hand, the government needs a healthy population but, on the other hand, the taxation and revenue systems must be fair. The government cannot expect people to pay a lot of tax and other charges for medications or treatment. For example, you can see here the figures for health expenditure in Scandinavian countries, showing percentage of GDP and spend per capita. They have a very good reputation for health care, but their taxation levels are very high. I don't think that every country wants to accept the same sort of relationship between high taxation and very large health and welfare costs.

Exercise D

Students should work in the same groups as their research groups from Lesson 9.3, Exercise F. They will need to have with them the research they have done individually on the group's chosen topic and countries.

1 Tell each group to discuss the information that they have found and agree on the main observations and conclusions from what they have researched.

2 In discussing these topics, students will need to decide who is going to speak when and what they are going to say. Encourage them to practise presenting to each other before talking to the whole class.

3 Allow each group a maximum of five minutes for the presentation. Then allow some time for questions. Remind the groups when discussing to use all the *good* techniques and phrases they have learnt.

Exercise E

Figure 1 shows health care indicators in the USA, France, UK and Singapore. The data are similar to what students will have presented and offer an opportunity to consolidate some of the language areas that have been used in the presentations. There are a number of differences which might be highlighted, even from a limited number of indicators from a selection of developed countries. The expenditure figures (US $100/per capita) are given thus to enable all data to fit on the same graph.

It is not necessary to give students the exact figures but if they are interested wait until they have completed the discussion.

See table below.

Answers

1 Possible answers:

You may want to give students sentences A and/or B as examples.

A As a proportion of GDP, the USA spends more than the other countries and Singapore spends less than the others.

B Life expectancy in all four countries is very similar, despite the differences in spending.

C The USA spends twice as much per capita on health care than France, and six times more than Singapore.

D Singapore spends the least on health care, approximately US $1,200 per capita annually.

E Singapore and the USA rely on private funding for their health services, 67% and 53% respectively.

F The private health care sector in the UK only provides 13% of total funding.

	Spending US $100 p/c	Life expectancy (years)	% from private funding	Child mortality*	% GDP
USA	72.9	78.1	52.8	67	16.0
France	36.01	81.0	20.8	48	11.0
UK	29.92	79.1	12.9	38	8.4
Singapore	12.28	79.7	67.4	21	3.4

*Child mortality per 100,000 live births

189

G Child mortality is highest in the USA, despite the fact that the USA spends most per capita on health.

H France spends more per capita than the UK, but child mortality is higher in France.

I Singapore has the lowest child mortality level, even though their health expenditure is the lowest per capita of the four countries.

2 Answers depend on the students.

Some of the sentences above highlight interesting and surprising information.

Exercise F

Put students in pairs (or threes). The data comes from an NHS trust in the South of England which had £429 million to spend in 2009–2010, or as the trust's publicity stated, 'around £815 for every minute of every day'. The data are based on a total population of about 600,000; mainly coastal towns (one large, several small, but with a lot of 'retirement' residents) and surrounding rural areas. The data given are important to a certain extent, but students should try to evaluate priorities and make decisions based on needs, efficiency and equity.

This activity should be fun and instructive for the students. It should not take a lot of time, but encourage students to discuss the various health care priorities and make serious choices. In their pairs, students should compare their ideas with another pair's.

Check students' answers, recording their assessments on the board if possible. Reveal the accurate figures to students and ask them to compare them with their own. Encourage comments on these figures, especially where there are big discrepancies between their figures and the real figures. Discuss any areas which the students find interesting.

Answers

1/2 Answers depend on students.

Priorities were as follows:

Of total £429 million budget:	%
Capital costs (equipment) and transfer payments (wages)	45
Management costs	4
Medicines	9
Community health services	15
Health promotion	2
Services for people with disabilities	11
Ambulance services	1
Primary health care including doctors (GPs), NHS dentists, pharmacists	11
Voluntary and community services	1

N.B. Owing to rounding of figures, the total in the above does not add up to 100%.

3 'Health promotion' and 'voluntary services' only take up a small portion of this NHS trust's budget. The first is important because it involves **prevention** of illness (which students heard about in the first part of the lecture). It might include clinics to stop smoking, sessions to reduce weight (often called 'weight watchers'), meetings and sessions about nutrition. Many publications (free leaflets or booklets available at libraries or doctors) focus on prevention. The economic advantages of 'prevention' are evident – less illness, less loss of working time, better motivation, fewer medications used.

Voluntary services are important in the UK as support for NHS work. They often involve people who, for example, raise money for the NHS trust or its activities or people who bring books to patients. Many hospitals have a café which is for visitors (and some patients) which is organized by volunteers. Some home visiting and activities with long-term patients are done by volunteers.

Again, economic advantages are evident as no wages are paid to volunteers. The NHS trust will (probably) not pay National Insurance contributions for the volunteers.

Closure

Use the *Vocabulary bank* at the end of the Course Book unit to check that the group can remember the meaning, spelling and pronunciation of the vocabulary from welfare economics. You may also want to refer students to their Cornell notes sections from the different parts of the lecture.

Extra activities

This unit contains a lot of technical and semi-technical vocabulary. Students will need lots of practice with the vocabulary.

1 Work through the *Vocabulary bank* and *Skills bank* if you have not already done so, or as revision of previous study.

2 Use the *Activity bank* (Teacher's Book additional resources section, Resource 9A).

   A Set the crossword for individual work (including homework) or pairwork.

   Answers

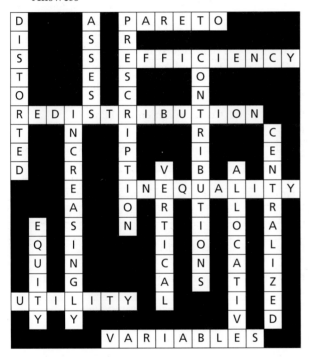

   B Ask students to look at the nouns in the table: are plural forms of the nouns possible? Tell students to use an English–English dictionary or online definitions to help them find out the answers to the following questions.

   1 Which forms are countable and which are uncountable?

   2 Do the countable and uncountable forms have different meanings?

Answers

Noun	Countable or uncountable?	Notes
allocation	U	
competitiveness	U	has special meaning of '*ability to compete*'; compare meaning of *competition*
coverage	U	
disabled	U	adjective used as noun and is uncountable; similar to *the unemployed, the poor, the needy*
discrimination	U	plural idea = *forms of discrimination*
efficiency	C/U	more frequently used in the singular
entitlement	C/U	technically countable, but usually used in singular to express concept
excess	C/U	used in singular form to mean *surplus*; plural usually implies something negative, e.g., *over-consumption, over-spending, over-reactions*
illness	C/U	more frequently used in singular (generic) way
norm	C	

3 Revise note-taking symbols – see the list at the back of the Course Book. Check back to Unit 5 if necessary. Give the meanings and ask students to write down the symbol (or do it the other way round). Then ask students to think about and discuss which ones they actually use. Are there any other ones that they have come across that they think are useful?

Alternatively, write the meanings on a set of cards. Put students in groups of about six with two teams in each group. Give each group a pile of cards. A student from each team picks a card and, without showing the members of his/her team, draws the appropriate symbol. The members of his/her team must say what the symbol stands for. If the student draws the correct symbol and the team gets the meaning right, the team gets a point. If the student draws the wrong symbol and/or the team gets the meaning wrong, the team loses a point. The teams take it in turns to pick a card.

4 Revise or identify abbreviations which will be useful for your students. Follow a similar procedure to Activity 3 if you have time. Otherwise, copy onto an OHT or other visual medium and cover the columns *Abbreviation* and *Meaning*. Show the clues. Students should work with a partner and try to identify as many abbreviations as possible. Reveal the *Abbreviation* column when checking answers, but keep the *Meaning* column covered until you have completed the feedback. Clarify any issues or uncertainties.

Clue	Abbreviation	Meaning
index of top UK companies	FTSE100	Financial Times top 100 companies in UK
regulatory body for finance and banking in UK	FSA	Financial Services Authority (UK)
leading financial newspaper in UK	FT	Financial Times
most important source of global finance	WB	World Bank
most powerful group of countries controlling a commodity	OPEC	Organization of the Petroleum Exporting Countries
body responsible for global health issues	WHO	World Health Organization
tax on goods	VAT	Value Added Tax
UN section responsible for analyzing trends in food production, distribution, etc.	FAO	Food and Agriculture Organization
measure of prices in UK	CPI	Consumer Price Index
European system of support and subsidies for farm products	CAP	Common Agricultural Policy
organization of 27 states in Europe	EU	European Union
group of 30 most developed nations	OECD	Organization for Economic Cooperation and Development
body responsible for global exports/imports, tariffs, etc.	WTO	World Trade Organization
measure of country's total production of goods and services	GDP	Gross Domestic Product
organization responsible for UK economic and social data	ONS	Office for National Statistics (UK)
government ministry responsible for health in UK	DH	Department of Health (UK)
a measure of how much demand changes when there is a rise in prices	PED	Price Elasticity of Demand
body responsible for organizing food aid to developing countries	UNWFP	United Nations World Food Programme
financial body which may give loans to countries in debt or with serious economic problems	IMF	International Monetary Fund
main financial authority in England	BoE	Bank of England
total planned expenditure/total of goods and services supplied	AD/AS	Aggregate Demand/Aggregate Supply

10 THE ECONOMICS OF SPORT

This unit considers the relationship between economics and sport. It shows that sport is a highly marketable product that generates large amounts of money worldwide, through the sale of tickets, sponsorship, television rights, active participation, sports clothing and other consumer items. The organization and financing of sport is therefore of particular interest to economists. This applies to mega-events such as the Olympic Games or World Cup, to other competitions such as Formula 1 motor racing and the (mostly) profitable football leagues around the world. Investment, sponsorship, media rights and licensing agreements are perhaps more widespread in sport than in any other sector of the global economy. Through the range of texts in this unit, students will be able to examine some of the economic connections to sport.

Skills focus

Reading

- recognizing the writer's stance and level of confidence or tentativeness
- inferring implicit ideas

Writing

- writing situation–problem–solution–evaluation essays
- using direct quotations
- compiling a bibliography/reference list

Vocabulary focus

- 'neutral' and 'marked' words
- fixed phrases from economics
- fixed phrases from academic English

Key vocabulary

administration (enter into ...)	ex-post analysis	procurement
bail-out	'externalities'	rocket (v)
bankruptcy	file (v)	slash
bid (n and v)	impact analysis	slump (n and v)
brand	insolvency	soar
budgetary	legacy	sponsorship
complementary	licensing	stage
concessions	lottery	staging
congestion	market failure	supplier
contingency	mega-event	tender (n and v)
creditor	monopoly	term (n)
derived	multiplier	undertaking
disposal	overhead	venue
ex-ante analysis	plummet	

10.1 Vocabulary

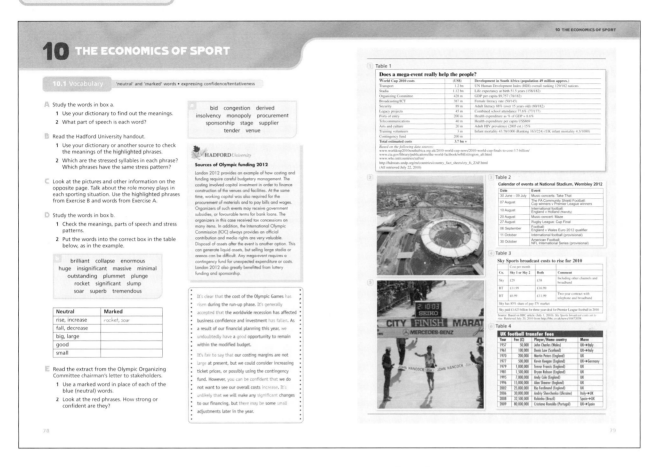

10 THE ECONOMICS OF SPORT

General note

Read the *Vocabulary bank* at the end of the Course Book unit. Decide when, if at all, to refer your students to it. The best time is probably at the very end of the lesson or the beginning of the next lesson, as a summary/revision.

Lesson aims

- understand when words are 'neutral' and when they are 'marked' (see *Vocabulary bank*)
- understand and use phrases expressing confidence/tentativeness (see *Vocabulary bank*)

Further practice in:

- fixed phrases/compound nouns from the discipline
- fixed phrases from academic English
- stress within words and phrases
- synonyms

Introduction

1 Revise words and phrases from economics encountered in the previous unit. Give definitions and ask students for the words/phrases. Slightly different wording is given here compared with definitions in Unit 8 Lesson 1, enabling students to practise listening skills. For example:

market forces – the factors within a market such as supply, demand, availability of capital and labour which work together

centralized economy – system of control over the economy, with the government making decisions on supply and production

vertical equity – concept from welfare economics where resources are redistributed to achieve efficiency and fairness

welfare economics – branch of economics dealing with how an economy distributes its resources efficiently and equitably for the benefit of society

Pareto efficiency – concept which relates to the equilibrium of resource allocation so that no redistribution can take place without making someone worse off

195

free market – economic system which allows the variables in an economy – demand, supply, price, labour, investment – to interact without government intervention

relative utility – a concept of how people value one good or service compared with others in order to gain maximum benefit for themselves

labour force mobility – the capacity of the workforce to move from one place to another to find new jobs

private sector – the section of the economy which is not funded by the government, but relies on motives such as investment for profit

2 Revise the following phrases used in academic writing. Ask students what sort of information will follow these phrases.

> *On the other hand*
>
> *In conclusion …*
>
> *To put it another way …*
>
> *As Smith (2002) pointed out …*
>
> *Research has shown that …*
>
> *Part of the difficulty is …*
>
> *To start with …*
>
> *This can be defined as …*
>
> *As a result …*
>
> *Finally …*
>
> *Given what has been shown above …*

Language note

It may be helpful to point out that the texts in this unit refer to *football* and do not use the American term, *soccer*. So, reference is made to the *football* World Cup. Americans use *soccer* to distinguish football from American football. Other English-speaking countries outside of North America may use the umbrella term 'gridiron', which again refers to American-style football. Where the focus is specifically on American football, this is made clear in the text. It should also be pointed out that *rugby* is *not* a version of American football, nor another name for it!

Exercise A

Set for individual work and pairwork checking. Feed back with the whole class.

Answers

Model answers:

Word	Part of speech	Meaning/synonym
bid	n (C), v (I/T)	offer to provide a good or service at a particular price, usually in competition with other bidders
congestion	n (U)	'traffic jam' or transport overcrowding which can cause delays
derived	adj	usually collocates with 'demand'; when demand for one good or service increases, demand for another good or service also increases. This is *derived demand* as it 'comes from' the main increase.
insolvency	n (U)	strictly speaking *not* bankruptcy; when debts are greater than liquid assets; inability of, for example, a football club to pay its costs, including wages, unless it sells players
monopoly	n (C)	usually used in singular form; dominant position of a single (sole) provider, supplier, employer that excludes competition from others
procurement	n (U)	acquisition process for goods and services required for a specified period
sponsorship	n (U)	financial arrangement between, e.g., a company (the sponsor) and a sports team or event. The company receives advertising, licensing and publicity rights as part of the deal.
stage	v (T)	to organize or to hold an event or competition
supplier	n (C)	company or organization which has a contract with the organizers of an event, but which may not have exclusive licensing agreements; they may have 'favoured' or 'preferred' status, such as an airline carrier for an event
tender	n (C), v (T/I)	an offer to provide goods and services at a specifically named price; the process of making such an offer (see **Language note** on p. 197)
venue	n (C)	location for an event; venues could be arenas (e.g., for cycling or basketball), swimming pools or stadia

Language and subject note

The words *bid*, *tender* and *procurement* are related in meaning but are not synonymous. *Bid* can mean the offer by a company to provide a good or service, in competition with others. However, *bid* is also found with reference to a country's expression of desire to stage a major event such as the Olympic Games. In this case, the country puts forward a bid, which obviously includes costing. However, this costing is not the main criterion for selection. This bid is often described as the country's *candidature*.

A *tender* is similar to a bid. A company or potential supplier submits an offer to provide specific goods or services under certain conditions of participation and documentation.

Procurement is the process of acquiring all the goods and services needed for an event or project and is usually seen from the perspective of the organizer. Here the emphasis is on obtaining the best value.

Exercise B

1 Set for individual work and pairwork checking. Other sources besides dictionaries could be business textbooks, other reference books, or the Internet.

2 Show students how they can draw the stress pattern for the whole word as well as just locating the stressed syllable. If they use the system of big and small circles shown in the Answers section, they can see the pattern for the whole phrase quite easily.

Answers

Model answers:

1 See table below.

2

budgetary management*	Ooo Ooo
capital investment	Ooo oOo
working capital	Oo Ooo
government subsidies*	Ooo Ooo
favourable terms	Oooo O
bank loans	O O
tax concessions	O oOo
media rights	Oo O
disposal of assets	oOo o Oo
liquid assets	Oo Oo
contingency fund	oOoo O
lottery funding	Ooo Oo

*Budgetary management and *government subsidies* have the same stress pattern.

Exercise C

Set for pairwork or class discussion. Encourage students to speculate about what is illustrated in the tables and photos. Students should use the highlighted phrases and other words that are useful from the text in Exercise B; they can also use words from Exercise A.

Feed back with the whole class. Accept anything reasonable.

Answers

Possible answers:

1 A table showing World Cup 2010 costs and data: South Africa has made significant progress according to the UN Human Development Index (HDI), and has made tremendous advances in education and literacy. It is obvious that massive problems remain, not least in health care and HIV treatment. Infant mortality remains high, while life expectancy is low. The question is whether $3.7 billion dollars including the large **contingency fund** for a prestige event is good value. As the table shows, 'legacy projects' (to improve the lives of local people) amount to only $45 million, while stadia construction is over $1 billion. Even huge

budgetary management	control of budgets
capital investment	the money paid to acquire (buy) a capital (fixed) asset
working capital	technically, current assets minus current liabilities; more commonly, capital which is readily available
government subsidies	support payments made by the public sector to offset the real cost of goods, services or projects
favourable terms	conditions for borrowing money which offer generous repayment schedules or low interest rates
bank loans	money lent by/borrowed from a bank
tax concessions	special tax-free or tax-reduced conditions
media rights	broadcasting rights sold to public and/or private media organizations
disposal of assets	when assets are sold, transferred or scrapped
liquid assets	money, or cash in hand, which can be used immediately to buy, sell, pay debt, etc.
contingency fund	an amount of money to be set aside for emergency or unexpected expenditure
lottery funding	money allocated to an organization or project from the National Lottery fund (as in the UK)

infrastructure expenditure such as for 'ports of entry' is likely to be of limited value for the majority of citizens unless external and internal tourism can really soar as a result of the event, with a positive impact on the labour market.

2   A stadium or construction site (Olympics 2012): The construction of the stadia and **venues** for the 2012 Olympics is likely to cost £1.3 billion (almost $2 billion). As South Africa 2010 and London 2012 illustrate, **budgetary management** is difficult to achieve with increasing costs for land and **procurement**. Organizers often need to use the **contingency funds**. For example, regarding the 2012 Olympics, increased VAT taxes in the UK, higher air fares and other factors emphasize how externalities have to be considered.

3   The table shows a calendar of events at Wembley Stadium. One key issue is what happens to stadia after a mega-event. For example, there is some concern as to what will happen to the South African 2010 World Cup stadia. The table shows how essential it is that people make maximum use of a major stadium, such as Wembley, that can **stage** important football matches and rock concerts in the same week. The venue is, after all, a major **asset**, but it is clear that it takes a long time to pay for itself from ticket prices, which is why merchandising and licensing to food and drinks **suppliers** is so important. **Disposal** of some major capital investments after a mega-event has proved problematic in the past. The Athens Olympics Games in 2004 were seriously over budget and sporting **venues** could not be sold easily afterwards. These factors contributed to the financial crisis in Greece which occurred in summer 2010.

4   This item illustrates the financial relationship between a broadcaster and **media rights**, especially for televised football. The monthly charges for subscribers mean that if you want to watch live sports, it can be expensive. Through licensing, a major licensee such as Sky sells on, and consequently shares, some of its rights with other companies who may offer a package with broadband and telephone components to their customers.

5   This photo of an athlete illustrates the relationship between sport and consumerism. The main product (e.g., the London Marathon) may be sponsored by one major and several minor companies. These companies receive advertising, logo and publicity and **media rights** for their **sponsorship**. Participation costs have soared in recent years and most big city marathons, for example, are always oversubscribed. It is difficult for an individual to pay a fee to participate unless he/she can guarantee to raise a certain amount of money for a charity. It is sometimes claimed that such events create a **monopoly** and exploit people who want to participate.

6   The table shows how UK transfer fees for footballers have rocketed over the past 60 years, with massive increases between 1957 and 1977 (10 times) and between 1979 and 1996 (15 times). It is unlikely that clubs ever get a return on their investment directly, for example, through increased attendances, so they rely very heavily on merchandising of official club goods and clothing. Most clubs also sell season tickets and this market is rather unique, economically speaking. Given the people costs involved (managers and footballers), many clubs are in serious debt, with some at risk of **insolvency**, which is why some UK clubs rely on rich owners to keep funding them.

Note: A useful book reference to give students for an insight into the complexities of the relationships between economics and sport is: Downward, P., Dawson, A., & Dejonghe, T. (2009). *Sports economics: Theory, evidence and policy.* Oxford: Butterworth-Heinemann.

Language and subject note

Insolvency and *bankruptcy* are not synonyms. The former means that an individual, company or other legal body cannot pay its bills or repay its debts. Possibly assets could be sold or the insolvent party may be able to generate cash. There are also legal options open to the insolvent party without applying for bankruptcy. Insolvency may lead to an application for bankruptcy by a company or individual, but this is not automatic or inevitable. Bankruptcy is a legal status with a number of conditions and restrictions attached. A company has to apply to a court for bankruptcy proceedings to begin. The debtor's assets will be disposed of equitably (fairly) to the creditors.

Exercise D

Introduce the idea of 'neutral' and 'marked' vocabulary (see *Language note* on page 199 and *Vocabulary bank*). Set for individual work and pairwork checking.

Feed back, discussing any differences of opinion about whether the words are marked, and in what sense they are marked. (Some students may argue that *minimal*, *significant* and *insignificant* are not marked, for example. Others may argue that they are marked, because they suggest not just that something is big/small, but that it is important/unimportant. Compare *There is a small problem with the program* and *There is an insignificant problem with the program*.)

Answers

Model answers:

Neutral	Marked
rise, increase	'rocket, soar (v)
fall, decrease	co'llapse (v and n), 'plummet (v), plunge (v and n), slump (v and n)
big, large	e'normous, huge, 'massive, sig'nificant, tre'mendous* (adj)
good	'brilliant, out'standing, su'perb, tre'mendous* (adj)
small	insig'nificant, 'minimal (adj)

*_tremendous_ can mean both very large and very good, so students may place this word in either category

Language note

One way of looking at vocabulary is to think about 'neutral' and 'marked' items. Many words in English are neutral, i.e., they are very common and they do not imply any particular view on the part of the writer or speaker. However, there are often apparent synonyms which are 'marked' for stance or opinion. Neutral words are usually thought of as basic vocabulary (the adjectives often have opposites, e.g., _big/small_; _light/dark_). Marked words tend to be less frequent and are therefore learnt later.

The marked words in Exercise D are not totally synonymous. Their appropriate use and interpretation will be dependent on the context and also on collocation constraints. For example, one can say that a building is 'massive', but not (in the same sense) 'significant'.

Exercise E

1 Set for individual work and pairwork checking. Make sure that students understand any words they are not sure of. Feed back with the whole class by asking individual students to read out a sentence. Make sure that the pronunciation and stress patterns of the marked words are correct.

2 Put the table from the Answers section on the board. Make sure that students understand _confident_ and _tentative_. Elicit answers from the whole class and complete the table. Point out that these phrases are usually found in conversation or in informal writing such as this. Academic writing also requires writers to show degrees of confidence and tentativeness. The mechanisms for this will be covered in the next lesson.

Answers

Model answers:

1 It's clear that the cost of the Olympic Games has (_risen_) soared/rocketed during the run-up phase. It's generally accepted that the worldwide recession has affected business confidence and investment has (_fallen_) plummeted/slumped/collapsed. As a result of our financial planning this year, we undoubtedly have a (_good_) tremendous/outstanding opportunity to remain within the modified budget.

It's fair to say that our costing margins are not (_large_) enormous/huge at present, but we could consider increasing ticket prices, or possibly using the contingency fund. However, you can be confident that we do not want to see our overall costs (_increase_) soar/rocket/escalate. It's unlikely that we will make any (_significant_) huge/massive changes to our financing, but there may be some (_small_) minimal/insignificant adjustments later in the year.

2

	Very confident	Fairly confident	Tentative (= not confident)
It's clear that	✓		
It's generally accepted that		✓	
we undoubtedly have	✓		
It's fair to say that		✓	
we could			✓
you can be confident that	✓		
It's unlikely that		✓	
there may be			✓

Closure

1 For further practice of neutral and marked vocabulary, ask students to write down some basic words, e.g., four verbs, four nouns and four adjectives. Put a list of these on the board and ask students if they are neutral or marked. See if you can find any opposites. Ask students to find some synonyms for neutral words – they can use a dictionary. A synonyms dictionary or Microsoft Word thesaurus can be useful here as well.

2 Ask pairs or groups to define as accurately as they can three of the fixed phrases from economics listed in the _Vocabulary bank_. Give them a few minutes to think of their definitions, then feed back and discuss as a class.

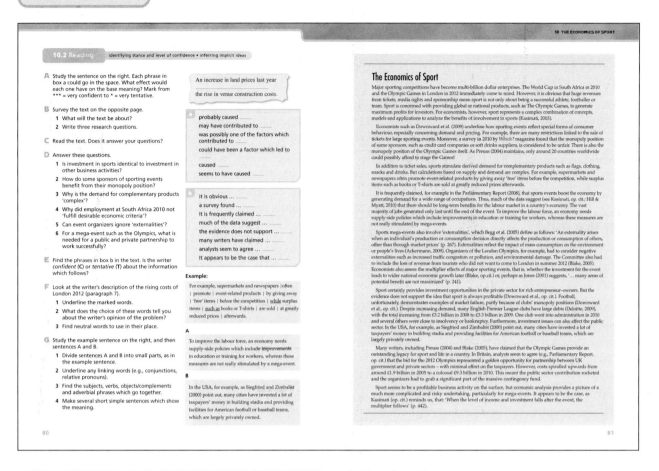

General note

Read the *Skills bank – Identifying the parts of a long sentence* at the end of the Course Book unit. Decide when, if at all, to refer students to it. The best time is probably at the very end of the lesson or the beginning of the next lesson, as a summary/revision.

Lesson aims

- identify the writer's stance on information from the use of marked words
- identify the writer's level of confidence in the research or information
- infer implicit ideas

Further practice in:

- finding the main information in a sentence

Introduction

Introduce the idea of degree of confidence in information, which is usually shown in academic writing. More often that not, writers will avoid very categorical statements such as 'X was the cause of Y' and will demonstrate the extent to which they are sure about something through various different linguistic devices such as modals and hedging words and phrases.

Put this table on the board to help explain the idea:

100% *** definitely true. The writer is very confident.	X caused Y
75% ** probably true. The writer is a little tentative.	X probably/is likely to have caused Y
50% * possibly true. The writer is very tentative.	X may/might/could have/ possibly caused Y

Exercise A

Set the exercise for pairwork. Students should refer to the table on the board to explain the rating system. Feed back with the whole class, pointing out the aspects of the language that contribute to the degree of confidence.

Answers

Model answers:

Word/phrase	Rating	Words which show less than 100% confidence
probably caused	* *	probably
may have contributed to	*	may contributed (i.e., there were other reasons)
was possibly one of the factors which contributed to	*	possibly one of the factors (i.e., there were several factors) contributed
could have been a factor which led to	*	could a factor (i.e., there were other factors)
caused	* * *	–
seems to have caused	* *	seems

Exercise B

Remind students that surveying the text means scanning and skim-reading to get an approximate idea of the text contents. They should:

- look at the title
- look at the first few lines and the final few lines of the text
- look at the first sentence of each paragraph

Note that this is in order to get a very approximate idea of the contents of the text. This will enable students to formulate questions about the text for which they might try to find answers. Students should be discouraged from reading deeply at this point, as they will be able to do this later.

Set for individual work and pairwork discussion. Each pair should agree three questions. Feed back with the whole class. Write some research questions on the board.

Exercise C

Set for individual work followed by pairwork discussion. Feed back with the whole class. Ask whether the questions you have put on the board have been answered in the text.

Exercise D

These questions require students to 'infer' information – that is, understand what is not directly stated.

Set for individual work and pairwork checking. Feed back with the whole class, making sure that students understand the answers.

Answers

Model answers:

1 With investment in sports, the objective is not only to make a profit, but also to provide a successful product which is recognized nationwide or worldwide. Success is not just measured in terms of profits. For example, most people would consider Chelsea or Manchester United 'successful' football clubs in the UK, but they both have enormous debts. An example of investment from the public sector is the way many countries have 'elite' athletes who are paid by the government (really with taxpayers' money!) for their sporting abilities, in the hope of, for example, winning a gold medal for the nation at the Olympic Games!

2 They pay to raise the profile of their product while their competitors' products are excluded. People who may not identify with the product are forced to accept it. This applies to situations relating to suppliers/providers of fast food, drinks or credit card use.

3 Demand is difficult to predict and depends on many factors, such as popularity of a team, its success, amount of exposure in the media and impact of (others') monopoly positions. For example, sales of a snack food product such as crisps (potato chips) may depend on the success/image of the players who advertise it. A service such as banking or mortgage provision may depend on the success of the team or individual it sponsors.

4 The question is partly answered by the theoretical argument which follows about 'supply-side policies'. However, students need to infer that employment at the 2010 World Cup in South Africa was for short-term, unskilled, low-wage construction workers and stadium or security staff. 'Supply-side policies' are designed to boost long-term productivity and economic growth, using investment in new equipment but also in training and upgrading workers' skills.

5 Yes, if the organizers have an extremely powerful position. In such cases, they can make decisions which, for example, cause more pollution, inconvenience, restrictions or extra costs for local people. They make their event the *only* priority.

6 Good cooperation and communication; openness in discussion; honesty in setting costs and deadlines; clear designation of responsibility; accountability; and a good balance between, for example, profit and legacy.

Exercise E

Set for individual work and pairwork checking. Feed back with the whole class. Point out that these phrases are very important in academic writing and will help to determine whether something is a fact or an opinion – an important aspect of reading comprehension. They are also used by writers in developing their arguments for or against a particular point of view.

Answers

Model answers:

However, it is obvious that huge revenues from tickets, media rights and sponsorship mean sport is not only about being a successful athlete, footballer or team.	C
Moreover, a survey in 2010 by *Which?* magazine found that the monopoly position of some sponsors, such as credit card companies or soft drinks suppliers, is considered to be unfair.	C
It is frequently claimed, for example in the Parliamentary Report (2008), that sports events boost the economy by generating demand for a wide range of occupations.	T
Thus much of the data suggest (see Kasimati, op. cit.; Hill & Myatt, 2010) that there should be long-term benefits for the labour market in a country's economy.	T
But the evidence does not support the idea that sport is always profitable (Downward et al., op. cit.).	C
Many writers, including Preuss (2004) and Blake (2005), have claimed that the Olympic Games provide an outstanding legacy for sport and life in a country.	T
In Britain, analysts seem to agree (e.g., Parliamentary Report, op.cit.) that the bid for the 2012 Olympics represented a golden opportunity for partnership between UK government and private sectors – with minimal effect on the taxpayers.	T
It appears to be the case, as Kasimati (op.cit.) reminds us, that …	T

Exercise F

Set for pairwork. Feed back with the whole class. Discuss any differences in students' answers, and whether neutral equivalents are hard to find for some of the words.

Answers

Possible answers:

1 Many writers, including Preuss (2004) and Blake (2005), have claimed that the Olympic Games provide an <u>outstanding</u> legacy for sport and life in a country. In Britain, analysts seem to agree (e.g., Parliamentary Report, op.cit.) that the bid for the 2012 Olympics represented a <u>golden</u> opportunity for partnership between UK government and private sectors – with <u>minimal</u> effect on the taxpayers. However, costs <u>spiralled upwards</u> from around £1.9 billion in 2005 to a <u>colossal</u> £9.3 billion in 2010. This meant the public sector contribution <u>rocketed</u> and the organizers had to <u>grab</u> a <u>significant</u> part of the <u>massive</u> contingency fund.

2 The choice of words emphasizes the dramatic rise in the costs of London 2012 and the writer's generally critical attitude towards the increases.

3

Marked word	Neutral alternative
outstanding	notable, important
golden	suitable, useful, ideal
minimal	minor, limited
spiralled upwards	rose, increased
colossal	substantial*
rocketed	increased
grab	use/utilize
significant	large
massive	substantial**, allocated, sizeable

*substantial collocates better here

**a good text would avoid *substantial* twice in such a short passage, so a very neutral expression such as *the contingency fund allocated* would work better.

Exercise G

Draw the table from the Answers section on the board. Ask students to look at the example sentence and say which box each part of the sentence should go in. Complete the table for the example sentence as shown. Point out how noun phrases may be made up of several words. In each case, elicit which words are the core of the noun phrases (shown in bold in the table in the Answers section). Do the same with the verb phrases. Ask students to suggest how the sentence can be rewritten in several short, very simple sentences in which noun phrases and verb phrases are reduced to the core meaning as far as possible.

Demonstrate with these examples if necessary:

Supermarkets promote products.

Items are sold.

Point out how in the actual sentences the noun phrases have been expanded so that there is:

supermarkets + newspapers (*and* is a coordinating conjunction)

event-related + products (adjective + noun)

surplus + items + such as + books or T-shirts (adjective + noun + example with coordinating conjunction, *such as*)

Point out how the verb phrases have been expanded, too.

often + promote + before the competition (time adverb + verb + time adverbial phrase)

by giving away 'free' items (preposition + gerund + noun phrase)

are sold + at greatly reduced prices + afterwards (verb + adverbial phrase + time adverb)

Point out that *whereas* is a subordinating conjunction which compares or contrasts information between the main and subordinating clauses.

Set questions 1–4 (relating to sentences A and B) for individual work and pairwork checking. Feed back with the whole class.

Answers

Model answers:

1–3

A To improve | the labour force, | an economy | needs | supply-side policies | which | include | improvements in education | or training for workers, | whereas | these measures | are not really stimulated | by a mega-event.

B In the USA, for example, | as Siegfried and Zimbalist (2000) point out, | many cities | have invested | a lot of taxpayers' money | in building stadia | and | providing facilities for American football or baseball teams, | which | are largely privately owned.

	Subject noun phrases	Verb phrases	Object/complement noun phrases	Adverbial phrases	Notes
Example	... **supermarkets and newspapers**	promote	event-related products	often by giving away 'free' items before the competition	in this sentence, *whereas* is a subordinating conjunction of contrast
	surplus items such as books or T-shirts	are sold		at greatly reduced prices; afterwards.	
A	An **economy**	needs	**supply-side policies;** to improve the labour force		*to improve the labour force* is the object complement; *which* acts as relative pronoun (for '*policies*') and subject of its relative clause
	(which)	include	**improvements** in education or **training** for workers		*or* is a coordinating conjunction
	these measures	are not (really) stimulated		really; by a mega-event.	*whereas* is a subordinating conjunction of contrast
B				In the USA; for example (*)	*as* is a subordinating conjunction of manner (*) these adverbials relate to the main sentence which comes after the subordinate clause
	(as) Siegfried and Zimbalist (2000)	point out			
	many cities	have invested ... in	(a lot of) **taxpayers' money** (direct object) building stadia and providing facilities for American football or baseball teams (indirect object)		*and/or* are simple coordinating conjunctions, but the use of *or* allows for ellipsis, so it is not necessary to write *teams* twice
	(which)	are (privately) owned.		(privately) (**); largely	*which* is (here) a subject relative pronoun (**) *privately* is an adverb attached to the verb

Language note

Some of the grammar in the table on the previous page is quite tricky. You may want to explain **if you think it is appropriate**. Verbs such as *believe, invest*, etc., are considered transitive so can take a direct object or they may be used with a preposition. They are not phrasal verbs. When they are used with a preposition, the phrase after the preposition functions as a form of indirect object. Give these examples of different structural formats:

believe/believe in

He believed the evidence completely. (subject + verb + direct object + adverb)

He believed in the capitalist system. (subject + verb + in + object)

He believed strongly in (supporting) the free market economy. (subject + verb + adverb + in + [gerund] + object)

invest/invest in

He invested his money wisely. (subject + verb + direct object + adverb)

He invested his money in Japan. (subject + verb + direct object + adverbial phrase of place).

He invested wisely in government bonds. (subject + verb + adverb + in + object)

A verb like *compete*, however, cannot take a direct object, i.e., it is intransitive. But the verb can be used with a few prepositions – *for, in, with* – but that does not make it transitive! Again, compare the structural differences:

The company usually competes quite openly. (subject + adverb + verb + modifier + adverb)

The company competes in the Asian market. (subject + verb + adverbial)

He always wanted to compete in the Olympic Games. (subject + adverb + verb + infinitive + adverbial)

The company is competing for a larger share of the South American market. (subject + verb + preposition + object)

4 Possible sentences:

   A An economy needs supply-side policies.

     It needs these policies in order to improve the labour force.

     The policies include improvements in education.

     They also include (improvements in) training for workers.

     These measures (education and training) are not stimulated by mega-events.

   B The information refers to the USA.

     An example is provided by Siegfried and Zimbalist (2000).

     Many cities have invested a lot of money.

     The money comes from taxpayers.

     The cities have invested money in building stadia and providing facilities.

     The stadia and facilities are for American football and baseball teams.

     These teams are privately owned.

Language note

1 Subjects and objects will nearly always be nouns, with or without modifying adjectives, or pronouns.

   Examples:

     To earn a lot of money is the aim of many people.

     Many people want to earn a lot of money.

   Complements can be

     ● nouns: *He is a doctor.*

     ● adjectives: *He is French.*

     ● adverbs: *He is ready.*

2 There are several types of conjunction in English.

   Coordinating conjunctions such as *and, or, but* link elements of equal grammatical status.

   Correlative conjunctions have two items: either ... or ... ; both ... and ... .

   Subordinating conjunctions relate clauses to each other using single words (e.g., *that* with verbs of saying, thinking, etc., *after, as, before, if, although, while*) or phrases (e.g., *as soon as, in order to, provided that ...*).

   See a good grammar reference book.

3 Adverbial phrases add information about the actions or processes described by the verb phrase.

Closure

Here are some newspaper headlines connected with sport. Ask students to identify marked vocabulary items in each sentence and to suggest more neutral words. Feed back, comparing answers and discussing any differences of opinion. Do the first item as an example for the students.

Example:

*City debts **soar** as Milanovic **slashes** funding!*

● Debts at City have increased sharply as (the owner) Milanovic has reduced funding considerably.

Massive injury list at United!

Ronaldo transfer value plunges!

Massive protests as owners throw out fans' favourite manager!

Spectator numbers plummet: City finances close to collapse!

Soaring costs: season ticket numbers plummet!

Taxpayers pick up new gigantic Olympic bills!

Possible changes:

- United have a long injury list.
- The transfer market value of Ronaldo has fallen dramatically.
- Supporters have protested in large numbers at the decision of the owners to dismiss their favourite manager.
- A severe decline in spectators means the financial situation for City is extremely serious.
- A large increase in season ticket prices has led to a decline in the number of tickets which have been bought.
- The public sector will be expected to pay more for the extremely high costs of the Olympic Games.

10.3 Extending skills

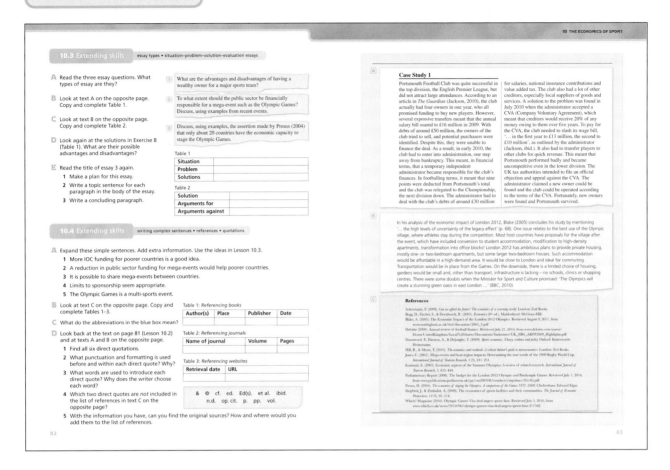

Lesson aims

- understand situation–problem–solution–evaluation structure in essays relevant to the discipline
- understand the use of information in this type of essay structure to:

  describe

  give cause and effect

  compare

  evaluate

  argue for

Further practice in:

- identifying required essay types
- producing an outline
- writing key sentences – which can be expanded in the next lesson into longer sentences

Introduction

Revise the different types of essay that were examined in Unit 8. Say or write on the board some key words or phrases from essay titles such as the following:

> *State …*
>
> *Outline …*
>
> *Describe …*
>
> *Compare …*
>
> *Evaluate …*
>
> *Discuss …*
>
> *Why …?*
>
> *How …?*
>
> *To what extent …?*
>
> *How far …?*

Ask students to say

- what type of essay is required
- what type of organizational structure should be used

If students find this difficult, refer them to the *Skills bank* for Unit 8.

Exercise A

Set for individual work and pairwork checking.

Feed back with the whole class. Point out that in real life, essays given by lecturers often involve several types of writing in one essay. This is the case with essay 3. Tell students that in fact a possible structure for essay 3 would be the following, which is commonly found in many types of writing (including newspapers and academic writing).

Situation: description of a state of affairs, often giving some reasons and background information	description
Problem(s): the problems which are caused by the state of affairs; plus the effects of these problems	description (cause and effect)
Solution(s): ways of dealing with the problems (i) which may have been tried in the past or are being tried now; (ii) which will, may or could be tried in the future; suggestions for further solutions	description (+ possibly suggestion)
Evaluation of solution(s): comparison of solutions; opinion on how successful the solutions are or could be + justification; an opinion on which is the best option + justification	comparison and argument

Tell students they will plan (and possibly write) this essay.

Answers

Model answers:

1 Comparison, plus some evaluation.
2 Evaluation then analysis.
3 Outline of viewpoint, evaluation/argument/opinion, suggestions plus support (see table above).

Exercise B

Set for individual work and pairwork checking. Feed back with the whole class.

Answers

Model answers:

Situation	Portsmouth in top English football league; but changes of ownership, low attendances, high wage bills, expensive transfers and debts with local creditors created an unstable financial environment
Problem	this meant the club faced bankruptcy, so to continue operating it had to enter into administration; points were deducted and the club was relegated to a lower division
Solutions	Short term – administrator agreed to a CVA Long term – seek a new (wealthy) owner

Exercise C

Set for individual work and pairwork checking. Feed back with the whole class.

Answers

Model answers:

Solution	use Olympic village for private housing after the Games
Arguments for	commuting distance to London; affordable prices; good transport
Arguments against	limited choice of accommodation type; infrastructure not appropriate

Exercise D

Set for pairwork discussion. Feed back with the whole class. Accept any reasonable suggestions. Common sense answers are also suitable here.

Answers

Possible answers: See table below.

	Advantages	Disadvantages
CVA	club continues to function will keep some players even if not the best supporters are happy gains time to find new owner creditors receive something (possibly more than if club goes bankrupt) perhaps successful in lower division	have to accept the administrator's evaluation of situation tax authorities objected; may be successful in their claims poor team performance might lead to even lower attendances local creditors/suppliers unhappy and so may avoid any future contact with the club
New owner	will inject much-needed cash into the business supporters will be optimistic of a return to the Premiership over time	difficulty for new owner to take over a nearly bankrupt club investment risk – is the new owner patient enough to be satisfied with long-term returns?

Exercise E

1 Set for pairwork discussion. Remind students to refer back to the text in Lesson 10.2 for ideas and information, as well as the texts they have discussed in this lesson. Remind students about the basic structure of an essay (introduction – main body – conclusion).

If you wish, you can give students the first two columns of the table in the Answers section, with the third column empty for them to complete. The table is reproduced in the additional resources section (Resource 10B) for this purpose.

Feed back with the whole class. Build the plan on the board, using the ideas in the Answers section to help.

2 Ask students to write some topic sentences for the four body paragraphs, using the information in the plan. Remind students that topic sentences need to be very general. Set for individual work.

Feed back with the whole class, writing some examples on the board.

3 Set for pairwork, then discussion with the whole class. Or if you prefer, set for individual homework. The ideas should be those of the students. Remind them to introduce their ideas with suitable phrases.

Note: Students will need their essay plans again in Lesson 10.4.

Answers

1 Possible essay plan below:

Introduction		Examples of ideas
introduce the topic area give the outline of the essay		mega-events → extremely high costs, so only advanced economies can afford ... *Preuss (2004) claimed ...* *In this essay, I will discuss the argument that ...* *I will illustrate/describe ... (examples)* *I will consider ... (solutions)* *Finally, I will suggest ... (best solution)*
Body	**Para 1:** situation/problems (general)	1. Olympic Games (OG)/World Cup (WC) are very expensive undertakings monopoly position of Games → International Olympic Committee selection of host mostly from richer countries 2. sport as business → profit motive 3. nature of the events – sponsors/media/licences (often for multiple events – OG/Winter Games (WG) over 10-year period) 4. change in policy? WC → South Africa (low-income country)
	Para 2: problems (specific examples)	examples of cases: OG held in USA in 1984 (Los Angeles), 1996 (Atlanta); and WG often in USA or Canada profit: legacy trade-off/impact for Games and WC often discussed, but no fixed criteria for analysis (Kasimati, 2003; Blake, 2005)
	Para 3: solutions	1. more IOC funding for poorer candidates 2. reduce government involvement 3. sharing across countries (e.g., as done for World Cup 2002) 4. sponsors pay more or limit to single mega-event 5. reduce number of sports in single Olympics
	Para 4: evaluations of solutions	1. idea seems appropriate, but legacy impact should be improved 2. limit to, e.g., 30% public, 70% private → better chance for poorer nations; less capital investment 3. if geographically OK; rich + poor? 4. seems suitable → different types of sponsors? business decision – would sponsors accept? 5. highlight of many a sportsman/woman's life – take away?
Conclusion		*In my view/As I see it, the best option is ... because ...* *Firstly ...* *Secondly ...* *Thirdly ...*

2 Possible topic sentences:

Para 1	It is, undoubtedly, an expensive undertaking for any country to host the Olympic Games or the football World Cup.
Para 2	There are a number of examples which illustrate how recent decisions to stage major sporting events have favoured richer countries.
Para 3	According to the IOC, there is a desire to locate the Olympic Games in countries with less economic influence, and a number of potential solutions have been put forward.
Para 4	A comprehensive evaluation of these possible solutions reveals a number of disadvantages as well as advantages, particularly in the current economic climate.

3 Students' own concluding paragraphs.

Language note

Although 'situation–problem–solution–evaluation of solution' is often said to be an organizing principle in writing, in practice it is sometimes difficult to distinguish between the situation and the problem: they may sometimes seem to be the same thing. The important thing is to be clear about the main *focus* of the essay – that is, the answer to the question *What am I writing about?* – and to structure the essay around this.

Closure

The cities listed in the table on page 210 are likely to be candidates for the 2020 Summer Olympic Games.

Tell students to check they understand the abbreviations at the bottom of the table.

The International Olympic Committee (IOC) will probably select the shortlist of candidate cities in summer 2013. Then a final selection will be made. If you do this activity before the selection, you can follow this procedure.

Divide the class into groups. Each group should discuss the candidate cities according to the following criteria:

suitable location

experience

economic strength

legacy impact

other factors

Make an OHT, or data show, with the information above for students to discuss. The data relate to several major sports events since 1948.

After a short discussion, ask students to vote as individuals. Count the votes and select the top two or three cities for a final vote. If the decision to stage the 2020 Olympic Games has already been made, remove the successful candidate, but keep the remaining candidate list as likely candidates for 2024. Remember, the IOC does not permit the same continent to be host for successive Summer Olympic Games.

Note: If time does not permit this to be completed as a class activity, try to set up the discussion part. Set the decision-making for homework and ask students to come to the next lesson with their vote.

Choosing a venue for the Summer Olympic Games, 2020	
City, country	Relevant information
Brisbane, Australia	OG 2000 (Sydney) and 1956 (Melbourne) RWC 2003 (Australia)
Doha, Qatar	On shortlist of seven for OG 2016, but bid rejected Selected for WC 2022
Dubai, United Arab Emirates	First bid ever for major sporting event
Tokyo, Japan	OG 1964 WG (not Tokyo) 1972 and 1998 On shortlist for OG 2016, but eliminated in Round 2 voting WAC 1991 and 2007 (Osaka) WC with South Korea 2002 Possibly RWC 2019
Busan, South Korea	OG Seoul 1988 Pyeonchang lost in last round for WG 2010 and 2014, but favourite for 2018 WAC 2011 (Daegu) WC 2002 with Japan
Budapest, Hungary	–
Athens, Greece	Note: *Regionally*, WAC 1997 Athens, Greece OG 2004 Athens, Greece
Rome, Italy	OG 1960 WG (not Rome) 1956 and 2006 WC 1990 EC 1968 and 1980 WAC 1987
Madrid, Spain	Lost OG 2012 and 2016 votes (second to Rio) OG 1992 (Barcelona) WC 1982 EC 1984
Lisbon, Portugal	EC 2004
Saint Petersburg, Russia	OG 1980 (Moscow) WG 2014 (Sochi) WAC 2013 (Moscow); city bid for OG 2004, but not shortlisted WC (Russia, 2018)
Mexico, Central America	OG Mexico City 1968 WC 1970 and 1986 (remember OG 2016 Rio de Janiero, Brazil, and WC Brazil 2014)
USA (four new candidate cities)	OG 1996 and 1984 WC 1994 Chicago shortlisted for OG 2016, but not candidate for 2020 WG different venues 1960, 1980 and 2002
Toronto, Canada	OG 1976 (Montreal) WAC 1991 (Edmonton) Toronto had unsuccessful bids for OG 1996 and 2008 WG, different venues, 2010 and 1988
Rabat, Morocco	No previous bid for a major sporting event
Cape Town/Durban, South Africa	WC 2010 (South Africa) Good chance of RWC 2015 or 2019

Abbreviations:
OG = Summer Olympic Games
WG = Winter Olympic Games
WC = Football World Cup
EC = European Football Championship (2012 Poland/Ukraine; 2016 France)
WAC = World Athletics Championships (200+ nations)
RWC = Rugby World Cup (20 nations)

10.4 Extending skills

10.3 Extending skills essay types • situation–problem–solution–evaluation essays

A Read the three essay questions. What types of essay are they?

B Look at text A on the opposite page. Copy and complete Table 1.

C Look at text B on the opposite page. Copy and complete Table 2.

D Look again at the solutions in Exercise B (Table 1). What are their possible advantages and disadvantages?

E Read the title of essay 3 again.
1 Make a plan for this essay.
2 Write a topic sentence for each paragraph in the body of the essay.
3 Write a concluding paragraph.

1 What are the advantages and disadvantages of having a wealthy owner for a major sports team?

2 To what extent should the public sector be financially responsible for a mega-event such as the Olympic Games? Discuss, using examples from recent events.

3 Discuss, using examples, the assertion made by Preuss (2004) that only about 20 countries have the economic capacity to stage the Olympic Games.

Table 1

Situation	
Problem	
Solutions	

Table 2

Solution	
Arguments for	
Arguments against	

10.4 Extending skills writing complex sentences • references • quotations

A Expand these simple sentences. Add extra information. Use the ideas in Lesson 10.3.
1 More IOC funding for poorer countries is a good idea.
2 A reduction in public sector funding for mega-events would help poorer countries.
3 It is possible to share mega-events between countries.
4 Limits to sponsorship seem appropriate.
5 The Olympic Games is a multi-sports event.

B Look at text C on the opposite page. Copy and complete Tables 1–3.

C What do the abbreviations in the blue box mean?

D Look back at the text on page 81 (Lesson 10.2) and at texts A and B on the opposite page.
1 Find all six direct quotations.
2 What punctuation and formatting is used before and within each direct quote? Why?
3 What words are used to introduce each direct quote? Why does the writer choose each word?
4 Which two direct quotes are *not* included in the list of references in text C on the opposite page?
5 With the information you have, can you find the original sources? How and where would you add them to the list of references.

Table 1: *Referencing books*

Author(s)	Place	Publisher	Date

Table 2: *Referencing journals*

Name of journal	Volume	Pages

Table 3: *Referencing websites*

Retrieval date	URL

& © cf. ed. Ed(s). et al. ibid.
n.d. op. cit. p. pp. vol.

Case Study 1

Portsmouth Football Club was quite successful in the top division, the English Premier League, but did not attract large attendances. According to an article in *The Guardian* (Jackson, 2010), the club actually had four owners in one year, who all promised funding to buy new players. However, several expensive transfers meant that the annual salary bill soared to £16 million in 2009. With debts of around £50 million, the owners of the club tried to sell, and potential purchasers were identified. Despite this, they were unable to finance the deal. As a result, in early 2010, the club had to enter into administration, one step away from bankruptcy. This meant, in financial terms, that a temporary independent administrator became responsible for the club's finances. In footballing terms, it meant that nine points were deducted from Portsmouth's total and the club was relegated to the Championship, the next division down. The administrator had to deal with the club's debts of around £30 million for salaries, national insurance contributions and value added tax. The club also had a lot of other creditors, especially local suppliers of goods and services. A solution to the problem was found in July 2010 when the administrator accepted a CVA (Company Voluntary Agreement), which meant that creditors would receive 20% of any money owing to them over five years. To pay for the CVA, the club needed to slash its wage bill, '… in the first year to £13 million, the second to £10 million', as outlined by the administrator (Jackson, ibid.). It also had to transfer players to other clubs for quick revenue. This meant that Portsmouth performed badly and became uncompetitive even in the lower division. The UK tax authorities intended to file an official objection and appeal against the CVA. The administrator claimed a new owner could be found and the club could be operated according to the terms of the CVA. Fortunately, new owners were found and Portsmouth survived.

In his analysis of the economic impact of London 2012, Blake (2005) concludes his study by mentioning '… the high levels of uncertainty of the legacy effect' (p. 68). One issue relates to the best use of the Olympic village, where athletes stay during the competition. Most host countries have proposals for the village after the event, which have included conversion to student accommodation, modification to high-density apartments, transformation into office blocks! London 2012 has ambitious plans to provide private housing, mostly one- or two-bedroom apartments, but some larger two-bedroom houses. Such accommodation would be affordable in a high-demand area. It would be close to London and ideal for commuting. Transportation would be in place from the Games. On the downside, there is a limited choice of housing, gardens would be small and, other than transport, infrastructure is lacking – no schools, clinics or shopping centres. There were some doubts when the Minister for Sport and Culture promised: 'The Olympics will create a stunning green oasis in east London …' (BBC, 2010).

References

Ackermann, F. (2009). *Can we afford the future? The economics of a warming world.* London: Zed Books.
Begg, D., Fischer, S., & Dornbusch, R. (2005). *Economics* (8th ed.). Maidenhead: McGraw-Hill.
Blake, A. (2005). The Economic Impact of the London 2012 Olympics. Retrieved August 9, 2011, from www.nottingham.ac.uk/ttri/discussion/2005_5.pdf
Deloitte (2009). Annual review of football finance. Retrieved July 21, 2010, from www.deloitte.com/assets/Dcom-UnitedKingdom/Local%20Assets/Documents/Industries/UK_SBG_ARFF2009_Highlights.pdf
Downward, P., Dawson, A., & Dejonghe, T. (2009). *Sports economics: Theory, evidence and policy.* Oxford: Butterworth-Heinemann.
Hill, R., & Myatt, T. (2010). *The economics anti-textbook: A critical thinker's guide to microeconomics.* London: Zed Books.
Jones, C. (2001). Mega-events and host-region impacts: Determining the true worth of the 1999 Rugby World Cup. *International Journal of Tourism Research, 3* (3), 241–251.
Kasimati, E. (2003). Economic aspects of the Summer Olympics: A review of related research. *International Journal of Tourism Research, 5*, 433–444.
Parliamentary Report (2008). The budget for the London 2012 Olympic and Paralympic Games. Retrieved July 7, 2010, from www.publications.parliament.uk/pa/cm200708/cmselect/cmpubacc/85/85.pdf
Preuss, H. (2004). *The economics of staging the Olympics: A comparison of the Games 1972–2000.* Cheltenham: Edward Elgar.
Siegfried, J., & Zimbalist, A. (2000). The economics of sports facilities and their communities. *The Journal of Economic Perspectives, 14* (3), 95–114.
Which? Magazine (2010). Olympic Games Visa deal angers sports fans. Retrieved July 5, 2010, from www.which.co.uk/news/2010/06/olympic-games-visa-deal-angers-sports-fans-217502

82 83

General note

This lesson focuses on writing references for a bibliography according to the APA (American Psychological Association) system. Before the lesson, it would be useful to familiarize yourself with this system. See the *Skills bank*, and for more detailed information, websites such as http://owl.english.purdue.edu/owl/resource/560/02/.

Lesson aims

- use quotations with appropriate punctuation and abbreviations such as ibid.
- write a reference list (APA system)

Further practice in:

- the reverse activity to Lesson 10.2, i.e., putting extra information into simple sentences in an appropriate way

Introduction

Introduce the idea of using sources in writing. Look back at the text in Lesson 10.2 and ask students to find all the places where a reference to a source is mentioned. Ask them to find a quotation and a paraphrase. What are the main differences?

Exercise A

Remind students of the essay plan in Lesson 10.3. If you wish, you can reproduce the following table for them. They should try to get all the information in each numbered point into one sentence.

This activity is based on Paragraph 4 of the essay plan from Lesson 10.3, Exercise E. Note that each sentence is an evaluation of the potential solutions discussed in paragraph 3.

Para 4:	1. idea seems appropriate, but legacy impact should be improved
	2. limit to, e.g., 30% public, 70% private → better chance for poorer nations; less capital investment
	3. if geographically OK; rich + poor?
	4. seems suitable → different types of sponsors? business decision – would sponsors accept?
	5. highlight of many a sportsman/woman's life – take away?

211

Do the first sentence with the whole class as an example on the board. Students should feel free to add words as appropriate to make a coherent sentence; they can also paraphrase (e.g., *seems appropriate* → *appears to be a persuasive argument*).

Set the remaining sentences for individual work.

Answers

Possible answers:

1 The suggestion that poorer countries might receive larger amounts of IOC funding appears to be a persuasive argument, but the legacy impact for that country should be maximized.

2 Regarding the reduction of government financial involvement for mega-events, it has been suggested that a ratio of 30% public to 70% private funding would lead to better chances for poorer nations as less capital investment would be required.

3 The proposal for two countries, possibly one rich and one less wealthy, to share the staging of a mega-event appears attractive if the countries are immediate neighbours and the transport infrastructure is suitable.

4 Sponsorship could be expanded, but sponsors have a strong business hold over mega-events and any increase in payment or restriction of licensing agreements, such as limiting to a single event, would probably be strongly opposed.

5 For many sportsmen and women, the multi-sports Olympic Games are the highlight of that person's sporting life, and any attempt to take that moment away by reducing the number of sports would be controversial.

Exercise B

Tell students that this is a list of references from the text in Lesson 10.2. Note that it is called 'References' because it lists all the references actually given (it is not a list of all the sources the author might have consulted but not referred to – that is a bibliography).

Set for individual work and pairwork checking. Note that these tables are intended to help students identify some key information. For a full set of categories to include in a reference list, see the *Skills bank*. Tell students that when writing a reference list, they will need to pay close attention to the detail of the layout which is in APA style (the American Psychological Association). See the *Skills bank* for a website which (at the time of writing) gives further details. In particular, students should note and will need to practise:

- putting the names of writers and multiple writers in the correct alphabetical order according to family name, with the right spacing and punctuation
- writing all numbers correctly, including dates and page references

- using punctuation including the role and placing of full stops, commas and colons
- laying out the references in the correct style with the correct positions (e.g., of indents and tabs)
- using standard APA style features such as italic and brackets

Answers

Table 1:

Author(s)	Place of publication	Date of publication	Publisher
Ackermann, F.	London	2009	Zed Books.
Begg, D., Fischer, S., & Dornbusch, R.	Maidenhead	2005	McGraw-Hill.
Downward, P., Dawson, A., & Dejonghe, T.	Oxford	2009	Butterworth-Heinemann.
Hill, R., & Myatt, T.	London	2010	Zed Books.
Preuss, H.	Cheltenham	2004	Edward Elgar.

Table 2:

Name of journal	Volume/	Pages Issue
International Journal of Tourism Research	3(3)	241–251
International Journal of Tourism Research	5	433–444
The Journal of Economic Perspectives	14(3)	95–114

Table 3:

Retrieval date	URL
August 9, 2011	www.nottingham.ac.uk/ttri/discussion/2005_5.pdf
July 21, 2010	www.deloitte.com/assets/Dcom-UnitedKingdom/Local%20Assets/Documents/Industries/UK_SBG_ARFF2009_Highlights.pdf
July 7, 2010	www.publications.parliament.uk/pa/cm200708/cmselect/cmpubacc/85/85.pdf
July 5, 2010	www.which.co.uk/news/2010/06/olympic-games-visa-deal-angers-sports-fans-217582

Exercise C

Many of these were covered in Unit 5, so ask students to check back if they are not sure, or they can refer to the list at the back of their books; they can also check online at the APA site and/or the other sites given in the *Skills bank*.

Set for individual work and pairwork checking.

Answers

Model answers:

&	and
©	copyright
cf.	compare
ed.	edition
Ed(s).	editor(s)
et al.	and other authors
ibid.	same place or same page in a work already referred to
n.d.	no date (used in a reference list if there is no date – as is often the case with web articles)
op. cit.	the work already referred to
p.	page
pp.	pages
vol.	volume

Exercise D

Remind students (if you have not done so already) of the two main ways in which students can use sources (i.e., references to other writers' work) in their writing:

- by giving the exact words used by another writer

- by paraphrasing another writer's ideas, i.e., rewriting the ideas using their own, different words but retaining the meaning

The first method is referred to as quotation or direct quotation. Short direct quotations should be in quotation marks, and incorporated into the paragraph. Quotations of more than one sentence should be 'display quote' style, i.e., on a new line, and indented.

The second method is referred to as paraphrase, summary or indirect quotation. Note that around 90% of the paraphrase should be new words.

Give students the framework for the Answer table opposite.

1 Set for individual work. Tell students to look for all six direct quotations and to identify the research sources in the reference list on page 83 of the Course Book. Writing the page numbers on the reference list may seem a mechanical exercise, but it is useful for students to get into the habit of doing this. It will enable them to find an original source book, refer to the relevant part of the book, and read more about the subject. Note that not all the direct quotations are listed (see 4/5 below).

2/3 Students should identify the punctuation and introducing phrases used.

Feed back with the whole class.

4/5 Remind the students that, for these searches, they are doing something which should really *not* be necessary, i.e., looking for missing information. Students should always keep a record of Internet articles and items they find with all the details. Otherwise, it can be tricky to search again!

Answers

Model answers:

See table on next page.

Quote	Source	Punctuation/ formatting before/ within each direct quote	Introducing phrase + reason for choice
From reading text in Lesson 10.2			
'An externality arises when an individual's production or consumption decision directly affects the production or consumption of others, other than through market prices'	Page 267 of Begg et al. (2005). *Economics* (8th ed.). Maidenhead, UK: McGraw-Hill.	colon + 'Xxx'	Sports mega-events also involve 'externalities', which Begg et al. (2005) define as follows: … reason: The authors want to provide a complete definition.
'… many areas of potential benefit are not maximized'	Page 241 of Jones, C. (2001). Mega-events and host-region impacts: Determining the true worth of the 1999 Rugby World Cup. *International Journal of Tourism Research*, 3(3).	'xxx'	Economists also assess the multiplier effects of major sporting events, that is whether the investment for the event leads to wider national economic growth later (Blake, op.cit.) or, perhaps as Jones (2001) suggests, … reason: The writer makes a comment which he/she supports by using a direct quote from Jones (2001).
'When the level of income and investment falls after the event, the multiplier follows'	Page 442 of Kasimati, E. (2003). Economic aspects of the Summer Olympics: A review of related research. *International Journal of Tourism Research*, 5.	colon + 'Xxx'	It appears to be the case, as Kasimati (op.cit.) reminds us, that: reason: The writer wants to reinforce an idea by using a direct quotation. The writer shows he/she is not very certain of the correctness of Kasmati's statement.
From texts A and B			
'… in the first year to £13 million, the second to £10 million'	*Students to complete in 4/5*	'xxx'	To pay for the CVA, the club needed to slash its wage bill, reason: The writer wants to reinforce the amounts involved.
' … the high levels of uncertainty of the legacy effect'	Blake, A. (2005). The Economic Impact of the London 2012 Olympics. Retrieved August 9, 2010 from www.nottingham.ac.uk/ttri/ discussion/2005_5.pdf	'xxx'	In his analysis of the economic impact of London 2012, Blake (2005) concludes his study by mentioning reason: This is the author's final viewpoint.
'The Olympics will create a stunning green oasis in east London …'	*Students to complete in 4/5*	colon + 'Xxx …'	There were some doubts when the Minister for Sport and Culture promised: reason: The writer wants to signal his/her doubts about the idea expressed by the Minister for Sport. It is important for the reader to know exactly what was said.

4/5 The 'missing' sources would be inserted alphabetically in the list of references and are as follows:

BBC News. (2010, January 26). London 2012 Olympic Park to be 'stunning green oasis'. Retrieved from http://news.bbc.co.uk/1/hi/ england/london/8481945.stm

Jackson, J. (2010, July 8). Balram Chainrai 'wants to be Portsmouth owner for second time'. *The Guardian*. Retrieved from www.guardian.co.uk/football/2010/jul/08/ portsmouth-balram-chainrai-andrew-andronikou

A search of the BBC website using '**stunning green oasis**' as the search term is sufficient.

The *Guardian* online article has an author and a year. The student could also go to the *Guardian* home page and use the direct quotation as given in the text. This is actually quicker than searching for **Jackson + Portsmouth Football Club.**

The searches illustrate how direct quotations can be located and serves as a reminder to students that plagiarism is not difficult to detect, even with a Google search. Most institutions have something like *Turnitin*® which is a powerful detection tool.

Language and subject note

An ampersand (&) is used with multiple authors, preceded by a comma.

The full stop at the end of the reference is omitted in the case of URLs.

Dates are (for example) April 7, not April 7th.

Closure

Refer students to the *Skills bank* for a summary of writing references. Study how the following are used:

- names (order)
- punctuation (capital letters, full stops, commas, colons)
- layout (indentation, spacing)
- style features (italics, brackets)

For further practice, use Resource 10C from the additional resources section. Ask students to check the references on a library database or on the Internet. Discuss which sources are likely to be the most accurate and give them all the information they need. Usually, the best way to check bibliographical details is to use a university library catalogue. Information found on the Internet is frequently inaccurate or incomplete. Students should also make any necessary changes to ensure the references fit the APA models used in this unit. If possible, they should use the online website references (see *Skills bank*) to help them. Remind students that they will also need to put the references in the correct alphabetical order.

Correct versions are:

Bracking, S. (2009). *Money and power: Great predators in the political economy of development*. London: Pluto Press.

Friedman, T. L. (1999). *The Lexus and the olive tree*. New York: Farrah, Straus Giroux.

Goldblatt, D. (2010). Footing South Africa's World Cup bill. BBC World Service *Focus on Africa* magazine. Retrieved from http://news.bbc.co.uk/1/hi/world/africa/8718696.stm

Organization for Economic Co-operation and Development (2010). Country statistical profiles 2010. Paris: OECD. Retrieved from http://stats.oecd.org/Index.aspx?DataSetCode=CSP2010

Sachs, J. E. (2005). *The end of poverty: Economic possibilities for our time*. New York: Penguin Books.

Stiglitz, J. E. (2002). *Globalization and its discontents*. New York: Norton & Company.

Tabachnik, B. G., & Fidell, L. S. (2007). *Using multivariate statistics* (5th ed.). Boston, MA: Pearson.

1 Work through the *Skills bank* and *Vocabulary bank* if you have not already done so, or as revision of previous study.

2 Use the *Activity bank* (Teacher's Book additional resources section, Resource 10A).

   A Set the wordsearch for individual work (including homework) or pairwork.

   Answers

   B Set for individual work (including homework) or pairwork. Accept all reasonable answers. Students should be able to explain the meaning.

   Answers

   Possible answers:

capital	investment/expenditure
disposal	of assets
favourable	terms
fixed	rate, assets, terms
impact	analysis
licensing/sponsorship	agreement
market	failure
medium-term	investment
private/public	sector
tax	concessions

3 Ask students to choose one of the other essays in Lesson 10.3 and make a plan. They can also write topic sentences for each paragraph in the essay.

11 LABOUR MARKETS

This unit looks in more detail at the importance of the labour market as an economic factor. The lecture provides students with an insight into some of the issues affecting global labour markets, including population growth, ageing populations, migration and changing patterns of work. The lecture allows students to develop their Cornell note-making skills. In the accompanying writing activities, students are provided with more practice related to organizing an academic essay and developing an argument. Students will also reinforce their speaking skills by analyzing the way information is signalled by a speaker, often using specific phrases, in order to construct the argument.

Skills focus

 Listening

- recognizing the speaker's stance
- writing up notes in full

Speaking

- building an argument in a seminar
- agreeing/disagreeing
- expressing and supporting opinions

Vocabulary focus

- words/phrases used to link ideas (*moreover*, *as a result*, etc.)
- stress patterns in noun phrases and compounds
- fixed phrases from academic English
- words/phrases related to labour market issues

Key vocabulary

See also the list of fixed phrases from academic English in the *Vocabulary bank* (Course Book page 92).

accountability	expansionary	migrate	reversal
ageing	exploit	migration	saturation
census	exploitation	monopolistically	slavery
contractionary	facilitate	net (adj)	strike (n)
crude	fertility	occupational	surpass
curb (n)	immigration	pension	trafficking
demographic	inflow	per annum	unlawful
departure	inhuman	predict	vulnerable
displaced	intermediary (n)	regime	workforce
dramatically	life expectancy	remittances	would-be (adj)
entitlement	manufacturing	retire	
exert	middlemen	retirement	

11.1 Vocabulary

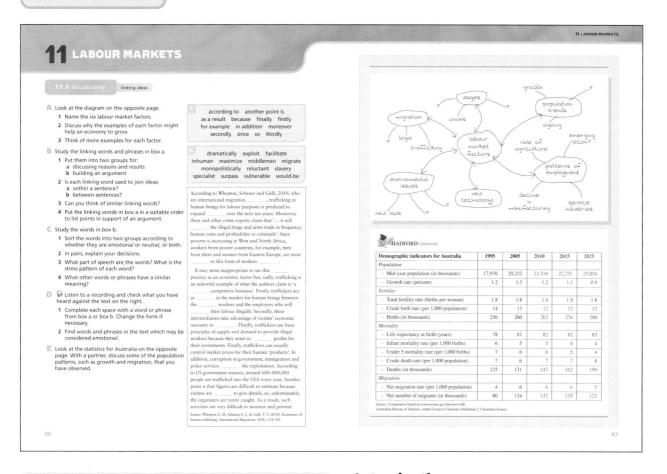

General note

Read the *Vocabulary bank* at the end of the Course Book unit. Decide when, if at all, to refer your students to it. The best time is probably at the very end of the lesson or the beginning of the next lesson, as a summary/revision.

Lesson aims

- use rhetorical markers: to add points in an argument; to signal cause and effect (between- and within-sentence linking)
- further understand lexical cohesion: the use of superordinates/synonyms to refer back to something already mentioned; building lexical chains

Further practice in:

- synonyms, antonyms and word sets from the discipline
- identifying emotional or neutral lexical use

Introduction

1 Revise some vocabulary from previous units. Give students some key words from the previous unit (in italics below) and ask them to think of terms connected with these words (for example, some key phrases from economics and/or economic factors in sport):

> *budgetary* management/control, *sponsorship* deal, *multiplier* effect, *contingency* fund/budget/plan, *complementary* products, *derived* demand, *impact* analysis, *legacy* impact/factors, *media* rights/agreements, *lottery* funding/money, *procurement* contract

2 Introduce the topic: before asking students to open their books, ask them what factors influence the effectiveness of labour markets. Accept any reasonable suggestions. Remind students that they have seen how labour markets represent one of the most important economic resources, but here they are going to consider this topic in more detail.

Exercise A

Ask students to open their books and look at the diagram on page 87.

Check the meaning of the words in the diagram. If necessary, outline the role of trade unions and discuss how important they are in students' own economies. Clarify ideas such as *trends*, giving some examples of growth (Chinese economy), rising unemployment (USA), increased carbon emissions (India, China), agricultural development (Brazil), population growth (India) and migration (USA, Australia).

1 Set for pairwork. Feed back with the class. Clarify any issues about the six factors.

2/3 With the whole class, discuss the *new technology* factors. What can they remember about technology from Unit 4? Ask students to explain how exactly computers play an important role in economics and finance. Discuss with the class other possible future technological developments and how they might affect labour markets.

Suggestions:

- new types of jobs, especially in service industries
- computer skills will be essential for many jobs
- less face-to-face contact
- technological changes may mean some countries are left (further) behind and become poorer
- new technologies in industry may improve production and efficiency, but not necessarily increase demand for labour

Add to the diagram accordingly. (See below for suggested methodology.)

Next, look at *population trends*. Discuss with the class the likely effects of ageing changing age structure, especially what an 'older' population means. Discuss what a 'young' population means.

How will these trends affect economies in different countries? Accept any reasonable suggestions.

Set the remaining factors (patterns of employment, environmental issues, wages and migration) and their effects on labour markets for pairwork discussion. It would be a good idea to ask each pair to think about a different factor and problems associated with them. Ask a few pairs to feed back to the class. Accept any reasonable suggestions.

Answers

Possible answers:

1 See diagram below.

2 Answers depend on the students, but the following should be discussed:

Wages

For an economy, to remain competitive, its *wage costs* must reflect the standard of living, the type of work people do and the pressure on jobs, based on supply and demand factors. The place of *unions* (often called *trade unions*) has become less important in advanced economies as a result of the decline in the traditional industries. However, services unions (for example, airport staff, public transport staff, maintenance personnel) are quite powerful.

Migration

Students may be familiar with workers going overseas to work, for economic reasons. They may also know about countries such as the USA or Germany which have, in different ways, developed economies where foreign workers play an important role. Some students may know about *trafficking* and this can be discussed briefly.

Patterns of employment

Students probably know that countries such as the USA, UK and other European countries have experienced a *decline in production industries*, such as automobile manufacturing, steel industry,

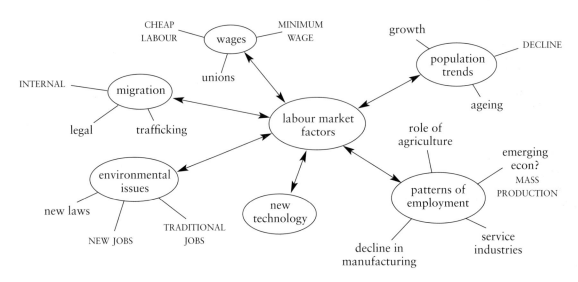

220

shipbuilding, electronics, etc., and have seen a *growth in service and financial industries.* *Agriculture* is an interesting sector in most economies and has been considered in depth in Unit 8. Students may know the approximate proportions of the population employed in agriculture, but most economists will maintain that the value of agriculture is estimated as much in human terms as through economic indicators.

3 For the question marks, the following may be included as factors or related aspects. A little prompting may be needed to bring out some of the links.

Population trends

- POPULATION DECLINE. (Students may not actually think some populations are in decline!) A declining population (especially if it means young people are leaving the country which causes a drop in the birth rate and a disproportion of older people in the population) usually means less revenue and less opportunity for expansion.

Wages

- CHEAP LABOUR in many emerging economies makes many consumer goods cheaper, but labour markets are highly competitive and global firms shift production frequently.

- A 'MINIMUM WAGE' level applies in many countries, but is it good for the economy? On the one hand, it helps unskilled workers to receive a reasonable wage; on the other hand, it adds extra wage costs for employers.

Migration

- INTERNAL MIGRATION. (Students may not think of internal migration as an important factor.) It is a concept which generally applies to developing economies, although many advanced economies (UK, USA, Japan) have experienced a form of internal migration. The type of internal migration students may know about is that experienced by China, Thailand, Indonesia, India, and many South American countries, where migration is often from rural to urban areas, with resultant problems such as overcrowding, lack of sanitation, pressure on infrastructure, etc.

Environmental factors

- TRADITIONAL JOBS. Climate change leads to loss of workplaces through desertification, pollution, flooding, and end of traditional working patterns, e.g., in forests and in local agriculture.

- NEW JOBS. There are often more jobs in leisure, services and tourism if the environment is protected (e.g., Costa Rica invests a lot in

eco-tourism to exploit its rainforests sustainably). However, multinational industries which exploit natural resources often pay low wages, and long-term damage to the environment is common.

Patterns of employment

- MASS PRODUCTION. Emerging economies have relied on mass-produced goods (e.g., cheaper electronic goods, textiles, shoes, toys, metal products). This helps to boost exports, but the labour force may not develop skills for the future.

Add these (and/or others) to the diagram, as students suggest them. It would be a good idea to make a large poster-sized copy of the diagram or put it on an OHT or other visual medium to which you can add more examples as the unit progresses.

Exercise B

1 Set for individual work and pairwork checking. Feed back with the whole class, building the table in the Answers section.

2 Explain what is meant by 'within' and 'between' sentences: 'within-sentence' linking words or phrases join clauses in a sentence; 'between-sentence' linking words or phrases connect two sentences. Demonstrate with the following:

Within-sentence linking words:

The workforce in many emerging economies has become highly skilled <u>because</u> their governments have invested in education.

Make sure students can see that 'within-sentence' linking words precede dependent clauses.

Between-sentence linking words:

The governments in many emerging economies have invested in education. <u>As a result</u>, the workforce has become highly skilled.

Point out that 'between-sentence' linking words usually have a comma before the rest of the sentence.

Note that some information may be placed differently to achieve a well-balanced sentence, in this case in *many emerging economies.*

Ask students to say which of the other words in box a are 'between' and which are 'within'.

3 Ask for suggestions for synonyms and add to the table.

4 First make sure that students understand the basic principle of an argument, which is:

> Statement

+

> one or more support(s) for statement
> (= more facts, reasons, results, examples, evidence, etc.)

Linking words/phrases	Use for	Within or between sentence	Other similar words/phrases
according to	building an argument by referring to a source	between (or at the beginning)	referring to … based on (research by) as X points out …
another point is	building an argument	between (or at the beginning)	moreover additionally and another thing
as a result	reasons and results	between	consequently
because	reasons and results	within	as
finally	building an argument	between	lastly
firstly	building an argument	between	to begin with/to start with for one thing
for example	building an argument	between	for instance
in addition	building an argument	between	also
moreover	building an argument	between	furthermore
secondly	building an argument	between	next then
since	reasons and results	within (or at the beginning)	as
so	reasons and results	between	therefore thus hence
thirdly	building an argument	between	after that then

Constructing a complex argument will usually entail a statement plus several supports.

With the whole class, elicit suggestions for how to use the linking words/phrases when constructing an argument. Build the table in the Answers section on the board.

Answers

Possible answers:

1–3 See table above.

4 A typical argument is constructed like this:

firstly	making the first major support point
for example	supporting the point with a specific example
in addition	adding another related point in support
secondly	making the second major support point
another point is	adding another related point in support
moreover	adding more information to the point above
finally	making the last point

Language note

1 Note that within-sentence linking words may be placed at the beginning of the sentence with a comma after the first clause, as in:

Because the governments have invested in education, the workforce in many emerging economies has become highly skilled.

2 Although the between-sentence linking words are described above as joining two sentences, they can of course link two independent clauses joined by coordinating linking words *and* or *but*, as in:

The governments in many emerging economies have invested in education and, as a result, the workforce has become highly skilled.

Exercise C

1 Set for individual work. Note that students should try to put each word into one of the two categories, even if it is not immediately clear how it could be relevant. If they are not sure which category to use, they should try to think of a phrase containing the word and imagine how it could be relevant to one of the categories.

2 Ask students to compare their answers and to justify their choices. Feed back with the whole class, discussing the words for which students feel the category is not obvious. If no decision can be reached, say you will come back to the words a little later.

3/4 Set for pairwork. Feed back with the whole class if you wish.

Answers

Model answers:

Word	Suggested categories	Part of speech	Other words/phrases
dra'matically	emotional	adv	extraordinarily, remarkably
ex'ploit	emotional	v (T)	misuse, take advantage of
fa'cilitate	neutral	v (T)	make easier, assist, help, permit
in'human	emotional	adj	cruel, heartless
'maximize	neutral	v (T)	increase as much as possible
'middlemen	neutral	n (C) here plural	intermediary, agent
mi'grate	neutral	v (I)	emigrate, travel/move from one place to another, go abroad
monopo'listically	emotional	adv	exclusively
re'luctant	emotional	adj	hesitant, unwilling
'slavery	emotional	n (U)	exploitation, servitude (formal)
'specialist	neutral	n (C)	expert, authority
sur'pass	neutral	v (T)	go further than, exceed
'vulnerable	emotional	adj	at risk, exploitable
'would-be	neutral	adj	intended, desired, aspiring to be

🎧 Exercise D

Note: Students may need to use dictionaries in question 2.

Students should first read through the text to get an idea of the topic.

1/2 Set for individual work and pairwork checking. Feed back with the whole class.

Language note

Tell students that a particular topic will have groups of words which are connected to or associated with it – known as 'lexical chains'. These lexical chains show us the themes that run through the text and which help 'glue' the ideas together to make a cohesive piece of text. It is a good idea, therefore, to learn vocabulary according to topic areas.

Answers

Model answers:

1 According to Wheaton, Schauer and Galli, 2010, who are international migration <u>specialists</u>, trafficking in human beings for labour purposes is predicted to expand <u>dramatically</u> over the next ten years. Moreover, these and other crime experts claim that '... it will <u>surpass</u> the illegal drugs and arms trade in frequency, human costs and profitability to criminals'. Since poverty is increasing in West and North Africa, workers from poorer countries, for example, men from there and women from Eastern Europe, are most <u>vulnerable</u> to this form of modern <u>slavery</u>.

It may seem inappropriate to see this <u>inhuman</u> practice as an economic factor but, sadly, trafficking is an unlawful example of what the authors claim is 'a <u>monopolistically</u> competitive business'. Firstly, traffickers act as <u>middlemen</u> in the market for human beings between the <u>would-be</u> workers and the employers who will <u>exploit</u> their labour illegally. Secondly, these intermediaries take advantage of victims' economic necessity to <u>migrate</u>. Thirdly, traffickers use basic principles of supply and demand to provide illegal workers because they want to <u>maximize</u> profits for their investments. Finally, traffickers can usually control market prices for their human 'products'. In addition, corruption in government, immigration and police services <u>facilitates</u> the exploitation. According to US government sources, around 600–800,000 people are trafficked into the USA every year. Another point is that figures are difficult to estimate because victims are <u>reluctant</u> to give details, so, unfortunately, the organizers are rarely caught. As a result, such activities are very difficult to monitor and prevent.

2 The emotional words have mostly been identified in Exercise C, but other emotional words in the text include: *illegal* (can be emotional), *sadly, take advantage of, corruption* (can be emotional) and *unfortunately*.

Transcript 🎧 2.13

According to Wheaton, Schauer and Galli, 2010, who are international migration specialists, trafficking in human beings for labour purposes is predicted to expand dramatically over the next ten years. Moreover, these and other crime experts claim that '... it will surpass the illegal drugs and arms trade in frequency, human costs and profitability to criminals'. Since poverty is increasing in West and North Africa, workers from poorer countries, for example, men from there and women from Eastern Europe, are most vulnerable to this form of modern slavery.

It may seem inappropriate to see this inhuman practice as an economic factor but, sadly, trafficking is an unlawful example of what the authors claim is 'a monopolistically competitive business'. Firstly, traffickers act as middlemen in the market for human beings between the would-be workers and the employers who will exploit their labour illegally. Secondly, these intermediaries take advantage of victims' economic necessity to migrate. Thirdly, traffickers use basic principles of supply and demand to provide illegal workers because they want to maximize profits for their investments. Finally, traffickers can usually control market prices for their human 'products'. In addition, corruption in government, immigration and police services facilitates the exploitation. According to US government sources, around 600–800,000 people are trafficked into the USA every year. Another point is that figures are difficult to estimate because victims are reluctant to give details, so, unfortunately, the organizers are rarely caught. As a result, such activities are very difficult to monitor and prevent.

Source: Wheaton, E. M., Schauer, E.J. & Galli, T. V. (2010). Economics of human trafficking. *International Migrations* 48(4), 114–141.

Exercise E

With a partner, take it in turns to ask and answer questions on the demographic statistics.

Language note

Students may be familiar with the term *net* from mathematics or everyday use. If they are unsure, clarify that net signifies the difference between two sets of related figures, for example, the salary that a person earns before tax (*gross* salary) and the amount after deductions for tax, etc., the *net* salary. With migration figures, it signifies the difference between the number of migrants who enter a country and those who leave the country.

Answers

Possible answers:

How much has the population grown?

By 1.2%–1.3% between 1995 and 2010. Growth is expected to slow after this, down to 0.9% by 2025.

How has the population grown?

Australia is a country which has grown steadily over the period in question by encouraging migration as a balancing process for mortality.

What can we see regarding birth rate and natural growth?

The fertility rate itself has remained static over the period and births (per 1,000) have remained fairly steady.

What has happened to life expectancy, even with a growing population?

Life expectancy has increased by four years since 1995.

Has infant mortality increased?

No, it has decreased over the period and is forecast to decrease more in the future, indicating the good health care programmes that have been maintained.

What pattern is evident for the migration programme?

The net number of migrants has actually increased between 1995 and 2010 and is expected to reduce only slightly for the next decade and more. Migration acts as a sort of balance for mortality levels.

What is the trend in death rates?

They are, in fact, increasing.

Of course, the implications of these statistics could be discussed further, if time permits, but Australia serves as an example for the closure activity.

Closure

Ask students to review the lesson and list the factors which affect global labour markets. Then ask them what examples they know of different forms of migration.

To focus further on migration, divide students into two groups, designating them A and B.

Group A will discuss the issues of trafficking – why it happens, who is involved, how it affects labour markets, how it might be prevented or reduced.

Group B will discuss the issue of conventional migration, for example to a country such as Australia. Why do people emigrate there? What controls should a country have over migration? How can a country acquire the skilled people it needs? How can a country ensure that immigrants are given a fair chance?

Then one student from Group A should pair up with a student from Group B to exchange their ideas and discuss further.

11.2 Listening

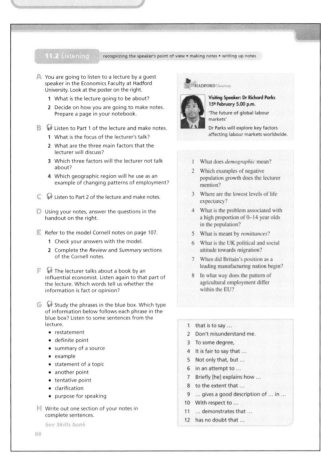

General note

Read the *Skills bank – Writing out notes in full* at the end of the Course Book unit. Decide when, if at all, to refer students to it. The best time is probably at the very end of the lesson or the beginning of the next lesson, as a summary/revision.

Lesson aims

- recognize and understand phrases that identify the speaker's point of view
- use background knowledge in listening comprehension
- convert notes into full sentences and paragraphs

Further practice in:

- making notes (use of heading systems and abbreviations)
- referring to sources
- general academic words and phrases

Introduction

1 Review phrases indicating a speaker's view of the truth value of a statement. Write a sentence such as the following on the board (i.e., a 'fact' about which there may be differences of opinion): *Many developed economies impose restrictions on economic migration to maintain labour force stability.*

Ask students to say whether they think this is true or not. Elicit phrases they can use before the sentence to show how certain they are about their opinion.

Dictate or write on the board the following phrases. Ask students to say what the effect of each phrase is when put before the sentence on the board. In each case, does it make the writer sound confident or tentative?

The research shows that …

A survey found that …

The evidence does not support the idea that …

It appears to be the case that …

The evidence suggests that …

The evidence shows that …

It is clear that …

It is possible that …

2 Revise the Cornell note-taking system. Elicit the R words. Ask students to describe how to divide up the page (refer to Unit 9). Revise the other ways to take notes (see Units 1 and 3).

3 Revise note-taking symbols and abbreviations (see Units 5 and 9, and Unit 9 extra activity 4).

Exercise A

Refer students to the Hadford University lecture announcement. Tell them to look at the title and the summary of the talk.

Set the exercises for pairwork discussion. Feed back with the whole class.

Answers

1 Accept any reasonable suggestions.

2 The lecturer is clearly going to outline major factors affecting the labour markets. As these factors may be seen as distinct from each other, a headed/numbered list would probably be most appropriate. A spidergram (as in Unit 1) might be appropriate, but each factor is likely to be presented in some detail, so the notes on the spidergram would have to be very precise. Remind students of the Cornell system (which is used here) as an additional resource, particularly when notes are made as a list.

🎧 Exercise B

Play Part 1 through once *without* allowing students time to focus on the questions.

Put students in pairs to answer the questions by referring to their notes. Feed back with the whole class, building a set of notes on the board if you wish.

Ask students which method they are going to use to make notes, now that they have listened to the introduction. They should make any adjustments necessary to the page they have prepared in their notebooks.

Answers

Model answers:

1 Factors affecting global labour markets.
2 Population (demographic aspects), migration and changing patterns of employment.
3 Wages, technological development and the environment.
4 The UK.

Transcript 🎧 2.14

Part 1

Good morning. My name is Dr Richard Parks and I'm an economic consultant for the private and public sectors. It's a pleasure to be here today. I am going to try to outline some of the major factors which will influence the labour markets over the next few decades; that is to say, I shall mainly be looking at how the world economy can recover and grow by using its human resources most efficiently.

Don't misunderstand me. I don't want to imply that labour has not been used efficiently over the past 50 years. In fact, industry and services have adapted and reshaped themselves many times during this period, especially through advances in technology. But as a consequence of the global financial crisis after 2008, labour market factors have gained in importance as economists plan ahead. To some degree, individual countries will be affected differently, but it is fair to say that the factors I am going to talk about will influence policies and politics worldwide. Not only that, but the pressure on the world's labour markets will encourage more cooperation between nations and force countries to revise their ideas about competition, trade and the environment.

So in an attempt to provide you with an overview of global labour market issues, I am going to talk about three major areas. There are, in fact, six in total but I think it is best to leave three other important factors – wages, technological development and the environment – until later in your course. So, we are going to concentrate on

three. Firstly, population or demographic structure, especially the challenges facing many countries about the age of their working populations. Secondly, I will discuss migration from various perspectives. Thirdly, I will talk about patterns of employment, using the UK as an example.

🎧 Exercise C

Play the whole of the rest of lecture through *once* without stopping. Students should make notes as they listen.

Answers

See the *Notes* section of the table in the Answers section for Exercise E.

Transcript 🎧 2.15

Part 2

So, to start with, then: what are the key demographic elements and how do they impact on the labour market?

This is a complex issue, so let's take a few simple examples. I'll talk first about population growth. Many of the fastest-growing populations are in the poorest countries in Africa where infant mortality is high. As a result, families have many children to make sure some survive. A few examples here are Burundi, Niger, Liberia, the Central African Republic and others, all with a growth rate of around 4% per annum. But there is also rapid growth in Asia, for example in Pakistan, Bangladesh and Afghanistan. Many of these countries are trying to recover from years of civil war or face other conflicts and challenges, notably climate change.

Interestingly, there is an opposite demographic development, a decline in population in some countries. Many Eastern European countries such as Ukraine, Moldova, Romania, Poland, Croatia and others, for example, have a negative population growth rate for a number of reasons.

Let's now consider another aspect – the average age of a population. Firstly, we have ageing populations in many advanced economies. This is a problem because there are fewer people in the labour market and the elderly make strong demands on the health and welfare services of a country. Mortality rates are lower than even 20 years ago because of better medical care and some lifestyle improvements. Therefore, life expectancy is higher. Japan, Australia, Switzerland, Canada, France, Italy, Norway, Spain and several others have life expectancies of over 80 years old! Several others, including Britain, will reach this figure in the next few years. Another age indicator is presented by measuring the proportion of the population over 60 years old. In this category, Japan, Italy, Germany, Sweden and Greece have approximately 25% of their population over that age. If a country has a high percentage of people who are too old to work and will probably live until they are 85 or 90, expenditure on medical care, special housing needs and pensions becomes a problem.

But, of course, countries with a low average age also pose a problem economically, for different reasons. The lowest life expectancy is to be found in Africa, with several countries around the 40–45 year-old mark which puts a strain on the labour-force. Even South Africa has a figure of only around 45 years old! Just to make the problem in Africa more acute, the continent contains the top ten countries with more than 40% of the population between the ages of 0 and 14. Understandably, economists are pessimistic about problems related to such young populations. They have high demands on education and health care, but limited employment prospects and so contribute little to national revenue.

So, most people say that the advanced economies and the developing economies really have to find solutions to deal with this age factor. The evidence shows that it certainly won't be easy, particularly for the young, emerging economies. However, I tend to agree with one influential writer, Phil Mullan, a social economist, who expresses doubts about the economic threats associated with ageing populations. Briefly, he explains how ageing is not the dramatic 'time-bomb' it has been labelled as. In his extremely interesting book, *The Imaginary Time-Bomb: Why an Ageing Population is Not a Social Problem*, written in 2002, he claims this demographic development is not presented as a social benefit but as a burden for the future. He, for one, has no doubt that a deeper examination of the issue from a more optimistic perspective will, quite rightly, enable economies to maximize human resources of all ages.

The second main area of focus in my lecture is migration. I will focus on three main aspects – political issues, economic migration and the conflict between economic necessity and public opinion. Firstly, there is a clear overlap between politics and decisions on migration, to the extent that sometimes political decisions take priority over economic reality. For example, most Western European countries have imposed limits on immigrants from outside the EU. However, they still allow free movement within the EU for all citizens. Another example … the USA spends billions of dollars each

year on preventing illegal immigration, especially from Mexico, but historically it has been the number one destination for migrants.

The second aspect relates to so-called economic migration. Understandably, many people are willing to leave their homes and families to find a better future elsewhere. However, there are many curbs and restrictions on movements of people. Moreover, migration is not only difficult, but it can also be dangerous. Thousands of would-be migrants die each year trying to enter Italy or Spain from North Africa. Several million workers are trafficked illegally every year, sometimes with tragic consequences, as happened in England in 2004. Yet many states, especially in the Middle East, rely on large numbers of temporary workers to support their economies. The International Organization for Migration, or IOM, is the agency which looks at global patterns, mainly to protect migrants against exploitation. The IOM states that, worldwide, there are 214 million international migrants. In 2009, these migrants sent home money, called remittances, to the value of an estimated $414 billion! The IOM also calculates that there are over 27 million people who are displaced internally. The IOM reports give a very good description of the complex issues related to migration and its economic implications.

The third aspect of migration relates to the conflict between economic necessity and public opinion. In Europe and Britain, for example, why do many people and politicians see immigration as a sensitive issue? Generally speaking, British people want curbs on immigration, but don't always consider the economic realities. Some of these relate to the patterns of work, which I'll talk about in a minute. Some people in Britain say that migration is a threat to jobs in the UK. About 1 million people came to the UK from so-called A8 Eastern Europe, the most recent group to join the EU, between 2004 and 2009. Most of these migrants came from Poland. The evidence shows that the impact of such an inflow of new workers is especially positive with respect to sustaining a growing economy. However, if the economy declines, as happened in 2009 in the UK, people return home. A report published in 2010 by the UK Office for National Statistics, or ONS, demonstrates that migration can be short-term. This report shows that A8 departures exceeded arrivals in 2009. There are a number of reasons for this reversal. Jobs that Polish workers were happy to take perhaps no longer exist. The other possibility is that, in a recession, British people began to accept jobs that they refused earlier because no other options were available. The Polish economy also improved during this period. Nevertheless, UK government politicians had no doubt that net immigration was still too high. So, as we can see, the effect of politics and public opinion on an economic issue can be quite important.

Now, let's turn to the third main topic of my lecture, the pattern of work, and here I will again use the UK as an example, focusing on industry and agricultural sectors. Historically speaking, since the mid-18th century, the UK economy has been based on the manufacturing sector. But in 2004, only about 12% of the workforce were in the manufacturing sector. By 2009, this had declined further to around 10.7% of workers actively engaged in production. Obviously, there are other employees in factories and workshops who assist the manufacturing process. So, in total, around 18% of the UK workforce make things! In agriculture, only around 1% of the working population are directly engaged in farming, either as skilled workers or as labourers. This means that the vast majority of workers are in different occupations which are sometimes classified together as 'services'. Compare that with other EU countries, where agriculture is a much more important employment sector. For example, in Poland, about 15% of the population is employed in farming, while in Romania the figure is over 23%. So, such differences can cause problems as employment priorities will be different across the EU, for example. But when you compare that with developing countries such as Thailand where the figure is over 40%, or China, where probably around 40–45% of the population still work in agriculture, you can understand how labour market patterns are important.

So, the pattern of work is changing, in the UK and elsewhere. But how can the global economy make sure that the balance in the labour market is efficient and sustainable? Now, I'm going to stop at this point, but I'd just like to tell you about an interesting website where you can really research population statistics. The US Census Bureau's International Data Base gives you a chance to create your own population growth profiles and compare across countries and time periods. The URL is: www.census.gov/ipc
It is well worth a look!

Exercise D

Put students in pairs to answer the questions by referring to their notes. Feed back with the class to see how much they have been able to get from the lecture. If they can't answer something, do not supply the answer at this stage.

Answers

Model answers:

1 Factors that relate to a population.

2 Eastern European countries, such as the Ukraine, Moldova, Romania, Poland and Croatia.

3 In Africa.

4 This age group needs access to main resources such as education and health, but may not have good employment chances; thus the group does not contribute much revenue to the economy. (Of course, students may point out that 'child labour' is quite common and that a lot of children contribute within their families through childcare, work in the home or on family farms, even if they continue to go to school.)

5 The money sent back home ('repatriated') by migrant workers which boosts the home economy by providing income for the workers' families. This money is then spent domestically, but the migrant workers may make demands on the 'host' economy's infrastructure for health, housing, energy, transport, etc.

6 Most people, including politicians, favour tighter restrictions on immigration, especially for non-EU migrants.

7 In the mid-18th century.

8 In some EU countries, the percentage of the populations engaged in agriculture is very small (UK 1%) but in other countries it is much higher (Poland 15%, Romania 23%). However, subsidy payments related to agriculture form the largest part of the EU budget.

Exercise E

1 Set for individual work.

2 Set for individual work and pairwork checking. Feed back with the whole class.

Answers

Possible answers:

See table on next page.

Review	Notes
	Six main factors, but three factors in lecture
How do factors interrelate?	1 demographic
	2 migration
	3 patterns of work
	(NOT wages, technological development and environment)
Wages/environment how/why	1 Demographic
different …?	1a population growth
Where can I check these	+ (Mainly Africa – high inf. mortality ➔ bigger families) e.g., Burundi, Niger, Centr.
countries?	Afr. Rep & Asia – Pakistan, Bangladesh, Afghanistan) approx. 4% p.a.
	– (Eastern Europe) e.g., Poland, Romania, Ukraine
	(unlikely to be 'new consumers' for W. Europe)
	1b ageing population ↗
	↗ life expectancy, e.g., Japan, Australia, Switzerland, Canada, etc., 80+ (UK soon!)
	cf. populations with 25%+ over 60 y.o., e.g., Japan, Germany, Italy
	(↗ demands – health care, special housing, etc.)
0–14 y.o. group … a problem for	Young population also a problem cf. Africa (many 40–45 y.o., e.g., South Afr. 45)
emerging countries?	N.B. Africa all top ten nations 0–14 y.o. group (40%+)
	Associated problems
	• high demands for eductn.
	• high health expenditure BUT
	• poor employment chances
	• limited contribution ➔ national revenue
Mullan's views … have they	BUT Mullan (2002) (social economist) ageing population ≠ a 'time-bomb'
changed? Have other economists	adv. econ. must re-examine social benefits of elderly population
accepted his position?	
	2 Migration (three main aspects)
	1 political aspect; e.g.,
	a) W. Europe – limits (but free movement for EU members)
USA continues to be a favourite	b) USA ($ billions to prevent illegal migration but historically destination for
destination …? Exclude	migrants!)
S. American/Mexican labour …?	2 economic aspect
Check what happened!	• danger for illegal migrants, e.g., N. Africa ➔ Spain, Italy
	• trafficking (exploitation of workers) e.g., incident in UK (2004)
	• (214 million migrants, $414 billion remittances + internal displacement)
	= complex issue
Migration statistics … politically	3 economic necessity vs political opinion, e.g., UK (A8 East European countries – 1 mill.
dangerous …?	➔ UK 2004–2009) but reversal after economic downturn; returned home BUT
	political and popular opinion 'net immigration too high'
UK figures … healthy	3 Patterns of work (e.g., UK)
development …?	industry
	historically (since mid-18thC) manufacturing nation BUT 2004 about 12% ↓ to about
	10.7% in 2009 in manufacturing; approx. 18% if support workers counted;
EU expansion ➔ such	agriculture
differences …? No problem …?	only 1% in agriculture in UK cf. some EU, e.g., Poland (15%) Romania (23%) but cf.
Advantage of specialization …?	China/Thailand (40%+)

Summary
Key economic factors are changing (especially related to population size and age); the mobility of workforces is also more complex with large numbers of migrants; patterns of employment, especially in the developed economies, are also changing, with decline in manufacturing sectors (in % terms of workers employed), but emerging economies are able to produce more because of cheap labour. However, the question is how to keep the balance for a sustainable future with appropriate growth and concern for people?

Note

Source references for lecture:

Mullan, P. (2002). *The imaginary time-bomb: Why an ageing population is not a social problem.* London: I. B. Tauris & Co. Ltd.

International Organization for Migration (IOM) (2010). World Migration Report. Retrieved August 3, 2010 from www.iom.int/jahia/Jahia/world-migration-report-2010

Office for National Statistics (ONS) (2010). Migration Statistics Quarterly Report Retrieved August 3, 2010 from www.statistics.gov.uk/pdfdir/mig0510.pdf

Office for National Statistics (ONS) (2010). Labour Force Survey, April–June 2009. Retrieved August 3, 2010 from www.statistics.gov.uk/STATBASE/Product.asp?vlnk =14248

🎧 Exercise F

Discuss the question with the whole class. Ask them if they can remember any phrases which signal whether comments are fact or just opinion.

Play the extract. Ask students to tell you to stop the recording when they hear key phrases. Write the phrases on the board.

Remind students that it is important to recognize when someone is giving only their opinion, which others might well disagree with.

Answers

Model answers:

See table below.

Transcript 🎧 2.16

So, most people say that the advanced economies and the developing economies really have to find solutions to deal with this age factor. The evidence shows that it certainly won't be easy, particularly for the young, emerging economies. However, I tend to agree with one influential writer, Phil Mullan, a social economist, who expresses doubts about the economic threats associated with ageing populations. Briefly, he explains how ageing is not the dramatic 'time-bomb' it has been labelled as. In his extremely interesting book, *The Imaginary Time-Bomb: Why an Ageing Population is Not a Social Problem*, written in 2002, he claims this demographic development is not presented as a social benefit but as a burden for the future. He, for one, has no doubt that a deeper examination of the issue from a more optimistic perspective will, quite rightly, enable economies to maximize human resources of all ages.

🎧 Exercise G

Allow students time to read the phrases and the types of information, making sure that they understand any difficult words. Remind students that 'type' of information tells you what the speaker *intends to do* with the words. The words themselves are something different.

Ask students to try to match the phrases and types of information as far as they can. Note that it is not always possible to say what the function of a phrase is outside its context, so they may not be able to match all the phrases and information types before hearing

… most people say that (the advanced economies and the developing economies …)	This phrase can be used to add weight to the speaker's own opinion and show that it is a widely held viewpoint.
The evidence shows that (it won't be easy) …	Sometimes, to put their case strongly, people will present assumptions or opinions as facts, very strongly stated, with no tentativeness.
However, I tend to agree …	Here, the lecturer expresses agreement with the author's opinion in a very tentative way.
… with one influential writer …	The adjective 'influential' reflects the lecturer's opinion more than verifiable fact.
In his *extremely interesting* book (*The Imaginary Time-Bomb: Why an Ageing Population is Not a Social Problem*) …	Whether something is 'interesting' is always a matter of opinion.
He, for one, has no doubt that …	The lecturer emphasizes the author's certainty of his position, but implies that other people may question Mullan's views.
… (a deeper examination of the issue) will, quite rightly (enable economies …)	This is the lecturer's strongly expressed opinion but it is linked to the author's own views to give the opinion more force. Whether something is 'right' or not is a matter of opinion.

the extracts. Note that some types of information are needed more than once.

When they have done as much as they can, play the extracts one at a time, allowing time for students to identify the type of information which follows. Check answers after each extract, making sure that students understand the information that actually follows the phrase. If possible students should also give the actual words.

Answers

Model answers:

Fixed phrase		Type of information which follows the phrase
1	that is to say …	restatement
2	Don't misunderstand me.	clarification
3	To some degree,	tentative point
4	it is fair to say that …	tentative point
5	Not only that, but …	another point
6	in an attempt to …	purpose for speaking
7	Briefly, [he] explains how …	summary of a source
8	to the extent that …	clarification
9	… gives a good description of … in …	summary of a source
10	With respect to …	statement of a topic
11	… demonstrates that …	an example
12	has no doubt that …	definite point

Transcript 🎧 2.17

Extract 1

I am going to try to outline some of the major factors which will influence the labour markets over the next few decades; that is to say, I shall mainly be looking at how the world economy can recover and grow by using its human resources most efficiently.

Extract 2

Don't misunderstand me. I don't want to imply that labour has not been used efficiently over the past 50 years.

Extract 3

To some degree, individual countries will be affected differently …

Extract 4

… but it is fair to say that the factors I am going to talk about will influence policies and politics worldwide.

Extract 5

Not only that, but the pressure on the world's labour markets will encourage more cooperation between nations and force countries to revise their ideas about competition, trade and the environment.

Extract 6

So, in an attempt to provide you with an overview of global labour market issues, I am going to talk about three major areas.

Extract 7

Briefly, he explains how ageing is not the dramatic 'time-bomb' that it has been labelled as.

Extract 8

Firstly, there is a clear overlap between politics and decisions on migration, to the extent that sometimes political decisions take priority over economic reality.

Extract 9

The IOM reports give a very good description of the complex issues with respect to migration and its economic implications.

Extract 10

The evidence shows that the impact of such an inflow of new workers is especially positive with respect to sustaining a growing economy.

Extract 11

A report published in 2010 by the UK Office for National Statistics, or ONS, demonstrates that migration can be short term.

Extract 12

Nevertheless, UK government politicians had no doubt that net immigration was still too high.

Exercise H

Use this section from the Cornell notes to demonstrate what to do:

> **Notes**
> 1b ageing population
> ↗ life expectancy, e.g., Japan, Australia, Switzerland, Canada, etc., 80+ (UK soon!)
> cf. populations with 25%+ over 60 y.o., e.g., Japan, Germany, Italy
> (↗ demands – health care, special housing, etc.)
>
> Young population also a problem cf. Africa (many 40–45 y.o., e.g., South Afr. 45)
> N.B. Africa all top ten nations 0–14 y.o. group (40%+)
> Associated problems
> • high demands for eductn.
> • high health expenditure BUT
> • poor employment chances
> • limited contribution → national revenue
> BUT Mullan (2002) (social economist) ageing population ≠ a 'time-bomb'
> adv. econ. must re-examine social benefits of elderly population

Elicit from students suggestions on how to write up the notes in complete sentences. Write the suggestions on the board.

Ask students to say what they need to add in to the notes to make a good piece of writing, for example,

Grammar: relative pronouns and *where* clauses; articles and determiners; prepositions, auxiliary verbs, linking words, *there has/have been* clauses (in italics in the model notes below) to show trends; phrases to discuss statistics (e.g., *increased by 4.5%; increased to over 25%*).

Vocabulary: some vocabulary may need to be added, particularly where symbols are used in the notes, or where extra words are needed to make sense of the information or give a good sense of flow in the writing (in bold below).

Note that this of course works the other way: when making notes, these elements can be excluded from the notes.

Possible rewrite of the notes:

The second demographic issue relates to ageing populations, **for example, increased life expectancy such as in Japan, Australia, Canada and in other countries,** *where* the average is now over 80 years old. **The UK will soon reach this figure.** *There has been* **another trend** in advanced economies such as in Japan, Germany or Italy, *where* the proportion of the population over 60 years old **has increased to over 25%. This places huge demands on health care and special housing resources. There is an opposite phenomenon** in Africa with populations which are too young. *There,* life expectancy for many people is **between 40 and 45 years old, even in South Africa the figure is 45 years old. The labour force is negatively affected by a low life expectancy.** But *there has also been* a growth in African populations so that the number of 0–14 year olds in the population is extremely high. **As an illustration of this,** Africa has all the top ten nations **with a proportion of 40% or more in this age group. In this situation,** there has been an increased demand for health and education in these countries but *these young people* have poor employment chances and are **unlikely** to make a large contribution to economic revenue. Ageing populations seem to be a problem for many advanced economies but the social economist, Phil Mullan, stated in his 2002 book that **this phenomenon** is not the 'time-bomb' *it* has been labelled and can be **beneficial** to a society.

Set another section for individual writing in class or for homework. Either ask students to refer to their own notes, or to the Cornell notes on page 107 of the Course Book.

Closure

1 Tell students to review and make a list of the main topics and arguments presented in this lesson. Then ask them to try and summarize the viewpoints, using some of the language they have practised.

2 They could also give a two- or three-sentence summary of anything that they themselves have read, e.g., *I read a useful article on X by Y. It said that …*

3 Ask students to do some research and to make a list of useful or interesting books/articles/websites on the topics in this lesson. They should draw up a list, including correct referencing, and share their sources with other students.

11.3 Extending skills

Lesson aims

- recognize stress patterns in noun phrases
- understand how to develop an argument:

  stating the issue

  giving a counter-argument

  rejecting a counter-argument

  giving opinions

  supporting opinions
- understand more general academic words and phrases mainly used in speaking

Further practice in:

- expressing degrees of confidence/tentativeness
- reporting back

Introduction

1 Revise the lecture in Lesson 11.2. Ask students to use the model Cornell notes on page 107 of the Course Book. They should cover up the *Notes* section and use the *Review* and *Summary* sections (which they completed in Lesson 11.2) to help recall the contents of the lecture. They could work in pairs to do this.

2 Revise phrases which express degrees of confidence in 'facts'. Dictate these phrases. Do they show that the speaker is certain or tentative?

> *There is no question that* (= certain)
>
> *We have to accept the evidence* (= certain)
>
> *Some people claim that* (= tentative)
>
> *What seems obvious is that* (= certain)
>
> *As everyone is aware* (= certain)
>
> *To some degree* (= tentative)
>
> *This means ultimately that* (= certain)
>
> *It's quite clear that* (= certain)
>
> *We could argue that* (= tentative)

🎧 Exercise A

1/2 Set for individual work and pairwork checking. This is an exercise in perceiving rhythm. At this point there is no need to distinguish between different levels of stress. Students can underline all the stressed syllables. They will also need to count all the syllables.

Feed back with the whole class, checking pronunciation of the phrases and meanings.

3 Discuss this with the class first. Demonstrate with *e͵merging e'conomies*, showing how if you say *e'merging e͵conomies*, it appears that a contrast is being made with another type of economy, for example, *advanced* economies, *rural* economies or *mixed* economies. Tell students that the usual pattern for the adjective + noun phrase is for stronger stress to go on the noun.

If a compound is made from a noun + noun, the stronger stress may be on the first noun, as in *'labour shortages* or *re'tirement age*, as the first noun acts like an adjective. However, with common noun + noun collocations, such as with *consumer*, *media* or *government* (see next page) or *computer* (*science/software/hardware/data/program*) or *university* (*education/teacher/course/degree*), the stronger stress is usually on the second noun. Set students to pick out the other adjective + noun patterns, writing each one on the board. Elicit the stress patterns and give students time to practise the phrases.

Answers

Model answers:

1/2 con,sumer 'power

   eco,nomic justifi'cation

   e,merging e'conomies

   environ,mental 'issues (stronger stress could be on *environ'mental* if a contrastive meaning is required, i.e., not *economic* or *social* issues)

   'government revenue

   in,ternal mi'gration

   'labour ,shortages

   'media attention

   occu,pational 'pensions

   po,litical moti'vation

   re'tirement age

   'welfare ,services

3 Adjective + noun (second word has stronger stress): economic justification, emerging economies, environmental issues, internal migration, occupational pensions, political motivation

Transcript 🎧 2.18

con,sumer 'power

eco,nomic justifi'cation

e,merging e'conomies

environ,mental 'issues

,government 'revenue

in,ternal mi'gration

'labour ,shortages

,media a'ttention

occu,pational 'pensions

po,litical moti'vation

re'tirement age

'welfare ,services

🎧 Exercise B

1 Look at the three topics. Discuss with the class what they know already about these topics and find out what opinions they may have. Put students in pairs and ask each pair to write down one question to which they would like an answer in the lecture.

2 Set for individual work.

3 Play Part 3 straight through; students make notes.

4 Put students in pairs to compare their notes and fill in any gaps they may have.

Transcript 🎧 2.19

Part 3

In this part of the lecture, I want to outline the debate on ageing populations in the developed economies. Secondly, I will present a brief overview of how China's labour markets might develop over the next decade and what this might mean for China's future status.

Now, as I mentioned earlier, an ageing population presents a major problem for many governments, especially in the developed economies. It is mainly seen as a revenue issue. That is to say, how will governments pay for larger, healthier populations that are likely to live longer and, quite rightly, have expectations of a decent and worthwhile life? The real question about ageing populations is: can governments find acceptable political and economic solutions to the issue? Well, it's quite clear that a solution based only on economic considerations will definitely not be popular. Research in several countries has concluded that people would like to retire early and enjoy a long retirement with a good state pension! But, some government economists claim that as people are healthier, they should work longer and retire later, at the age of 67, for example. Well, I'm afraid that just isn't acceptable, as state pensions are already quite low and work stress increases as people get older. The evidence lies in the fact that people who have worked in stressful jobs do not live so long after retirement anyway.

Now, one solution might be for people who are in work to pay higher contributions for their welfare services, for their own pensions and to pay more tax. It is sometimes argued that this is the best option. But people must be motivated to continue in work, so governments cannot take too many chances. If workers accept this, it could generate sufficient government revenue.

As another option, government could restrict pay increases and make many jobs part-time, temporary or only paid at minimum wage levels. Well, that's not going to be popular, is it?

Finally, a combination of all the solutions might work – later retirement, limited state pensions, higher pension contributions and higher taxes! Not very popular, I'm sure you'd agree? Well, all things considered, this is, in my opinion, the most likely choice of strategy in Western Europe at least. But critics of the strategy say it is based more on political motivation than economic justification.

Now, let's consider my second topic which presents a quite different economic perspective. This is the issue of the impact on global labour markets of the rapidly expanding new economies.

Cheap labour has been their key to success over the past 20 years. China has benefitted from internal migration and labour laws which strengthened the government's position. But things are changing. For example, the Chinese authorities have to face a number of environmental issues. You might remember how the Beijing Olympic Games in 2008 made the Chinese authorities very aware of environmental concerns. Moreover, the government has to accept greater accountability and more open debate. China participates in big economic conferences, and discusses world trade issues and labour laws. It has accepted its status as a 'global economic player'. This has benefitted the workers in China, where, for example, a new law which is more favourable to workers was introduced in 2008. As an indication of changing patterns of work-related behaviour, some strikes and protests have even been registered over the past few years. These attracted global media attention and China is aware that the world is watching carefully! Moreover, it may sound strange, but there is even a shortage of workers in some areas of China. It is true that workers' wages have increased steadily, but they are still way below OECD levels. It is argued that giving China's workers more consumer power will be a key factor in global economic recovery and growth. But this will not be easy. One writer in *The Economist* magazine, July 29th 2010, has no doubt that China's labour market needs to change. I quote: '... as it runs dry of crude labour, China will have to increase its supply of skilled workers. That will require a stable workforce that stays with its employers long enough to be worth investing in. In similar fashion, the older economies, such as the USA, Germany, UK and Japan will also have to raise skill levels or they will see emerging economies moving ahead with even more determination and success.'

Now, I'm going to set you a task which will involve investigating some of the points I've raised. I want you to do some research into some of the challenges facing the new economies, other than China. So, here, we might consider, for example, India, Brazil, Vietnam, Venezuela, South Africa, Indonesia, Thailand or Singapore to name several possible choices. I want you to focus firstly on demographic issues – population growth – migration, mortality rates, etc. Secondly, I'd like you to consider economic indicators related to growth, employment sectors, the role of agriculture, unemployment, etc., some of which we have heard about with reference to China. This is quite a challenging research task. Later in the course, you will be asked to include environmental issues in your analysis but here you should concentrate on the demographic and economic factors, especially the labour market issues. Good luck!

Exercise C

Set for individual work and pairwork checking. Feed back with the class on question 7 to make sure that it is clear.

Answers

Model answers:

1 If you have an older population, there are fewer workers contributing to government revenue through taxes and insurance payments, but more people who have access to welfare and health services as well as receiving state and/or occupational pensions.

2 Pensions could be reduced; people in work might have to pay more tax; people might be obliged to work longer (until the age of 67, for example).

3 Because people want to retire as early as possible and enjoy a longer retirement.

4 China benefitted from a large labour force, mobility of labour, favourable labour laws and low wages paid, initially at least, to workers in mass-production manufacturing.

5 China has to face environmental issues, as it is a major source of CO_2 emissions; it has to be accountable at international trade conferences and workers are demanding better wages and conditions. There have been strikes and protests, but also some improvements in labour laws and wages.

6 China, according to economic experts, needs to raise the skills level of its workers. It also needs to address trade, workers' rights and environmental issues.

7 Each group should focus on a different emerging economy. They should examine demographic background and look at the economic indicators for that country.

Exercise D

1 Set for pairwork discussion. Point out that there is no one 'correct' order; students should try to identify the most logical sequence for the argument. Explain that a 'counter-argument' means an opinion which you do not agree with or think is wrong. 'Issue' means a question about which there is some debate.

2 Set for individual work and pairwork checking.

Do not feed back with the class at this point but move on to Exercise E where the answers will be given.

🎧 Exercise E

1 Play the extract. Tell students to stop you when they hear each item. Make sure students can say exactly what the words are in each case. Ask them also to paraphrase the words so that it is clear that they understand the meanings.

2 If necessary play the extract again for students to check that they have the phrases and types of statement correct. Ask how many students had the stages of an argument (Exercise D, question 1) in the same order as the recording/model answers below. Discuss any alternative possibilities (see *Language note* below).

Answers

Model answers for Exercises D and E:

See table below.

Language note

A common way in which an argument can be built is to give a counter-argument, then reject the counter-argument with reasons and evidence. There are, of course, other ways to build an argument. For example, the counter-arguments may be given after the writer/speaker's own opinion. Or all the arguments against may be given followed by all the arguments for an issue (or vice versa), concluding with the speaker/writer's own opinion.

Transcript 🎧 2.20

The real question about ageing populations is: can governments find acceptable political and economic solutions to the issue? Well, it's quite clear that a solution based only on economic considerations will definitely not be popular. Research in several countries has concluded that people would like to retire early and enjoy a long retirement with a good state pension! But some government economists claim that as people are healthier, they should work longer and retire later, at the age of 67, for example. Well, I'm afraid that just isn't acceptable, as state pensions are already quite low and work stress increases as people get older. The evidence lies in the fact that people who have worked in stressful jobs do not live so long after retirement anyway.

Exercise F

Set for individual work – possibly homework – or else a pair/small group writing task. If the latter, tell students to put their writing on an OHT or other visual medium, so that the whole class can look and comment on what has been written. You should correct language errors on the OHT.

Exercise G

Set students to work in groups of three or four. Make sure they understand that they should choose to focus on one emerging economy per group. Allow each group to choose their country, but be prepared to adjudicate between groups who want to consider the same country. Ask one or two group members to present the results of the group's discussion.

Tell the class that they should carry out research into their respective countries. You will also need to arrange the date for the feedback and discussion of the information, and how the members will present it. This is the focus of Exercise G in Lesson 11.4.

Type of statement	Phrase	Lecturer's words
c stating the issue	The real question is …	The real question about ageing populations is: can governments find acceptable political and economic solutions to the issue?
b giving your opinion	it's quite clear that …	Well, it's quite clear that a solution based only on economic considerations will definitely not be popular.
f giving a reason for an opinion	Research has concluded that …	Research in several countries has concluded that people would like to retire early and enjoy a long retirement with a good state pension!
a giving a counter-argument	Some government economists claim …	But some government economists claim that as people are healthier, they should work longer and retire later, at the age of 67, for example.
e rejecting a counter-argument	I'm afraid that just isn't acceptable …	Well, I'm afraid that just isn't acceptable as state pensions are already quite low and work stress increases as people get older.
d supporting the reason with evidence	The evidence lies in the fact that …	The evidence lies in the fact that people who have worked in stressful jobs do not live so long after retirement anyway.

Closure

Arguments, counter-arguments and giving opinions:

Ask students to think about the methods seen earlier to build an argument. As they do this, write the statements below on the board or display them on an OHT or other visual medium. Ask them to think about whether they agree with the statements below. They should prepare a brief summary of their viewpoints on the topics; they should also try and use some of the phrases used in this lesson.

1 As the world's second biggest economy, China should take responsibility for the pollution it causes.

2 The IOM and UN should aim for global standards of employment conditions, locally appropriate minimum salaries and more workers' rights.

3 An economy that relies on service industries for over 60% of its economic activity cannot be healthy in the long term.

4 London and New York's dominance of the world financial markets should be ended.

5 Immigration should be a socio-economic issue, not a political one.

6 There is no way that trafficking in human beings can be controlled.

7 All economies should include a minimum proportion (e.g., 15–20%) of older workers (over 65, for example) in their labour force.

8 Environmental interests should take priority over economic growth.

11.4 Extending skills

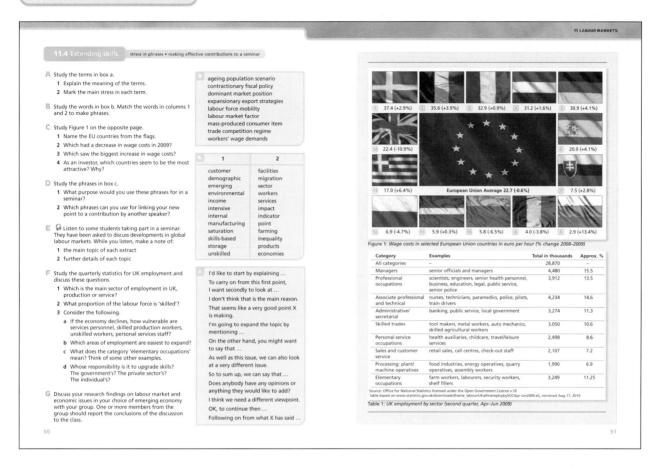

11.4 Extending skills — stress in phrases • making effective contributions to a seminar

A Study the terms in box a.
1 Explain the meaning of the terms.
2 Mark the main stress in each term.

B Study the words in box b. Match the words in columns 1 and 2 to make phrases.

C Study Figure 1 on the opposite page.
1 Name the EU countries from the flags.
2 Which had a decrease in wage costs in 2009?
3 Which saw the biggest increase in wage costs?
4 As an investor, which countries seem to be the most attractive? Why?

D Study the phrases in box c.
1 What purpose would you use these phrases for in a seminar?
2 Which phrases can you use for linking your new point to a contribution by another speaker?

E Listen to some students taking part in a seminar. They have been asked to discuss developments in global labour markets. While you listen, make a note of:
1 the main topic of each extract
2 further details of each topic

F Study the quarterly statistics for UK employment and discuss these questions.
1 Which is the main sector of employment in UK, production or service?
2 What proportion of the labour force is 'skilled'?
3 Consider the following.
   a If the economy declines, how vulnerable are services personnel, skilled production workers, unskilled workers, personal services staff?
   b Which areas of employment are easiest to expand?
   c What does the category 'elementary occupations' mean? Think of some other examples.
   d Whose responsibility is it to upgrade skills? The government's? The private sector's? The individual's?

G Discuss your research findings on labour market and economic issues in your choice of emerging economy with your group. One or more members from the group should report the conclusions of the discussion to the class.

Box a
ageing population scenario
contractionary fiscal policy
dominant market position
expansionary export strategies
labour force mobility
labour market factor
mass-produced consumer item
trade competition regime
workers' wage demands

Box b

1	2
customer	facilities
demographic	migration
emerging	sector
environmental	workers
income	services
intensive	impact
internal	indicator
manufacturing	point
saturation	farming
skills-based	inequality
storage	products
unskilled	economies

Box c
I'd like to start by explaining …
To carry on from this first point, I want secondly to look at …
I don't think that is the main reason.
That seems like a very good point X is making.
I'm going to expand the topic by mentioning …
On the other hand, you might want to say that …
As well as this issue, we can also look at a very different issue.
So to sum up, we can say that …
Does anybody have any opinions or anything they would like to add?
I think we need a different viewpoint.
OK, to continue then …
Following on from what X has said …

Figure 1: Wage costs in selected European Union countries in euro per hour (% change 2008–2009)

① 37.4 (+2.9%) ② 35.6 (+3.9%) ③ 32.9 (+0.9%) ④ 31.2 (+1.6%) ⑤ 30.9 (+4.1%)
⑭ 22.4 (-10.9%) ⑥ 20.0 (+4.1%)
⑬ 17.0 (+6.4%) European Union Average 22.7 (-0.6%) ⑦ 7.5 (+2.8%)
⑫ 6.9 (-4.7%) ⑪ 5.9 (+0.3%) ⑩ 5.8 (-6.5%) ⑨ 4.0 (-3.8%) ⑧ 2.9 (+13.4%)

Category	Examples	Total in thousands	Approx. %
All categories	–	28,870	–
Managers	senior officials and managers	4,480	15.5
Professional occupations	scientists, engineers, senior health personnel, business, education, legal, public service, senior police	3,912	13.5
Associate professional and technical	nurses, technicians, paramedics, police, pilots, train drivers	4,234	14.6
Administrative/ secretarial	banking, public service, local government	3,274	11.3
Skilled trades	tool makers, metal workers, auto mechanics, skilled agricultural workers	3,050	10.6
Personal service occupations	health auxiliaries, childcare, travel/leisure services	2,498	8.6
Sales and customer service	retail sales, call centres, check-out staff	2,107	7.2
Processing: plant/ machine operatives	food industries, energy operatives, quarry operatives, assembly workers	1,990	6.9
Elementary occupations	farm workers, labourers, security workers, shelf fillers	3,249	11.25

Source: Office for National Statistics licensed under the Open Government Licence v.10
Table based on www.statistics.gov.uk/downloads/theme_labour/UKallInemployby/SOCApr-Jun2009.xls, retrieved Aug 17, 2010

Table 1: UK employment by sector (second quarter, Apr–Jun 2009)

90   91

Lesson aims

- recognize stress in compound phrases
- link a contribution to previous contributions when speaking in a seminar
- understand vocabulary in the area of environmental issues

Further practice in:

- taking part in seminars:
  introducing, maintaining and concluding a contribution
  agreeing/disagreeing with other speakers

Introduction

1 Remind students that they are going to be presenting their research findings later in this lesson. Check that they can remember the main points from Lesson 11.3 lecture extracts; key phrases and rhetorical strategies from the lecture could be used as prompts, e.g.:

So, to start with, then, what are the key demographic elements and how do they impact on the labour market? (growth, age, ageing, mobility)

Not only that, but will the pressure on the world's labour markets encourage more cooperation between nations … and force countries to revise their ideas about competition, trade and the environment? (possibly within the EU; unlikely to become more generous to Africa or, in the case of the USA, to South America)

In Europe and Britain, why do many people and politicians see immigration as a sensitive issue? (people feel uneasy because of rising immigration, especially in an economic recession; nationalism, racism)

So, the pattern of work is changing, but how can the global economy make sure that the balance is efficient and sustainable? (international cooperation on environmental issues, climate change, trafficking, etc.)

2 The following activity is a good way to check that students are familiar with the terminology and vocabulary from Lesson 11.3. Ask students to write down 5–10 words or expressions from the previous lesson relating to labour markets and the current issues. Then use two or three students as 'secretaries'. Ask the class to dictate the words so that the secretaries can write the vocabulary on the board. Use this as a brainstorming session.

Exercise A

These are more complex noun phrases than in Lesson 11.3, since they are made up of three words. In some cases the pattern is noun + noun + noun. In this case, there may be a compound made from the first two nouns, or the last two nouns. In other cases, the pattern is adjective + noun + noun, in which the second and third words make a compound. These patterns should become clear once the meaning is understood.

1 Discuss *ageing population scenario* with the class as an example. Elicit that it is a scenario (or model) that relates to an economy where the population is becoming (disproportionately) older. The adj + noun (*ageing population*) would have standard stress, thus *ageing popu'lation* (with a stronger stress on the second noun element). By adding the third element, the stress remains strong there, too: *ageing popu'lation sce'nario*. Set the remaining phrases for individual work and pairwork discussion. Feed back with the whole class, writing each phrase on the board and underlining the words which make a compound noun.

2 Tell students to try to identify where the main stress should come in each phrase. The key to this is finding the two- or three-word compound which is at the base of the three-word phrase. The stress will normally fall in the same place as if this two-word compound was said without the third word. Demonstrate this with *workers' wage demands*. The two-word compound here is not *workers' wage* but *wage demands*. This is a noun + noun compound, so the rules say this will normally be stressed on the first noun 'wage demands. The main stress remains in its original place when the third word is added.

Tell students only to identify the syllable on which the heaviest stress in the phrase falls. (See also *Language note*.)

Answers

Model answers:
See table.

The basic compound is underlined in each case.

ageing <u>popu'lation scenario</u>	a model relating to an economy where the population is ageing disproportionately
contractionary <u>'fiscal policy</u>	(a contrastive meaning, highlighting *contractionary* rather than *expansionary*, is also possible)
dominant <u>'market position</u>	a strong or leading position in a market
expansionary <u>'export strategies</u>	export strategies that are expanding (as for *contractionary* above; this could be contrastive)
<u>'labour force</u> mobility	ability of workers to be flexible/mobile (unless *mobility* needs to be contrasted or emphasized)
<u>'labour market</u> factor	something which influences the availability or cost of labour in a particular market
mass-produced <u>con'sumer item</u>	a consumer item produced in high volumes
<u>trade compe'tition</u> re'gime	(*regime* receives strong stress here because the listener needs to know more about what is referred to; not trade competition *regulations* or trade competition *changes*, but trade competition *regime*)
workers' <u>'wage demands</u>	wage demands made by employees

Language note

Stress placement, especially in complex compound noun phrases, is notoriously unstable. There will be apparent exceptions or variations to the rules, as explained in Exercise A. For example, in the phrase *company spending review*, there are two possible stress placements, which might produce slightly different interpretations.

company spending (compound) + *re'view* (i.e., a review of a company's spending, perhaps carried out by an independent agency) or *company* + *spending review* (compound) (i.e., the spending review carried out by a company).

Stress may often move, depending on the context: for example, *She is well 'known* but *She is a well-known e'conomist*. It is also possible that some native speakers may not agree about some of the phrases above. The main point is to try to notice where the main stresses fall.

Exercise B

Set for individual work and pairwork checking. Tell students that although in some cases it will be possible to make a phrase with more than one option, they must use each word once, and they must use all the words.

Feed back with the whole class. Check that the meaning of all other phrases is understood. Check pronunciation.

Answers

Model answers:

customer	services
demographic	indicator
emerging	economies
environmental	impact
income	inequality
intensive	farming
internal	migration
manufacturing	sector
saturation	point
skills-based	products
storage	facilities
unskilled	workers

Language note

Although in most noun–noun compounds the main stress comes on the first element, there are some compounds where this is not true. Definitive pronunciation of compounds can be found in a good pronunciation dictionary.

Exercise C

Refer students to Figure 1 on page 91 of the Course Book. Set for pair or small group discussion. Students should work in pairs to identify the countries and answer the questions.

Answers

1 1) Denmark, 2) Belgium, 3) France, 4) Netherlands, 5) Germany, 6) Spain, 7) Slovakia, 8) Bulgaria, 9) Romania, 10) Lithuania, 11) Latvia, 12) Poland, 13) Greece and 14) United Kingdom

2 9) Romania (-3.8%), 10) Lithuania (-6.5%), 12) Poland (-4.7%) and 14) UK (-10.9%), as well as overall in the EU (-0.6%)

3 8) Bulgaria, although the wage costs there are still the lowest in the EU

4 This is a difficult question, but if labour costs are the deciding factor, then Eastern Europe (Poland, Romania or Bulgaria) or the Baltic countries (Latvia, Lithuania), all with low wage costs, would be attractive to investors. More careful demographic examination would reveal, for

example, a younger workforce, with greater skills and technological expertise. This might persuade investors to choose a medium-level wage regime such as in Slovakia, although wage costs rose there between 2008 and 2009.

Exercise D

This is mainly revision. Set for individual work or pairwork discussion. Feed back with the whole class.

Answers

Model answers:

I'd like to start by explaining ...
= beginning

To carry on from this first point, I want secondly to look at ...
= maintaining/continuing a point

I don't think that is the main reason.
= disagreeing

That seems like a very good point X is making.
= confirming

I'm going to expand the topic by mentioning ...
= adding a new point to someone else's previous contribution

On the other hand, you might want to say that ...
= disagreeing

As well as this issue, we can also look at a very different issue.
= adding a new point to someone else's previous contribution

So to sum up, we can say that ...
= summarizing/concluding

Does anybody have any opinions or anything they would like to add?
= concluding

I think we need a different viewpoint.
= disagreeing

OK, to continue then ...
= maintaining/continuing a point

Following on from what X has said ...
= adding a new point to someone else's previous contribution

🎧 Exercise E

Before students listen, tell them to look at the exercise and questions. Check that students understand the topic for the seminar discussion. Ask them what they might expect to hear.

Play each extract one at a time and ask students to identify the main topic and some further details. Feed back with the whole class.

Answers

Model answers:

	Main topic	Further details
Extract 1	workers' wages	cheap labour in developing economies has kept wages low in developed economies; increase in income inequality
Extract 2	workers' skills	skilled workers in developed economies produce export and trade goods; get wage rewards; cheap imports mean unskilled workers in developed economies at a disadvantage; inequality gap widens
Extract 3	technology	technology can help economy to expand; can give other economies a chance to catch up; example of India given
Extract 4	environmental concerns	example of fish products in Vietnam; economic expansion often puts the environment at risk

Transcript 🎧 2.21

Extract 1

MAJED: The lecturer we listened to last week introduced a number of interesting issues. In my part of the seminar, I would like to expand the topic by mentioning a number of factors related to workers' wages, especially in the advanced economies. We know that cheap labour has been a factor in emerging countries such as China, India, Bangladesh or Vietnam. It's obvious that these populations depend to a large extent on mass-produced consumer items, such as clothes, shoes, some food products and so on. But, on the other hand, you might want to say that it has also affected wages in the developed economies. I think it has exerted a downward pressure on wages there. This has kept wages low and has contributed to income inequality. If you add this factor to the ageing population scenario, you can see that the revenue issue which the lecturer talked about can't easily be solved. Not only do you have more people who live longer, you have more *poor* people who live longer!

Extract 2

EVIE: OK, following on from what Majed has just said, I'd like to start by mentioning another factor which relates to skills and trade. The lecturer said it is important for all countries to develop skilled workers. Yes, I agree. But, with the present trade competition regime, there is a difficulty. For example, you have a lot of skilled workers who manufacture skills-based products for export, like engineering or automotive products made in

Germany. But there is a danger that unskilled workers in that country lose out! Their wages remain much lower than skilled workers' wages, which increases income inequality and poverty. That is true especially if there are cheap imports from countries with a lot of unskilled labour. So, to sum up, you can see that governments may have to pay more in welfare benefits, as well as equip the labour force with new skills.

Extract 3

JACK: Right. Thank you, Evie, that seems like a very interesting point you're making. But I'm going to expand the topic a bit by mentioning another important factor in globalized labour – technology. Every country tries to create a dominant market position and technology can be the key to success. Let me try and make this clearer with an example. Brazil has used technology to expand its agriculture to grow more sugar and soy beans than any other country. It has become the leading global producer of bioethanol, an important biofuel. Similarly, India has developed its own computer and telecommunications industries. The computers or mobile phones used by students in India are just as advanced as those from America, South-East Asia or Europe. The difference is that they were probably manufactured in the consumer's own country! Does anyone have any opinions on that or anything else to add?

Extract 4

LEILA: Yes, I think that what you have all said is quite correct, but I think we need a different viewpoint – the environmental impact of expansionary export strategies. To give an example, … erm … I'm sure you know that Vietnam exports a lot of prawns and other fish products to Western Europe. Many rivers and coastal regions have been transformed by this expansion and quite a lot of people have gained financially. But what about the increased water pollution from such intensive fish farming? What about the fact that these markets soon reach saturation point and many businesses fail? To carry on from this first point, I want secondly to emphasize that most of these emerging economies have had the advantage of labour force mobility. But this also creates many problems, especially for overcrowded urban areas and through depopulation of rural areas. I recently read Partha Dasgupta's book from 2007, *Economics: A Very Short Introduction*. It really opens your eyes to the conflicts between growth and the environment. Many economists argue that the environment should take priority over growth or expansion.

Exercise F

1/2 Set for pairwork. Tell students to study the UK employment statistics on page 91 of the Course Book. Feed back with the whole class.

3 Set for small group discussion. Feed back with the whole class.

Answers

Possible answers:

1 As students will observe, employment in production industries is much less than in service industries in the UK economy.

2 This is a matter for debate. Students might like to define what a 'skilled' worker actually is or does. Only one category actually uses the word 'skilled', but we can assume that the top four categories plus 'skilled trades' all require skills. However, some people might claim that other skills, such as 'people skills', are equally important as, for example, basic computer skills.

3 a This is a difficult question and depends on the type of economy. In a recession, people have less disposable income and reduce spending. Production usually declines. The government will, most likely, reduce public spending on welfare and health. If the economy is services-based (as in the UK), this sector is hardest hit. If there is a more production-based economy (as in Germany), then *unskilled* workers in industries attached to production are most vulnerable. Skilled workers are valuable to companies and so they are less vulnerable. Personal services staff are very vulnerable because people don't spend on leisure, travel and personal health (e.g., hairdressers, beauticians, health club staff).

b Probably service industries because so many service occupations are based on 'person-to-person' contacts and skills. There is less investment in capital items such as machinery.

c Ask students to focus on their daily lives – perhaps bus drivers, ticket office staff, shop assistants, cleaners, grounds or building maintenance workers, gardeners.

d Answers will depend on the students.

Exercise G

In their groups, students should now present their research findings on the demographic, economic and environmental indicators for an emerging economy. One or more group members should present the information to the class.

Students have had some experience of collecting data using World Bank, CIA, UN (Human Development Reports) or the International Monetary Fund (IMF). This time, they might use other organizations such as IOM, World Wildlife Fund (WWF), Friends of the Earth, Greenpeace or the Food and Agriculture Organization (FAO), or charities such as Oxfam or Water Aid.

They might also have expanded their search by drawing on specific sites relating to their country, such as for India:

Human Development Report for India: http://hdrstats.undp.org/en/countries/profiles/IND.html

India Development Service: www.idsusa.org/

Information and statistics on India and details of programmes: www.wateraid.org/india

Encourage students to use the seminar language practised in this unit and earlier. They should be looking at, or at least mentioning, some or all of the following:

- population structure: growth and age factors; status of women in the economy; proportion of young/old; levels of unemployment; education indicators; GDP spending on education; literacy, raising level of skills; university education percentage; status of female education; mobility; internal and migration overseas; level of remittances

- economic indicators: GDP growth; patterns of employment, especially agriculture: production; status of services; opportunities for skilled workers; types of industries and other activities; status of production industries; technology situation; level of foreign direct investment (FDI) and/or government investment in infrastructure; availability of micro-finance; role of multinational enterprises; role of trade unions; workers' rights; health and safety issues at work

As a group, students should try to come to an overall conclusion as to the prospects for their respective countries. This conclusion should be presented to the rest of the class, together with supporting evidence from students' own research.

Closure

Ask students to imagine that they are 10–15 years in the future. What differences do they think there will be in the labour markets worldwide? How will situations have changed? Ask them to think about the following:

expansion of industrial activities – where/why?

financial services activities – expansion?

role of technology – rapid expansion or slow growth?

environmental protection – growing/declining?

labour force mobility – greater/less?

restrictions on migration/immigration – more/fewer?

skilled workers – more/fewer?

role of agriculture – more localized/more international?

workers' rights and protection – improved/worse?

Encourage students to use the 'future perfect' form with *will have* + past participle. For example:

I think agriculture will have grown in importance.

I think environmental protection will have become stronger.

Extra activities

1 Work through the *Vocabulary bank* and *Skills bank* if you have not already done so, or as revision of previous study.

2 Use the *Activity bank* (Teacher's Book additional resources section, Resource 11A).

A Set the crossword for individual work (including homework) or pairwork.

Answers

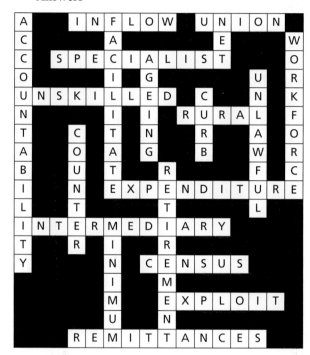

B Set for individual work (including homework) or pairwork. Check students understand the meanings.

Possible answers

ageing	population
environmental	issues
expansionary	policies
human	trafficking
internal	migration
labour	mobility
manufacturing	sector
occupational	pension
retirement	age
saturation	point

3 Tell students to add other words to each of the words below to make as many two-word phrases as possible. Elicit one or two examples, then set for individual work or pairwork.

- immigration
- pension
- demographic

Possible phrases:

immigration controls, immigration figures/statistics, immigration levels (but better, *curbs on immigration* and *restrictions on immigration*)

pension entitlement, pension payments, pension plan/scheme, pension rights

demographic change, demographic outlook, demographic picture, demographic indicators, demographic developments

4 Use an extended activity to allow students to practise some of the concepts they have studied in this unit. Tell students to work in groups. They are going to design a labour force development strategy. The following scenario should be used:

A steel factory has had to close. Four thousand workers are now unemployed in a relatively small area. The steel industry had been the only major employer in the town. The age structure of the former workforce is approximately:

18–35 years old: 1,500 workers

36–55 years old: 2,000 workers

Over 55 years old: 500 workers

Divide the activities into stages as follows:

a Identify the various stages involved in developing a strategy to deal with this problem. The stages might include discussions, consultations, planning, training, implementation, monitoring, evaluation, etc.

b The groups should make specific suggestions for:

- the type of training/retraining needed
- the type of skills which will need to be upgraded/introduced
- help for workers other than financial support
- agencies involved in this programme
- the types of jobs which could be created
- environmental issues which must be solved
- the type of problems (other than financial) which might occur

c Draw up an action plan showing the various stages of the labour force development strategy. (Plans can be put onto A2 sheets, flipcharts or another visual medium and displayed for other groups to compare.)

12 STRATEGY, POLICY AND ECONOMIC CHANGE

This unit provides an opportunity for revision of many of the concepts and vocabulary items used in the book. It introduces students in more detail to the principles of Corporate Social Responsibility (CSR) and features a case study of a bank that has its own CSR programme. As part of the case study, the unit concentrates on processes of data gathering and analysis for the purposes of compiling a research report, similar to authentic student assignments. Composition of the text forms a central part of the unit, with sections on cohesion, and writing suitable introductory and concluding sections. In addition, students are introduced to the idea of the SMART approach to goal-setting, which is frequently used in economics and business planning processes.

Skills focus

Reading

- understanding how ideas in a text are linked

Writing

- deciding whether to use a direct quotation or a paraphrase
- incorporating quotations
- writing research reports
- writing effective introductions/conclusions

Vocabulary focus

- verbs used to introduce ideas from other sources (*X contends/suggests/asserts that ...*)
- linking words/phrases conveying contrast (*whereas*), result (*consequently*), reasons (*due to*), etc.
- words for quantities (*a significant minority*)

Key vocabulary

bail-out (n)	data	mortgage	'repos' (repossessions)
beneficiary	economic cycle	mortgagee	respondent
bequest	ecosystem	product range	retail (outlet)
case study	findings	questionnaire	sample
corporate social responsibility (CSR)	foreclose (v)	recession	SMART framework
creditor	integrity	recoup	survey
customer loyalty	interest rates	(make someone) redundant	trustworthy
	loyalty		

12.1 Vocabulary

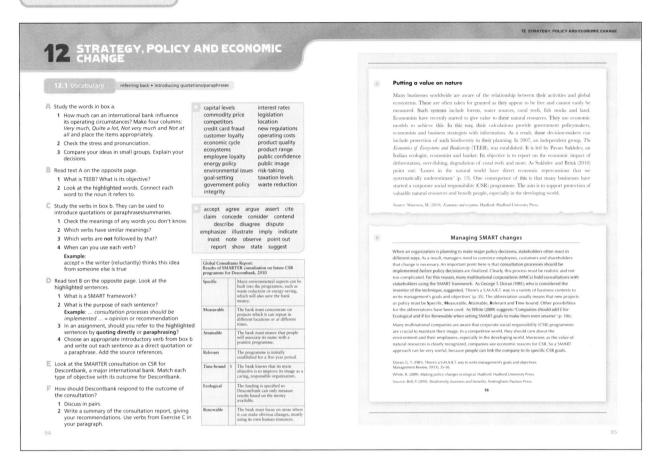

General note

Read the *Vocabulary bank* at the end of the Course Book unit. Decide when, if at all, to refer your students to it. The best time is probably at the very end of the lesson or the beginning of the next lesson, as a summary/revision.

Lesson aims

● understand deictic reference – pronouns and determiners

● refer to sources: the choice of introductory verb and stance of writer towards reference

● choose whether to quote or paraphrase

Further practice in:

● words and phrases from the discipline

Introduction

1 Revise the following words and phrases from the two previous units. Ask students to say which grammar class the words belong to and to provide definitions of them.

insolvency (n, U)

contingency (n, U)

plummet (v, I)

externality (n, C)

licensing (n, U – used as adj)

insignificant (adj)

exploit (v, T)

legacy (n, C)

migration (n, U)

demographic (adj; n, C)

monopoly (n, C)

renewable (adj)

stage (v, T)

2 Introduce the topic of the unit: write the words *strategy*, *policy* and *change* on the board. Ask students: what do these signify for economics? How do banks and companies develop strategy for change? How do they make decisions? What factors do governments need to take into consideration when they are thinking about economic policy? What processes will they all need to go through in order to decide their plans for the future? Have a class discussion on what factors

247

private sector companies and governments need to consider when they are thinking about future development. Accept any reasonable suggestions. Do not elaborate but tell students that this will be the topic of this unit.

Exercise A

1/2 Set for pairwork. Warn students that they may find it difficult to decide how much a bank may influence some of the items listed. Ask students to mark the most strongly stressed syllable in compounds.

Feed back with the whole class, checking meanings.

3 Set for individual work and pairwork checking. Feed back with the whole class. Accept any placings as long as they can be justified. Ask students which items they placed at each end of the scale. Compare views and discuss some of the possible reasons for the answers.

Answers

Possible answers:

See table below.

Other possibilities may be acceptable. The main idea is to generate discussion and give the students a chance to activate the vocabulary, clarifying any unknown words or concepts.

Exercise B

Introduce the idea of textual cohesion, created by referring back to words or ideas already mentioned with pronouns such as *it* and *this* (pronouns and determiners). Say that this is an important way in which the sentences in a text are 'held together'. In reading and understanding it is important to know what is being referred to by such words.

You can build up the answers to question 2 by copying Resource 12B in the additional resources section onto an OHT or other visual medium.

Set for individual work and pairwork checking. Feed back with the whole class, building the table below. Establish why a writer might use a particular referring word (see table on next page).

		Explanations/Justifications
Very much	'goal-setting in'tegrity 'product range 'risk-taking	All these are under the control of the bank. *Goal-setting* is fundamental to the bank's strategy. The bank needs to have *integrity* (honesty, correctness and transparency) in its dealings. It can also influence the *range* of *products* it offers and the degree of *risk-taking* that it is prepared to accept.
Quite a lot	'capital levels 'customer loyalty 'employee loyalty lo'cation 'operating costs 'product quality public 'confidence public 'image 'waste reduction	The bank obviously wants strong *levels* of *capital* to ensure its own stability. It can influence both *customer* and *employee loyalty* by its policies and service. *Location* is tricky as property prices for prime sites can be high, but it should be able to control its *operating costs*. The *quality* of the *products* is possibly less under the bank's influence than the *range*. The bank can influence *public confidence* and its own *public image*, but customers are often unpredictable and may not react the way the bank expects! Surprisingly perhaps, *waste reduction* is an area which a well-run bank should control reasonably well.
Not very much	com'modity price 'credit card fraud economic 'cycle 'energy policy environmental 'issues 'government policy 'interest rates legis'lation new regu'lations tax'ation levels	These items are less under the control of a bank as they relate to external factors. *Taxation levels* depend on government policy, while *commodity prices* depend on the market and the bank should always avoid speculation. *Economic cycles* may affect banks, but are not usually caused by them! Similarly, *environmental issues* and *energy policy* may be dealt with locally by a bank, but they are not controlled at national or international level by the bank. The bank may modify its own *interest rates*, but is often influenced by the general trend and by its competitors. *Credit-card fraud* can be reduced by good bank security practices, but it is not fully under the bank's influence. *Legislation* and *new regulations* are subject to influence by banks, but usually only to delay, modify or minimize an impact rather than to prevent it.
Not at all	'ecosystems com'petitors	These could be in the 'Not very much' column. Most students would say that *ecosystems* are not influenced by a bank's activities at all. However, text A suggests that all businesses have an interest in protecting and preserving them. So there is, in fact, an indirect influence *if* a bank chooses to adopt an ecological approach. A bank is not usually able to influence its *competitors* but, in banking, it is often the case that when one bank leads, another bank follows.

Answers

Model answers:

1 TEEB is an independent group of scientists and economists who, since 2007, have been active in examining the economic value of biodiversity and the world's ecosystems.

2 Putting a value on nature:

Many businesses worldwide are aware of the relationship between their activities and global ecosystems. These are often taken for granted as they appear to be free and cannot easily be measured. Such systems include forests, water sources, coral reefs, fish stocks and land. Economists have recently started to give value to these natural resources. They use economic models to achieve this. In this way, their calculations provide government policymakers, economists and business strategists with information. As a result, those decision-makers can include protection of such biodiversity in their planning. In 2007, an independent group, *The Economics of Ecosystems and Biodiversity* (TEEB), was established. It is led by Pavan Sukhdev, an Indian ecologist, economist and banker. Its objective is to report on the economic impact of deforestation, over-fishing, degradation of coral reefs and more. As Sukhdev and Brink (2010) point out: 'Losses in the natural world have direct economic repercussions that we systematically underestimate' (p. 13). One consequence of this is that many businesses have started a corporate social responsibility (CSR) programme. The aim is to support protection of valuable natural resources and benefit people, especially in the developing world.

Subject note

The objective of TEEB is to provide research-based information on biodiversity and to bring the economic issues of species loss, climate change and pollution to the attention of stakeholders. TEEB has presented a number of reports and has its own website: www.teebweb.org

As the group was formed as a result of a G8+5 meeting and is funded by a number of European governments, the EU site is a useful resource: http://ec.europa.eu/environment/nature/biodiversity/economics/

Word	Refers to	Comments
the + noun	a previously mentioned noun	one of several ways in which choice of article is governed
it, they	a noun	generally refers to the nearest suitable noun previously mentioned or the subject of the previous sentence
its, their	a previously mentioned noun, indicating possession	other possessive pronouns used in text for reference: *his, her, hers, theirs*, etc.
this	an idea in a phrase or a sentence	• often found at the beginning and sometimes at the end of a sentence or a paragraph, e.g., *to achieve this*; a common mistake is to use *it* for this purpose • also used with prepositions (e.g., *for this*)
this/these + noun	a previously mentioned noun/ noun phrase	also used with prepositional phrases (e.g., *in this way*)
those	a previously mentioned noun/ noun phrase	• also used with prepositions • *those* – not *these* – is used to show distance between the writer/speaker and the objects/concepts themselves
such + noun	a previously mentioned noun	one meaning is: 'Xs like this' if the noun is plural, e.g., *such problems* Note that when referring to a singular countable noun, *such a X* is used (e.g., *in such a situation*); in this text, *such biodiversity* indicates that *biodiversity* is uncountable.

Language note

Clearly, in this text, there are also relative pronouns which refer back to previously mentioned nouns in relative clauses. However, the grammar of relative pronouns is not covered here.

This is a complex area of written language. The reference words here are commonly found and, arguably, students should be able to use them in their writing. There are, of course, various other ways to refer back to a word or idea, such as when comparing: *the former ... the latter ...; some ... others ... .*

For more information on this, see a good grammar reference book.

Exercise C

1–3 Set for individual work or pairwork. Feed back. Discuss any differences of opinion in question 2 and allow alternative groupings, with reasonable justifications. Establish that not all verbs have equivalents.

  4 Discuss this with the whole class, building the table in the Answers section. Point out to students that the choice of introductory verb for a direct or indirect quote, or a paraphrase or summary, will reveal what they think about the sources. This is an important way in which, when writing essays, students can show a degree of criticality about their sources. Critically evaluating other writers' work is an important part of academic assignments, dissertations and theses.

Point out also that some verbs have a degree of markedness, that is, extra meaning or connotation (as in the final column).

Answers

Possible answers:

  2 accept, agree, concede

     argue, assert, claim, contend, imply, insist

     consider, note, observe, point out, state

     disagree, dispute

     illustrate, indicate, show

3/4 See table below.

Exercise D

Discuss with the students when it is better to paraphrase and when to quote directly. Refer to the *Skills bank* if necessary.

1–3 Set for individual work and pairwork checking. Feed back with the whole class.

  4 Set for individual work. Remind students that if they want to quote another source but to omit some words, they can use three dots (...) to show some words are missing.

		Used when the writer ...
accept	that	(reluctantly) thinks this idea from someone else is true
agree	that	thinks this idea from someone else is true
argue	that	is giving an opinion that others may not agree with
assert	that	is giving an opinion that others may not agree with
cite	+ noun	is referring to someone else's ideas
claim	that	is giving an opinion that others may not agree with
concede	that	reluctantly thinks this idea from someone else is true
consider	that	is giving his/her opinion
contend	that	is giving an opinion that others may not agree with
describe	how; + noun	is giving a description
disagree	that; with + noun	thinks an idea is wrong
dispute	+ noun	thinks an idea is wrong
emphasize	that	is giving his/her opinion strongly
illustrate	how; + noun	is explaining, possibly with an example
imply	that	is suggesting something which may be rather controversial
indicate	that	is explaining, possibly with an example
insist	that	is giving an opinion that others may not agree with
note	that	is giving his/her opinion
observe	that	is giving his/her opinion
point out	that	is giving his/her opinion
report	that	is giving research findings
show	that	is explaining, possibly with an example
state	that	is giving his/her opinion
suggest	that; + gerund	is giving his/her opinion tentatively; *or* is giving his/her recommendation

Language note

When deciding between quoting directly and paraphrasing, students need to decide whether the writer's original words are special in any way. If they are, then a direct quote is better – for example, with a definition, or if the writer has chosen some slightly unusual words to express an idea. If the writer is giving factual information or description, a paraphrase is better. Opinions also tend to be paraphrased.

A page reference should be given for a direct quotation but is not necessary for a paraphrase.

Answers

Possible answers:

1 A S-M-A-R-T framework refers to an abbreviation (an acronym) which acts as an evaluation mechanism for new policies or projects. It is useful in management and usually refers to how SPECIFIC, MEASURABLE, ATTAINABLE, RELEVANT and TIME-BOUND the objectives are.

2–4 See table below.

Exercise E

This is an exercise in relating some of the vocabulary discussed in Exercise A to meanings in financial economics. It will help prepare students for work later in the unit. Remind students of the reference to SMART frameworks or analysis. This exercise extends the framework with *E* for Ecological and *R* for Renewable. Sometimes it is quite difficult to identify if an element is, for example, Attainable or Relevant. This is not a problem, as it will give students a chance to develop their critical thinking. Set for pairwork discussion. Feed back with the whole class if necessary.

Answers

Model answers:

Global Consultants: Results of SMARTER consultation on future CSR programme for Descontbank, 2010	
Specific	The bank knows that its main objective is to improve its image as a caring, responsible organization.
Measurable	The funding is specified so Descontbank can only measure results based on the money available.
Attainable	The bank must focus on areas where it can make obvious changes, mostly using its own human resources.
Relevant	The bank must ensure that people will associate its name with a positive programme.
Time-bound	The programme is initially established for a five-year period.
Ecological	Many environmental aspects can be built into the programme, such as waste reduction or energy saving, which will also save the bank money.
Renewable	The bank must concentrate on projects which it can repeat in different locations or at different times.

Original sentence	The writer is …	Direct quote or paraphrase?	Suggested sentence
a When an organization is planning to make major policy decisions, stakeholders often react in different ways.	making a statement of fact	paraphrase	Bell (2010) points out that stakeholders may respond differently to planned changes in organizational policy.
b … consultation processes should be implemented *before* policy decisions …	giving an opinion or recommendation	paraphrase	Bell (2010) asserts that there is a need for careful consultation before any changes are introduced.
c For this reason, many multinational corporations (MNCs) hold consultations with stakeholders using the SMART framework.	making a statement of fact	paraphrase	Bell (2010) considers that the SMART framework provides MNCs with a valuable consultation instrument.
d As George T. Doran (1981), who is considered the inventor of the technique, suggested,	quoting from another writer; the other writer is making a strong statement	quote the other writer directly but omitting some of what the original author wrote	Bell (2010) cites Doran, who stated that: 'There's a S-M-A-R-T way … to write management goals and objectives' (Doran, 1981, p. 35).
e As White (2009) suggests: 'Companies should add *E* for Ecological and *R* for Renewable when setting SMART goals to make them even smarter' (p. 186).	quoting directly from the original writer because the opinion is quite special	quoting directly but omitting some of what the original author wrote; inserting words in [ ] to clarify	Bell (2010) quotes White, who suggests that: 'Companies should add *E* for Ecological and *R* for Renewable … to make them [SMART goals] even smarter' (White, 2009, p. 186).
f … people can link the company to its specific CSR goals.	making a statement of fact	quoting directly	As Bell (2010) emphasizes, SMART has advantages because '… people can link the company to its specific CSR goals' (p. 16).

Exercise F

1 Set for pairwork discussion, followed by class discussion.

2 Before setting the students to write, tell them they should refer to both texts A and B and use the primary source for text B (Bell, 2010), to support their answer. You might want to put the paragraph on an OHT or other visual medium as an example to illustrate what students might include.

Answers

Possible answers:

1 Accept any reasonable suggestions.

2 As Bell (2010) indicates: '… Corporate Social Responsibility (CSR) programmes are crucial to maintain their [multinational companies] image' (p. 16). From the information in the SMARTER consultation (Global Consultants, 2010), the report emphasizes that Descontbank wants to review its own CSR programme in the near future. The report points out that Descontbank intends to make its public image stronger and more positive. The report also asserts that, because funding is limited to five years, Descontbank needs to ensure that results are measured according to financial criteria, and that bank employees are used wherever possible. The report considers that small but significant changes to people's lives are attainable. To ensure sustainability over the time period, the report suggests that a renewable CSR programme for Descontbank should focus on projects which can be transferred to other locations or repeated. It is likely that Descontbank can improve customer loyalty by its association with environmental or waste-reduction projects which will 'save the bank money' (ibid., p. 16). However, because CSR programmes should focus on benefits to the developing world and environmental issues, I recommend that Descontbank should consult with employees on their participation and also conduct a survey to establish customers' priorities for Descontbank's CSR programme.

Closure

1 Ask students to think again about strategy, policy and change.

How can SMART help a company to develop a strategy? (*It provides a framework and all stakeholders can participate in using it.*)

When might a strategy lead to a policy for an MNC? (*If it is acceptable economically and politically.*)

Ask them to list reasons why Descontbank might have a CSR programme. They might mention, for example:

image/good publicity

strengthen their market position

potential new markets and customers

employee loyalty

customer loyalty

desire to help the developing world

2 Refer students to the additional material on page 108 of the Course Book.

See table below.

Ask students to study the table.

Discuss the meaning of the various values related to ecological factors.

Clarify any difficulties and deal with any queries. Students should observe there are three USE and two NON-USE values. For example, DIRECT USE VALUE relates to consumption of the natural resources but INDIRECT USE VALUE relates to the way the environment regulates itself to assist humans: for example, rivers that flood leaving new soil or provide natural irrigation; forests that prevent soil erosion; or using the sun for energy or for assisting evaporation in making salt.

Putting a value on nature:

How can the economic value of nature be assessed?			
Total economic value	Use values	Direct use value	Consumption benefits e.g., sight-seeing, fishing, agricultural products
		Indirect use value	Ecosystem benefits e.g., chemical self-regulation of water supplies
		Option value	Future availability benefits e.g., genetic manipulation
	Non-use values	Bequest value	Legacy benefits e.g., habitat/landscape/cultural conservation
		Existence value	Existence benefits e.g., knowledge of biodiversity/programmes

Adapted from: OECD (2001). *Valuation of Biodiversity Studies*. Paris: OECD Publications, p. 159.

OPTION VALUE might need to be discussed but the example given is useful. So improvements in breeding cattle or creating hybrid versions of plants as well as genetically improved organisms can benefit humans in the future and so the improved version has an added value.

In the NON-USE category, the division is into BEQUEST VALUE and EXISTENCE VALUE, which again may need to be discussed a little. Students should be familiar with the idea of 'legacy' from Unit 10. Here, it relates to conservation so natural resources can be passed on to future generations. EXISTENCE VALUE is a little more complex and relates to the knowledge and awareness of ecosystems through education and information. The value of an entity increases if more people know about it and more people become aware of the interconnectedness of, for example, land exploitation and wildlife conservation.

If you wish, you may refer students to a useful resource which adapted the original table.

This is a presentation by Gernot Bäurle entitled 'Putting Economic Value to Nature Protection', available at the time of writing at:

chm.moew.government.bg/nnps/upload/Common/ Costs_and_Benefits.ppt

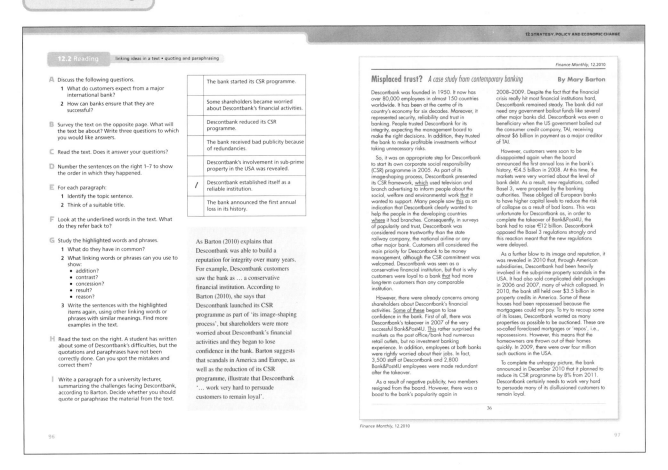

General note

Read the *Vocabulary bank* and *Skills bank* at the end of the Course Book unit. Decide when, if at all, to refer students to them. The best time is probably at the very end of the lesson or the beginning of the next lesson, as a summary/revision.

Lesson aims

- understand rhetorical markers in writing (*but* and *so* categories)
- use direct quotations from other writers:

  common mistakes

  missing words

  fitting quotations to the grammar of the sentence

  adding emphasis to a quote

  continuing to quote from the same source

Further practice in:

- indirect quotations/paraphrases/summaries
- summarizing with a series of topic sentences
- rhetorical markers (adding points)
- deictic reference and relative pronouns

Introduction

Revise the main SMARTER concepts from Lesson 12.1. What does each letter stand for?

To prepare students for the lesson's theme, ask them to think of any experiences they (or members of their family) have had with a bank recently. They might like to consider, for example, quality of service, efficiency, information from the bank, the bank's communication with customers, or banking products such as investments. They might know some of the problems and challenges facing banks in general, in their country or globally.

Exercise A

Set for pairwork or class discussion. Accept any reasonable suggestions.

Answers

Possible answers:

1 Customers might expect good service; efficiency; good communication; a policy of safe investments without risk; a high standard of ethical practice (integrity).

2 As with all sectors, banks have to look for growth. They have to decide what their customers want

from them; they have to deal with competition; and they have to make the most of the political and economic climate (regulation/deregulation, changes in government policy, consumer trends and behaviour). Banks are also very conscious of their image, particularly after the financial collapse of 2008/2009. They have to minimize risk and offer products which are responsible and secure. Many banks have seen a reduction in customer loyalty, as they switch banks to find better deals.

Exercise B

Remind students about surveying a text (skim-reading to get an approximate idea of the text contents by looking at the title, looking at the beginning few lines and the final few lines of the text, and by looking at the first sentence of each paragraph).

Set for individual work and pairwork discussion. Each pair should agree three questions. Feed back with the whole class. Write some questions on the board.

Exercise C

Set for individual work followed by pairwork discussion. Feed back with the whole class. Ask whether the questions you have put on the board have been answered in the text.

Exercise D

Set for individual work and pairwork checking. This activity could also be done using Resource 12C in the additional resources section. Photocopy and cut up the sentences and hand them out in a jumbled order. Tell students to put them in the correct order.

Answers

Model answers:

2	The bank started its CSR programme.
3	Some shareholders became worried about Descontbank's financial activities.
7	Descontbank reduced its CSR programme.
4	The bank received bad publicity because of redundancies.
6	Descontbank's involvement in sub-prime property in the USA was revealed.
1	Descontbank established itself as a reliable institution.
5	The bank announced the first annual loss in its history.

Exercise E

1/2 Set for individual work and pairwork discussion. The topic sentences should suggest a suitable title.

Answers

Possible answers:

	Topic sentence	Para title
Para 1	Descontbank was founded in 1950.	The beginning of Descontbank
Para 2	So, it was an appropriate step for Descontbank to start its own corporate social responsibility (CSR) programme in 2005.	Descontbank and CSR
Para 3	However, there were already concerns among shareholders about Descontbank's financial activities.	Shareholders' concerns
Para 4	As a result of negative publicity, two members resigned from the board.	Results of bad publicity
Para 5	However, customers were soon to be disappointed again when the board announced the first annual loss in the bank's history, €4.5 billion in 2008.	First annual loss
Para 6	As a further blow to its image and reputation, it was revealed in 2010 that, through American subsidiaries, Descontbank had been heavily involved in the sub-prime property scandals in the USA.	Descontbank's involvement in US sub-prime property market
Para 7	To complete the unhappy picture, the bank announced in December 2010 that it planned to reduce its CSR programme by 8% from 2011.	Descontbank cuts back its CSR programme

Exercise F

Set for individual work and pairwork checking.

Answers

Model answers:

Word	Refers to
which	CSR framework
that	(the bank's) social, welfare and environmental programmes
this	the decision (step) that Descontbank had undertaken
where	in the developing countries
that	the bank
some of these	shareholders
this	the decision to take over Bank&Post4U

Exercise G

1 Refer students to the highlighted words. Elicit that they are all linking words and phrases.

2 With the whole class, elicit from the students some linking words or phrases that can be used for:

- contrast and concession (i.e., words which have a *but* meaning)
- result and reason (i.e., words which have a *so* or *for* meaning)

  Build the table in the Answers section on the board, reminding students of the difference between between- and within-sentence linking words (refer to Unit 11 *Vocabulary bank*).

3 Set for individual work. Encourage students to rewrite the sentences using a different type of linking word from the original (i.e., swapping between- and within-sentence linking words).

Answers

Possible answers:

2 See table below.

3 Possible answers:

Furthermore, it represented security, reliability and trust in banking.

Moreover, they trusted the bank to make profitable investments without taking unnecessary risks.

Therefore, it was an appropriate step for Descontbank to start its own corporate social responsibility (CSR) programme in 2005.

As a result, in surveys of popularity and trust, Descontbank was considered more trustworthy than the state railway company, the national airline or any other major bank.

In spite of the fact that customers still considered the main priority for Descontbank to be money management, the CSR commitment was welcomed.

OR

The CSR commitment was welcomed, *despite the fact that* customers still considered the main priority for Descontbank to be money management.

Descontbank was seen as a conservative financial institution. *Nevertheless*, that is why customers were loyal to a bank that had more long-term customers than any comparable institution.

At the same time, there were already concerns among shareholders about Descontbank's financial activities.

Additional practice in paraphrasing these sentences is given in Resource 12G.

Exercise H

Set for individual work and pairwork checking. Feed back with the whole class.

Answers

Model answers: See table on next page.

	Between-sentence linking words/phrases	Within-sentence linking words/phrases
Addition (*and*)	Furthermore, … In addition, … Additionally, … Moreover, …	… and … … too … also … … along with … … together with …
Contrast (*but*) used when comparing	However, … In/By contrast, … On the other hand, …	… but … … whereas … … while …
Concession (*but*) used to concede/accept a point which simultaneously contrasts with the main point of a sentence or paragraph	However, … At the same time, … Nevertheless, … Despite/In spite of (*this*/noun), … Yet …	… although … … despite/in spite of the fact that …
Result (*so*)	So, … As a result, … Consequently, … Therefore, …	…, so … … so that … … with the result that …
Reason (*for*)	Because of (*this*/noun), … Owing to (*this*/noun), … Due to (*this*/noun), …	… because … … since … … as … … due to/owing to the fact that …

Corrected version	Comments
As Barton (2010) explains,	Note the grammar here: either *As Barton explains* or *Barton explains that* but not both. This is a common mistake.
as '*a conservative financial institution*' (p. 36) [emphasis added].	1. The words are the same as the original and therefore need quotation marks. 2. It is not really necessary here to use three dots to signify omission as it is a key phrase which is directly cited. 3. The page number should be given in brackets at the end of the quote. It could also be (ibid., p. 36), but it is clear that the writer is quoting Barton directly. 4. If you want to emphasize a part of a quote, use *italics* and then put [emphasis added] after the quote.
According to Barton (ibid.), Descontbank …	1. You do not need a verb of saying with *According to*. 2. When referring to the same place in the same source, use *ibid.* instead of repeating the source reference. If it is the same publication (but not the same place in the text), use *op. cit.*
Descontbank launched its CSR programme 'as part of its image-shaping process',	The quotation marks must be added to the *exact* words which are the same as the original source.
… but shareholders were already worried about some of Descontbank's dealings and their trust in the bank's decision-making began to decline.	1. The words in the student's version are almost identical to the original version. 2. Paraphrasing is a better option as the information is fairly basic.
… illustrate that Descontbank must 'work very hard to persuade … customers to remain loyal'. OR … illustrate that Descontbank has a difficult task to convince some of its customers to stay with the bank.	1. It is important to make a quotation fit the grammar of a sentence. Failing to do this properly is a common mistake. 2. Here, the … omission is signalled. 3. Again, paraphrasing is a good option here.

Exercise I

Set for individual work, possibly for homework. Alternatively, set for pair or small group work. Students can write the paragraph on an OHT or other visual medium, which you can display and give feedback on with the whole class.

Answers

Possible answers:

It seems that Descontbank faces a serious examination of its integrity, particularly now it has announced reductions in its CSR programmes. In her recent article, Barton (2010) claims that the bank established a good reputation over 50 years and was seen by stakeholders as a symbol of '… security, reliability and trust in banking' (p. 36).

According to Barton (ibid.), it seemed a logical step that a CSR programme should be launched in 2005. However, as a result of a badly managed takeover of Bank&Post4U in 2007, Descontbank received negative publicity because of thousands of redundancies. Consequently, shareholders and customers were dissatisfied with Descontbank's dealings. Barton asserts further that the bank's opposition to new regulations, known as Basel 3, made the markets uncertain once again. Moreover, Barton (ibid.) points out that its involvement in the American sub-prime mortgages scandal has left Descontbank in a poor financial position, with over $3.5 billion still tied up in property credits. She suggests that this may be a reason for its

CSR reductions. As Barton (ibid.) observes, Descontbank must now '… work very hard to persuade … customers to remain loyal'.

Closure

Ask students to discuss these questions.

1 To what extent should an international bank like Descontbank be concerned about an aspect of its operations such as CSR?

2 Imagine you work for Descontbank's strategy development department. What strategies should Descontbank develop to improve its profile and ensure customer loyalty?

Answers

1/2 Accept any reasonable suggestions.

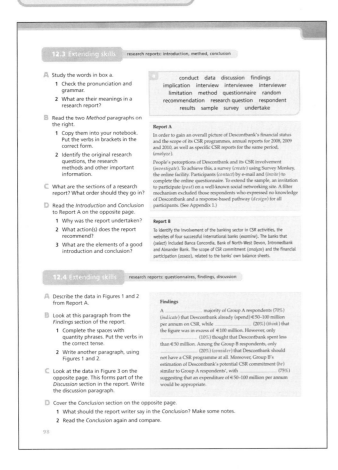

Lesson aims

- structure a research report:

  introduction

  method

  conclusion

Further practice in:

- essay structure
- research methods

Introduction

In preparation for looking at the structure of a research report, revise the sections for an essay: introduction, body, conclusion.

Ask students what should go in each section. Elicit ideas for introductions and conclusions. Do not correct at this point.

Remind students about the methods for doing research (see Unit 5). Ask students what kinds of research would be appropriate if you want to find out what stakeholders think of a bank's performance and policies. Remind students that stakeholders might include shareholders, management and staff, as well as customers. (Primary sources are best: survey, questionnaire, interview, quantitative and qualitative methods.)

Ask students what kinds of research would be appropriate if you want to find out whether a bank has a CSR programme in place and any ethical policies. (Secondary sources are the easiest, e.g., Internet research, company reports, trade magazines.)

Tell students that the next two lessons will focus on writing up research in reports. Ask for suggestions for suitable sections of a research report. Do not correct at this point.

Subject note

In the model presented here, the report is executed at a fairly simple level. For instance, in a real academic research report, there will be a literature review section before the methods section, and the research questions will be linked with this review. There are also different formats for reports, although the one given here is widely acceptable.

For example, an economic analysis of a company or country, a form of case study, may also have sections with the headings, findings and recommendations. A more narrow analysis of an economic issue, such as those listed in the closure activity might involve academic research and a summary of findings plus possible consequences. Students in economics may have to do group reports, but this approach is not considered here. For the complete text of the report, see Resource 12D in the additional resources section.

Exercise A

Set for individual work and pairwork checking. Feed back with the whole class.

Answers

Model answers: See table at top of opposite page.

Word	Notes on pronunciation and grammar	Meaning in a research report
con'duct	v (noun is pronounced: 'conduct)	do (some research, a survey, an experiment)
'data	pl n	information; can be numerical (quantitative) or verbal (qualitative)
dis'cussion	n (U/C)	the title of the section in a research report which discusses the findings. Sometimes the discussion is included in the *Findings/Results* section.
'findings	pl n	the title of the section in a research report which details what has been found out; each finding should be linked with a research question. The title *Results* can also be used for this section.
impli'cation	n (C)	possible effect or result of the findings
'interview	n (C), v	noun: a type of research in which the researcher asks someone a series of questions to gain information/opinions on a certain subject(s) verb: conduct this type of research
interview'ee	n (C)	the person who answers the questions in an interview
'interviewer	n (C)	the person who asks the questions in an interview
limi'tation	n (C)	a restriction related to the research methods; an aspect which the research could not address
'method	n (C)	title of the section in a research report which explains how the research was carried out. In the plural it refers to the research methods used.
question'naire	n (C)	a written set of questions
'random	adj	in no fixed order; with no organizing principle
recommen'dation	n (C)	suggestion for action as a result of the findings of the research
re'search question	n (C)	what the researcher wants to find out
re'spondent	n (C)	a person taking part in a questionnaire survey
re'sults	pl n	Same as *Findings*. Used more or less interchangeably.
'sample	n (C), v	noun: the group of people taking part in the research verb: ask research questions to a selected group of people
'survey	n (C), v (sur'vey)	noun: a type of research in which the researcher sets out to describe a situation or set of ideas or behaviours by reading a variety of documents or asking people questions verb: conduct this type of research
under'take	v	do (some research, a survey)

Exercise B

Explain to the students that this paragraph is an example of the *Method* section of a research report.

1 Set for individual work. Ask students to copy the text into their notebooks and put the verbs into the correct form. Feed back with the whole class, drawing students' attention to the use of the past tense when reporting methods of research, as well as the use of the passive.

2 Set for individual work and pairwork checking. Tell students that they should transform the research questions into real, direct questions. Feed back with the whole group, pointing out that the information given in the *Method* section should include these types of details.

Answers

Possible answers: See table on next page.

Exercise C

Use this to confirm that students understand the organization of a research report. Elicit the answers from the whole class.

Answers

Model answers:

Section	Order in a research report
Introduction	1
Method	2
Findings/Results	3
Discussion	4
Conclusion	5

	Research questions	Research method	Other important information
Report A In order to gain an overall picture of Descontbank's financial status and the scope of its CSR programmes, annual reports for 2008, 2009 and 2010, as well as specific CSR reports for the same period, (*analyze*) <u>were analyzed</u>. People's perceptions of Descontbank and its CSR involvement (*investigate*) <u>were investigated</u>. To achieve this, a survey (*create*) <u>was created</u> using Survey Monkey, the online facility. Participants (*contact*) <u>were contacted</u> by e-mail and (*invite*) <u>(were) invited</u> to complete the online questionnaire. To extend the sample, an invitation to participate (*post*) <u>was posted</u> on a well-known social networking site. A filter mechanism excluded those respondents who expressed no knowledge of Descontbank and a response-based pathway (*design*) <u>was designed</u> for all participants. (See Appendix 1.)	1 What is Descontbank's overall financial status? 2 How much has Descontbank invested in CSR programmes? 3 What are people's perceptions of Descontbank and its CSR programmes?	Library research Online survey	Descontbank's annual reports and specific CSR reports were analyzed. Participants were contacted directly and invited at random. (targeted and random response)
Report B To identify the involvement of the banking sector in CSR activities, the websites of four successful international banks (*examine*) <u>were examined</u>. The banks that (*select*) <u>were selected</u> included Banca Concordia, Bank of North-West Devon, Intromedbank and Almander Bank. The scope of CSR commitment (*analyze*) <u>was analyzed</u> and the financial participation (*assess*) <u>(was) assessed</u>, related to the banks' own balance sheets.	1 How strongly is the banking sector committed to CSR? 2 What is the scope of CSR programmes in the four banks? 3 How much do they commit to CSR activities?	Online investigation	Descontbank was not selected for examination of its CSR commitments.

Subject note

Different disciplines and reports for varying purposes may have different section names or organization. The model suggested here is a rather general one, and is a pattern commonly adopted in an academic context, though there are variations depending on the level of the writing (whether, for example, it is a Master's or PhD dissertation). If students are going to write about 500 words only, you may wish to include *Discussion* with *Findings/Results* or with the *Conclusion*.

Exercise D

Explain to the students that these are examples of a typical introduction and conclusion. The introduction explains why the report was undertaken.

Set for pairwork discussion. Feed back with the whole class. Bring the class's attention to the tenses that are used here (present perfect, present simple, future) as well as the use of the passive.

Answers

Model answers:

1 To examine people's perceptions of Descontbank's CSR programme.

2 The report recommends that Descontbank should increase its CSR commitments in the developing world; reduce the amount of employee labour used; and increase the expenditure on CSR overall.

3 See table on next page.

Language note

The impersonal use of the passive for research reports is not absolutely required. It is often possible to find students' work (assignments, dissertations) which contains the use of the first person singular. However, in more formal writing, such as in journal articles, the passive is usually used.

Good introduction	Example sentence(s)
Introduce the topic. Give some background information.	Many private sector companies have developed extensive corporate social responsibility (CSR) programmes over the past decade.
Say why the topic is important.	Such commitments are valuable in terms of improved public image and raised international profile, as well as enhanced employee loyalty.
Mention any previous studies or research and what they have contributed. (Note: This section may not always be necessary.)	A number of studies (Amiss, 2006; Bryant, 2007; Young, 2009) have shown that the perception of these programmes depends on the respondents' overall experience of the company, its image, reputation and integrity.
Say what you will do in the report. Give a general statement of the purpose of the research.	This study will present an investigation, using an online survey, into how people perceive the CSR activities of Descontbank. First, the financial aspects and specific CSR activities of the bank will be focused on. After that, the results of the online survey will be analyzed, and some recommendations for development and improvement of the bank's CSR programmes will be proposed.
Good conclusion	**Example sentence(s)**
Give a general summary/restatement of findings.	Descontbank is clearly not associated with extensive CSR activities. A majority of those surveyed did not attribute CSR programmes to the bank at all. Nobody had the correct picture; on the one hand, many people didn't know there was a programme. However, the ones who did, thought it was bigger and more generously funded than in reality. Descontbank was also linked more to projects in the developing world than is, in fact, the case. It is clear that Descontbank focuses primarily on its domestic markets. However, Descontbank operates mainly in the developing world.
Say what your recommendations are.	It is therefore strongly recommended that the bank should raise its overseas commitments and spend more to alleviate poverty there. It should also rethink the use of so much employee voluntary work at a time when job security is a serious issue. Moreover, it should reconsider if a figure of 0.57% of its total profits in 2010 is really a serious CSR commitment.
Say what the implications might be.	If Descontbank fails to act decisively soon, it may find that its integrity has declined significantly in the global marketplace and customers and investors will look for an alternative.

Closure

1 Refer students to the *Skills bank* to consolidate their understanding of the sections of research reports and their contents.

2 In economics, students might be expected to look at a specifically defined topic, with underlying economic principles and concepts, e.g.:

tackling budget deficits in Western Europe and North America

encouraging investment through fiscal incentive

China and its relationships to South America

recession in Japan

the importance of training and education in OECD countries

the arguments for a minimum wage

the role of national central banks

the Internet economy

competition in the energy industry

agricultural commodity prices

or even looking at a TEEB group topic such as *the economics of natural resources.*

Ask students to work in groups of three or four and decide how they might plan one of these titles. It is

likely that it would be a research report (library and Internet based). They would need to formulate their own research question and indicate limitations of their investigation. As well as collecting data from sources, students might also have to include diagrams (curves, figures) to illustrate their arguments. Some information would undoubtedly be placed in Appendices.

Another option would be for some students to do a case study of an organization or enterprise according to specific economic principles which underlie its activities, such as a national airline (Lufthansa, Air France) or the French nuclear industry, German or Danish state railways, an organization such as the BBC or utilities companies in the USA or UK. A public sector employer such as the National Health Service in the UK, or a state-run insurance institution such as the German health and pensions system, might also be interesting. Such studies would be a little different from a 'normal' business case study.

Again, planning such a report is good practice for students and, in this way, they might have an opportunity of developing qualitative data-gathering instruments.

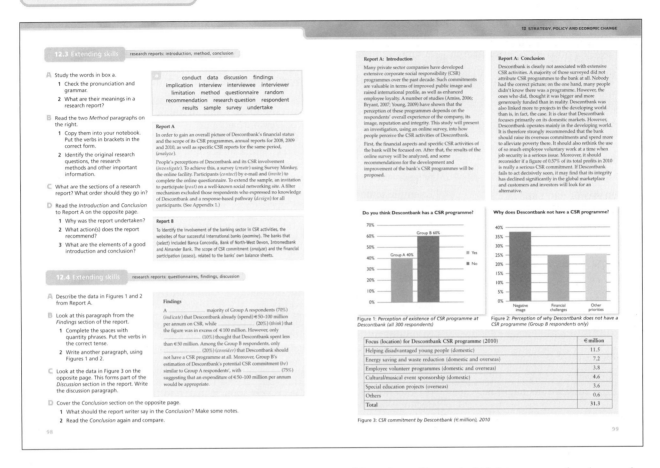

12.3 Extending skills research reports: introduction, method, conclusion

A Study the words in box a.
1 Check the pronunciation and grammar.
2 What are their meanings in a research report?

conduct data discussion findings implication interview interviewee interviewer limitation method questionnaire random recommendation research question respondent results sample survey undertake

B Read the two *Method* paragraphs on the right.
1 Copy them into your notebook. Put the verbs in brackets in the correct form.
2 Identify the original research questions, the research methods and other important information.

C What are the sections of a research report? What order should they go in?

D Read the *Introduction* and *Conclusion* to Report A on the opposite page.
1 Why was the report undertaken?
2 What action(s) does the report recommend?
3 What are the elements of a good introduction and conclusion?

Report A

In order to gain an overall picture of Descontbank's financial status and the scope of its CSR programmes, annual reports for 2008, 2009 and 2010, as well as specific CSR reports for the same period, (*analyze*).

People's perceptions of Descontbank and its CSR involvement (*investigate*). To achieve this, a survey (*create*) using Survey Monkey, the online facility. Participants (*contact*) by e-mail and (*invite*) to complete the online questionnaire. To extend the sample, an invitation to participate (*post*) on a well-known social networking site. A filter mechanism excluded those respondents who expressed no knowledge of Descontbank and a response-based pathway (*design*) for all participants. (See Appendix 1.)

Report B

To identify the involvement of the banking sector in CSR activities, the websites of four successful international banks (*examine*). The banks that (*select*) included Banca Concordia, Bank of North-West Devon, Intromedbank and Almander Bank. The scope of CSR commitment (*analyze*) and the financial participation (*assess*), related to the banks' own balance sheets.

12.4 Extending skills research reports: questionnaires, findings, discussion

A Describe the data in Figures 1 and 2 from Report A.

B Look at this paragraph from the *Findings* section of the report.
1 Complete the spaces with quantity phrases. Put the verbs in the correct tense.
2 Write another paragraph, using Figures 1 and 2.

C Look at the data in Figure 3 on the opposite page. This forms part of the *Discussion* section in the report. Write the discussion paragraph.

D Cover the *Conclusion* section on the opposite page.
1 What should the report writer say in the *Conclusion*? Make some notes.
2 Read the *Conclusion* again and compare.

Findings

A _____ majority of Group A respondents (70%) (*indicate*) that Descontbank already (*spend*) €50–100 million per annum on CSR, while _____ (20%) (*think*) that the figure was in excess of €100 million. However, only _____ (10%) thought that Descontbank spent less than €50 million. Among the Group B respondents, only _____ (20%) (*consider*) that Descontbank should not have a CSR programme at all. Moreover, Group B's estimation of Descontbank's potential CSR commitment (*be*) similar to Group A respondents', with _____ (75%) suggesting that an expenditure of €50–100 million per annum would be appropriate.

Report A: Introduction

Many private sector companies have developed extensive corporate social responsibility (CSR) programmes over the past decade. Such commitments are valuable in terms of improved public image and raised international profile, as well as enhanced employee loyalty. A number of studies (Amiss, 2006; Bryant, 2007; Young, 2009) have shown that the perception of these programmes depends on the respondents' overall experience of the company, its image, reputation and integrity. This study will present an investigation, using an online survey, into how people perceive the CSR activities of Descontbank.

First, the financial aspects and specific CSR activities of the bank will be focused on. After that, the results of the online survey will be analyzed, and some recommendations for the development and improvement of the bank's CSR programmes will be proposed.

Report A: Conclusion

Descontbank is clearly not associated with extensive CSR activities. A majority of those surveyed did not attribute CSR programmes to the bank at all. Nobody had the correct picture; on the one hand, many people didn't know there was a programme. However, the ones who did, thought it was bigger and more generously funded than in reality. Descontbank was also linked more to projects in the developing world than is, in fact, the case. It is clear that Descontbank focuses primarily on its domestic markets. However, Descontbank operates mainly in the developing world. It is therefore strongly recommended that the bank should raise its overseas commitments and spend more to alleviate poverty there. It should also rethink the use of so much employee voluntary work at a time when job security is a serious issue. Moreover, it should reconsider if a figure of 0.57% of its total profits in 2010 is really a serious CSR commitment. If Descontbank fails to act decisively soon, it may find that its integrity has declined significantly in the global marketplace and customers and investors will look for an alternative.

Do you think Descontbank has a CSR programme?

Figure 1: *Perception of existence of CSR programme at Descontbank (all 300 respondents)*

Why does Descontbank not have a CSR programme?

Figure 2: *Perception of why Descontbank does not have a CSR programme (Group B respondents only)*

Focus (location) for Descontbank CSR programme (2010)	€ million
Helping disadvantaged young people (domestic)	11.5
Energy saving and waste reduction (domestic and overseas)	7.2
Employee volunteer programmes (domestic and overseas)	3.8
Cultural/musical event sponsorship (domestic)	4.6
Special education projects (overseas)	3.6
Others	0.6
Total	31.3

Figure 3: *CSR commitment by Descontbank (€ million), 2010*

98   99

12.4 Extending skills

Lesson aims

- write part of a research report: *Findings* and *Discussion*
- analyze and use research data and information

Further practice in:

- talking about numbers and quantities

Introduction

Reproduce the table below on the board. Give some example phrases and ask students to say approximately what percentage they represent, e.g., a large majority = 80% approximately?

A/An	overwhelming large substantial significant small	majority	
		minority	
		number	(of + noun)
Over Around		half a quarter a third	
(Slightly)	More Less	than	x%

Note that *of* is needed if the category for the numbers is given: *A small minority of respondents said that …* but *A small minority said that …*

Ask students: *What is the difference between many and most?*

Exercise A

Set students to work in pairs to talk about the key elements of the numbers shown in the charts. If you wish, ask students to write some sentences. Feed back with the whole class, writing some example sentences on the board. Ask the class what these results show about the perceptions of Descontbank.

Answers

Possible answers:

Figure 1

A significant minority (40%) said that Descontbank had a CSR programme. These were termed Group A respondents.

A substantial majority (60%) of respondents (Group B) said that Descontbank had no CSR programme.

The total number of respondents was 300, all of whom knew about Descontbank.

Figure 2

The total number of Group B respondents was 180.

Three main reasons were given by Group B respondents as to why they thought Descontbank had no CSR programme. A quarter of Group B respondents specified financial challenges facing the bank. More than a third (35%) stated that the bank had other priorities. A significant minority (40%) gave the bank's need to improve its domestic image as the reason why it had no CSR programme.

Exercise B

1 Set for individual work and pairwork checking. Tell students that each space may be for more than one word. They will also need to practise the expressions they used for quantity in Exercise A.

   Feed back with the whole class, pointing out the use of past tenses when reporting findings.

2 Set for individual work. Remind students to use linking words and to begin with a topic sentence. This paragraph continues the *Findings* section of the report.

Answers

Possible answers:

1 Findings

   A <u>significant majority</u> of Group A respondents (70%) (*indicate*) <u>indicated</u> that Descontbank already (*spend*) <u>spent</u> €50–100 million per annum on CSR, while <u>a small minority</u> (20%) (*think*) <u>thought</u> that the figure was in excess of €100 million. However, only <u>a small proportion</u> (10%) thought that Descontbank spent less than €50 million. Among the Group B respondents, only <u>a small minority</u> (20%) (*consider*) <u>considered</u> that Descontbank should not have a CSR programme at all. Moreover, Group B's estimation of Descontbank's potential CSR commitment (*be*) <u>was</u> similar to Group A respondents', with <u>an overwhelming majority</u> (75%) suggesting that an expenditure of €50–100 million per annum would be appropriate.

2 The survey revealed some interesting results. Firstly, a substantial majority of the respondents (60%) thought that Descontbank had a CSR programme, but, on the other hand, a significant minority (40%) said that Descontbank had no CSR programme. Secondly, three main reasons were given by Group B respondents as to why they thought Descontbank had no CSR programme. A quarter of Group B respondents specified financial challenges facing the bank, whereas more than a third (35%) stated that the bank had other priorities. A significant minority (40%) gave the bank's need to improve its domestic image as the reason why it had no CSR programme.

Exercise C

Tell students to look at Figure 3 on page 99 of the Course Book. Ask checking questions about the information there, e.g.:

What were Descontbank's main spending commitments in its CSR programmes?

How much was spent in the developing world?

What is the proportion of its domestic focus compared with its overseas commitments?

How do these figures relate to people's perceptions of how much Descontbank spends (Group A) or ought to spend (Group B)? (Refer to that part of the Findings section you have completed in Exercise A.)

Tell students that the *Discussion* section of a report is where they interpret findings and therefore can give their opinions on the findings. They should write a paragraph using the ideas in Figure 3. Set for individual work.

Answers

Possible answers:

Discussion

It is clear from the results of the analysis of CSR expenditure for 2010 that Descontbank spends more than half of its CSR programme on domestic projects. It only spends a small proportion of its CSR commitments exclusively for the developing world, namely for special education projects. Expenditure for domestic cultural projects amounts to over 14% of its total spending, compared with around 11% for its overseas school projects. Moreover, the environmental programmes are in the bank's interest as part of cost reductions, so its expenditure of €7.2 million (or 23% of the total) is only a small commitment to improving the environment in the developing world. When the actual spending (€31.3 million) in 2010 is compared with the responses in the survey, it is clear that respondents from Group A ('Yes, Descontbank has a programme') and Group B ('No, Descontbank does not have a programme, but should have one') believe spending is (or should be) much greater than the real commitment. Clearly, the perception among many participants in the survey is that Descontbank has or should have a strong commitment to CSR. Though it may be argued that 'something is better than nothing', it would be beneficial to Descontbank's image if it launched a better funded programme with revised targets.

Exercise D

1 Get students to cover the *Conclusion*. They may well remember what it said, but, even if they don't, they can work out what it *should* say based on the *Findings* and the *Discussion* and, of course, on the *Introduction*. Set for individual work and pairwork checking. Do not confirm or correct.

2 Refer students to the *Conclusion* to check their ideas.

Closure

1 Ask students to work out the original questions used in the Descontbank online survey on CSR.

First, suggest some question types for questionnaires. Elicit the following:

- yes/no
- multiple choice
- open-ended

Tell students to concentrate on the *yes/no* or *multiple choice* types (open-ended questions will elicit qualitative information which is often hard to analyze) and to look at the data in Figures 1 and 2 and the sample *Findings* paragraph. They should try to formulate the actual questions given in the customer survey questionnaire.

Set for pairwork. Feed back with the whole class, writing examples of good questions up on the board. Refer to the model questionnaire in the additional resources section (Resource 12E).

2 Set a research report based on a questionnaire survey for homework. Students can use the ideas they have already discussed in this unit. They should write questionnaires, carry out the research among a suitable group of participants (20–40 respondents would be fine) and then write up the report. Some possible topics have been mentioned in Closure for Lesson 3. Alternatively, students might like to design a questionnaire survey (in pairs or in small groups) to investigate the opinions of their fellow students and others about future economic policies and changes. There are some ideas in Resource 12F. If you ask students to design such a questionnaire, they need to think particularly of:

- how to formulate the questions
- the scale they might use to investigate level of agreement (refer students to the 'Likert scale' for more information if desired)
- what time period(s) they might choose
- how many questions/respondents they will choose
- how they will analyze their data
- how an analysis package such as SPSS might be used (if applicable)
- how they will write the report, especially findings and conclusion
- how they will record the data in their report (graphs, tables, charts, etc.)

3 If you wish, students could follow up some real CSR programmes inside companies to see what information they can find about the scope of their programmes. They could look at the following websites (URLs correct at time of writing) to research the companies registered:

www.csreurope.org/news.php?type=csr_europe

www.csreurope.org/members.php

On the environmental issues, www.greenbiz.com/home/ is a good starting point.

www.ftse.com/Indices/FTSE4Good_Environmental _Leaders_Europe_40_Index/index.jsp might be helpful for how CSR may be measured.

An interesting approach is offered by the Swiss textile company, Switcher, at www.switcher.ch/english/about-switcher/ or that of one of the largest MNCs in the world, RTZ, the mining company, at www.riotinto.com/index_ourapproach.asp and www.riotinto.com/annualreport2009/pdf/resources/ sustain_develop_review.pdf

The Dow Jones Sustainability Index should also give students the chance to investigate various programmes. See www.sustainability-index.com.ø

Extra activities

1 Work through the *Vocabulary bank* and *Skills bank* if you have not already done so, or as revision of previous study.

2 Use the *Activity bank* (Teacher's Book additional resources section, Resource 12A).

A Set the wordsearch for individual work (including homework) or pairwork.

Answers

B Set for individual work and pairwork checking.

Answers

95%	the great majority
70%	a significant majority
53%	just over half
50%	half
48%	slightly less than half
10%	a small proportion
2%	a tiny minority

3 Set Resource 12G for individual work and pairwork checking.

The table shows the simple replacement of the linking device from the original in the reading text. Ask students to try a full paraphrase of the sentences.

Possible answers: See table on next page.

Original	**Moreover,** it represented security, reliability and trust in banking.
Replacement	*Furthermore,* it represented security, reliability and trust in banking.
Paraphrase	*More specifically,/More importantly,/More than that,/In addition,* the bank was viewed as an example of trustworthy and reliable banking.
Original	**In addition,** they trusted the bank to make profitable investments without taking unnecessary risks.
Replacement	*Moreover,* they trusted the bank to make profitable investments without taking unnecessary risks.
Paraphrase	*Moreover,/What's more,/Additionally,* customers knew that the bank was conservative in its investment and risk acceptance policy.
Original	**So,** it was an appropriate step for Descontbank to start its own corporate social responsibility (CSR) programme in 2005.
Replacement	*Therefore* it was an appropriate step for Descontbank to start its own corporate social responsibility (CSR) programme in 2005.
Paraphrase	*Therefore,/Consequently,/As a result,* Descontbank considered that it was a suitable time to launch a CSR programme of its own.
Original	**Consequently,** in surveys of popularity and trust, Descontbank was considered more trustworthy than the state railway company, the national airline or any other major bank.
Replacement	*As a result,* in surveys of popularity and trust, Descontbank was considered more trustworthy than the state railway company, the national airline or any other major bank.
Paraphrase	*As a result,/So,/Therefore,* regarding popularity and integrity, Descontbank came out ahead of all its banking competitors and of the major national transport companies.
Original	Descontbank was seen as a conservative financial institution **but** that is why customers were loyal to a bank that had more long-term customers than any comparable institution.
Replacement	Descontbank was seen as a conservative financial institution. *Nevertheless,* that is why customers were loyal to a bank that had more long-term customers than any comparable institution.
Paraphrase	Descontbank had a reputation for conservative transactions. *Nevertheless,/Despite this fact,* customers showed much more loyalty to Descontbank (than to its banking competitors).
Original	Customers still considered the main priority for Descontbank was money management **although** the CSR commitment was welcomed.
Replacement	Customers still considered the main priority for Descontbank was money management *despite the fact that* the CSR commitment was welcomed.
Paraphrase	*In spite of the fact that* Descontbank's CSR programme was well received, customers saw financial activities as the bank's main priority.
Original	**However,** there were already concerns among shareholders about Descontbank's financial activities.
Replacement	*At the same time,* there were already concerns among shareholders about Descontbank's financial activities.
Paraphrase	*On the other hand,* shareholders were worried about some of Descontbank's dealings.

Activity bank

A Solve the crossword.

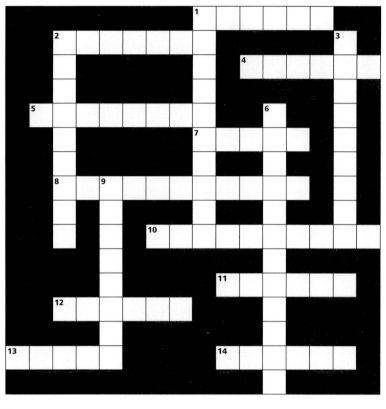

Down

1 … are long-term government bonds which are traded.
2 When we talk about capital, we mean financial and human … .
3 A … is an economic decline where production and demand decrease.
6 When banking and finance are supervised less by the government or authorities.
9 A … is a special form of loan or credit to buy a house or other property.

Across

1 … and demand are two basic principles in economics.
2 The money which a government collects in taxes and other payments is known as … .
4 Taxes paid to the government for certain goods are known as … .
5 A … is a person who buys goods or services.
7 A list showing share, commodity or currency prices.
8 The name given to metals, oil or agricultural products which are traded.

10 A financial … is a type of investment in a financial product.
11 A company may issue … to raise capital.
12 *The … of Nations* is Adam Smith's most famous work on economics.
13 A … is a mathematical figure or line showing economic trends and developments.
14 The GDP of a country is a measurement of … .

B Play noughts and crosses. Use the words in context or explain what they mean.

supervision	influential	misjudge	interest	econometrics	capital
repetition	quantitative	elasticity	trading	prediction	expenditure
employment	sub-prime	interdependent	currency	sector	investment

Activity bank

A Find 20 words from this unit in the wordsearch.

- Copy the words into your notebook.
- Check the definition of any words you can't remember.

V	Y	C	O	M	P	E	T	I	T	O	R	X	U	A	G	I	M
V	T	T	G	U	M	S	C	I	E	N	T	I	F	I	C	V	X
T	Z	S	H	B	I	K	E	M	P	I	R	I	C	A	L	L	Y
U	R	E	C	E	J	S	O	P	E	L	G	H	D	L	K	Y	S
M	F	C	A	S	O	F	P	X	R	T	I	Z	C	Y	P	C	A
N	I	U	P	U	X	R	X	E	O	E	R	D	T	N	I	I	Z
L	N	R	I	B	F	E	E	C	F	S	D	I	F	M	M	R	M
I	S	I	T	S	R	O	A	T	E	V	N	I	O	E	E	T	B
Q	U	T	A	I	C	W	F	K	I	U	L	N	C	D	N	J	Y
U	R	Y	L	D	X	O	U	R	T	C	O	N	L	T	T	Q	E
I	A	B	M	I	B	Y	M	R	C	C	A	O	S	P	Y	G	S
D	N	B	Q	E	L	E	O	M	E	P	H	L	L	V	A	Y	E
I	C	W	B	S	J	P	N	G	O	E	E	V	Q	R	O	L	R
T	E	F	A	P	P	C	U	E	K	D	Q	P	E	N	E	E	V
Y	U	Z	R	O	M	U	X	A	F	Z	I	V	Z	A	R	N	I
H	U	G	A	S	S	E	T	S	U	I	E	T	R	K	T	D	C
C	S	M	K	G	M	S	P	B	G	L	T	A	Y	B	G	W	E
C	H	R	L	I	A	B	I	L	I	T	Y	I	K	Z	P	W	S

B Do the quiz.

1 The person who works in a branch of economics is an … .
2 A branch of economics which looks at the more practical aspects.
3 Capital which a company needs to allow it to take over or buy another company.
4 Government payments to farmers or industries.
5 Oil is a very important … .
6 Capital and other property that a company has which it can use to obtain credit.
7 What does the abbreviation IMF stand for?
8 Which economic system is now the most important globally?
9 What date (year) is usually given for the end of communism?
10 OPEC is responsible for which world commodity?
11 What should governments not do in a free market economy?
12 What name is given to those businessmen who own companies or enterprises?

Economics is considered by many people to be organized in a scientific way.	There are several reasons for this idea. Firstly, people point out that economists use a lot of economic theories. These are based on observation of the ways money, goods, services and people interact. Secondly, there are economic models or equations to explain or predict economic behaviour. For example, it is important to analyze how consumers think and behave. It is also essential to understand the financial markets. In addition, statistics and data are very important for economists. They have developed the special area of econometrics to focus on analysis of economic patterns or developments.
However, opponents say these reasons are not enough to demonstrate the scientific status of economics.	In chemistry, physics or biology, it is possible to prove results and outcomes empirically, using experiments. In economics, it is much more difficult. Economics refers to human needs. This is an important idea in economics and relates to a person being satisfied! It is called utility. Human needs can be for goods, such as a new computer game or a new bicycle. They could also be for services – a visit to the sports centre or a meal in a restaurant. A successful economy organizes a system to benefit the majority of the citizens. This is known as economic welfare.
Different economic systems have developed over time.	A centralized system, such as communism, decides which goods and services the citizens need. There is little choice and no competitors for the government's goods and services. This system has declined in importance since 1989. Capitalism is the most important world economic system nowadays. A central idea in capitalism is liquidity. This means capitalism uses liquid assets, including money, but also investment and labour, to make profits. However capitalism must consider human needs and behaviour. Economics cannot always predict the way people will think or act. This makes economics less scientific.
Economics has an accepted structure with a number of branches or divisions.	In fact, economists generally agree that there is a division into 'macro' economics and 'micro' economics. Macroeconomics considers the bigger aspects of growth. It examines government or international policies on trade or employment, inflation and the money markets. Microeconomics looks at the decisions that individuals or families make about consumption or saving. It also examines how companies establish prices for their products or how a special area of the labour market works in practice.
However, both macroeconomics and microeconomics can examine the same problem or issue at a different level.	For example, the government might have a health policy based on insurance – a macroeconomic policy – but want to increase workers' insurance payments – a microeconomic application. This will have an effect on individuals and on companies.
A further division seems to be between theory and practice.	Economists talk about theoretical and applied economics but again, the division is not simple. For example, a government announces a change in taxation policy for macroeconomic reasons. However, the collection of the tax from the people is an application of the theory at the microeconomic level.
Finally, the division between national and global economics seems to be important.	However, there are connections here, too. For example, a country might pay subsidies to farmers to produce certain crops and support national agriculture. But this will have an effect on the world market price, perhaps with serious consequences for the developing world.
In conclusion, it is sometimes difficult to draw dividing lines in economics.	Economists do not always agree about the structure. However, global relationships mean that countries are no longer economically isolated. This is the new economic reality.

Economics is considered by many people to be organized in a scientific way.

However, opponents say these reasons are not enough to support the scientific status of economics.

Different economic systems have developed over time.

Economics has an accepted structure with a number of branches or divisions.

However, both macroeconomics and microeconomics can examine the same problem or issue at a different level.

A further division seems to be between theory and practice.

Finally, the division between national and global economics seems to be important.

In conclusion, it is sometimes difficult to draw dividing lines in economics.

Economics is considered by many people to be organized in a scientific way.

However, opponents say these reasons are not enough to support the scientific status of economics.

Different economic systems have developed over time.

Economics has an accepted structure with a number of branches or divisions.

However, both macroeconomics and microeconomics can examine the same problem or issue at a different level.

A further division seems to be between theory and practice.

Finally, the division between national and global economics seems to be important.

In conclusion, it is sometimes difficult to draw dividing lines in economics.

For an economist, it is essential to understand who the stakeholders are in any economy.	Stakeholders are those people (or institutions) who have power or influence in the economic structure. The most important groups are described here.
In advanced economies, consumers are powerful stakeholders who have the ability to choose goods and services.	However, they are not really organized and patterns of consumption are difficult to predict. In capitalism, economists emphasize that resources are limited for a number of reasons. Economists also see consumers as people who make rational decisions. In other words, they make the correct choices for the resources available. In reality, consumer choices are not based on rationality.
As most people have limited money to spend, they must set priorities.	For example, a family decides to save for a holiday. As a result, they do not spend money on visits to the cinema or a theme park. This is called an 'opportunity cost'. It means that a good or service is **not** chosen because something else is chosen. Economists must calculate or predict such opportunity cost factors.
Another way to make economic decisions is as members of a group.	The family is an informal group. Workers in a particular company or union have a more formal structure. They often want the same results. Usually workers want higher wages but sometimes better working conditions or more job security are important, too. In most industrialized countries, unions represent the interests of workers. They act for employees to improve the workers' economic welfare.
The owners and managers of companies are crucial stakeholders in any economy.	These people are entrepreneurs who link up all the economic factors – capital, labour and other resources – to produce goods or services. These are called the 'factors of production'. When economists examine the actions of entrepreneurs or their enterprises, they look at risk. Enterprises want to make profits so calculating risk is very important. In capitalist countries, individuals, shareholders in a company or other investors carry the risk. The government does not usually intervene in a 'free market economy'.
However, governments themselves are very important economic stakeholders.	One example is the decision to intervene. In an economic crisis, the government might act to support banks or companies. Many governments intervened as a reaction to the global crisis beginning in 2008. But this intervention does not show a complete change in their macroeconomic principles.
When governments make decisions, they are acting as stakeholders.	Most governments want a healthy economy to meet the needs of their citizens. But their decisions are often 'opportunity cost' calculations. Governments must try to balance advantages and disadvantages. For example, building a new motorway will bring transportation benefits but it changes the landscape, creates noise and pollution and affects the lives of local residents. A good government should be accountable for its decisions, economically and politically.
Financial institutions such as banks are similar to companies but rather more complicated.	However, they are very important stakeholders. They want to make profits, usually for shareholders. They also take risks, especially as financial markets can fluctuate a lot. However, in an economic crisis, people ask difficult questions about the power of banks. They say the banks are too powerful and they take too many risks. The banks sometimes make decisions on lending or investing money which are too risky. For these reasons, banks will probably have to accept more regulations to limit their activities in the future.
A final example of economic stakeholders is the group of international or regional institutions or agencies.	These bodies have enormous economic power. They can influence policies on, for example, world trade, the global supply of money, lending to developing countries or economic cooperation. Nowadays, it is hard to imagine how the world economy would function without the World Bank (WB), the International Monetary Fund (IMF), the World Trade Organization (WTO), the Bank of International Settlements (BIS) or the regional development banks. Think of the importance of a special interest group such as the Oil Producing and Exporting Countries (OPEC) which is a powerful economic stakeholder.
In conclusion, the position of all the main economic stakeholders has an influence on the wider political economy.	Economists will continue to examine their status carefully.

Activity bank

A Solve the crossword.

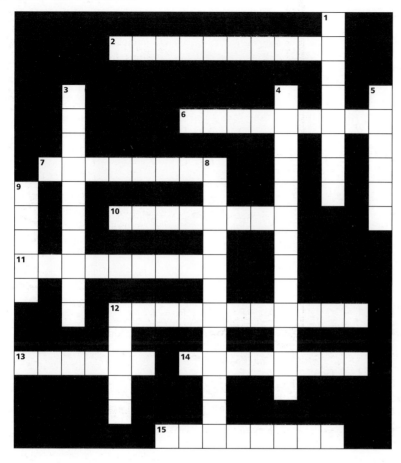

Down

1 When consumers actually buy goods, we talk of ... demand.
3 Consumers often buy ... goods if they are similar and cheaper.
4 Goods which are different but closely related are known as ... goods.
5 Supply and ... represent key principles in economics.
8 An ... is someone who uses capital to expand his/her business.
9 A demand ... occurs when a complete demand curve moves.
12 Economists use a ... as a diagram to show changes.

Across

2 The money a consumer has to spend is usually called his/her ... income.
6 When a good has more than one use, we talk of ... demand.
7 A producer cannot always calculate demand exactly. Sometimes he has to ... .
10 If there is a ... of some essential food product, some people buy more than they really need out of 'panic'.

11 Oil prices ... on a regular basis for political as well as economic reasons.
12 A ... occurs when demand declines.
13 When prices decrease, there is an ... movement in demand.
14 Banks will pay ... to customers who have savings in their banks at different rates.
15 A ... is a form of credit or loan which is provided for a person over a 20- or 25-year period to buy a property.

B Play bingo.

- Think of words for each of the categories and write them on card 1. Think of a word from another category for the last square ('another word').

- Each student says one of their words. Cross the squares on card 2 when you hear a word from that category.

1

a type of demand	an effect of recession	a market factor
_____	_____	_____
a reason for demand shift	a verb of market movement	another word
_____	_____	_____

2

a type of demand	an effect of recession	a market factor
a reason for demand shift	a verb of market movement	another word

---

Activity bank

A Find 20 verbs from the first four units in the wordsearch.
- Copy the words into your notebook.
- Write the noun for each verb.

C	V	O	G	J	R	R	E	D	U	C	E	Q	E	L	E
Q	O	A	D	J	U	S	T	E	A	N	R	T	P	V	M
X	I	O	N	O	J	D	D	V	E	M	A	Q	O	D	C
K	N	T	R	O	C	I	M	V	W	V	Z	M	T	Q	V
I	T	D	R	D	V	O	R	K	I	O	R	N	F	N	M
U	E	P	G	I	I	E	N	T	D	E	V	E	L	O	P
E	R	R	D	W	T	N	O	S	E	R	L	G	U	E	U
X	A	N	M	N	W	M	A	U	U	R	Y	P	C	M	L
P	C	L	I	I	G	C	M	T	C	M	A	P	T	P	I
A	T	I	S	T	S	W	X	J	E	X	E	H	U	L	N
N	J	M	T	S	U	B	S	I	D	I	Z	E	A	O	V
D	R	V	E	I	N	P	L	W	W	B	A	C	T	Y	E
B	V	S	R	S	A	L	L	O	C	A	T	E	E	T	S
D	S	V	H	E	X	W	X	P	R	O	M	O	T	E	T
A	X	L	P	W	J	T	E	Z	E	X	T	E	N	D	H
L	V	I	D	E	N	T	I	F	Y	O	G	O	B	K	B

B Play noughts and crosses. You must say the abbreviation or acronym and give the original words to place your symbol in a square.

DVD	JPEG	HTTP
PPT	RAM	CAL
ROM	PC	HTML

PIN	USB	URL
WWW	LCD	ISP
CPU	RTF	PDF

Most human activities have undergone an enormous technological change over the past 40 to 50 years, and economics is no exception.

It may be hard for students of economics nowadays to imagine how finance, business and economic research could manage without technology, but things were very different 40 years ago.

There are many additional examples of how technology has revolutionized the world of economics at every level and, generally speaking, the advances have been positive.

Nowadays, statistical data are so much easier to compile and analyze as the technology is widely available all over the world.

In banking and investment, time is money, so institutions must have access to financial data immediately.

When we consider technology at the microeconomic level, businesses, too, can plan better.

However, technological progress has some drawbacks and, unfortunately, these can have serious economic consequences.

Most human activities have undergone an enormous technological change over the past 40 to 50 years, and economics is no exception.

It may be hard for students of economics nowadays to imagine how finance, business and economic research could manage without technology, but things were very different 40 years ago.

There are many additional examples of how technology has revolutionized the world of economics at every level and, generally speaking, the advances have been positive.

Nowadays, statistical data are so much easier to compile and analyze as the technology is widely available all over the world.

In banking and investment, time is money, so institutions must have access to financial data immediately.

When we consider technology at the microeconomic level, businesses, too, can plan better.

However, technological progress has some drawbacks and, unfortunately, these can have serious economic consequences.

CAL	DVD
JPEG	HTML
HTTP	ISP
LCD	PIN
RAM	ROM
URL	USB
WAN	WWW

Card 1

Abbreviation	Currency	Correct?
GBP	Great Britain Pound	
AUD	Australian Dollar	
DKK	Danish Kroner	
HKD	Hong Kong Dollar	
JPY	Japanese Yen	
SGD	Singapore Dollar	

Card 2

Abbreviation	Currency	Correct?
USD	American Dollar	
NZD	New Zealand Dollar	
SEK	Swedish Kroner	
ZAR	South African Rand	
CHF	Swiss Franc	
EUR	Euro	

Activity bank

A Solve the synonyms crossword. Find words with the same meaning as the clues.

Down

2 replace
3 wealth
4 reduce
5 naturally (2 words)
6 aid
8 barrier
12 mining
15 decline
17 increase
18 influence

Across

1 goods
7 talk about
9 shift
10 small-scale
11 location
13 advantage
14 diversify
16 stimulate
19 fall sharply
20 migration

B Play opposites bingo.

• Choose six words from the box and write one word in each square of your bingo card.

• Your teacher will call out some words. If you have the **opposite** word on your card, cross it out.

• The first person to cross out all the words on their card is the winner.

access   affluence   assets   consumer
dangerous   degradation   dependent
destroy   drawback   efficient   exactly
expenditure   globalization   growth
job security   multinational   profit
rural   shortage   slow down

Verbs	Nouns	Adverbs	Adjectives
rise		gradually	
increase		sharply	
grow		slightly	
improve		markedly	
fall		significantly	
decrease		rapidly	
drop		steeply	
decline		steadily	

Poor contributions	Student A	Student B	Student C
disagrees rudely			
doesn't explain how the point is relevant			
doesn't understand an idiom			
dominates the discussion			
gets angry when someone disagrees with them			
interrupts			
is negative			
mumbles or whispers			
says something irrelevant			
shouts			
sits quietly and says nothing			
starts a side conversation			
other:			

Good contributions	Student A	Student B	Student C
allows others to speak			
asks for clarification			
asks politely for information			
brings in another speaker			
builds on points made by other speakers			
contributes to the discussion			
explains the point clearly			
gives specific examples to help explain a point			
is constructive			
links correctly with previous speakers			
listens carefully to what others say			
makes clear how the point is relevant			
paraphrases to check understanding			
says when they agree with someone			
speaks clearly			
tries to use correct language			
other:			

5.4 Student A

Economic and environmental background: [Brazil]

Give some background about the economy, including GDP/per capita, labour force, unemployment, poverty, exports and import commodities and partners.

Outline the main environmental issues for this country.

Use https://www.cia.gov/library/publications/the-world-factbook/index.html to find out about FDI and Brazil.

5.4 Student B

Economic and environmental background: [Ghana]

Give some background about the economy, including GDP/per capita, labour force, unemployment, poverty, exports and import commodities and partners.

Outline the main environmental issues for this country.

Use https://www.cia.gov/library/publications/the-world-factbook/index.html

Try to find more about FDI and Ghana from:
www.unctad.org/sections/dite_dir/docs/wir10_fs_gh_en.pdf

5.4 Student C

Economic and environmental background: [Indonesia]

Give some background about the economy, including GDP/per capita, labour force, unemployment, poverty, exports and import commodities and partners.

Outline the main environmental issues for this country.

Use https://www.cia.gov/library/publications/the-world-factbook/index.html to find out about FDI and Indonesia.

5.4 Student D

Economic and environmental background: [Rwanda]

Give some background about the economy, including GDP/per capita, labour force, unemployment, poverty, exports and import commodities and partners.

Outline the main environmental issues for this country.

Use https://www.cia.gov/library/publications/the-world-factbook/index.html

Try to find out more about FDI and Rwanda from:
www.unctad.org/sections/dite_dir/docs/wir10_fs_rw_en.pdf

Activity bank

A Find 20 verbs from this unit in the wordsearch.
- Copy the words into your notebook.
- Write the noun for each verb.

S	O	M	V	T	Q	C	O	M	M	I	T	K	B	M	D	E	E
J	Z	U	B	A	S	V	S	O	S	G	I	J	S	G	H	T	O
Q	S	D	A	S	U	C	C	E	E	D	J	Z	P	U	A	F	N
V	A	G	V	E	S	A	T	U	R	A	T	E	Z	U	S	Q	G
I	T	A	P	Q	R	P	C	Q	M	W	Y	C	L	C	B	R	A
V	E	M	P	X	O	F	B	B	X	R	B	A	F	M	P	F	V
A	N	F	R	P	O	P	D	R	J	W	V	X	M	U	Y	G	I
A	F	D	U	Q	R	Q	R	N	O	E	Q	W	N	R	D	R	N
H	B	W	Y	N	H	O	N	E	U	A	W	N	B	C	T	O	Q
C	O	Y	C	M	D	I	V	T	D	C	D	S	R	U	Z	W	V
N	R	E	S	C	A	P	E	E	M	I	Z	C	K	U	U	E	V
E	R	S	T	T	K	L	A	I	A	X	C	Y	A	T	F	I	T
O	O	R	N	N	P	R	O	V	I	D	E	T	M	S	V	M	C
V	W	I	G	T	F	A	C	O	N	T	R	A	C	T	T	P	Z
T	A	A	S	S	E	S	S	A	P	P	R	O	A	C	H	L	J
M	S	O	G	C	A	W	B	S	V	P	Q	M	Q	Y	J	Y	N
L	E	Y	I	R	R	E	F	U	S	E	B	B	O	R	I	W	V
M	V	Q	R	E	J	E	C	T	N	P	R	E	S	E	R	V	E

B Think of a word or words that can go in front of or after each of the words below to make a phrase from economics. Explain the meaning.

Examples: commitment: *social commitment, long-term commitment, commitment to buy*

approval	expenditure	range
available	fair	rate
benefits	growth	research
commitment	guarantee(d)	small-scale
community	market	term
craft	message	underserved
cycle	phase	valuable
ethical	policies	
entrepreneurial	poverty	

1 The economy _____ every year between 2007 and 2010 except in 2008 when _____ .

2 Actual GDP growth in _____ was _____ than expected except in 2007.

3 The economy _____ in the years 2009 and 2010.

4 The GDP trend figures suggest _____ in the whole economy over the period.

5 Government spending over the period was _____ than actual GDP growth.

6 The government increased spending _____ .

1 The economy grew every year between 2007 and 2010 except in 2008 when it contracted.

2 Actual GDP growth in all years was worse than expected except in 2007.

3 The economy expanded in the years 2009 and 2010.

4 The GDP trend figures suggest stability in the whole economy over the period.

5 Government spending over the period was lower than actual GDP growth.

6 The government increased spending every year except for 2008.

a In the period shown, actual GDP performance was below predictions with the exception of 2007.

b After the downturn in 2008, the economy recovered and expanded again, although less than predicted.

c GDP trend expectations were for stable and sustained economic growth over the four years.

d The government was unable to proceed with its expenditure plans for 2008 but otherwise these commitments were fulfilled.

e With the exception of 2008, when the economy did not expand, positive actual growth was sustained over the period.

f Government expenditure commitments always remained below actual growth.

Original sentence	Student A	Student B
For example, it refuses investment in companies involved in the production or sale of weapons.	One UK microfinance institution, for example, refuses investment in companies linked to weapons production.	For instance, investments in armaments manufacture or trade are rejected by one specialist British microfinance bank.
	not satisfactory: not enough changes: this is patch-writing	*acceptable paraphrase:* ● *use of the passive (it refuses investment → investments are rejected)* ● *lexical changes 'weapons' → 'armaments'; 'production' → 'manufacture'*
It will also not invest in the tobacco industry or tobacco products.	It also rejects investment in the tobacco industry or tobacco products.	Moreover, it has refused participation in any financial involvement in tobacco production or marketing.
	completely unacceptable: only some words have been changed	*acceptable paraphrase:* ● *note that although there is a tense change here, ultimately this makes no difference to the meaning in the context* ● *lexical changes are minor but acceptable; 'investment' → 'financial involvement'; 'refuse to participate' to replace 'not invest'* ● *use of 'Moreover' as a reinforcing adjunct to replace 'also'*
In addition, it rejects investment in companies which do not uphold basic human rights in countries where those enterprises have business activities.	This microfinance institution also rejects any investment in companies which do not support human rights in the countries where they have commercial activities.	Investment is not approved in multinationals with poor human rights records in their overseas operations.
	not satisfactory: not enough changes: this is patch-writing	*acceptable paraphrase:* ● *use of the passive, e.g., 'investment is not approved'* ● *prepositional phrase (with poor human rights records) in place of simple noun phrase* ● *changes in lexical selection, e.g., 'overseas operations' to replace 'countries where those enterprises have business activities'*

Original sentence	Student A	Student B
It also does not invest in companies which have caused serious environmental pollution.	There is also no investment in companies which have polluted the environment seriously.	If the activities of the enterprise result in any severe pollution, this leads to a refusal of financial commitment by the bank
	not satisfactory: not enough changes: this is patch-writing	*acceptable paraphrase:* ● *information order has been changed* ● *verb 'refuse' becomes noun 'refusal'* ● *lexical changes – 'serious' becomes 'severe'* ● *paraphrase of idea of 'invest'* → *financial commitment*
So, microfinance institutions have developed a real sense of social responsibility, which normal banks are starting to admire.	These microfinance institutions have a real social responsibility which other banks admire.	It is their strong commitment to society, which is now more appreciated by their financial rivals, that is frequently emphasized by the microbanks.
	not satisfactory: not enough changes: this is patch-writing	*acceptable paraphrase:* ● *empty 'it': so (they) have developed ... e.g., it is their ...* ● *lexical changes: strong commitment (to replace 'responsibility'); appreciated (to replace 'admire')* ● *word form change: ... to society (to replace 'social')* ● *use of the passive (which [they] admire becomes 'is now more appreciated')* ● *use of the passive + time adverbial (is frequently emphasized)*

Microfinance is different from normal banking because microfinance banks understand the special needs of their poorer customers.

Microfinance has expanded considerably from the original idea of Muhammad Yunus, the founder of the Grameen Bank, Bangladesh, who was the pioneer of microcredit from the 1970s.

A useful definition of microfinance is a partnership for sustainable development between banks and unserved individuals or communities, that is, for those people who have never had access to financial services.

Moreover, it is the high ethical standards of microfinance banks, such as those in the Global Alliance for Banking on Values (www.gabv.org) which makes them really special.

However, microfinance is not the *only* way for people to escape poverty.

In recent developments, however, university research focusing on sustainable development has made some controversial suggestions.

In conclusion, microfinance has become an economic reality.

Microfinance is different from normal banking because microfinance banks understand the special needs of their poorer customers.

Microfinance has expanded considerably from the original idea of Muhammad Yunus, the founder of the Grameen Bank, Bangladesh, who was the pioneer of microcredit from the 1970s.

A useful definition of microfinance is a partnership for sustainable development between banks and unserved individuals or communities, that is, for those people who have never had access to financial services.

Moreover, it is the high ethical standards of microfinance banks, such as those in the Global Alliance for Banking on Values (www.gabv.org) which makes them really special.

However, microfinance is not the *only* way for people to escape poverty.

In recent developments, however, university research focusing on sustainable development has made some controversial suggestions.

In conclusion, microfinance has become an economic reality.

	Main subject	Main verb	Main object/ complement	Other verbs + their subjects + objects/ complements
A	they	support	development projects	which are sustainable and environmentally friendly
B	it	refuses	investment in companies	involved in the production or sale of weapons
C	microfinance institutions	have developed	a real sense of social responsibility	which normal banks are starting to admire
D	a normal bank	gives	1. someone 2. a loan or credit	only when there is security
E	a high rate of interest	is demanded	–	which must be paid by the borrower
F	microfinance	supports	small entrepreneurs	providing possibilities for them to become self-sufficient and escape poverty

A actual	A expenditure	A seasonal
A agricultural	A fair-trade	A social
A craft	A fixed-term	A sustainable
A customer	A human rights	A underserved
A microfinance	A market	A minimum
A economic	A entrepreneurial	A environmentally
A ethical	A predicted	
B growth	B cycle	B plans
B sector	B initiative	B product
B enterprise	B sustainable	B loan
B choice	B standards	B policy
B employment	B commitment	B development
B institution/bank	B price	B growth
B prices	B individuals/groups	

Activity bank

A Solve the crossword.

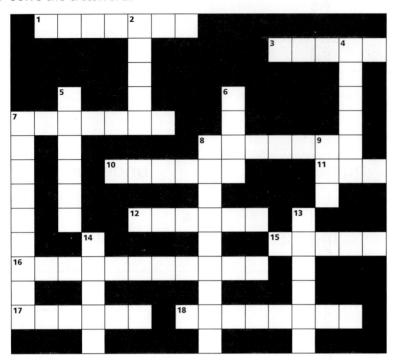

Down

2 The yield is a measure of how much profit an investor … or gains on a financial product.
4 One way for a government to raise money is to … taxes.
5 I'd like to make two … .
6 A 'gilt' is another name for a government … .
7 … demand refers to total demand in the economy.
8 When money such as investment is introduced into the economy, it is known as an … of capital.
9 Maturity of an investment comes at the … of the period or term.
13 Government policy related to taxes and revenue is known as its … policy.
14 Business expectations often depend on the … of interest rates.

Across

1 People in Britain pay a … of taxes.
3 The smallest measurement of growth as shown in a stock market index is a … point.
7 When a government wants to remove import duties permanently, it plans to … such duties.
8 The plural of index is … .
10 Can you … on that, please?
11 The surplus between, e.g., export and import revenue is … income.
12 Investors must … the risks before investing.
15 A cautious investor does not want to take too many … .
16 The relationship between more consumer income and investment is known as the … effect.
17 A balanced budget means government expenditure does not … its revenue.
18 When economists predict growth or expenditure they make a … .

B Think about the topic *'Studying effectively'*. List a few bullet points related to what you have to/must/should do. For example:

- *make good notes*
- *buy a good dictionary*
- *revise carefully*
- *practise listening*

Then in pairs transform the bullet points into sentences beginning with *Wh~*. For example:

Student A: *I have to revise my notes regularly*

Student B: *What you have to do is to revise …*

Student B: *I have to listen more to native speakers*

Student A: *What you have to do is to listen …*

	Fixed phrase	Followed by ...	Actual information (suggested answers)
1	In this way ...	a concluding comment giving a result of something	
2	As you can see, ...	a comment about a diagram, figure or picture	
3	In economic terms, ...	a general idea put into a specific context	
4	An important concept (is) ...	a new idea or topic that the lecturer wants to discuss	
5	Say ...	an imaginary example	
6	Looking at it another way, ...	a different way to think about the topic	
7	What do I mean by ...?	an explanation of a word or phrase	
8	The point is ...	a key statement or idea	

STUDENT A

PS = Public sector (civil servants = workers in public sector)

Give the other members of the group information about your list of proposed savings.

Your group should select a total of six items: ONE transfer item, TWO capital expenditure items, ONE current expenditure item, ONE revenue item and ONE additional NON-REVENUE item.

Transfer payments (A)	freeze PS pay, i.e., no pay increases	2.5 bn
Capital expenditure (A1)	abandon plans to introduce identity cards	500 m (for next five years)
Capital expenditure (A2)	delay construction of two new hospitals	1 bn (for next five years)
Current expenditure (A)	improve efficiencies in PS activities, e.g., police, health service through more careful recruitment, training and employment conditions (incl. reducing absenteeism)	200 m
Revenue (A)	sales of government assets – building, land, etc.	3 bn (for next five years)

STUDENT B

PS = Public sector (civil servants = workers in public sector)

Give the other members of the group information about your list of proposed savings.

Your group should select a total of six items: ONE transfer item, TWO capital expenditure items, ONE current expenditure item, ONE revenue item and ONE additional NON-REVENUE item.

Transfer payments (B)	reduce bonus payments to civil servants	100 m
Capital expenditure (B1)	cancel plans for new IT system in National Health Service	250 m (for next five years)
Capital expenditure (B2)	delay government involvement in new electricity-generating stations	1 bn (for next five years)
Current expenditure (B)	abolish regional industrial business promotion agencies	2 bn
Revenue (B)	increase airport landing charges	1.5 bn (for next five years)

STUDENT C

PS = Public sector (civil servants = workers in public sector)

Give the other members of the group information about your list of proposed savings.

Your group should select a total of six items: ONE transfer item, TWO capital expenditure items, ONE current expenditure item, ONE revenue item and ONE additional NON-REVENUE item.

Transfer payments (C)	reduce salaries by 15% of PS employees already earning over 100,000/year	100 m
Capital expenditure (C1)	reduce waste in defence procurement	200 m (over next five years)
Capital expenditure (C2)	delay construction of two new prisons	2 bn (for next five years)
Current expenditure (C)	reduce activities of regional skills training councils	300 m
Revenue (C)	increase personal income tax	1.2 bn

STUDENT D

PS = Public sector (civil servants = workers in public sector)

Give the other members of the group information about your list of proposed savings.

Your group should select a total of six items: ONE transfer item, TWO capital expenditure items, ONE current expenditure item, ONE revenue item and ONE additional NON-REVENUE item.

Transfer payments (D)	impose higher employee pension contributions AND increase retirement age by two years	1.8 bn
Capital expenditure (D1)	cancel orders for new fighter aeroplanes, military transport planes and nuclear submarines	3 bn (for next 20 years)
Capital expenditure (D2)	delay construction of new bridge	500 m (for next five years)
Current expenditure (D)	decentralize aspects of education planning and administration	600 m
Revenue (D)	increase business taxes	2 bn

Activity bank

A Find 15 words from this unit in the wordsearch. All the words are uncountable nouns in the texts in this unit.

P	C	A	W	Z	Z	T	H	W	F	V	R	B	M	I	T	M	I
Y	R	I	G	D	O	W	A	S	T	A	G	E	R	N	O	Y	T
G	X	O	N	R	R	V	E	X	C	D	C	G	Y	E	E	U	B
R	N	B	D	F	I	G	A	R	H	N	S	D	Y	L	K	B	S
M	C	C	Q	U	R	C	Y	L	A	B	X	H	L	A	J	Z	E
M	O	W	H	P	C	A	U	T	L	T	J	I	L	S	C	M	C
A	N	K	F	E	V	E	S	L	C	E	B	V	F	T	L	H	U
V	S	U	U	R	T	I	M	T	T	V	V	V	T	I	Y	A	R
A	U	S	P	I	S	P	P	S	R	U	Y	I	S	C	Q	Z	I
I	M	T	Z	S	Y	F	O	T	Z	U	R	U	A	I	V	L	T
L	P	A	A	H	X	K	V	O	V	N	C	E	B	T	S	B	Y
A	T	R	O	A	A	E	E	R	E	G	U	T	Z	Y	I	T	W
B	I	V	U	B	N	H	R	A	Z	V	W	F	U	X	A	O	J
I	O	A	I	I	G	O	T	G	W	N	Q	I	Q	R	W	O	N
L	N	T	U	L	Z	U	Y	E	M	F	R	N	W	M	E	Y	O
I	U	I	A	I	P	E	S	F	R	W	P	V	N	F	J	Q	E
T	H	O	K	T	Z	R	Z	V	I	M	P	H	F	O	A	T	S
Y	U	N	Z	Y	F	S	U	B	S	I	S	T	E	N	C	E	K

B Rearrange the letters in the words to form a correctly spelt word from this unit.

Jumbled word	Correct spelling
lfubeoi	
naatssubeli	
elspat	
atrffi	
ybusisd	
chsanmemi	
iiiflcatse	
tyovpre	
ncotissnte	
tskcos	

Activity bank

A Solve the crossword.

Down

1 When a situation is changed by some exceptions, then the picture is … .
2 When we evaluate, judge or measure a situation, we … the circumstances.
3 A patient gets a … from a doctor or hospital for medications and medicines.
5 The payments made for health insurance are called … .
7 When you observe a trend, you might say, ' … we see that …' .
8 Communist countries relied on … economies.
9 Economists talk about … equity to emphasize efficient allocation and appropriate redistribution of resources.
10 When resources are allocated appropriately for the activities of a company or government department, this is known as … efficiency.
12 The concept of … means fairness.

Across

3 Influential Italian economist who proposed an important efficiency theory.
4 The concept of … is one key factor in deciding distribution or redistribution of resources.
6 If resources are unfairly allocated, there must be a … .
11 If a society has many forms of discrimination, then there will be a lot of … .
13 When economists talk of … , they think of consumer well-being or satisfaction, not spiritual happiness!
14 In economics, supply, demand, labour and price are the main factors or … which can change to affect the others.

B Are the nouns countable or uncountable? Use a dictionary to check.

Noun	Countable or uncountable?	Notes
allocation		
competitiveness		
coverage		
disabled		
discrimination		
efficiency		
entitlement		
excess		
illness		
norm		

Review reduce + recite + review	**Notes** record
Here you write only important words and questions; this column is completed *after* the lecture. Later this column becomes your study or revision notes. You can use it by covering the right hand column and using the cue words and questions here to remember the contents on the right.	This column contains your notes. You should underline headings and indent main ideas. After the lecture or reading you need to identify the key points and write them in the review column as questions or cue words.

Summary

reflect + recite + review

After the class you can use this space to summarize the main points of the notes on this page.

Review	Notes
Two principles in w/e are …?	Welfare economics (w/e) = how efficiently an economy works to *allocate* resources.
Why not just supply and demand in health care?	w/e NOT only supply/demand, but *equity* and efficiency Health care (h/c) = high priority for govts. (different problems)
Are care and prevention really different?	Two ways to consider h/c 1) about diseases, illness, medicine, hospitals, 2) but also about *prevention* of disease N.B. h/c = physical AND *mental* health issues
How are norms established?	Establishment of social *norms* (standards & values) → econ. concept of *relative* utility (people's satisfaction/well-being).
Social analysis by whom?	Three aspects of relative utility: 1) economists' explanation (to compare social values/factors) 2) person's/group's utility compared with another's (happiness, satisfaction, priorities) 3) social values and fixing social norms
Can a free market assess the value of a job fairly?	Illustration – how society *values* your job (incl. salary level), e.g., doctor vs. cleaner. Maintain norms – free market society has *mechanisms*, e.g., pay salary/raise tax. H/c reflects priority for govts. How much of *GDP* to be spent on health?
Why is expenditure more sustainable in advanced economies?	In advanced economies, public sector h/c paid for by taxes and national insurance *contributions*. Advisable to use, e.g., from advanced econs. (*sustainable* expenditure).

Summary

Welfare economics relates to *equity* (fairness) and efficiency. Health care is a good example of welfare economics. This branch of economics considers norms, values (including utility) and distribution. Health care reflects government *priorities* in terms of expenditure.

Activity bank

A Find 20 words from this unit in the wordsearch.

- Copy the words into your notebook.
- Check the definition of any words you can't remember.

C	L	O	P	A	P	U	H	B	O	W	B	A	I	L	O	U	T
R	U	J	G	R	C	O	M	P	L	E	M	E	N	T	A	R	Y
S	F	T	B	N	O	Z	L	E	Y	L	T	D	N	K	X	G	H
D	V	V	H	A	I	C	T	E	F	N	E	H	V	J	O	A	S
C	I	Y	E	O	N	B	U	Y	G	V	D	F	M	C	K	D	Y
T	C	N	M	X	C	K	Z	R	I	A	W	J	T	O	Y	M	N
M	R	P	U	Y	T	W	R	R	E	F	C	N	Z	N	P	I	K
B	E	D	L	D	T	E	E	U	K	M	E	Y	V	T	O	N	S
U	D	Q	T	E	O	D	R	Z	P	V	E	U	X	I	M	I	P
D	I	L	I	O	U	V	Q	N	E	T	W	N	U	N	O	S	O
G	T	S	P	Z	R	C	V	A	A	N	C	G	T	G	N	T	N
E	O	T	L	C	N	V	G	N	D	L	B	Y	E	E	O	R	S
T	R	A	I	B	A	E	V	F	L	K	I	D	E	N	P	A	O
A	E	G	E	A	M	Q	G	N	Z	Z	X	T	D	C	O	T	R
R	A	E	R	N	E	K	W	B	Q	Z	J	M	I	Y	L	I	S
Y	M	C	D	I	N	S	O	L	V	E	N	C	Y	E	Y	O	H
U	I	E	D	W	T	W	L	O	T	T	E	R	Y	O	S	N	I
F	N	U	Z	D	V	E	N	U	E	J	N	K	D	P	X	Y	P

B Think of a word or words that can go before or after each of the words or phrases below to make a phrase used in economics. Explain the meaning.

Examples: fixed: *fixed rate, fixed assets, fixed term*

capital

disposal

favourable

fixed

impact

licensing/sponsorship

market

medium-term

private/public

tax

Introduction	Examples of ideas
introduce the topic area give the outline of the essay	

Body	Para 1: situation/problems (general)	
	Para 2: problems (specific examples)	
	Para 3: solutions	
	Para 4: evaluations of solutions	

Conclusion	

T. L. Friedman (1999). The Lexus and the Olive Tree. New York: Farrah, Straus Giroux

Goldblatt, (2010). Footing South Africa's world cup bill. BBC world service 'Focus on Africa' magazine. From: http://news.bbc.co.uk/1/hi/world/africa/8718696.stm

Tabachnik, B. G. and Fidell, L.S. 2007. Using multivariate statistics (5th Edition). Boston, MA: Pearson.

Organisation for Economic Co-operation and Development (2010). Country statistical profiles 2010. OECD: Paris. http://stats.oecd.org/Index.aspx?DataSetCode=CSP2010

Stiglitz J. E. (2002). *Globalization and its discontents.* New York.

J.E. Sachs (2005). *The end of poverty: economic possibilities for our time.* New York, Penguin Books.

S. Bracking. *Money and Power: Great predators in the political economy of development.* London: Pluto Press.

T. L. Friedman (1999). The Lexus and the Olive Tree. New York: Farrah, Straus Giroux

Goldblatt, (2010). Footing South Africa's world cup bill. BBC world service 'Focus on Africa' magazine. From: http://news.bbc.co.uk/1/hi/world/africa/8718696.stm

Tabachnik, B. G. and Fidell, L.S. 2007. Using multivariate statistics (5th Edition). Boston, MA: Pearson.

Organisation for Economic Co-operation and Development (2010). Country statistical profiles 2010. OECD: Paris. http://stats.oecd.org/Index.aspx?DataSetCode=CSP2010

Stiglitz J. E. (2002). *Globalization and its discontents.* New York.

J.E. Sachs (2005). *The end of poverty: economic possibilities for our time.* New York, Penguin Books.

S. Bracking. *Money and Power: Great predators in the political economy of development.* London: Pluto Press.

Activity bank

A Solve the crossword.

Down

1 When people talk about … , they refer to a high level of responsibility and openness.
3 When we make something happen more easily, we … the result or effect.
5 A statistical term to indicate the difference between two figures; a total or *gross* amount minus a second statistic. For example, the difference between imports and exports is the … trade revenue or between migrants arriving and leaving the country shows … migration.
6 The employees of a factory are known as the … .
8 An … population usually means a reduction in revenue for governments.
9 Another word for *illegal* is … .
11 Many people in Britain want a … on immigration.
13 When someone presents an argument which opposes your opinion, it is known as a … argument.
14 The end of a person's active working life is followed by his/her … from work.
17 When someone is paid the lowest possible wage, he/she receives a … wage.

Across

2 An … is the term for the movement of immigrants into a country.
4 An organization which represents the interests of workers is known as a … .
7 Someone who is an expert in a particular field is a … .
10 A person who works in an elementary occupation is likely to be … .
12 Migrants often move from … areas to the cities.

15 The amount of money which a government spends is known as its … .
16 Someone who acts as an agent between a buyer and a seller is an … .
18 A … is a method of collecting demographic information about a population.
19 If a person is trafficked, then some employers will try to … this worker.
20 Migrant workers send home money known as … to their families.

B Match a word in the first column with a word in the second column to make a two-word phrase. Make sure you know what they mean.

ageing _____	sector
environmental _____	pension
expansionary _____	migration
human _____	mobility
internal _____	age
labour _____	policies
manufacturing _____	trafficking
occupational _____	population
retirement _____	point
saturation _____	issues

According to Wheaton, Schauer and Galli, 2010, who are international migration specialists, trafficking in human beings for labour purposes is predicted to expand dramatically over the next ten years. Moreover, those and other crime experts claim that '... it will surpass the illegal drugs and arms trade in frequency, human costs and profitability to criminals'. Since poverty is increasing in West and North Africa, workers from poorer countries, for example, men from there and women from Eastern Europe, are most vulnerable to this form of modern slavery.

It may seem inappropriate to see this inhuman practice as an economic factor but, sadly, trafficking is an unlawful example of what the authors claim is 'a monopolistically competitive business'. Firstly, traffickers act as middlemen in the market for human beings between the would-be workers and the employers who will exploit their labour illegally. Secondly, these intermediaries take advantage of victims' economic necessity to migrate. Thirdly, traffickers use basic principles of supply and demand to provide illegal workers because they want to maximize profits for their investments. Finally, traffickers can usually control market prices for their human 'products'. In addition, corruption in government, immigration and police services facilitates the exploitation. According to US government sources, around 600–800,000 people are trafficked into the USA every year. Another point is that figures are difficult to estimate because victims are reluctant to give details, so, unfortunately, the organizers are rarely caught. As a result, such activities are very difficult to monitor and prevent.

Source: Wheaton, E. M., Schauer, E. J., & Galli, T. V. (2010). Economics of human trafficking. *International Migrations*, 48(4), 114–141.

Activity bank

A Find 20 words from this unit in the wordsearch.
- Copy the words into your notebook.
- Check the definition of any words you can't remember.

I	N	T	E	G	R	I	T	Y	S	G	N	E	E	U	Y	P	Q
V	S	M	I	C	O	N	C	E	D	E	N	E	T	S	E	M	N
T	I	B	F	M	J	S	X	C	N	V	G	V	Y	T	L	P	S
U	H	A	P	H	A	D	U	X	D	A	W	G	S	G	B	T	P
J	R	I	M	C	L	G	P	B	G	Z	J	A	N	B	N	U	E
P	X	L	R	V	C	E	E	T	S	C	W	I	M	E	I	J	C
S	R	O	Q	E	J	R	R	C	P	I	M	O	D	G	V	I	I
A	E	U	V	N	G	O	E	T	R	L	D	N	D	T	D	S	F
T	D	T	U	E	M	U	C	P	E	E	O	I	T	Q	G	Y	I
T	U	Y	D	N	V	U	L	H	O	P	D	L	A	N	N	H	C
A	N	F	A	I	D	D	W	A	S	S	E	I	I	R	U	A	N
I	D	W	W	N	S	R	E	E	T	A	S	D	T	P	Y	J	X
N	A	C	O	H	E	A	R	U	X	I	N	E	O	O	T	C	O
A	N	C	V	V	E	X	G	E	S	I	O	N	S	B	R	V	J
B	T	U	O	C	L	I	U	R	F	W	S	N	M	S	Y	X	L
L	R	A	N	G	E	T	Q	G	E	U	W	L	S	Q	E	V	G
E	Q	R	T	N	P	J	I	I	H	E	M	B	O	N	H	D	U
Y	S	N	L	O	Y	A	L	T	Y	L	T	K	P	E	C	Z	K

B Match the percentages with a suitable phrase to describe numbers of respondents.

95%	....	a significant majority
70%	....	a small proportion
53%	....	a tiny minority
50%	....	half
48%	....	just over half
10%	....	slightly less than half
2%	....	the great majority

Many businesses worldwide are aware of the relationship between their activities and global ecosystems. These are often taken for granted as they appear to be free and cannot easily be measured. Such systems include forests, water sources, coral reefs, fish stocks and land. Economists have recently started to give value to these natural resources. They use economic models to achieve this. In this way, their calculations provide government policymakers, economists and business strategists with information. As a result, those decision-makers can include protection of such biodiversity in their planning. In 2007, an independent group, *The Economics of Ecosystems and Biodiversity* (TEEB), was established. It is led by Pavan Sukhdev, an Indian ecologist, economist and banker. Its objective is to report on the economic impact of deforestation, over-fishing, degradation of coral reefs and more. As Sukhdev and Brink (2010) point out: 'Losses in the natural world have direct economic repercussions that we systematically underestimate' (p. 13). One consequence of this is that many businesses have started a corporate social responsibility (CSR) programme. The aim is to support protection of valuable natural resources and benefit people, especially in the developing world.

The bank started its CSR programme.

Some shareholders became worried about Descontbank's financial activities.

Descontbank reduced its CSR programme.

The bank received bad publicity because of redundancies.

Descontbank's involvement in sub-prime property in the USA was revealed.

Descontbank established itself as a reliable institution.

The bank announced the first annual loss in its history.

The bank started its CSR programme.

Some shareholders became worried about Descontbank's financial activities.

Descontbank reduced its CSR programme.

The bank received bad publicity because of redundancies.

Descontbank's involvement in sub-prime property in the USA was revealed.

Descontbank established itself as a reliable institution.

The bank announced the first annual loss in its history.

Report A

Report on perception of Descontbank's CSR programme

Introduction

Many private sector companies have developed extensive corporate social responsibility (CSR) programmes over the past decade. Such commitments are valuable in terms of improved public image and raised international profile, as well as enhanced employee loyalty. A number of studies (Amiss, 2006; Bryant, 2007; Young, 2009) have shown that the perception of these programmes depends on the respondents' overall experience of the company, its image, reputation and integrity. This study will present an investigation, using an online survey, into how people perceive the CSR activities of Descontbank.

First the financial aspects and specific CSR activities of the bank will be focused on. After that, the results of the online survey will be analyzed and some recommendations for development and improvement of the bank's CSR programmes will be proposed.

Method

In order to gain an overall picture of Descontbank's financial status and the scope of its CSR programmes, annual reports for 2008, 2009 and 2010, as well as specific CSR reports for the same period, were analyzed.

People's perceptions of Descontbank and its CSR involvement were investigated. To achieve this, a survey was created using Survey Monkey, the online facility. Participants were contacted by e-mail and invited to complete the online questionnaire. To extend the sample, an invitation to participate was posted on a well-known social networking site. A filter mechanism excluded those respondents who expressed no knowledge of Descontbank and a response-based pathway was designed for all participants. (See Appendix 1.)

Findings

In the studies of its general financial performance, Descontbank showed profits of almost €4.7 billion in 2008, a loss of €4.5 billion in 2009 and in 2010 made a profit of €5.6 billion. Its turnover in the three years was €22.5 billion (2008); €21.2 billion (2009) and €24.6 billion (2010). Allocations for its CSR programmes amounted to €32 million, €31.5 million and €31.3 million respectively.

As far as the online survey is concerned, 300 respondents who fulfilled the basic criterion of having heard of Descontbank were filtered to continue. However, from this group, only 40% confirmed their belief that Descontbank had a CSR programme. These are designated Group A below. Of the 60% who did not think Descontbank had a CSR programme (Group B), 40% indicated that the bank had a negative domestic image and had to concentrate on its core customers, 25% replied that the bank faced too many financial challenges, and 35% replied that the bank had different priorities. Among the Group A respondents, when asked about Descontbank's CSR focus, 60% specified education projects in the developing world, 45% mentioned environmental programmes in the developing world, 25% mentioned domestic education support, and 30% mentioned volunteer programmes. (Multiple responses were possible.)

A significant majority of Group A respondents (70%) indicated that Descontbank already spent €50–100 million per annum on CSR, while a small minority (20%) thought that the figure was in excess of €100 million. However, only a small proportion (10%) thought that Descontbank spent less than €50 million. Among the Group B respondents, only a small minority (20%) considered that Descontbank should not have a CSR programme at all. Moreover, Group B's estimation of Descontbank's potential CSR commitment was similar to Group A respondents', with an overwhelming majority (75%) suggesting that an expenditure of €50–100 million per annum would be appropriate.

Discussion

It is clear from the results of the analysis of CSR expenditure that Descontbank spends more than half of its CSR programme on domestic projects. It only spends a small proportion of its CSR commitments exclusively for the developing world, namely for special education projects. Expenditure for domestic cultural projects amounts to over 14% of its total spending compared with around 11% for its overseas school projects. Moreover, the environmental programmes are in the bank's interest as part of cost reductions, so its expenditure of €7.2 million (or 23% of the total) is only a small commitment to improving the environment in the developing world.

When the actual spending (€31.3 million) in 2010 is compared with the responses in the survey, it is clear that respondents from Group A ('Yes, Descontbank has a programme') and Group B ('No, Descontbank does not have a programme, but should have one') believe spending is (or should be) much greater than its real commitment. Clearly, the perception among many participants in the survey is that Descontbank has or should have a strong commitment to CSR. Though it may be argued that 'something is better than nothing', it would be beneficial to Descontbank's image if it launched a better funded programme with revised targets.

Conclusion

Descontbank is clearly not associated with extensive CSR activities. A majority of those surveyed did not attribute CSR programmes to the bank at all. Nobody had the correct picture; on the one hand; many people didn't know there was a programme. However, the ones who did, thought it was bigger and more generously funded than in reality. Descontbank was also linked more to projects in the developing world than is, in fact, the case. It is clear that Descontbank focuses primarily on its domestic markets. However, Descontbank operates mainly in the developing world. It is therefore strongly recommended that the bank should raise its overseas commitments and spend more to alleviate poverty there. It should also rethink the use of so much employee voluntary work at a time when job security is a serious issue. Moreover, it should reconsider if a figure of 0.57% of its total profits in 2010 is really a serious CSR commitment. If Descontbank fails to act decisively soon, it may find that its integrity has declined significantly in the global marketplace and customers and investors will look for an alternative.

Online survey on Descontbank International

1 Have you heard of Descontbank?   YES ☐   NO ☐

If you answered YES to this question please go to Question 2. If you answered NO, you do not need to complete the survey and we thank you for your time.

Background information:
In 2010, Descontbank made a pre-tax profit of €5.6 billion on a turnover of €24.6 billion. It operates in 146 countries worldwide and has over 80,000 employees.

2 Many companies now have a corporate social responsibility (CSR) programme. Do you think Descontbank has such a programme?   YES ☐ (Go to Question 6.)   NO ☐ (Go to Question 3.)

3 If NO, why do you think this is? (Tick one answer only.)
  a Descontbank has had a very difficult time lately and faces many financial challenges. ☐
  b It wants to concentrate on its own domestic customers. ☐
  c It has rejected such programmes completely. ☐
  d It has established different priorities and objectives. ☐
  e It has tried such programmes in the past but these were unsuccessful. ☐
  f It is satisfied with its present profile and does not want to extend it. ☐

4 Do you think Descontbank should develop a CSR programme?   YES ☐   NO ☐

5 If you answered YES to Question 4, how much should Descontbank spend on CSR programmes?
  a €10–20 million per annum ☐
  b €21–49 million per annum ☐
  c €50–100 million per annum ☐
  d €100 million + per annum ☐
  e Other amount. Please specify: _____

At this point, participants who answered Questions 1, 2, 3, 4 (and possibly 5) are thanked for their participation and the questionnaire is closed.

6 If you answered YES to Question 2, which of these activities form part of Descontbank's CSR programme? (Please tick or specify other activities up to a maximum of four responses.)
  a Improving education in developing countries ☐
  b Energy saving and waste reduction in its home country ☐
  c Helping disadvantaged young people and adults in its home country ☐
  d Helping disadvantaged young people and adults in the developing world ☐
  e Sponsoring musical and cultural groups domestically ☐
  f Encouraging employee volunteer programmes worldwide ☐
  g Environmental improvement projects in the developing world ☐
  h Water and sanitation projects in developing countries ☐
  i Other projects. Please specify: 1) _____ 2) _____

7 If you answered YES to Question 2, how much do you think Descontbank spends on CSR programmes? (Tick one answer only.)
  a €10–20 million per annum ☐
  b €21–49 million per annum ☐
  c €50–100 million per annum ☐
  d €100 million + per annum ☐
  e Other. Please specify: _____

Thank you for taking part in this survey. All responses are, of course, confidential.
Names will not be used in any report based on the survey, or communicated to a third party.

Designing a questionnaire

With your partner(s), design a short questionnaire to investigate the opinions of other students and respondents regarding certain key economic changes and how likely they might be.

Examples of topics which might be addressed include:

- revaluation of the Chinese currency against the US$
- insolvency or bankruptcy of major banks or insurance companies
- re-nationalization in developed countries of key industries or services
- stability of oil prices over a certain period
- sale of gold reserves by China
- strength of American government bonds
- lowering of trade barriers to help the developing world
- withdrawal of countries from the European Monetary System (countries using the euro)
- stabilization of commodity prices
- cheaper access to health care

Other topics may, of course, be selected.

The table shows the simple replacement of the linking device from the original in the reading text. Write a full paraphrase of the ideas expressed in the sentences.

Original	**Moreover**, it represented security, reliability and trust in banking.
Replacement	*Furthermore*, it represented security, reliability and trust in banking.
Paraphrase	
Original	**In addition**, they trusted the bank to make profitable investments without taking unnecessary risks.
Replacement	*Moreover*, they trusted the bank to make profitable investments without taking unnecessary risks.
Paraphrase	
Original	**So**, it was an appropriate step for Descontbank to start its own corporate social responsibility (CSR) programme in 2005.
Replacement	*Therefore* it was an appropriate step for Descontbank to start its own corporate social responsibility (CSR) programme in 2005.
Paraphrase	
Original	**Consequently**, in surveys of popularity and trust, Descontbank was considered more trustworthy than the state railway company, the national airline or any other major bank.
Replacement	*As a result*, in surveys of popularity and trust, Descontbank was considered more trustworthy than the state railway company, the national airline or any other major bank.
Paraphrase	
Original	Descontbank was seen as a conservative financial institution **but** that is why customers were loyal to a bank that had more long-term customers than any comparable institution.
Replacement	Descontbank was seen as a conservative financial institution. *Nevertheless*, that is why customers were loyal to a bank that had more long-term customers than any comparable institution.
Paraphrase	
Original	Customers still considered the main priority for Descontbank to be money management, **although** the CSR commitment was welcomed.
Replacement	Customers still considered the main priority for Descontbank to be money management, *despite the fact that* the CSR commitment was welcomed.
Paraphrase	
Original	**However**, there were already concerns among shareholders about Descontbank's financial activities.
Replacement	*At the same time*, there were already concerns among shareholders about Descontbank's financial activities.
Paraphrase	